IDITAROD ALASKA

For John
An adventursome
man! Burt Bomhoff
Aug 31, 20/13

Burt Bomhoff, Long Distance Sled Dog Musher. *Jeff Schultz Photo*.

IDITAROD ALASKA

THE LIFE OF A SLED DOG MUSHER

BURT BOMHOFF

FORWARD BY
LIBBY RIDDLES

PO Box 221974 Anchorage, Alaska 99522-1974
books@publicationconsultants.com—www.publicationconsultants.com

ISBN 9787-1-59433-296-8
Library of Congress Catalog Card Number: 2012940464

Manufactured in the United States of America.

DEDICATION

I dedicate this book to four people who were my inspiration, and who set examples by the way they lived their own lives. All had an impact on me.

To my father, Reverend Harold O. Bomhoff, Lutheran pastor, who raised me to do the right thing and to follow my dreams. He believed I could accomplish anything if I was willing to work hard and earn it.

To my mom, Mildred Wilcke Bomhoff, who understood me better than anyone. She was always there to tolerate my shenanigans, and give me lots of love and room to grow. A sensitive, perceptive mother, she recognized my destiny while I was still in grade school.

To Colonel Norman D. Vaughan, a great adventurer and dog-driver, and a princely gentleman who dreamed big and dared to fail. He believed that the only death you die is the death you die every day by not living.

To Joe Redington Sr., Father of the Iditarod, a traditional Alaskan and a dog man to the core of his soul. Miles of winter dog-trails and nights by a campfire with Joe were like a time machine transporting me to a time in Alaska now almost gone.

All four are dearly loved, though now gone, and sorely missed.

ACKNOWLEDGMENTS

I offer my sincere gratitude to the people listed below. I could not have written this book without them.

- ➤ Libby Riddles for what she added to my book and for what she's done for sled dog racing and Iditarod.

- ➤ My family, especially my children, Brad, Jeff and Jill, for always loyally supporting my passion for adventure.

- ➤ Great friends, many who came all the way to Nome to cheer me on, including Terri McWilliams, Ed and Bette McMillan, Sandy and Susanne Williams, Fred Rosenberg, Floyd Tetpon, Bob Snider, Dave Burke, Jack Felton, and many more, too numerous to list here.

- ➤ Friends who helped me fund this expensive habit by sponsoring me, including Bruce Campbell, Dr. Paul Sayer, Bill Pargetter and others.

- ➤ To the great people of the Iditarod family—friends, mushers, fans and volunteers—who by their very presence helped me to build my warm and precious life.

- ➤ Puddin, Tiger, and all my dogs, who are what much of this book is about.

➤ The Iditarod staff, for archival material and help with my facts.

➤ My editor, Sheryl Oldham, for tightening my verbiage and making it best tell my story. With the patience of Job, she polished the film off the lens and made the view clear.

➤ Marthy Johnson for her expertise in modern sentence structure and word usage.

➤ Publisher Evan Swensen of Publications Consultants for making it easy to publish my book.

➤ Photographer Jeff Schultz for pictures that help tell my story.

FOREWORD

Burt Bomhoff is a typical Alaskan character in that there is not much typical about him. Businessman and musher, Burt placed respectably in the Iditarod and was friends with Joe Redington Sr. and Col. Norman Vaughn during an important era of the race. He also did a stint as President of the Iditarod Trail Committee, putting his business experience to work for the race.

I met Burt when we were both running the 1981 Iditarod. It was my second time in the race, Burt's first Iditarod. He has a hair-raising story about heading up the river instead of jumping off to the buffalo tunnels out of Rohn that year, open water, getting lost and drenched. Jeff King, Martin Buser, and DeeDee Jonrowe were a few of the mushers just starting to race about this time, and the memoir has some great stories about other mushers from those days as well, characters like Gene Leonard.

Burt's memoir gives a taste of training for the Iditarod and racing during those days when Joe Redington was busy trying to create as many Iditarod addicts as possible. It has some great mushing stories and race fans will recognize many of the racers that are part of these tales. It offers another take on why people are crazy enough to want to run the Iditarod, and the connection that many of us have to the spirit of the old timers that traveled the trails in days gone by.

This memoir has some great stories and good laughs that I think all Iditarod fans will enjoy, from the days when we actually used our snowshoes and had time to make campfires.

Libby Riddles

Contents

BOOK ONE

Iditarod, the Race and the Life

BOOK TWO

APPENDICES

Iditarod Alaska

Sled Dogs, Sourdoughs, and Life in the Bush

BOOK ONE

Chapter One
Reflections in an Old Log Cabin

A warm, nostalgic feeling swept over me as I sat in the rocking chair in the quiet of my cabin. It was located at Petersville, which is a tiny gathering of cabins, and a roadhouse in the wilderness foothills south of Mount McKinley in Alaska. I had purchased the antique rocker for one dollar sixty years earlier when I was ten years old and my dad had restored it for me. Dad was a Lutheran pastor, but he could do a lot more than preach. He did such a good job of restoring the rocker that a local reporter heard about it and wrote an article for the local paper. Now, the news article with a picture and story of Dad finishing the chair was pasted under the seat. So many great memories.

Years earlier, I had built this cabin with my former wife out of logs taken from the land nearby. Her CB moniker was Fireweed. Easy to see where the name came from by the splash of purple fireweed blanketing the meadow outside the picture windows.

Memories of so many good times and warm moments swirled about the place, almost as though it was haunted. I noticed the quiet. Gone were the sled dogs that once raised a ruckus in the yard out front. And gone were my buddies, such as Norm, and Joe Redington Sr. Joe had talked me into moving to Petersville in 1982 after a second year with no snow at my cabin down on the Kahiltna River. We needed snow to train sled dogs. Alaska's bare ground terrain was too rough to drive dogs on without snow cover. Without snow the trails, many of them oil exploration seismic trails, were rugged with humps and ruts churned up by heavy equipment.

My move to the Peters Hills country had been a good move for a couple of reasons, much more snow, and much more company. Down in the Kahiltna River valley, the country was remote back then, not many neighbors—mostly trappers and some seasonal workers—and none who mushed dogs. These solitary folks traveled by snowmachines not dog teams. This meant there was no one to help break trail and no one to help when danger threatened. But, mostly, there was almost no one to stop by for dinner or a cup of tea.

Joe Redington Sr. visited with Burt while Burt did chores during a quiet moment at Skwentna checkpoint on a warm, sunny day during the 1981 Iditarod. The Coleman stove was perched between the sled runners so it wouldn't melt into the snow while water boiled in the cook pot. The snow was firm so the snowshoes lay by the sled. The dogs were up and alert and enjoying the activity of the checkpoint, a good sign they were well rested and that it's time to leave again.

At Petersville there were many friends, including long-time Alaskans. Tough men that could get the job done in the Great Alone. And good women who could face down the challenges of this great land. There was Joe Redington Sr., who came to Alaska in 1948 to mush dogs. His cabin was a quarter mile up the trail from ours. We traveled many hundreds of miles together both in the hills near our cabins and along the Iditarod Trail at race time. Joe and I often talked dogs, trails, gear, and other things mushing long into the night. Sometimes we would agree to meet twenty or thirty miles out on the trail where we would build a fire and brew some tea while the dogs rested. Traditions from a time long past were always important to me, so these trips were special. I sometimes imagined that the ghosts of pioneers long gone had joined us by our crackling campfire for conversation and a cup of tea. I imagined they liked our company and didn't want to leave the warm campfire any more than we did. But eventually it would be time to leave and we'd hike up our dogs and head home with the ghosts hot on our heels. Whenever Joe and I trained together, we raced each other like there was some big trophy at stake. So much fun for a couple of guys who never could quite make peace with the loss of a truly basic life that was Alaska a century ago.

Then there were Joe and Vera Duhl, who ran the roadhouse at the Forks. Vera waitressed and cooked while Joe tended bar and cut firewood for the barrel stove. He also kept the worn Witte generator going. He'd been a boxer so couldn't hear well from getting his ears thumped. We'd sit at the bar and yell at each other. He cussed a lot, usually under his breath so Vera couldn't hear it.

His double-barrel stove was special. The Forks Roadhouse was a big log and frame building that went back to the mid-thirties, built to serve sourdoughs headed for the gold mines along Cache Creek to the north. The weathered building needed lots of heat to keep it warm and cozy. That big double-barrel stove was important. The lower barrel was kept stoked with seasoned birch that burned white-hot. The stovepipe went up to another barrel a foot above it, which served as a heat trap. Both barrels gave off serious heat that left you serene after a chilly sled dog run up in the Peters Hills. The Duhls were in their seventies, authentic Alaskans, and full of beans.

Col. Norman Vaughan and Burt reminisced at Vaughan's log cabin at Petersville on a beautiful fall day. Norm had slowed down by then, but his memory bank was full.

My pals Norman Vaughan and his wife Carolyn lived in the cabin I'd built next door. It was just across the meadow. Norm had told me if I ever decided to sell it to let him know. I said, "Hell, let's do it now and I'll build another one next door."

I had been privileged to perform their wedding ceremony at the Forks Roadhouse years earlier. What an event that was. Guests, all adventurers, came by dog team, airplane, snowmachine and helicopter. I'd driven my dog team over from the cabin to perform the ceremony. Norm was eighty-two when he married Carolyn and they loved each other until Norm died at the age of 100. Norm was adamant about not wanting to end up in a retirement home, and Carolyn made sure that didn't happen.

My memories flooded back to a time when we used to visit nearly every day to talk dogs, trail conditions and other important things. Norm would spin yarns all evening while we sat in privileged awe and hung on every word. He had been Admiral Byrd's chief dog handler on his expedition to the South Pole. He had one adventure after another from then until he was a hundred. He never wanted *stuff*—*he* wanted *adventure*. Several years later, my wife Rhea and I had a small birthday party at our house for Norm with a few of his closest friends. It was just two weeks before his 100th birthday. Riley and Marge came down from Nenana, and Masek came all the way from Panama. Shannon was there with Mike. All were long-standing dog mushing buddies. Norm made his goal of living to a hundred but then died a couple of days later.

Dear friend Joe Redington Sr. was gone, too. I had the sad privilege to serve as pallbearer at the funerals of Joe, his wife Vi, and Norm.

I had visited and mushed with these great old-timers, long and often. They have all passed on and were sorely missed.

I just don't make it up to Petersville much anymore. It's too quiet without dogs in the yard and my pals to visit and chase down a cold winter trail. It was 1992 when I last ran a serious team of sled dogs in the Iditarod Race. I've been working in town since then, two decades later.

As I sat in the quiet cabin, a smile flickered across my face. Those memories were just too good. I enjoyed them. Many of these memories were of a time now gone. *A lifestyle now gone.* At the same time, I had a feeling somewhat like you get when a dear friend dies.

I realized that I had a choice. I could feel sad that those days were gone or grateful that I had friends and a life so good that I miss them this much.

In the words of that great philosopher, Dr. Seuss, "Don't cry because it's over. Smile because it happened."

I felt happy and grateful just to be here again and to have the memories. And they do come flooding back as I look around this cabin where so much of the good life was lived. Not the good that money can buy but the good that comes with friends, family, and doing something that absorbs every particle of my being. It was a life complicated in some ways but basic and simple in ways important. When I awoke each morning, I knew that most likely any problem that arose that day would be solved by nightfall. It might be serious, even life-threatening, but if it weren't behind me by day's end, it just wouldn't matter anymore.

It wasn't just the lifestyle. All of this training led to race time, and what an adventure that had been. I'd made eight trips down the precipitous Happy Valley steps, eight trips down the dreaded Dalzell Gorge, and seven finishes across the ice pack of Norton Bay, some through blinding blizzards. All of that was very different from my years as an engineer in Anchorage. I had loved my work but had longed for adventure.

As my eyes swept the cabin, the logs that reflected the warmth of a cozy fire caught my attention. Every inch of every seam in those logs that composed the lower half of the cabin walls had been caulked by hand. Using a caulking gun, we had run a bead of silicone along the seams and smoothed it with rubber-gloved fingers. Two coats of log oil were rubbed into every square inch of log, inside and out. Hard work had left the logs with the soft luster of velvet. When you'd spent that much effort, something of you would remain there forever.

As my eyes wandered over the walls and out the windows, memories of this other life were everywhere. A hundred dog posts jutted out of the jungle of fireweed outside the window and a huge pile of doghouses, neatly stacked, gave mute testimony to a yard that once was full of swirling, barking dogs that went insane at the sight of a bundle of harnesses. The dogs were gone and so was Fireweed. Evidence this hadn't always been a bachelor pad was a tiny basket of silk flowers hanging from a cabinet near the window over the kitchen sink, clearly a woman's touch and not easy for a man living alone to copy. She must not have wanted the reminder, so left it behind.

As I soaked it all in, I began to realize the danger of getting hung up on what was a most enjoyable time of my life. This cabin brought back wonderful memories but it could be a trap. As I sat there and soaked it all in, I realized that I was in peril just being there. Looking back can be good, but not if it distracts from the road ahead. The life that had been here could not be duplicated, but one just as good or better and full of new adventures and other great relationships, were there, just over the next ridge. Sure, there would always be moments that would be relived repeatedly from memory. But let's look at them as inspiration for what could be, not a place to rest and then stagnate.

A group of Norm's close mushing buddies celebrated his 100th birthday at Burt's home. Norm was still sharp and fun, and the gang traded Norm stories until the wee hours of the morning. Left to right standing: Rhea Bomhoff, Margie Riley, Jan Masek, Carolyn Vaughan, Shannon (Chase Poole) Gribbon. Seated: Burt, Norm, and Gerald Riley.

As my thoughts followed one after another, I reached for a book Norm had written. Norm had not only been my neighbor but my dear friend and inspiration. He never lost sight of life's important goals, not his own goals, and not those of his pals, not until the day he died. The book was *My Life of Adventure*. I opened it and read the inscription dated June 21, 1995. It read:

Trapper Creek, Alaska 21 June, 1995

To Burt – A most loyal friend. Come back into sled dog mushing.
You have out-lived one team – now build an Iditarod Team as good as you
did. I want all your cast-offs. The pup on the jacket cover was one of yours.
The only death you die is the death you die every day by not living.
I'm going to live to 100 because not many people die after that.

Norman D. Vaughan

At that moment, the dream of a new place was born. Maybe a cabin where the ghosts didn't inhabit every corner and the yard was just as beautiful. A spot with trails that traveled this great wilderness with an occasional glimpse of the Talkeetna Mountains or the Alaska Range or even Mount McKinley, to make your heart swell with the glory of Alaska and a lifestyle that was common a hundred years ago. There might be a few detours along the way, but they'd be good detours. I still had an airplane and cabins in remote wilderness Alaska. A feeling of exhilaration overcame me as I arose from my rocking chair, picked up my book and my jacket and headed for my dusty red Chevy pickup.

There were many great adventures ahead, which may not even include dogs. But for now, Dear Reader, sit back and let me tell you about the good old days, before my memory fades . . . or I leave to join my dear pals. I must write them down now before they're gone forever. The dreams, the learning, the mistakes, the rookie becoming a veteran musher, the triumphs and the tragedies, the friends, the kindnesses and the chicanery, some by my good friends, and yes, the jerks, all must be written down honestly because they are all part of the tapestry of mushing in the wilds of Alaska. I hope you enjoy my story.

The beauty and stillness of Alaska on a warm sunny day, and a strong
dog team to pull your sled.

Chapter Two
Lloyd's Leaders

I am a dog musher. I've been many other things in my life, challenging things. I've been a professional engineer, designing miles of roads and highways and water systems and sewer systems. I've managed multi-million dollar construction projects. I've been a surveyor, laying out subdivisions and staking massive construction projects, including much of the TransAlaska pipeline. I've been a commercial pilot, flying the Alaska wilderness through white-outs, blizzards, teeth-rattling turbulence and tortuous mountain passes. I've been a U. S. mineral surveyor, staking hundreds of claims. Now I am a dog musher and I'm excited.

Find a comfortable place to relax, and I'll tell you the story.

The sun shone brightly and the grass was still green as I drove to work that first Monday in October 1980. I scanned the sky looking for some sign that Alaska wouldn't pick this year to torture me with no snow. Most Alaskans love to have fall weather last as long as possible before winter's icy blasts chill the soul. We Bomhoffs were a family of skiers, snowmachiners, and campers; we loved the outdoors and we loved winter. But this year was special—there I was with a dog team to train and I needed snow. I wasn't set up to cart-train, so snow was an essential part of the plan.

Our balmy weather lasted the entire month of October. Nothing came, not even a cloud in the sky.

It seemed like we'd *never* get our first snow. My handler, Neal, and I finally moved the dogs and supplies into my cabin on a small pond near the Kahiltna River. It was November 1, and I had hoped to begin mushing immediately; however, while the pond was frozen, there was no snow. So we waited, day after day.

Camp had been only half finished when we'd moved in so we had lots to do. But the top priority was training dogs and that wasn't happening.

I'd flown all the materials for my cabin and everything inside it to the site in my Cessna 206 because the only surface access to this area was by trail during winter. All the interior items such as cook stove, woodstove, cabinets, mattresses, tables, chairs, couch, propane bottles, gas lamps, and canned goods were hauled inside the airplane's cabin. So was the roofing material and nails. All the lumber was tied to my floats and hauled in. Getting it all to the site took many trips, but it was a great little cabin and worth the trouble. The cabin still wasn't accessible over the trails this early in the season. The Kahiltna River hadn't frozen over yet and there was no snow for snowmachines, but we had to get moved in so we could finish the camp.

The only thing complete was a shell of a cabin with a woodstove. This late freeze-up had created problems with transporting some of the items. I'd put the airplane on skis but couldn't land on the pond until now for fear of breaking through the ice. I'd landed with my Cub first to check the thickness of the ice. Landing close to shore minimized the risk, but it was still dicey. The ice was five inches thick, which was strong enough to land the bigger ski-equipped Cessna 206. I made several trips with building supplies, then dog food, dogs, and sleds, and last, the handler.

Flying the dogs was an interesting challenge. None had flown before and all were hyperactive. I loaded a sled and several boxes of frozen hamburger into the airplane and then tied the dogs off short to anything I could inside the airplane, including the sled. There was a lot of growling but no fights until we were halfway to camp when a huge fight erupted. I had a broom handle handy for just such an event. I grabbed the handle and started banging away on the fighters who totally ignored me in their frenzy. I couldn't leave my seat and still fly the airplane, so I was momentarily helpless to stop the melee.

A thought occurred to me. I hauled back hard on the wheel throwing the airplane into a steep climb and then pushed the wheel hard forward. Everything in the airplane was suddenly weightless. It scared the bejeebers out of the dogs and they all hunkered down with a look that said, "What the heck was THAT?" They behaved the rest of the way into camp.

With an occasional prayer to the snow gods, we filled our days with finishing camp and, of course, taking care of the dogs. First, there was an outhouse hole to dig. Neal needed a pickaxe for that because the ground was frozen. And there was an outhouse to construct. There was a porch to enclose and shelves to build. The list went on and on, with bunk beds, kitchen cabinets, counter, sink, and well, propane cooking stove, propane lights and a lot, lot more.

The author hauling dogs to the Kahiltna cabin in his ski equipped Cessna 206. The camp was remote so transportation was by airplane only unless you wanted to spend a day mushing the team out to the road in winter. The airplane was always full to the ceiling and the trip only took 45 minutes. This load includes a dog sled, boxes of frozen beef and as many dogs as would fit.

Every morning when we awakened, we headed for the window to see what was happening outside. Nothing. Nothing happened until, finally, on November 16, we woke up to find the landscape covered with white. It was the most beautiful sight imaginable. A beautiful, clean, white blanket of snow covered everything. The surface of the lake, which had been a sheet of wind-glazed ice, was fluffy and white. Spruce boughs were heavily laden with the wet white stuff, as were the dog-houses, woodpile, storage shed, and everything else. We forgot about our chores.

We could hardly wait to get breakfast cooked and eaten. The flattest, clearest area for a dog lot was an area approximately a hundred yards above the cabin on a low ridge. We'd cleared a trail from there that angled down to the lake. I drove the snowmachine from the dog lot down the trail and across the pond to pack the snow and break a trail for the teams to follow. I continued from the pond for a half mile along the edge of a slough, where we connected with a seismic trail called Oil Well Road. This enabled us to join the trail system we hoped to establish around our camp. Our area was crisscrossed with seismic trails, but neither snowmachines nor dog teams used them—we just didn't have any close neighbors back then. Never having mushed in this area before, we didn't want the dogs to become confused and drag us off into the brush.

25

The author loads dog food into his Cessna 206 airplane at his home on Campbell Lake. He'll fly it to the Kahiltna camp and unload it there. The dogs were kept there all year the first year, with the neighbors taking care of chores while Burt worked in town. The entire cabin and lumber for doghouses and even the dogs were all hauled in with the Cessna.

I'd long since prepared a team list for Neal and me that showed the locations for hitching every dog so we would know which dogs to hitch and where to put them in the teams. We rigged sleds with gang lines and snow hooks, and filled sled bags with ballast. Everything was in place up in the dog lot behind the cabin. We each grabbed a bundle of harnesses and headed for the dogs.

For the first time, we were hitching my new Iditarod dog team. I was nearly done putting the harnesses on my dogs and hitching them into the gang line when most of Neal's dogs, minus his sled, came charging into my team. I turned around to see Neal in hot pursuit, hollering and yelling at his dogs to "whoa." One of his dogs had bitten his gang line in two in its excitement and eagerness, turning the rest of the team loose. Sled dogs could chew like wolverines.

I ran back to the cabin and got him another gang line so he could begin all over again. I asked him to hitch the culprit last and not take his eyes from that dog until we were ready to go. Then he could dash back to his sled, release the snow hook and away we would go. He rigged up the new gang line and began hitching the dogs. When he got them all ready to go, he turned his back for an instant to tell me he was ready and the whole thing happened again.

There were compounds a musher could use to eliminate this problem. Bitter Apple was one and a product called Chew Check was another. These chemicals taste so bad that if a dog bites the line when this stuff had been sprayed on it, he won't likely do it again. That was my first experience mushing dogs, however, and I still had a lot to learn. We later learned how to thread a small steel cable into our gang lines, making it much harder for a dog to chew through the line.

We were finally ready to mush out of the yard on about the third try. I released my snow hook, hollered "Giddyap," and hung on for dear life. I don't think I ever came so close to getting killed in my life. Those dogs took off at a furious gallop with me standing on the brake with all of my weight. I guess the dogs were even more eager than I was. The first fifty feet was on smooth level ground, so I had a moment to stow the snow hook and settle on the runners. Then the dogs broke over the lip where the trail pitched steeply down toward the lake. From there, the trail was *really* rough. Things got out of control in a hurry. There wasn't enough snow to smooth out the irregularities in the rough ground, so the sled was bouncing up and down like a jeep through a boulder patch, keeping me airborne most of the time. The brakes were almost useless since they weren't in contact with the ground.

When we'd used our axe and chainsaw to cut the trail, we thought our new trail was nice and straight. That wasn't the case at all. There was a huge spruce tree about a hundred feet down the trail on the left, whose root system encroached into the trail. When the sled hit the root, I was thrown to the right side of the trail, where another spruce tree was equally close. This threw the sled to the left into a birch tree, which threw me off the sled and capsized it. I managed to hang on as the dogs dragged the sled careening down the hill. I hung on with all my might by one arm with the other arm flailing wildly as I attempted to get a better hold of the sled. The sled bounced violently and I was dragged along so roughly it nearly tore my clothes off.

Meantime, I was trying to glance up at where we were going so I wouldn't slam my head into a tree or bust my knuckles should the hand bow slam into a tree. The sled continued careening wildly along. Like some primitive snowplow, I swept the new snow from our trail, right down to bare ground. There wasn't much snow, but that ground was frozen hard.

We finally reached the lake and the dogs dragged me pell-mell across the ice. At the far shore, I dragged myself up onto the sled and with my weight pushing down managed to get them slowed and then finally stopped. I set the snow hook to anchor the team and turned it on its side to be sure nothing could move. I sat down on the overturned sled to catch my breath and started picking the twigs and leaves off my arms and from down my neck. Then, I pulled my sleeves back down to my wrists from somewhere up around my shoulder. It took awhile, first my long johns, then my shirt, then my sweater, and finally my parka sleeve.

I was to capsize my sled on that damned hill every time we ran dogs for that first week until I finally came to my senses and prepared a new dog yard down near the lake. The spot next to the lake was full of hummocks and stumps, but it was off the hill. It took a lot of work trying to get poles in the frozen ground, but our trips out of the yard were a whole lot less exciting. By mushing directly onto the pond, we had a nice straight, level path for a quarter mile or so until the dogs had used up that first explosive burst of energy. By the time we got to the rougher section of the trail off the pond, they'd slacked off a little bit.

Snicking a winter supply of kindling at the Kahiltna cabin, 1981 season. Cabin heat was provided by a wood stove while meals were cooked on a propane stove. All seasonal chores needed to be completed by snowfall so that nothing would stand in the way of training. Firewood needed to be cut and the pile of lumber to the right had to be turned into doghouses. Note the snowshoes, dog harnesses, gang lines and snow hooks hanging in readiness on the cabin walls, ready for that first sign of snow.

We increased our mileage gradually and occasionally gave the dogs a day off. We tried to travel different trails as much as we could to make it more interesting for us and for the dogs. Each morning we eagerly awakened to look for the next snowfall, but day after day, week after week, it didn't come. Soon, what little snow we had was gone and we were mushing on trails that were virtually bare. The ground was rough and frozen so the sled was constantly jumping and pitching, making it difficult to hang on. The constant battering beat the sleds apart so we were always replacing broken parts. Also, there was always the possibility that the brake would catch on a frozen hump and rip it right off the sled.

Glaciation caused problems on some of our trails, with water seeping out of the ground and freezing. The ice never froze nice and level. Humps and side slopes were the norm. It was difficult for the dogs to maintain their footing and the sled tended to want to skid sideways in whatever direction the ice sloped. When the sled skidded off the ice back onto bare ground, the sudden jolt made it difficult to hold the sled upright so the driver was often hurled to the ground with terrible force. Iditarod teams were trained to be powerful and fast, so if you didn't have adequate snow cover to smooth things out, a dangerous situation developed.

Our training trails traversed several areas that scared us half to death every time we approached. I told Neal what I used to tell my kids, "It's okay to be scared, but we need to overcome fear to get the job done." In one area, our trail angled down through a slough full of hummocks the size of bushel baskets with a curve toward the bottom that was covered with a huge glacier. The dogs invariably broke into a lope when heading downhill because the sled was easier to pull. We would start hitting those huge hummocks just as the dogs started to lope and, because the sled was clattering from one hummock to the next, our brakes were virtually useless. Faster and faster we would go, careening over those hummocks until it was almost impossible to stay upright. How many times we spilled as we clattered down through that trail I'll never know. Sooner or later, as the sled bounced higher and higher, over it went and one of us went crashing to the ground.

Getting dragged a hundred feet or so over those big frozen hummocks was no fun. If we managed to make it through the hummocks, a big thrill always came when we hit the glacier. By then the dogs were galloping full tilt. The ice started right at the curve and sloped downward toward the outside of the curve. Little stubs of roots and small bushes stuck up through the ice. The sleds skittered sideways toward the outside of the curve and then struck one of these little stubs, stopping sideward motion abruptly. The first time it happened, I was thrown violently from the sled down onto the hard ice on my knees. Then I was dragged across these stubs with no way of stopping the sled until we were on bare ground on the far side. The pain was so excruciating it brought tears to my eyes.

I tried nearly everything during those weeks as I learned to drive that sled and not get thrown. I tried leaving one foot on a sled runner while skidding my other foot along like an outrigger, first using the uphill foot, then the downhill foot.

I tried crouching as low as I could. After a couple of weeks, we could make it through that patch of hummocks and then over the glacier without falling at least part of the time and then, eventually, all of the time. Before we were done, we would drive the team down through the most violent trails as relaxed as though mushing across the pond. These are important skills that mushers need when descending the dreaded Happy Valley Steps and the Dalzell Gorge during the Iditarod Trail Sled Dog Race.

Wienies need not apply.

Another trail gave me fits. The hummocks and the glacier were painful but not likely to injure us seriously. But this other hill was downright dangerous. It was only about thirty-feet high and a hundred feet long but was rougher than a stucco bathtub. It had a gully about a foot wide and a foot deep running down the middle of it where the rain had washed and there were three or four huge, frozen hummocks toward the bottom end. The first time we approached it, I slowed the team down somewhat as we neared the descent, but it was so short that it just didn't look that dangerous. As usual, the dogs began picking up speed as they broke over the edge and were soon moving at full gallop. I was standing on the brake with absolutely no effect at all. The brake wouldn't bite in the frozen ground.

The sled was bouncing and skittering in and out of the little gully making it extremely difficult to hang on, much less remain upright. When we hit the first clump at the bottom, the sled rose into the air and did a snap roll to the right. Moving at full speed, I was slammed to the ground so hard that it knocked me unconscious. I came to moments later and tried to get out of the way of my handler's sled, which wasn't far behind. I did manage to crawl off to the side just as the following team broke over the edge of the hill and came clattering down. He'd had enough sense to slow his team down to a walk before he got close to the hill, so he was able to keep things at a slower pace and remain upright.

As I began to come to, he loaded my battered body onto his sled and we mushed on home where we found my dogs wagging their tails. They were looking at me as though to ask, "Gee whiz, Boss. What happened to you?" By the next morning, I had a lump on the side of my head that extended from below my ear to above my temple. During the week that followed, I broke a toe on my right foot on that hill. I also got slammed to the ground a few more times so hard that I was in constant pain for a couple of weeks.

With these painful experiences, I began to get about half psyched-out over that short hill. I knew I had to conquer it, but it seemed like no matter how I slowed the dogs down as I approached it, things always got out of control before I reached the bottom. I finally began to slow them down to an absolute walk before we got to the hill, and I would stand on the brake with all my might until we reached the bottom. After that, I was never thrown again, but I certainly didn't think I was approaching things with much finesse.

When people asked me why I was doing Iditarod during that period, I told them that you just had to be the kind of person who enjoyed slamming your thumb with a hammer and feeling pride that you could stand it. It hurt like the dickens, but at least you were stalwart enough to take it. There was one benefit of learning to mush dogs on those terrible trails. No part of the Iditarod Trail was as bad as the trails we mushed on that first year of training, including the steep descent down the Happy Bluffs and the trip down the Dalzell Gorge out of Rainy Pass. Both those areas were notoriously intimidating, but I never had a problem with them.

Aside from rough trails and too little snow that first year, the one thing we did have was cold—thirty below zero and more. Neal had come to Alaska from California. He had worked for a friend of mine as an assistant guide and packer and then came to work for me as a handler. He had a tremendous desire to be accepted as a true Alaskan outdoorsman. After all, he had worked for a guide the previous fall, which was proof of his prowess as a hunter/outdoorsman. He wanted to stand out as a guy who was capable, equal to anything, and a great hunter. Whenever company showed up, he brought out his photo album and showed pictures of his big game exploits. He would tell tales of great "derring-do."

Eventually, when he really warmed up, he would dig out his chrome-plated .44 Magnum as proof that he was the real thing. If he noticed anyone snickering, he became offended and once or twice even stomped out of the cabin, not to return until our company had gone. I think he'd been able to impress his clients from the big city with hunting tales and that big chrome-plated pistol, but these mushers were a different story. They lived out here in this harsh environment and knew what "tough" was.

After about the third time he brought out that chrome-plated .44, I asked him if he would please keep it hidden while company was around, because I didn't want any of my friends thinking I had a pimp for a handler.

He had such a low tolerance for low temperatures that he would take a Coleman lantern to the outhouse with him rather than a flashlight. He would set it between his legs to warm up the outhouse and to keep his hands warm. When we kidded him about it, he insisted it was just for the light. When he took the lantern out there during the daylight, it proved the point. We teased him so much about the lantern that he hardly dared go to the bathroom during daylight when we had company. We wondered what would happen if we ran out of fuel for the lantern, but it seemed a bit cruel to hide the fuel just to torment Neal.

I quit thinking Neal was funny one day when the temperature was thirty degrees below zero. We were on a long run and I began to see tiny spots of blood on the trail from the dogs' feet. Snow is quite granular during extremely cold weather and can become as sharp as bits of broken glass. I had stopped to examine the dogs' feet and asked Neal to do the same. We discovered that the snow was beginning to chafe several dogs' feet. I asked Neal to put booties on his dogs while I proceeded to do the same with mine.

I've always been blessed with an active metabolism and the exertion of bending over and working on the dogs was keeping me plenty warm. Even my bare hands were comfortable and within fifteen minutes or so, I was done booting up my dogs. I turned around to see how Neal was doing and was somewhat alarmed with what I saw. He had his hands tucked under his armpits and was jumping up and down, his face almost pure white. I asked him to come on up where I could look at him and asked him how he was doing. He reluctantly admitted that he was terribly cold. Normally, I would have teased him about being a California model, but his obvious misery made that inappropriate.

I said, "Neal, go on up ahead of my team and jog back and forth and see if you can get your blood circulating while I go back and boot up your dogs." I wanted him ahead of my team so they wouldn't run off and leave me while I was back working on his dogs.

I began booting his dogs and found that he had been able to boot only two out of the twelve before he had become too cold to continue. I've always felt a great responsibility for my dogs and the people who work for me. Neal had gotten into a situation he wasn't able to cope with. He had too much pride to complain and was trying to survive without my noticing. His pompous attitude made him an easy target, but that experience ended the teasing.

When his dogs were booted, I loaned him my heavy mitts and told him that we would mush on up to the next place where we could turn around and head home. I also told him to hang on to the sled and run along behind it to get his blood circulating. That'd warm him up.

For the next couple of days, I checked Neal before we went out to be sure he was dressed warmly; however, those low temperatures just didn't suit him. Sometimes the reality of this icy wilderness far exceeds what the inexperienced might envision.

One evening after another difficult run, when the dogs had been fed and the dinner dishes done, Neal began pacing the cabin with a wild look in his eye. He started to rant. He just wasn't going to be pinned down in this frigid desolate place another day. He announced that he was through. He just wasn't enjoying being cold all the time and he wanted to leave.

The dog yard was a mess during spring break-up. Dog houses are continually moved up on top of the snow as winter advances—then the snow melts out from under them during spring break-up leaving a topsy-turvy pattern.

"Neal, I'm really sorry this didn't work out for you. We can load up first thing in the morning and I'll fly you into town."

"No, Burt, I'm out of here. I want to go now. I'm packed and I could be in that airplane in five minutes."

"Neal, it'll be dark in a half hour or so and the airplane engine needs to be heated. We're in the middle of nowhere, and it is colder than hell out there. If we have any problems, they'll be harder to deal with in the dark with this minus thirty-degree cold."

"Burt, we *gotta* go." Neal was inches from my face talking through gritted teeth. Bits of spittle hit my face.

It was obvious that this had been bothering Neal since that first cold run and now he was over the edge. We call it "cabin fever," and everyone in bush Alaska knew what it was.

I'd heard of cases where people got so worked up over feeling trapped that bad things had happened. I had no intention of Neal getting out of hand in the middle of the night in that tiny cabin, not with that .44 Magnum under his pillow. Getting the airplane ready to go would take an hour or so, not what

I wanted to deal with in the dark at thirty below. On the other hand, I wasn't going to be trapped with Neal possibly going off the deep end while I was asleep and helpless.

"No problem, Neal. I'll call town to check on the weather and go put the heater in the airplane."

Years later, I read this explanation in Wikipedia. In part, it says, "Cabin fever is a claustrophobic reaction that takes place when a person is isolated and shut in a small space for an extended period. Symptoms include restlessness, irritability, irrational frustration with everyday objects, distrust of anyone they are with, and an urge to leave even in the rain, snow, or dark." True enough.

I called my wife on the HF radio and she said there should be no problem getting into Campbell Lake where we lived. "I can see all the way to the mountains."

I said to her, "We can leave in about an hour and a half."

When an airplane engine is cold, the propeller feels stiff when turning it by hand because of the cold oil. An hour or so later the prop turned easily and I told Neal to toss his bag in the back and hop in. We taxied to the end of the lake in the dark of night and took off without incident.

In the dim light of the moon, we could see the lights of Anchorage and Wasilla off in the distance. As we got closer, I called Anchorage tower for a clearance through their airspace to Campbell Lake. The controller said that Campbell Lake was completely socked in, as was Anchorage International. He recommended that we pick an alternate and that we do it quickly as the fog was spreading rapidly. A glance over my shoulder showed Wasilla and Palmer both wide open with no fog in sight. We weren't in any danger with those alternates, but I wanted to find a place to land closer to home.

I called home again, this time on the airplane's HF radio, and my wife again said that it was okay. "I can see clear to the mountains."

As I repeated my request to the tower for a clearance, we encountered a solid deck below us near the inlet. We could see streetlights and the runway lights at International through the fog. We proceeded over Anchorage International Airport and then Sand Lake, which was only half fogged in, but by then Campbell Lake was completely covered. I headed back to Sand Lake, which now only showed about a hundred yards open at the west end. That fog *was* moving fast! I made a beeline for the opening and was relieved when the skis touched the snow. My Super Cub was still rolling out when I hit the fog bank. I taxied over to Ralph Garrifola's house, squinting through the fog as we moved slowly along the frozen shore. I borrowed Ralph's phone and called my wife for a ride home. When we got to Campbell Lake, only a couple of miles from Ralph's house, I could in fact see clear to the mountains. Unfortunately, the fog was a solid layer about a hundred feet above the surface.

I flew back to camp the next day with my new handler and found the thermometer nearly bottomed out.

I'd experienced temperatures as low as sixty-five degrees below in the oil patch on Alaska's North Slope and in Fairbanks on various engineering and surveying projects, but that was an entirely different story. Not to take anything away from working outside in those temperatures no matter what you do, but in construction camps and obviously in any city, shelter is fairly close at hand. Lunch breaks and coffee breaks are normally taken inside where a person can warm up. The cabs on heavy equipment are heated. People can usually get inside immediately if experiencing frostbite or any other injury.

In long-distance sled dog racing, vast distances must be covered at slow speeds, even in training, through areas without habitation. No help is available and in some cases, search efforts are severely hampered by the vast areas and poor weather. In training, the only other person who knows where you are is probably your handler, but he's with you.

The point is that there are few things you could do during winter in the Arctic that place a greater demand on a person than long-distance sled dog racing. The Iditarod is a sport where the individual must know his limits and be prepared to be totally self-sufficient within those limits. Except during training, the sport does not lend itself to the buddy system, although mushers occasionally work together during a race in an effort to extend their capabilities.

Anything that required taking off one's mittens required the greatest of care. I wore prescription glasses then, which were a tremendous inconvenience at those low temperatures because of their tendency to frost up when my breath touched them. Wearing a face mask tended to deflect breath upward, making the problem of fogging glasses constant. If you sneeze or cough, you fog your glasses and instantly experience the sensation of mushing in a dense London fog.

When you need to perform tasks with the dogs, your disadvantage is twofold. You take off your mitts, so you're in danger of frostbiting your hands. When you bend over, face down, your warm breath rises and is collected by your parka hood, fogging up glasses or goggles. Then you can't see what you're doing.

THE NEW HANDLER, JOE

I replaced Neal with a new handler, Joe Daugherty. He was the super heavyweight Golden Gloves boxing champ of Alaska. He was quite a contrast to Neal.

He was so big and strong and sure of himself, he often mushed dogs in only a sweater and a pair of gloves, with no hat on. At the end of a long day after hours of standing on a sled and feeding the dogs, he would take off for an hour or so to do roadwork. His strength was awesome. When we went out cutting down trees to break trail or for firewood, he would grab logs as long as he was and a foot and a half through and pitch them around like kindling wood.

Dogs are given a break on long training runs. It keeps them happy and teaches them to lie down and rest when they get the chance. All dogs here are tired and resting with a few working on their paws. When they jump up and start pestering each other, you know it's time to leave.

He loved to fight. I don't believe he often picked a fight, but if someone was stupid enough to go after him, he was more than happy to oblige. Although I showed up at a couple of his Golden Gloves events, I never was lucky enough to see him in the ring. His opponents would take one look at him and scratch.

The rough-hewn side of him was a minor part of his personality. He was a gentle man. He loved to spend his evenings visiting with friends and playing his guitar. He'd been a professional guard dog trainer in Denver before coming to Alaska and knew a whole lot about training dogs. I'm sure that many times he could see better ways of doing things than I could, but he never once pushed his ideas nor argued about what we were doing. He knew there were a lot of things I wanted to try and respected that. Also, I was new at this and needed to discover things on my own.

LLOYD'S LEADERS

Kathy, my handler, takes a moment to snack the dogs on a long run north of the Kahiltna camp. The dogs seem to know when it's just a quick stop and most don't bother to lie down, although there's always a few who plop down the moment the sled stops anywhere.

I stretched mightily and lay there for a moment relishing the warmth of my down comforter. In the cabin's coldness, the tip of my nose felt like an icicle, making the warmth of my bed even cozier. I'd banked the fire just before bedtime the night before so it would burn slowly and not go out before morning. The price we paid for not having to restart the fire in the morning was a chilly cabin.

I rolled out of the top bunk and opened the door slightly on the little wood-burning Earth Stove. Before I could turn around, the fire roared to life. Heat began to push the cold out of the tiny cabin. I laid a couple of logs in the stove and pulled on my britches. The logs were seasoned birch from a tree I'd cut down the previous spring before the sap began to rise. Birch logs burned hot and long, about the best firewood we had in the woods around the cabin.

The one drawback was the sooty pitch they deposited in the chimney. Stack fires were common in the Alaska bush because of this pitch. If the pitch began to burn when no one was watching, it could get so hot that it burned right through the chimney and could then burn the cabin down.

We burned the pitch out of the stack every week to be sure that it didn't collect to the point of *accidentally* catching fire. The technique was to wad a paper grocery bag up and toss it in the stove. With the stove door slightly open to create a strong draft, the bag burned so hot that the pitch in the stack caught fire. We then ran out to watch the fireworks as the fire and sparks shot ten to fifteen feet into the air above the cabin. Oh, well. Small pleasures excite those living in the bush . . . no TV back then.

Bacon and eggs sizzled on the stove as the handler went out to water the dogs. The dogs needed water every morning to assure hydration during our training runs. A full meal would make them sluggish out on the trail. We watered them before breakfast to give their stomachs a few moments to settle before training began.

As the delicious aroma of frying bacon filled the air, I cast a weather eye out the window to see if the weather had lifted. I'd been stuck for days in my dog camp on that small pond west of the Kahiltna River. Low ceilings and short visibility made flying impossible. No road came close, so the only practical way in and out was to fly. To go by land involved driving the dog team fifty miles on the Oil Well Road trail. I would then have to load the dogs and sled into my dog truck and drive for three hours to get home. That was if I had a truck parked at the end of the trail, which I didn't. It was at my home on Campbell Lake in Anchorage.

With all the inconvenience of land-based transportation, I'd committed to flying back and forth in my ski-equipped PA-18 Super Cub. This made it a forty-five-minute trip rather than an all-day trip. In case of an emergency, I'd of course get out any way I could.

Now the weather had lifted somewhat. By the time we'd finished breakfast, I could see to the end of the pond. If the weather lifted, I'd fly home; if not, we'd train dogs. I watched the weather as I removed the wing and engine covers from the small bush plane. It looked like visibility would be okay, but the ceiling was low, almost in the trees. I would take off and check things out, intending to return immediately to the pond if the weather didn't look safe.

I stuffed the airplane covers into the airplane in case I was forced down on the way to town, and removed the catalytic heater from the engine compartment. As mentioned earlier, it was necessary to preheat an airplane engine in Alaska's winter to be sure that it would start and run like it was supposed to. I reflected on the inconvenience of flying airplanes in an Alaska winter.

I decided to take off and see how things looked. As I turned the small plane south toward Anchorage, I glanced down and saw Joe already jogging down the South Trail, sparring as he went. He was as eager as I was to get out of the cabin and away from the dogs for a little while.

Forty-five minutes later, my red and white Cub touched down gently on Campbell Lake in south Anchorage. Home sweet home.

A note to return a call from Dick Mackey lay in the pile of papers on my desk. This was my first season training my own dog team and there was so much to learn. I'd been told repeatedly that I would need more than one lead dog if I ever hoped to make it to Nome on the Iditarod Trail.

Every musher drops a few dogs during a race. This isn't near as bad as it sounds. If a dog is injured or becomes sick or overly tired, mushers "drop" (leave) that dog at the next checkpoint, where it receives loving attention from volunteers and veterinarians, after which it is flown home where it can rest and relax. If the dog you dropped happened to be your only leader, though, you'd likely need to scratch from the race. Lead dogs are the steering wheels of a team, as well as the pace setters. Without that lead dog, the team will go wherever it chooses, which might be right back to the starting line or off into an open hole in the ice.

After I began training, it wasn't long before most of my spare time at home was spent making phone calls and writing letters to everyone possible who might know of a decent lead dog for sale. I owned just one lead dog that would take commands. Her name was Black and she was part of the team I had bought from Duke. I'd bought his entire team before he raced it in the 1980 Iditarod Trail Sled Dog Race with the understanding that I would take delivery after the 1980 race. Duke had scratched this team from the race the year before but was a heck of a salesman. He assured me the team was capable of finishing at the front of the pack. Naturally, I was disappointed when he scratched again in McGrath during the 1980 race. When I expressed concern over this to my mushing buddies, they told me it probably wasn't the dogs. They said Duke just didn't seem like the finishing kind.

The mushers I talked with said many of the dogs had been to Nome a number of times and Black had been one of the most famous leaders in Iditarod history. Though Duke may not have been much of a musher, he'd bought dogs from some good teams. Black had a reputation for being a solid gee/haw leader that would keep you out of trouble, so she bordered on indispensable. It was possible that I'd be carrying her in the sled much of the time to make sure the she had a relatively pleasant trip. During those periods, I'd need a sub for her. And if the time came when she'd had enough, I would definitely need a substitute to move up into her place. Also, it was nice to be able to rotate your leaders to give each one a little break back in the team. Many leaders do fine in double lead but hate being up there alone.

Trying to separate a good lead dog from a musher is danged near impossible. There are few perfect leaders. Some will back off a little and slow the team when they get tired of it. Others will suddenly turn deaf when they don't want to go where you command them. Some will perform flawlessly until they got tired of it. This could be from too many commands getting in or out of a village, which makes the leaders a little frazzled. It could mean bucking into a strong wintery headwind on the Yukon River, especially if there's a skiff of snow blowing along the surface. This blowing snow bothers the dogs' eyes and even gets into the musher's eyes. It feels like icy, fine sand. Some leaders will mutiny when they've had enough and just lead the team off into the bushes.

Good solid leaders with true grit are hard to find and are literally worth their weight in gold. When I returned Mackey's call, he asked me if I'd called Lloyd Haessler. Dick Mackey had won the 1978 Iditarod and was a good dog man.

"Who's Lloyd?" I asked.

"Lloyd loves to train leaders. He isn't much of a racer, but he has won several lead dog contests. You should be able to get a good leader out of him."

What I didn't know then was that leader competitions don't have much to do with racing or even mushing. Racing involves not only obedience, but also speed and stamina and athletic ability. You can develop speed and stamina through conditioning if a dog has natural athletic ability, but leader competitions are more like obedience trials. These dogs are judged on their ability to complete a course following commands from their trainer.

Now it was time to find a couple of leaders. If I didn't get this done soon, my team would be too far into training to add dogs with no prior conditioning. New dogs would be hard to get up to speed.

I called and said, "Lloyd, this is Burt Bomhoff. Dick Mackey suggested I give you a call. I need a good gee/haw leader or two. We're well into training so I would need dogs that could be brought up to speed quickly, preferably with a few miles on them already."

"I've got just what you need," he said. "I've got two outstanding leaders right out of Emmitt Peters' Nugget breed. I didn't plan to sell them, but I guess I could let them go to the right musher. I'll need to be sure that they'll be well cared for."

"Have they got some miles on them?" I asked. "I've already got a thousand miles on my dogs so they're in pretty good shape. Any new leaders would have to be fast enough to stay ahead of my team."

"That would be no problem," Lloyd said. "These dogs have at least a thousand miles, maybe even fifteen hundred miles, on them in the last few months."

I said, "I've got one veteran leader named Black. She was bred and trained by Isaac Okleasik out in Teller. She's an excellent leader but she's been around the block and may not be able to make it all the way to Nome. I need a second command leader to be sure I can make it to the finish line."

"These dogs are proven, and out of the best stock possible," he said. He went on, "I've been one of the leading trainers of lead dogs in Alaska for many years. You could ask Dick Tozier or any of the leading mushers and they'll say the same."

The Kahiltna camp was remote with only the Meyers clan as neighbors, so it was always exciting when company came. Burt's handler Kathy Turko, Dewey Halverson's Swedish handler, Dewey, and his friends, Jane and Chris, gather for dinner at Burt's Kahiltna cabin.

Dick Tozier, a close friend of mine, was the race marshal for the Anchorage Fur Rondy races and was one of the most highly respected dog men in Alaska. This sounded like a good reference. *Wish I'd called him right then.*

Lloyd continued, "I've got fifty dogs in my yard here, and every one of them is a top, outstanding leader. The two that I'll sell are among the best that I've got. I've got breeding down to such a science that virtually all of the dogs that I breed turn out to be outstanding leaders."

Lloyd told me how to get to his yard, and I was on my way. The sign on his driveway said, "Lloyd's Leaders." How could I go wrong? I knocked on the door and a small gray-haired man answered. "You must be Burt."

"I am, and I sure hope you can help me out."

"I'm Lloyd. Let's take a walk through the yard and I'll introduce you to some of the finest lead dogs in existence. I believe I've won more lead dog contests with these dogs than any man alive."

When the runs get longer, the dogs become more relaxed about stops out on the trail. These dogs are perfectly at home and immediately relax and start exploring wherever we stop. The leaders learn to hold the team straight as training progresses.

As we walked through the yard, each dog had his own tale of excellence. Each was a born and bred champion.

"Burt, this leader won three state lead dog championships before he retired to sire more champions. This dog won the 1978 championship. She had to pull the entire team across the finish line they were so spent. But she did it! That pair of dogs over there are the best double leaders that I've ever driven. I never lost a race with them in lead."

We worked our way through the yard, Lloyd introducing each and every dog as we went. Each story was better than the last.

As I swallowed the story, hook, line, and sinker, I began to make my plan to dicker over the price of the two new leaders. I hadn't seen them yet but was already committed. I would have to be at my sharpest to pull this off.

Lloyd saved the best two dogs for last. It took us an hour, but we finally made it through Lloyd's dog yard to the ones he had set aside for me. "These are the two dogs I'm thinking about selling. I'm not sure yet. I'll need to be sure they're well taken care of."

I promised Lloyd from the bottom of my heart that the dogs would be well taken care of.

Here were two little dogs tied to their posts, which consisted of two-inch pipe driven into the ground. The dogs raced around their posts, again and again, so fast one would think they'd turn to butter like those tigers in the fairy tale. They never slowed down as they spun around on their six-foot chains. It was dizzying to watch. The paths where they ran were worn six inches deep in the gravel from their constant running. What energy! What enthusiasm!

When I approached the dogs to pet them and get acquainted, they nearly went berserk trying to get away.

"Little bit spooky, aren't they?" I asked.

"Not really," Lloyd responded. "All top racing dogs are high-spirited. This could appear as spookiness to the inexperienced dog man. I assure you, you would be totally happy with these leaders. And they are *guaranteed!* If you aren't satisfied for any reason, just bring them back."

Lloyd strolled over to the nearest dog as I watched fascinated. The dog tried to avoid Lloyd just as frantically as it had me.

"Lloyd, are you sure those dogs aren't just a little spooky?"

"Naw, just high-strung racing stock. Like I said, these dogs are right out of Emmitt Peters' Nugget."

"What are you asking for them?"

"Five hundred dollars apiece. I was asking seven hundred fifty dollars, but I really like your looks. I love these dogs, but I know they'll have a good home with you."

I gave each dog my most careful scrutiny. I stepped close. Then I stepped back to get the broad view. I walked around each dog and finally, with my most critical eye, I stepped well back to judge his gait.

"I'll give you eight hundred dollars for the pair. They are guaranteed now, aren't they?"

"Done! You take that one and I'll grab this one," he said. "And they are guaranteed. If you don't like them, just bring them back."

With a little fancy footwork, I was able to grab the dog assigned me and lead it wiggling and squirming through the yard to the truck. I boosted the dog up to one of the holes in the dog box, but the dog wouldn't go in it. He spread those four scrawny legs so wide so fast that I couldn't even get one foot into the box. Bear in mind, I'd had lots of practice loading spread-eagled dogs when I handled for Dick. I was no amateur. Lloyd was having the same wrestling match with his.

"These dogs don't seem to be too familiar with this dog box routine, Lloyd. How'd you get all those miles on these dogs without getting them into the dog box on your truck?"

"Right out of the yard, Burt. I drove them right out of the yard. Never needed to load them or take them anywhere. They'll be fine."

I decided it would be easier to just drop into nearby Nancy Lake with my Cub when I flew back to dog camp than get these danged mutts into my truck.

"Lloyd, would you mind bringing the dogs over to me at Nancy Lake in a couple of days? When I'm ready to fly back to my camp, I'll swing over here, circle your house a couple of times and then go land on the lake. If you could do that, it'll save us trying to load the dogs now and I won't have to worry about them in town."

"No problem, Burt. Just circle the house and I'll know it's you. I'll bring them right over."

With that happy assurance, I now had plenty of leaders to take me to Nome. I wrote Lloyd a check for eight hundred dollars. I felt like quite the astute dog buyer. I was the proud owner of not one but two fine new leaders, right out of Lloyd Haessler's yard from the Emmitt Peters' Nugget breed. Also, I was proud of myself for shaving a little off the price.

Two days later, I circled his house in my Super Cub and then landed on Nancy Lake. In twenty minutes, Lloyd showed up with the two new lead dogs, which I attempted to put in the airplane. I never saw such wild dogs in my entire life. I took one of the dogs and tried to put it into the backseat. It promptly spread-eagled itself over the edges of the door and hung on by its toenails with such tenacity that I couldn't even push it inside the airplane. This struggle went on for ten minutes, after which I took it away from the airplane.

"Lloyd, would you hold the damn dog while I try to guide its legs into the airplane?"

I took its front legs in one hand and its hind legs in the other and laid the dog upside down in the airplane. Holding it thus, I tied it to a ring at the back of the tiny airplane and went for the other dog. The moment I let go, the first dog started careening around the inside of the airplane like a half-crazed monkey at the end of a string.

"Lloyd, this dog is a little bit wild!"

"No, Burt, these are just high-strung racing dogs. They're all like this. Just be patient. All of this energy is what will get you to Nome in first place!"

We repeated the same exercise with the other dog and I was on my way to my dog camp. The dogs tussled wildly the entire flight to camp. They didn't fight; they simply never stopped their frantic attempts to escape. Heaven help them if they'd ever slipped their collars and managed to push the door open.

Joe came out to help me with the airplane. The moment I shut the engine down, Joe could hear the clatter and banging of those two leaders as they flailed around trying to get loose.

We grabbed the dogs and tied them to their new homes in the yard. After tying the airplane down and eating a quick lunch I said, "Joe, let's hitch some dogs and see how these new leaders do."

Joe readied the sleds and laid out the gear while I worked up the team lists. We never hitched a new leader in the lead position during the first few runs with a strange team. It is always a better idea to put them somewhere back in the team until they get used to their new master and their new teammates.

Grabbing a bundle of harnesses, we began hitching dogs. The first dog hitched was Black, my faithful leader, after which came three or four of my experienced dogs. I then went to get one of "Lloyd's Leaders." Even though the dog was chained to a post, it was nearly impossible to catch. I finally grabbed the chain at the post and started reeling him in. I took him over to the team, harnessed him, and snapped him onto the gang line.

"Joe," I said, "I believe that's the wildest dog I ever put in harness! I can't believe a good lead dog could develop from such a wild creature. I'll bet it would be easier to hitch a coyote than that dog."

While Joe started hitching his team, I went to retrieve the other dog and the same rodeo occurred all over again. When I was able to get the dog under control and lead it over to the waiting team, the first dog was nowhere to be found. Its collar lay there empty, as did its harness. Never had that happened to me before, but I dutifully hitched the second dog and then went looking for the first one. I searched everywhere, through the dog yard, under the cabin, behind the cabin, behind the outhouse, through the dog lot again. I finally began searching dog-houses one at a time. I finally found the little monster, standing on its hind legs and backed into the far corner of a doghouse.

I coaxed her out of there by the scruff of her neck and took her back to harness her only to find that the second of "Lloyd's Leaders" had disappeared. I called for Joe and asked him to stand and watch the one in harness while I found the other one. It didn't take long since this dog was also hiding, plastered to the far back corner of a doghouse. We finally got them both hitched with Joe and I both standing there.

I drove the team off across the lake to see how they would run, but they didn't run at all. They were so busy tugging and pulling and jumping over each other that soon one and then the other had backed out of their collars and harnesses and scooted back down the trail for home. When I returned to camp, they were both plastered to the back corners of their doghouses, hiding.

When I went to return these guaranteed leaders to Lloyd the following week, and asked for my money back, he'd already spent it.

"Lloyd," I said, "you guaranteed these dogs and said that I could return them if I wasn't satisfied."

"Burt, I said that you could bring them back, but I *never* said I'd give you your money back. I'll be happy to take them off your hands, but I *never* said anything about returning your money!"

"Well, then, Lloyd, give me a couple of other leaders to try."

"Burt, I never said I'd trade dogs. All I ever said was that you could bring them back."

"Lloyd, were you telling me that your idea of a guarantee is that you'd simply take the damned dogs off my hands?"

"Well, yah."

"Lloyd, how'd you live so long? You can't go around cheating people like this. Now either give me my money back or give me a couple of replacements!"

"Burt, all I *ever* said was that you could bring them back!"

"How'd you get all those miles on them?"

"Running around their posts. They had to have run at least 1,000 miles, maybe 1,500. Look at the grooves they wore in the dirt."

I left the dogs with the old pirate saying that he'd try to pay me back when he could, but to this day, I've never heard from him. The next winter I saw a "for sale" ad in a mushing publication advertising two leaders out of Emmitt Peters' famed Nugget stock. "Just call Lloyd Haessler," the ad said. I couldn't help but wonder if he wasn't still selling those same two leaders to this year's crop of green-horns. I'll bet he's made a bundle selling those *guaranteed* leaders over and over.

I learned then that there were two kinds of people selling sled dogs, just as there were selling horses and mules to my uncles on the farms back in Iowa. There were people you could count on to be fair and honest, because that's the kind of people they were and they wanted to continue dealing with you. And there were others who would give you a lesson because that was half the fun of the transaction.

I made a mental note to always buy dogs from people who were friends or who were honest and wanted me happy with this dog so they could sell me the next. I earned my BS degree in dog buying during that deal. The eight hundred dollars was the tuition. Little did I know. I learned later that you need an MS degree to buy dogs from some people.

The training season advanced and we continued training for the 1981 race. The trail south of our cabin to the Kahiltna River went through an area thick with fur-bearing animals, so it was my favorite place to train after a fresh snow. It was always interesting to see what kind of animals had passed through. We would see the tracks of squirrels, rabbits, marten, otters, and coyotes. In fact, reading sign was almost like reading the morning paper. All of the neighborhood activity was there. Who had been where and done what was all clear.

My good friend Floyd Tetpon was an Eskimo born over near Unalakleet. He was one of the finest outdoorsmen I knew and we shared a moose-hunting camp over in the Stony River country. He was an excellent pilot and hunter. During 1981, when I was training for my first race, I was still in the engineering business. Floyd was one of my managers at that time. He spent every weekend in his airplane flying here and there as he tended his trapline. He occasionally did a little hunting. Once while I was in town, Floyd said that a pack of five wolves was working its way up towards my cabin and ought to be in our country sometime in the next three or four days. I flew back to my camp at the beginning of the week and awoke the next morning to find five or six inches of fresh snow. We naturally took the route south, which had once been a seismic trail that had not been traveled in years before we arrived. In fact, it had taken several days of hard work to clear all the brush and downed trees just to make it passable. We considered it ours.

We were delighted to find the tracks of a small pack of wolves running along our trail just as Floyd had predicted. The small pack included a couple of adult wolves and several half-grown pups. The wolves generally traveled in a single file along the trail. Even with a few inches of fresh snow, the trail was like a highway compared to the deep snow on either side. As we mushed along, we noticed that a wolf would occasionally wander off into the deep snow on a scouting mission and then rejoin the others further on. Wolves were always hunting and there were a lot of moose in the area.

After our run, the neighbors stopped by for coffee and a visit. We took great delight in telling them about all the tracks we had seen and how much fun it was to mush down the south trail after a snowfall. Telling them turned out to be a mistake. We were mushing down that way a few days later and came across three or four marten sets alongside the trail. Although we certainly didn't own the land, we'd begun to think of it as our own. No one else had traveled that way in years, so it was a little bit hard not to resent the traps. That was the day I should have learned to keep my mouth shut.

Fortunately, our neighbor, Mike, was probably the lousiest trapper in the valley. He managed to trap just one marten the entire winter.

The next fall I finally did learn discretion. I was at my cabin getting things ready for winter when Mike and his son, Mikie, paddled their canoe across the lake for a visit and some tea. I told them about a covey of spruce hens I'd found a hundred yards or so behind the cabin. The young were just about full-grown but were still with their mother. I'd watched them for an hour or so as they rustled around in the leaves playing and looking for goodies.

Summer dog camp near Willow was functional with the training wheel on the far left where the author could watch it from his office cabin. The dogs ran in endless circles while Burt worked on his fishing lodge business. The 3-wheeler sits ready to cart train on the back roads behind the cabin, and the handler's cabin is on the far side of the yard.

Now, I'm a hunter. But I'm often torn between shooting an animal for the freezer and just enjoying the sight of critters doing what they do. I sure as hell would never shoot any creature still with its mother. It didn't occur to me that anyone else would either.

The next week when I returned to finish preparing for winter, the boys came paddling across the lake. They could hardly contain themselves as I put the water on to boil for tea. "Burt, we came back a couple of days ago and found that covey of spruce hens. We managed to shoot the entire covey!"

I went ballistic. "Mike, you son of a bitch! You ever come over here with a gun again and I'll shoot you on sight!" He never did figure out why I was so angry.

That was the day I *did* learn to keep my mouth shut.

Chapter Three
Lost on the South Fork

A tremendous effort is required to bring a team of long distance sled dogs to the start line. Months of preparation go into that first day. The dogs are trained to peak at race time so their speed, strength and enthusiasm are at maximum. It's a relief to get safely out of town. While the Alaska wilderness can be an intimidating, dangerous place for the uninitiated, it's a place of beautiful solitude and serenity to the long distance musher.

The ceremonial start of the 1984 Iditarod on Fourth Avenue in Anchorage was the most exciting day of the year, the day we'd all been working toward. Everybody was focused to make sure the team left without tangles and had a smooth run to the first checkpoint at Eagle River. Even the dogs sensed the excitement. Close friend, Jack Felton, Burt and Ed McMillan are there. Burt's son Jeff and wife Jan are to the right. The racing team included way more than just Burt and the dogs.

The team was trucked from Eagle River to the re-start at Settlers Bay near Knik. Burt's team is in the holding area for the Settlers Bay restart. Straw was laid down for the dogs to lie on while waiting to be harnessed.

The dogs are harnessed one at a time and taken to their place on the gang line. The leaders are hitched first and are expected to keep the line straight as the other dogs are hitched. The sled is packed and Burt's parka lies in readiness for the call to the starting line.

Here Burt stepped on the runners just as the starter said "GO" at the restart at Settlers Bay. Race Marshall Dick Tozier is at Burt's right and Terri McWilliams is ahead of Burt to the right. Starter Orville Lake holds the mike.

Skwentna was the first remote checkpoint along the trail and was just before the trail started its climb toward the Alaska Range. Joe Delia, a true sourdough, checks Burt in as the dogs grab some rest. Joe was the postmaster at Skwentna, as well as a trapper and a fisherman.
Jeff Schultz Photo

The trail winds in and out of the trees as it leaves Skwentna, with much of it across open swamps and lakes. The trail is packed well below the level of the surrounding snow, an indication that this section doesn't get much use except at race time. Trail breakers on snow machines sink deep into the fresh powdery snow. Few things stir the soul of a dog man like a team of good dogs moving across Alaska.

If there are cardinal sins in dog mushing, losing one's sled must be at the top of the list. It is bound to happen when you first begin mushing—there's just too much to learn. A distraction at the wrong moment and you may find yourself frantically hotfooting it down a cold, lonesome trail. It could even happen to a seasoned musher. But you don't want it to happen during a race, which is exactly what happened to me. But for the help of a couple of kind and discreet mushers, it could have been more embarrassing than it was.

It was the second day of the 1981 race, the first sled dog race I'd ever entered. I'd stopped to rest my dogs the first night of the race near Rabbit Lake. I had been too keyed up to get any sleep myself, so I was exhausted the next day. As I mushed along, I spotted a survey lath just six inches off the trail. It had something written on it. Then I saw my name and the message, "Go, Burt." That gave me a lift. A little further along was another lath, this one with the message, "1st to Nome, Burt." One of my survey crews had left me these messages as they surveyed through here.

The previous spring, Ted Smith, Director, Alaska State Division of Lands had called me in to ask if I were interested in surveying the Iditarod Trail from Knik all the way to Skwentna. The trail was an historic route across Alaska and had prescriptive rights across all lands that it passed through. To preserve those rights, the route would need to be surveyed and plats filed with the local recording district. In that way, any land subdivided along the route would have to preserve the right-of-way of the Iditarod Trail. He explained that the Iditarod Trail Sled Dog Race provided the motivation to get this done, but that a host of potential users needed their rights protected also. These users included recreational users, from cross country skiers to hikers and snowmachiners, and sporting events including all sorts of winter marathon events.

It was an honor to be asked and I jumped at the chance. He asked me if I had any thoughts on how we could assure that we surveyed the authentic Iditarod Trail. We discussed it for a few moments and then I suggested Joe Redington Sr. He'd lived next to the Iditarod Trail for years at Flathorn Lake and he was passionate about all things Iditarod. And he was probably the most prominent Iditarod personality in history with his founding of the Iditarod Trail Sled Dog Race. We wrote my contract with a proviso that I hire Joe Sr. to act as trailblazer for the project. He also jumped at the chance to be involved.

Joe had come out onto the trail in early winter when wilderness travel was possible using snowmachines and dog teams, and he had blazed this trail. My survey crew was still out here doing their work. Field work had to be done in winter because the trail crossed swamp after swamp as it wended its way toward Iditarod—difficult terrain during summer.

The first order of business had been to select the route and get approvals up the chain of command so that no changes would be made once field work had begun. Joe drew the route on USGS maps and we met with Ted to discuss and approve it. We asked Joe why he went cross country through Rabbit Lake instead of up the Susitna River where the trail was easy because it was flat and direct. He responded, "No way would those early guys have gone up that river. It's dangerous, especially during freeze-up and break-up when it's not frozen solid." Those early mushers were smart enough to find a place where the river froze up early and stayed frozen longer to make their river crossing. They didn't want to be on the river any more than they had to. They wanted to be safe all the way to where the trail crossed the Skwentna River near the old Skwentna Roadhouse. Joe wanted his race to follow the actual Iditarod Trail to Iditarod and Ted required that we be on the historic trail because of legal issues involving prescriptive rights, both good reasons. Now the crew was getting the job done. We surveyed the alignment from Knik Lake to Skwentna, a total of eighty-six miles.

These memories filled my consciousness as I mushed along. It was about nine o'clock in the morning; the day was crystal clear. My dogs were putting along only seven or eight miles from Skwentna when ahead of me loomed a large birch tree leaning across the trail. I'd driven under so many of those during training that it was hardly worth noticing. It was as simple as gliding along until the tree was right there, leaning slightly to the right, to avoid the tree, and continuing.

My reflexes were a bit slow, however. I approached the tree and just as I was ready to duck, the tree slammed me from my sled. I hit the ground hard but was quickly up and running after the team. When I say running, it's a little misleading—I lumbered. I've never been fast. I didn't make a sound as I lumbered along, fearing that if I did the dogs would know they'd lost me and would start picking up speed. It was not that they wanted to get away, it was just that anything different seemed to give them a little adrenaline boost and they went faster. Meanwhile, I was puffing along behind the sled as fast as I could, gaining inch by inch. I figured that, as soon as I got as close as I could and started dropping back, I'd make one diving lunge for the sled and hope to grab enough of it to hang on and slow it down.

Well, I got as close as I was going to get and the sled started drawing slowly away so I made my mad leap. My hand slammed into the ground about a foot behind the sled. By then, of course, the dogs realized that I was no longer a passenger and began picking up speed. I started trudging as rapidly as I could along the trail behind them but, of course, they disappeared. As I marched along, I suddenly heard the sounds of a team approaching and turned to see Gene Leonard coming from behind. My predicament was obvious. As his sled drew abreast of me, Gene asked if I would like to hitch a ride on his sled and see if we couldn't catch my dogs. I hopped aboard. Gene and I together probably weighed four hundred pounds. With that extra weight on his sled and no weight on mine, the distance between us would grow.

Soon Bruce Denton from Juneau came mushing up behind us. Again, my predicament was obvious. Bruce passed us and said he'd see if he could catch my team. He whistled to the dogs and they quickly broke into a lope. Gene and I mushed along for another mile or so enjoying the sunshine and having a little visit.

As we mushed along, Gene said, "Burt, I think we *better* catch that sled of yours. Skwentna is going to be jammed with volunteers, officials, fans, and reporters who are there to watch the teams. It's only a hundred miles from Anchorage and it's the last easily accessible checkpoint before the trail heads off into the bush. This could get embarrassing."

Soon we found my team anchored firmly in the trail with Bruce nowhere in sight. It was a remarkable feat that he could catch my team without my weight on the sled. He must have had fast dogs. It was nice to arrive at Skwentna on the runners of my sled. Gene Leonard and Bruce Denton have my eternal thanks.

LOST ON THE SOUTH FORK

We continued through the checkpoints at Finger Lake, Rainy Pass, and then on to Rohn. In Rohn, the dogs and I loaded up on good food and rest. It would be a long seventy miles across the burn to Nikolai. This would be a demanding run and I wanted us ready. It would turn out to be one of the most demanding, dangerous runs I would ever experience.

The team began to stir as I started to load my sled. Joe Redington Sr. and I had declared our required twenty-four-hour layovers when we arrived at the Rohn checkpoint in case we decided to stay. Now we had decided to leave early. Mandatory gear went in first, including snowshoes in the bottom of the sled, eight booties for each dog, my axe, and my sleeping bag. We were also required to carry a small package of mail to be postmarked in Anchorage and again in Nome. The caches we carried would be sold later as part of a fund-raising project.

The rest of the pile, dog food, my food, and some survival gear, were tossed in last. Not a lot of survival gear, since most of what we needed was included in the mandatory gear. And we didn't need much, just the logical items like matches and a small tarp for shelter. It was winter in the Alaska wilderness, but a competent woodsman could get by with remarkably little. Besides, we didn't plan to get stuck out there—we were racing.

We picked a nice clean spot in the open to camp during this nice weather, although we might have picked a sheltered spot in the trees during a blizzard. Joe Redington Sr. snapped this picture of Burt as they camped together on a lake heading toward Rainy Pass.

As the items hit the sled, the dogs readied themselves, each in his own way. Igor and Porky, my wheel dogs, just ahead of the sled, began to bark and lunge with tremendous force as they saw me working. Like cheerleaders, they incited the other dogs and their enthusiasm began to infect the others. Sundance, Dotty and Tippy were always the slowest to react. They were a little more sensitive than the other dogs and didn't like all this rowdy commotion. They were like college kids in a biker bar, excited but a little intimidated. Vegas and Black, my leaders for this leg, stood with quiet professional patience, waiting for my command to hike on out. A couple of soft yips out of Black was all the excitement I'd seen from her. The experienced dogs knew the responsibility and pressure that would be on them as we wended our way over the seventy miles across the Farewell Burn to Nikolai.

Things went nuts as I tossed the last of my camping gear into the sled and pulled my beaver mitts on. Now all the dogs were on their feet as Joe Sr. blasted out of the checkpoint ahead of me. I wanted to be hot on his heels. Our dogs were evenly matched, but his years of experience gave him an edge over my rookie status. I could learn from him and he just might save me from some stupid mistakes. He had invited me to travel along with him for mutual benefit and I took him up on it. We had taken turns at breaking trail to save on our leaders and it was always nice to share a campfire.

I pulled the hook and we charged out of the checkpoint behind Joe. We left the comforts of a warm cabin and friendly conversation behind and entered a frozen lonely wilderness to travel a trail not much populated.

We careened through a forest of huge, stately spruce trees for the first quarter mile out of Rohn and then dropped down onto the hard icy surface of the South Fork of the Kuskokwim River. I stood on the brake with both feet to slow the dash, fearful that the dogs might slip and sprain something on the slick ice in their eagerness to catch Joe. I was determined to finish in the money and had trained hard to do so.

Out of Rainy Pass and then through Rohn checkpoint, Burt heads onto the infamous South Fork of the Kuskokwim River. It's balmy at times but then the wind will howl and blow the icy river surface and the gravel bars clear of snow. Burt took a wrong turn and traveled this river across endless gravel bars, glare ice and thin ice that cracked and failed under the weight of Burt and his sled. It was 24 hours before he regained the trail into Nikolai.
Jeff Schultz Photo

Joe Sr. had said to stick with him during the race and he'd show me some things about racing Iditarod. We had climbed Rainy Pass and descended the treacherous Dalzell River Gorge out of Rainy Pass together. I'd made a valiant effort to keep up with Joe and had managed well. We had arrived at the Rohn cabin together at ten in the morning. The dogs ate, first a wet mixture of commercial dog food and meat followed by all of the cold meat snacks they would eat. I wanted their tanks full for the long run ahead.

While the slurp was cooking for the team, I grabbed a quick snack from the tiny log cabin where race checkers had laid out a feast of chili, cheese and crackers along with lots of Tang to get me hydrated.

Now we drove our teams from the checkpoint at two o'clock, hoping to make it well out into the Farewell burn before darkness. The edge of the burn was fifteen miles away over rugged trail. They call this first stretch the Buffalo Tunnel because the trail is narrow and twists through buffalo country. Much of the trail slants to the right causing the sled to slide sideways, constantly banging it into the stunted black spruce trees.

Rookies are always cautioned to consult with checkers and other race personnel at the checkpoints to glean whatever information is available for the route ahead to the next checkpoint. This is one bit of advice that rookies and veterans alike usually follow. When I made this standard inquiry at Rohn, the checker, Don Burt, told me to expect lots of bare gravel, lots of ice, and lots of overflow. It sounded like river travel to me and the Kuskokwim River did flow from Rohn to the next checkpoint. The fact was that anyone who had traveled this route before knew that the trail wouldn't be on the river again until Nikolai, seventy miles away, too dangerous to start with. As I punched out of Rohn behind Joe, visions of mushing my team over bare gravel, lots of ice and overflow danced in my head. I wasn't disappointed.

About half a mile out of the checkpoint, I realized I hadn't informed the checker that I was breaking my twenty-four-hour stop. As we bounced out onto the river, I couldn't remember what the rule required as to notifying the checker if I decided to leave my twenty-four-hour layover early. Could I simply leave or must I check back out again? I hurriedly turned my team around and headed back for Rohn as Joe Redington mushed across the icy surface of the South Fork and into the trees on the far bank. When I arrived at the checkpoint moments later, the checker informed me that it wasn't necessary to check out. I once again swapped ends and headed back toward the Farewell burn and Nikolai, the next checkpoint. Unless I could catch him, I wouldn't be able to shirttail on Joe's familiarity with the trail.

Less than an hour later, we descended a steep high bank onto the Post River, which flowed into the Kuskokwim River just a half a mile to the east. The Post was a sheet of glare ice with no markers on its broad expanse. Scrapes and scratches showed where other teams had preceded us. As the dogs trotted swiftly to the far bank, a natural channel seemed to proceed northeasterly to my right and toward the mighty Kuskokwim River.

Trees and bushes along the far bank to my left contained numerous survey ribbons, which in my inexperience were totally misinterpreted. Instead of directing the dogs into the trees near the ribbons, I allowed them to follow the natural drainage course northeasterly. Black's nose dipped down to sniff the surface, likely checking the scent left by a team ahead. An icy blast of wind hit us as we left the shelter of the trees along the Post River and wound our way out onto the slick ice of the South Fork of the Kuskokwim River. This river was known to be one of the most treacherous in Alaska.

Something felt wrong. The survey ribbon and the tripods used to mark the trail no longer appeared. Uncertainty nearly forced me to turn back once or twice, but then the scratches and scrapes of runners preceding me, and the occasional dog tracks, showed that another team had been here before me. I didn't want to turn back again and let Joe get even farther ahead. My mind was swirling in an effort to determine whether I was lost and should go back, or whether I should proceed the way I was going.

My eyes scanned ahead for some sign of a trail but all I saw was a wide, braided river reaching a width of more than half a mile in some places. Numerous sand and gravel bars divided the many broad, icy river channels. A strong bitter-cold tail wind pushed me like a sail. Extreme winds blowing northerly from the mountain passes of the Alaska Range blew the river completely clear of snow and polished the ice so its surface was glazed and hard. My brakes were nearly useless on the hard, icy surface, allowing the sled to blow forward in helter-skelter fashion, often bumping the wheel dogs, sometimes blowing sideways ahead of the wheelers.

I saw open water ahead and commanded Black to gee to the right around the water, but she forged ahead, refusing to heed my direction. Again, I commanded her to gee. Again, no response. We were now just a hundred yards away from serious peril. The water appeared absolutely smooth, indicating either deep water or overflow. Neither was good, but deep water was deadly. Shallow water usually contained riffles that were easy to see and a whole lot safer. We hurtled closer and closer.

I stood on the brakes with both feet, lifting up on the sled's hand bow to add the sled's weight to my own but the brake hardly scratched the hard polished ice. We didn't slow down at all. As we approached to within thirty yards, the imminent need for a decision blasted into my consciousness. How far should I ride this sled to oblivion before I bailed? Or should I go down with the team? Rookies pondered these issues; veterans didn't. Just as the leaders were about to plunge into the icy depths, the illusion morphed into reality and the open water turned into the polished surface of rock-hard ice. My heart still pounded as Black turned and gave me that look. The shallow sun's rays had created the illusion of water, which was actually ice. This mirage effect plagued me the rest of the afternoon.

We continued mushing north, the dogs alternately traversing gravel bars, then ice. The gravel was much harder pulling, but gave the dog's better footing. The ice was easy pulling but made it hard for the dogs to stay upright.

Egypt Mountain, a prominent landmark, appeared slowly ahead to the left. The dogs were trotting briskly across an icy expanse when the sled began a slow sideways skid to the left. That fierce wind was blowing me forward. The team was trotting briskly, so I should have been trailing along in a nice straight line, but soon I was even with the wheelers and still in a slow skid to the left. The wind was howling and my big parka acted like a sail.

Then it became evident that the force of gravity had added a component. The ice sloped to the left so gently that it was hard to see. But slope it did to a point ahead and fifty yards to my left. The dropping ice formed the bottom of a trough, from which the ice began to angle back up toward the far shore. As we continued, the sled caught up with the second pair of dogs ahead of the wheel dogs. The leaders and swing dogs had moved over to the gravel bar for better footing as they felt the dogs behind them pulling to the left. That was all that kept the entire team from sliding in a tangled mess down this gentle but extremely slick slope.

Then ahead the trough began to open slightly, just a crack, and I saw open water. There was no mistaking it this time. The soft sound of flowing water began as a pleasant sound. At first it was a gentle rushing sound but it developed into a roar as the crack opened wide and the sled began to accelerate its sideways skid down the ever-steepening slope. The ice had frozen when the water was higher. As the water level subsided, the ice slumped with it, forming a big deadly trap. The resulting break in the middle of the channel caused this open glory hole.

We continued with all the dogs except the leaders and swing dogs strung out in a straight line that angled down the slope, and me on the sled pulling us all down. Only Black and the three other dogs trotting along the gravel bar kept us all from skidding headlong down the icy slope. If they lost their footing or if Black decided to move off her gravel bar, there was not much to stop us. I dug my Buck knife out of my pocket and opened it. If things cut loose, I'd bail off the sled and try to jam the knife into the ice. I hoped it would hold, and not just leave a big scritch mark all the way to the hole. I was now skidding sideways along with most of the team as we approached the glory hole. Then, slowly, the yawning fissure closed up, and we moved on to a stretch of flat level ice. The team and sled again tracked normally.

Still in the mountains, Burt continues down the South Fork of the Kuskokwim River. Note the wind-glazed ice on the river and the snow blowing off the peaks hinting of high winds to come. This beautiful, serene day turned rough when Burt made a wrong turn and traveled for miles down the treacherous river.

The persistent lack of marking continued to be a cause for concern, but the checker's prediction of glare ice and gravel kept me on course downriver. The occasional scratch from a sled brake and a dog's paw print helped validate my location. I knew that the next checkpoint at Nikolai was on the South Fork of this river. It all made just enough sense to a rookie.

Black, my most experienced leader, was leading us mile after relentless mile downstream. She was a remarkable leader, bred by famed Eskimo musher Isaac Okleasik. During her prime, she had led many famous mushers to victory in sled dog races all over Alaska and had made several trips to Nome along the Iditarod Trail. She was now within a year or two of retirement. She was much too tired and slow to be in a top competitive team, but she was perfect for a rookie musher looking for a finish in the top twenty. She was trail savvy and smart enough to keep me out of danger, I hoped.

I'd heard tales of smart leaders that did all the thinking during hazardous times. Thin ice, obliterated trail, overflow, or being lost with no landmarks were all occasions when a musher could turn the decision making over to that trusted leader. The dog would know what to do when you didn't.

Overflow could be one of the most hazardous conditions. It occurred when water flowed over ice and could be caused by a number of conditions, possibly an open area in a swift river or a place where ice had settled sufficiently to allow water from the river to flow over the ice. It also could be the result of heavy snowpack on a lake, forcing the ice down and allowing water to cover it, or it might develop from warm springs along the edges of a lake or river flowing out over the ice. Sometimes a warm spring flowing out over the ground could freeze causing glaciation.

If there was a problem with Black, it was that she'd been around the block once too often. Past her prime, she'd had several drivers, including the guy I bought her from, who were not that proficient. She'd learned how to put one over on a rookie musher like me and sometimes took things into her own paws. Black was truly remarkable but more than a handful.

Black continued leading us farther and farther downstream, alternately skittering across glare ice, and sand bars, where the drag was exhausting, then more glare ice and then through overflow. I jumped off the runners and ran on the gravel bars to reduce the drag. The current was so swift in some places that ice couldn't form. Areas of open water were common, some of it was shallow, but some looked deep and dark. Black didn't like the dangerously slick glare ice and especially hated it when water over the ice made it even more slippery. I hated it as much as she did. The sled still wouldn't track straight since the runner bottoms were slick, soft plastic, which wouldn't track at all on the hard, polished ice.

Sudden gusts of wind continued to hit us so hard that the sled with me on it often caught up with the dogs, passing several dogs in the team. Occasionally, the wind blew so hard that the sled was blown sideways and strung the whole team out to the side. We occasionally proceeded apace down the river, the dogs all even with each other trying to run sideways to the gang line. All the while, I stood on the brake, a rooster tail of shaved ice spewing out behind with no noticeable braking affect whatsoever. It was like trying to cut diamonds. Several times during these sideways skids, we slid into an exposed rock or stick and the sled crashed on its side throwing me headlong onto the frozen surface. It was difficult righting the sled as the team continued unabated, seeming to enjoy the spectacle of me struggling. If we ever started skidding sideways into one of those glory holes, there'd be no tomorrow. Between the brakes, made dull by so much gravel, the hard ice and the strong tailwind, there was no stopping the sled, even when I stood on the brake with both feet. Theoretically, the harder the drag, the more the team would track in a straight line, but it wasn't working here.

The team made its way slowly down the river attempting to avoid sandbars and the bare ground as much as possible because of the added drag. The lack of any kind of trail markers was painfully obvious; however, each time I considered turning back, a telltale scrape from someone's brake appeared on the ice ahead of me. With other teams ahead, this *had* to be the trail.

It was rough going no matter where we ran. It was slow, heavy pulling across bare sand and gravel or so slick that the dogs and I could hardly keep our footing. We occasionally mushed the wrong way down a slough and found ourselves in a dead-end thicket of tangled spruce and willow. Each time, I untangled the dogs, and we retraced our steps to try again.

As we traveled along, we began to skirt a huge glory hole. The slumped area was a hundred feet across, consisting completely of glare ice. A deep, dark torrent of icy water raged at its apex. By now I'd become painfully aware of the lack of braking ability on my sled. The dogs came nearer and nearer to the edge, where the ice began its dangerous descent toward the open hole in the center.

Black had already heard so many commands as we traversed the open ice that she had begun to ignore my presence. As we approached the danger zone at the glory hole's edge, the rushing, thundering water became louder and louder until it filled the air with a roar that I could feel as much as hear. My hackles were up. The opening, approximately ten feet across and 200 feet long, was filled with a deep, black, raging torrent of water. Anything trespassing beyond the sloping edge of the glory hole would be doomed to a quick, nonstop skid into the water, which would instantly swallow it beneath the ice.

The dogs instinctively seemed to know they should skirt the edge, but the powerful wind blowing the sled from behind continually caused the sled to swerve from side to side, getting ahead of the wheel dogs. The dull brake was not effective. The skidding sled created a frightening spectacle as we mushed closer and closer to the edge of the hole.

I frantically pawed through my pocket for my Buck knife and again opened the blade. If the sled, which was now out of control, swerved onto the slope, I could at least try to jump free and stop myself by jamming the knife's blade into the ice. With my weight off the sled, the dogs would have little problem reaching safety themselves. If the ice immediately underfoot did not break through with my weight no longer spread by the sled's runners, I might somehow recover my team and continue.

We approached the glory hole's edge with me standing on the brake with both feet in a futile attempt to keep the sled behind the dogs. This hole was similar to the earlier ones but far more dangerous. With so little drag, a crack-the-whip situation began to develop. This was definitely something I hoped to avoid as we approached the dangerous edge.

Closer and closer we came. As we were almost safely past, a gust hit the sled and pushed us over the edge onto the gentle but deadly slope. Even with all my weight on the brake and my urgent, shrill whistles to quicken the pace, the sled lurched sideways and began to accelerate sideways down the icy slope. My sideways skid took me directly toward a frozen piece of driftwood stub as big as my wrist, which would surely upend the sled and hurl me onto the ice, even more out of control. At the last instant, I twisted my body like a skier in a turn and the sled lurched. We miraculously avoided the stub. Still skidding sideways with Buck knife in hand, I whistled the dogs up and asked for everything they had. Sensing my alarm, the dogs leaned their shoulders to the task and picked up the pace.

The leaders reached another small gravel bar and thankfully didn't try to stay on the ice. They must have felt the added pull from behind. Gravity and the icy slope began working quickly against them. Although it made their job harder, I needed to continue putting all my weight on that brake, doing everything possible to stop the accelerating sideways skid into that swirling torrent of icy, black water. Knowing something extra was needed, they stayed where the traction was best and continued to dig for everything they had.

We were about ten feet from the water's edge when our sideways skid slowed and then nearly stopped. With the dogs on solid ground, I determined to hang onto the sled at all cost. The Buck knife was a poor substitute if the dogs could do it. Slowly the sled began tracking behind the wheelers and I eased up on the brake. Now the dogs could pull us up and away from the deadly hole. My heart pounded for ten minutes with thoughts of what might have been. Drowning aside, a drenching could be deadly with this icy wind.

The light began to fade as the team wound its way south along the expanse of the ever-widening river. To the left, the winter sun was nearing the western horizon. As darkness settled, it would become more and more difficult to tell the water from the glare ice, thus increasing the chance of a soaking. Dealing with that problem, especially in the dark, would be tricky to say the least. The only things visible would be those things illuminated by the dim rays of one's headlight. A soaking would likely render any lights inoperative anyway. Survival meant finding a way off the middle of the South Fork and into trees that would shelter us from the wind and provide firewood until dawn. The sooner the better, as night was approaching.

After a day on the South Fork, Burt regains the Iditarod Trail as it proceeds towards Nikolai. Burt and the dogs appreciated a beautiful smooth trail. Notice the drifts from the incessant wind blowing out of Rainy Pass.

After a mile or so, a small grove of black spruce trees showed up on the east bank approximately a quarter mile away. From this distance, it appeared to be a perfect spot to seek shelter for the night. The dogs responded immediately to my command to "gee" and turned sharply to the right heading across a series of gravel bars and glare ice. They had caught on to the fact that we were heading off this miserable river and made a beeline for the trees. The dogs were as frazzled from the conditions as I was. My faithful leader, Black, was now totally blitzed by the constant gee-haw commands that had been necessary to guide her through the unfamiliar glare ice, open water, and gravel.

Once Black realized that we were heading ashore, she ran for the safety of that grove of trees with iron determination. She'd had it, and took matters into her own paws. I knew she wouldn't get away with this if Isaac was on the runners, but she'd had enough of rookies telling her what to do. It was again necessary to stand with all my weight on the brake. This time it was to slow things down. Our pell-mell run was leaving a rooster tail of ice chips and gravel as we headed from the river's icy surface across gravel bars and then back again onto glare ice. We were all eager to get off the treacherous river and into the trees, so I wasn't particularly alarmed over the breakneck speed of our run. Then I spotted open water ahead.

As we drew closer, it became obvious that the water was a shallow rapid approximately a foot deep and about seventy-five feet across. A gee command to direct the team upstream to what appeared to be solid ice was totally ignored. Black had taken command at the wrong moment. So much for trusting your lead dog. That theory was hogwash. Your leader might do the right thing ninety percent of the time, but those were thin odds when your life was at stake.

Much of the time, a good leader will do the right thing and will be uncanny about judging thin ice. But Black was on a mission. Without veering left or right, she headed for the open water, totally ignoring my commands. She leaped into the water looking like a black lab heading for a duck. The whole team plunged across the riffle, water splashing in all directions. The water was almost too deep for the dogs to maintain their footing. Any deeper and they would have been swimming, a dangerous situation considering the stiff current.

Then the sled reached the edge of the ice and I gave it a good push into the water. I tried to land on the runners. The inertia of the sled pulled me off my feet and I was dragged through the water on my belly, hanging on to the sled for dear life. Twelve frantic huskies never missed a beat as the icy water flooded down my neck and through my parka. I was drenched to the skin. I regained my footing but even my bunny boots and pockets were filled with water. In an instant, Black clambered up on the ice and each dog in turn climbed out behind her with the sled following.

One of the most deadly perils of Arctic travel is water or moisture. The temperature was sub-zero and there wasn't a moment to lose. I had to build a fire and get into dry clothes immediately. My wet clothes would draw heat from my body at a bone-numbing rate. Not only did my body's core temperature plummet, but also the surface of my clothes quickly froze. My fingers became too numb to undo zippers, unlace boots, or strike a match. You couldn't thaw your fingers by sticking them into pockets or mitts filled with icy water.

An icy blast of winter wind instantly froze the outer shell of my parka and mitts making the need for a warm fire urgent. Cold would quickly penetrate to my skin with my clothes soaked. There had been good reason for my concern at the prospect of an icy bath and now the worst had happened.

But the gods of the north weren't about to let us off. As we clambered up on to what I hoped was our last hurdle, an even more dangerous problem loomed ahead. Directly in our path, the last channel of the river took a sharp bend at the shore along a cut bank. The current was too swift to freeze. Even from fifty yards away, the water appeared swift, deep and dark. The open channel was only ten feet across and approximately thirty feet long, an easy obstacle to avoid if the dogs would listen. But they wouldn't. They had found that my brake had no affect on the glare ice. I couldn't get up there to discipline them as long as they maintained their headlong rush. The relatively small patch of water fooled the dogs into thinking they could get across it as easily as the riffle just passed. They couldn't have been more wrong.

Black plunged into the water with perfect form. She again reminded me of a big black lab launching after a duck. The current swallowed her instantly and she disappeared from sight under the water. Then I saw her tug line being swept under the ice. The swift current had pinned Black under the ice with no way to reach the surface. Seeing her disappear so quickly, the swing dogs screeched to a stop and, for once, I was able to keep the sled from making further progress. The first pairs of dogs were holding back with all their might to avoid disappearing with Black into the water while the big wheelers, Porky and Igor, apparently unaware of the problem ahead, strained with all their might to go forward.

As I continued to stand on the brake, I attempted to set the snow hook, an anchoring device on the end of a rope. The glare ice made it difficult to get a bite. Stomping on the hook with all my might achieved limited success. Each time I felt it catch, I allowed the dogs to put a little pressure on the snow hook in an effort to set it. Each time, it chinked loose just as it seemed it would hold.

Suddenly Black's head broke the surface as she paddled frantically. She screamed in fear, a panicky cry that begged for help. She sounded more like a terrified woman than a dog. Just as suddenly, she disappeared again, swept back under the ice by the raging current.

I needed the hook to hold so I could move forward along the sled and then the gang line to pull Black from the swift current. The hook finally held. I worked my way forward along the gang line, holding the dogs back as best I could. As I advanced, I feared that the hook would jerk loose and pull us all into the deadly water or that the treacherous ice beneath my feet would break loose and I would plunge into a watery grave.

I advanced first past Porky and Igor, then past the other dogs, applying just the right amount of pressure to keep the hook set. Black again surfaced and was able to get her paws on the ice, letting out a tortured scream. She could get her feet up on the ice but she couldn't make it any further. Then she was swept under again. After what seemed like an eternity, I reached the swing dogs, Zorro and Vegas, just behind Black. All the while, I talked to the dogs in low soothing tones hoping to keep them calm so they wouldn't yank against the snow hook and pull it loose. I had no way of knowing how thick the ice was under my feet, but I prayed it would hold.

Finally, I was able to grab Black's tug line and gave it a yank, pulling her up onto the ice to safety. She stopped there, hunkered down on the ice, not moving a muscle. Scared witless, she didn't even attempt to shake the water from her fur.

I looked around for a safe route to shore. The only safe path appeared to be back across the riffle and then upstream and back across solid ice to the edge of the trees. Black took off like a shot when I told her to go. Following every command flawlessly, she headed back into the riffle the way we had come. Once out of the water, I commanded her to haw, she obeyed with the precision of a drill team sergeant and we arrived at the edge of the trees. I drove the dogs right into the heart of the thickest nest of black spruce I could find. It was only then that the dogs took time to shake the water out of their fur. They snuggled up as warm and cozy as they could be with warm steam rising from their fur.

The ice penetrated deep into my clothes. The frozen shell began to sound like a suit of armor when I moved. While the excitement of the moment kept my blood racing, a cold numbness began to penetrate my fingers and face. I quickly chopped a dead spruce into kindling wood. Even with my active metabolism, I needed to keep moving. Within minutes, a roaring fire made everything okay. Soon, all my clothes lay in a pile as I warmed up and dried my naked body in front of the toasty blaze. I poured the water from my boots and put them back on my feet. The beauty of bunny boots is that they will keep your feet warm, even when wet. I wrung the water out of my clothes and then, still naked, I hung them to dry in the freezing wind at the edge of the trees.

Since we were heading into the longest run between checkpoints on the entire Iditarod Trail Sled Dog Race, I'd packed an abundant supply of succulent, tasty food for my trail mates. I put the cook pot over the blazing fire. Within twenty minutes, the meat was thawed and a delicious stew was ready for the dogs. Each had a big pan full, which they slurped down. Eagerly they finished the first course, which was followed by nice, fatty lamb and then finally some beef liver. Their cares were forgotten and so were mine. While they had dinner, I dined on a grilled cheese sandwich, hot cider, and crackers. The dogs were again nestled in with steam rising from their bodies.

I crawled into my sleeping bag, which I'd spread before the roaring fire. Even with two trips through the water, none of the gear on my sled was wet, having been safely wrapped in a waterproof sled bag. My nice dry sleeping bag felt like heaven.

I awakened often during the night to check for headlamps of other teams on the river but saw none. By morning, it was obvious that my turn off the trail yesterday at the Post River had led me far astray. I had no idea how to get back to the trail except to retrace my steps up the treacherous river.

As the sun created its first glow over the mountains to the east, I stirred. I stretched and nestled down a little lower in my warm bag, enjoying the last moments before this day began. Yesterday was the nastiest day of my mushing career and I knew I had to retrace the entire miserable path again today.

Crawling out of my bag, I hustled into my dry bunny boots and hotfooted it to my makeshift clothesline. The biting wind added urgency to getting my naked body dressed. The clothes were chilled to below zero. A delicious feeling came over me when putting my chilled clothes onto my rapidly cooling body. They were cold but dry. The exercise of feeding my dogs another slurpy meal and loading the sled warmed me up.

We were well rested and ready for most anything the day could bring. I had my doubts about mushing back up the river, but there was no choice. We headed south, back toward the starting line but into a dying wind. The trip back to the trail was almost a carbon copy of the trip down yesterday, without the drenching. Lots of gravel bars to cross, glare ice and frequent areas of overflow. The terrifying glory holes were still there and still gave me a chill each time we put one behind us. It was impossible to retrace our steps exactly on the untracked river, so each mile was a new surprise.

My error on the Post River and my ignorance in not turning back when the trail markers played out weighed heavily on my mind. My goal was to finish in the money, and my team and I had worked hard all winter to make it happen. Now I'd let the dogs down as well as my sponsors, workmates, and friends.

We were making good progress and I could see the Post River off to my right. But this Alaska winter wilderness still hadn't given up on me. The dogs suddenly began acting different. They weren't picking up their feet in their normal frisky trot. Instead, they seemed to slide their feet rapidly along the ice, almost seeming to pussyfoot along, but at a fast pace that was not quite a trot or a lope. They acted as though they were running on eggshells. Their heads were down and their ears were cocked forward as though they were listening to something below the ice. Suddenly the ice lurched downward and then continued to settle as though the sled was going to break through into the deep rushing water below. The ice was too thin to support us.

A quick glance back showed open water and floating ice chunks in the path we had just traveled. We were about to plunge through. The dogs knew it, and I had no idea how deep the water might be or how swift the current was. I whistled and called urgently for the dogs to pick it up fast. As long as we kept moving, there was a chance we would plane along like a water skier and wouldn't fall through into the icy depths below. I stood perfectly still on the runners so as not to upset the delicate balance as we moved rapidly forward. I could feel the sled lurch as the ice broke away beneath us. The ice, only an inch thick, continued to crackle and pop and settle as the heavy sled followed the now fast-moving team. It was obvious the dogs had heard the ice cracking and felt it settling beneath them before I did. They adjusted their pace, somehow knowing that any extra jolting could send us all into an icy grave.

My two hundred pounds on the back of the sled was still causing the tails of the runners to crack the ice, sometimes to the breaking point. I was alarmed each time the sled started breaking through. I could feel it lurch downward. The bow of the sled seemed to plane along like a surfboard but the runner tails where I stood continued breaking through, sometimes leaving floating ice chunks and a swirling current in our wake. There seemed to be no end to it.

In disbelief, Jack London's frightening stories raced through my mind. This couldn't be happening to me. Then, as quickly as it had begun, it ended. The ice felt firm, and the dogs broke into a happy lope as though they knew how close we'd come to disaster.

We pulled into the mouth of the Post River where it entered the South Fork of the Kuskokwim River. It was now obvious that we had mistakenly continued out onto the South Fork while the trail markers clearly showed where we should have made a haw turn to the left and up a steep bank. I'll share blame with Black for that goof up. With a nose like a bloodhound, Black had to know where most of the teams ahead of us had gone. Smart bitch that she was, however, she'd taken the easy route downriver rather than scramble up that steep bank. I kicked myself for misinterpreting the trail markers. That was when I learned the fallacy of the infallible leader.

We had no time for regrets. We'd been on the most treacherous river I'd ever been on before or since, and we had survived it. Independent though she was, Black took command after command as we wended our way through one hazard after another until her last, stubborn run for shore. She hadn't forgotten that drenching and obeyed all the way from there to Nome. We'd made some mistakes but were equal to the task and I was proud of my team. All we'd lost was a day on the trail. It could have been a whole lot worse, but that's partly why we did this. It wouldn't be adventure without the danger.

I learned later that a musher had in fact been ahead of us on the river. When he decided to leave the river for the night, he headed west up a slough instead of east, as we did, and miraculously ran right into the race trail.

Two things made me squirm worse than the danger of being on that river. First was the razzing we took from the ham radio operator at Nikolai who claimed I'd set a new record for the longest time reaching Nikolai from Rohn River. According to him, I'd demolished the previous record set by my good pal Col. Norman Vaughan, who was known far and wide for his leisurely sled dog trips to Nome.

The final embarrassment occurred later after I arrived in Shaktoolik. Several of us were at the checkpoint in Lyn Takak's house watching TV over a cup of hot chocolate, when Joe Redington appeared. His face was battered as though he'd been in a prizefight. The interviewer asked him what happened to his face.

Joe replied, "I was heading out of Rohn toward Nikolai and turned around to look for my good friend Burt Bomhoff. We were traveling together. He had a good team and I thought he could win 'Rookie of the Year.' When I turned back to the trail, a three-inch tree limb banged me right in the face and darn near knocked me off my sled!"

I was embarrassed.

Back in Nikolai, I left the checker and got down to my checkpoint business. I was somewhat chagrined at the checker's razzing but needed to get busy.

My normal procedure at a checkpoint was to first find a water supply, get my Coleman stove cranked up and put water on to boil. Boiling water tended to be the most time-consuming part of my act, so it was the one thing I liked to get at first.

I then tried to locate my food bags and opened the appropriate ones to get myself resupplied. I normally sent two or three gunnysacks full of supplies to each checkpoint putting certain items in certain bags depending upon anticipated need. Bag number one always had my personal food in it and the dog food that I would need if all was normal. There was enough dog food there to feed my dogs at the checkpoint and provide additional meals along the way to the next checkpoint depending upon the distance. Clean socks and a fresh hanky were included along with new batteries for my headlamp.

While the dog water was coming to a boil, I sorted through all these items, taking out the ones I needed for the next leg, and putting them in my sled. I then rested a little bit and was on my way. The dogs had slept virtually the entire period of the stop, waking only long enough to eat and then fall back asleep. The result was that the dogs got a good rest before we proceeded toward Nome.

Bert:
Sorry we got seperated.
You are doing okay.
The Trail will be a lot
Better, I still say you'll
be in the money. I hope to see
you up the Trail.
                    Joe Sr.

Joe Redington Sr. was concerned and left Burt a note of encouragement with the McGrath checker. Try as he might, Burt couldn't catch up, even with encouraging words from Joe all along the trail.

Chapter Four
The Anvik River

B lack led my team up the bank above the Yukon River into the tiny village of Anvik. The soft sound of gang line and traces was muffled by the snow that was still deep after a long winter. The afternoon had been warm and the snow was wet and sticky. Black didn't need me to tell her where to find the checkpoint in this village or any other along the Iditarod Trail. She'd been here often before. I'd also been here before, but not racing sled dogs. I had done the engineering for the Anvik Airport and the Grayling Airport just downstream, ten years earlier. Anvik didn't look the same to me as it did back then.

Warm temperatures had created an early break-up, making the Anvik River extremely dangerous during the day. The race marshal stopped teams at Anvik on the Yukon River and then allowed them to leave as evening approached and temperatures dropped, which made it safe for teams to proceed up the river. The teams found many places where the river ice had slumped in the warm temperatures, leaving deep swirling open water.

The checker inspected my gear and a veterinarian asked if I needed medical attention for the dogs. The dogs were fine, so I found a place to park them next to a small house where we could roll out our sleeping bags for a snooze. It was a little too warm for racing sled dogs and they let me know it. They immediately plopped down on their bellies, legs spread wide to cool down.

Before I could sleep, the dogs needed to be fed. I readied their food and dropped a frozen, precooked New York steak into the boiling water for my own hot meal. I enjoyed the tender steak and, when all were fed, I crawled into my sleeping bag for a good rest.

After having been lost on the south fork of the Kuskokwim River for nearly twenty-four hours early in the race, I rejoined the race but found myself way at the back of the pack. It is funny how the teams sort themselves out. By the time the race reaches halfway, mushers have fallen into fairly well-defined groups. The serious contenders are, of course, right up front and usually number about half a dozen. Behind them are a dozen or so that might be called "contenders." These first two groups generally contain the serious competitive mushers. These are the premier long-distance mushers of the world. The middle of the pack includes "hopefuls" and the back of the pack includes what we call "campers." I was now a camper.

I didn't want to be a camper and, in fact, was trying like hell to catch up. I wanted to finish in the money, but the reality was that even doing my best I would not be able to make up the lost time and get ahead. I was having a great time, though, and there's absolutely nothing wrong with being a camper. That's where many mushers travel during their first race and some have the ability to ultimately be competitive mushers. You don't have to be traveling a whole lot more slowly than the contenders to find yourself back there. In any case, my goal now was to finish.

When I awoke, I learned that seven or eight of us had arrived in the village in the middle of what appeared to be spring breakup. The Anvik River valley, which made up the first half of our journey from Anvik toward Unalakleet, had experienced extremely high daytime temperatures and was beginning to open up. Warm sunshine had made the trails so punchy that dogs found themselves wallowing up to their chests in soggy wet snow. Worse yet, sections of river ice were disappearing from sight into the black rushing current, creating an extremely dangerous situation.

The trail manager had frozen the race at Anvik, preventing any mushers who were there or who had not yet arrived there from continuing beyond that checkpoint up the Anvik River. With clear skies developing, it was possible that temperatures would drop during the night and firmly freeze things up along the river and allow us to continue. All but one of us accepted our fate. We took care of our dogs, visited with newfound friends, or rolled out our sleeping bags and took a nap hoping for things to improve. Our best bet was for the cloud cover that had plagued us for several days to disappear. Clear skies result in warm days, but temperatures drop when night falls.

With gear scattered about, Burt stops to cook and give the dogs a good rest. It's a good sign that the dogs aren't very tired when they refuse to lie down. Tough old Tiger didn't even bother to sit. The dogs have been fed and Burt is boiling a pot of coffee.

When the race freeze was announced, Jan Masek angrily refused to comply. Jan was an immigrant from the Czech Republic who had been a race car driver and a pilot in Europe. He'd made a daring escape from communist Czech Republic driving a race car at high speed through an Iron Curtain checkpoint. Guards had fired automatic weapons at him as he barged through.

"I vil not put up with theese bool sheet," he screamed. "I paid my money. I go ven I vant."

This was my first experience with Jan and I sat back in amazement as he stormed around the checkpoint waving his arms and shouting at the top of his lungs to all who would listen.

"Dey vant to hold us so dat ve don't catch up mit da leaders whose teams vill burn out because dey push too hard."

The trail has left the Anvik River Valley and runs across wind-blown glaze and crust into a stiff winter wind in the high tundra on the way to Unalakleet.

After noon, I crawled into my sleeping bag for a nap but couldn't begin to sleep with Jan stomping around the small house. I finally told him to either get out or shut up so we could get a little sleep. Jan slammed the door as he left and kept up his tirade as he stormed about the village yelling at anyone who would listen. He eventually hitched his team and drove off up the Anvik River defiant and alone. The day was sunny and warm with melt-water dripping off the eaves of the small house.

I rolled over and went back to sleep while most of the remaining mushers wandered around making new friends and enjoying the warm weather. An hour later, Jan was back, considerably subdued. It had taken him nearly forty-five minutes to mush a mile up the Anvik River wallowing in deep snow. His dogs had overheated and he had finally overheated himself. Much calmer, he came back to Anvik to wait for cooler weather that evening. It was pretty obvious that the trail manager didn't need to freeze anything—the problem solved itself.

My first impression was that I'd just met the biggest pain in the neck I'd ever seen in my life. I did not intend to get within one hundred miles of Jan ever again. That impression changed as we left Anvik together with two other mushers, Jim Strong and Dennis Boyer. We had agreed to stay together for reasons of safety until we had traversed the dangerous portions of the Anvik River. The moment the sun went down, the temperature plummeted to well below zero and the trail began to tighten up.

It was amazing how the trail, punchy just a couple of hours earlier, was now firm and fast. I chuckled to see where Jan had wallowed along the trail. He had stayed on the trail for a few hundred yards, but the trail was soft. The tracks showed where he'd tried to find firm footing off the trail with no success. About a mile out, his tracks made a small loop back toward Anvik.

Now the trail was as hard as stone and the dogs made good time. A few miles out, Jan commanded his team off the trail to detour around open water. Now we knew why Dick had held us up and we appreciated him watching out for us. A section of river ice had slumped and completely disappeared from our path. A gaping hole remained. The water in that hole was roiling, deep, and swift and dark, almost black in appearance. Neither dogs nor man would have survived a plunge into that fearsome hole.

We came to four similar holes directly in our path. The trail just disappeared for fifteen feet to almost forty feet in some cases. No musher wanted to be at that spot when the ice collapsed into the raging water. Each time, Jan guided his dogs around the danger. His leaders obeyed instantly without hesitation. My respect for him grew with each new demonstration.

As we mushed further up the Anvik River away from its mouth at the Yukon River, the ice became firmer until the danger was behind us.

About sixty-five miles out of Anvik, the trail suddenly veered toward the east and the dogs quickly followed the trail up the bank to Beaver checkpoint. The checkpoint was located at a small fishing lodge that was normally closed during the winter. The owners had opened it to Iditarod so we had a place to stop and regroup during the long haul to Unalakleet. The checker appeared from a small frame lodge building and directed us to a place where we could park our teams. A water hole in the river provided cooking water for the dogs.

With chores done, we gathered in the warmth of the lodge to visit with our new friends. As I filled my coffee mug, I thought I noticed the checker giving Dennis a subtle signal. They were both sprint mushers and longtime friends. Moments later, the checker got up, stretched elaborately and moseyed outside. Then Dennis stood up and mumbled something about drinking too much coffee. They were obviously up to something, so I followed them out and overheard muffled talk.

Ah-ha! It didn't take a genius to figure out the plan. Dennis was going to pull a sneak. The checker told Dennis to slip out ahead of us and make a run for it. If he could get some distance between us at this point, he could probably hang on to his lead all the way to Nome. My dogs needed a rest so I'd just have to wait until morning to see what developed.

We spent that night at Beaver checkpoint, and what a night it was. There is nothing as much fun as sitting around a cabin in the middle of the Alaska wilderness with a bunch of dog mushers trading stories. A wood fire crackled in the hearth, giving off the cozy warmth only a wood fire can give. The subtle smell of wood smoke wafted through the cabin.

Before Burt is even in sight of Nome, his family and friends hang banners on the burled arch at the finish line in Nome.

We had agreed to all leave together, but when we awoke the following morning, Dennis was already up and had fed his dogs. In fact, he was already packed and ready to go. We approached him just before he left and asked him what he was up to.

He replied, "I had trouble sleeping and just decided to get up and get going. I didn't want to disturb the rest of you. I planned to stop for lunch and wait for the rest of you to catch up."

Mushing up Front Street in Nome during unseasonably warm temperatures. Weather at the finish in Nome could be anything from the warm rain shown here to beautiful sunshine or a bitter coastal blizzard.

We saw right through it. With advice from his buddy, he'd decided he'd had enough of this togetherness and it was time to make the big sneak. He knew that if he could just gain a little distance on us, he could probably make it to Nome with us all trailing along behind. Since he'd just had a nice, long rest at Anvik during the race freeze and had slept well here at Beaver Creek, his dogs were perfectly capable of running the rest of the way to Unalakleet virtually nonstop. If the rest of us continued to putt along in our normal fashion, Dennis would establish a big enough gap between us to preclude our catching him before Nome.

We were so far back in the pack that we had no hope of finishing in the money, so Jan and I weren't in a big hurry. One thing was certain, fans remembered the mushers who finished in the money and the guy who finished last. The first twenty mushers are awarded trophies and the last musher to finish is awarded a symbolic red lantern. Traditionally, officials hung a lantern on a post at the finish line to welcome the last mushers in. With much hoopla, the last musher got the red lantern. I knew I wouldn't win a trophy, but I sure as heck didn't want to be remembered for coming in last. Even though we were at the back of the pack, we were still racing.

So off Dennis went, while Jan, Jim, and I finished feeding our dogs and packed our gear. Jan and I were ready to leave first, so we told Jim we would see him further on, and we left. We decided we'd be damned if we would let Dennis get away with this. We were determined that since he was pulling a sneak, we were going to turn the tables and beat him. The true test would be if we found him waiting for us at lunchtime. If we didn't, the race was on.

We left at 9:30 and by 1:30 had found no sign of Dennis. We stopped to snack our dogs and grab a bit of lunch ourselves and to palaver over what would be our best strategy.

We decided we would push onward until we caught him, at which time we would try to pass him in an effort to demoralize him. Since both of our teams had appeared to be faster than his, we figured we would get away from him far enough to where he would decide he couldn't beat us. Maybe then he would stop and rest. If he did this, we would stop and rest and things would be back to normal with him in our pocket. The four of us would then putt along to somewhere near the finish, at which time we would, by mutual agreement, make a mad dash for Nome. May the best man win.

We continued for the remainder of the afternoon, maintaining a steady pace, stopping shortly after dark to build a fire and cook a good meal for the dogs. We still hadn't seen Dennis.

We continued and then sometime before midnight, Jan switched on his headlight and stopped to wait for me to catch up. When I did, he pointed to fresh grizzly bear tracks! They crossed the trail from right to left and appeared to be smoking hot. I turned on my headlight and we scanned the surrounding woods to see what we could see. The bear tracks were extremely fresh; in fact, it appeared that the bear had been disturbed by our passage.

As Jan's light flashed across the west bank of the river, it suddenly illuminated the bear partly hidden in the trees. His eyes glowed like hot coals in the dark night, reflecting our headlights' strong beams. We had no idea what the temperament of a bear would be that had come out of hibernation in winter, but we weren't the least bit interested in finding out. Bears normally come out of hibernation in the spring when things turn a little green and food is available. Warm weather the past few days must have triggered something and caused the bear to awaken early. Now he was on the prowl with food hard to find. Assuming he was hungry and irritable, we mushed out of there with all possible haste. Neither of us was about to turn our headlight off for the next few miles.

Always faithful and always there to the finish in Nome, Tiger leads the team up Front Street toward the finish line with old Black at his side.

We continued, occasionally stopping to rest and snack our dogs. Sometime after midnight, Jan shouted back at me in his thick Czech accent, "Ve got heem! Ve got heem! Turn out de light. Turn out de light."

I quickly extinguished my headlight as we raced silently along, gliding through the trees and along the low ridges. I couldn't see Dennis's headlight yet, so I assumed that Jan had seen it flash somewhere ahead. Finally, I too saw Dennis's light playing on the trees and then on the snow. Neither of us uttered a sound until Jan's lead dog had his nose in Dennis's hip pocket. Then Jan turned on his headlight and at the top of his lungs, shouted, "Passing by, passing by!"

Dennis was so startled he seemed to nearly fall off his sled. He stopped to let Jan go by and then I went by. The three of us continued with Jan and me drawing slightly ahead as the miles rolled on.

Although Jan hadn't been a top competitive musher, he was a good dog man and an excellent trainer of leaders. And he had a loony sense of humor. His leaders would virtually thread a needle for him if he told them to. We'd been traveling along, the three of us, for a couple of miles when Jan hollered, "Gee," and his team shot off to the right across unbroken snow. The snow had a crust on it and was capable of supporting Jan and his team. A sled runner's weight, however, would cause the surface to crack somewhat so the next team had a more difficult time and the third team would punch through and wallow in the deep powdery snow beneath. Dennis's leader instinctively followed the freshest scent from the teams ahead, which put him in our wake on the treacherous snow off the trail.

Burt's gang gave him a bundle of balloons to carry up Front Street to start the hoopla. The fun of being a fan at the finish in Nome was welcoming your favorite musher.

We could see his dogs and his sled punching through the fragile crust. His dogs wallowed up to their necks with his sled tipping over in the light, fluffy, unstable snow beneath. Jan then commanded his team to turn left, across a shallow creek and up the other side and back to the trail. We stopped there in hysterical glee while Dennis shouted commands, and pushed and struggled with his sled. It was my first look at Jan's sense of humor and I was delighted.

Figuring we had Dennis right where we wanted him, we mushed on for another hour or so and then camped. While we slept, Dennis mushed silently by and we didn't see him again until Nome, where he had the last laugh.

Jan and I had our ups and downs as we continued toward Nome, occasionally getting on each other's nerves. Being short on sleep, we found ourselves with tempers short. Most of the time, however, Jan made things interesting and at times had me nearly hysterical with laughter. We became friends as we mushed toward Nome. Somewhere along the way, Jan and I came to the conclusion that one of us was going to have to be last. We decided that it might as well be Jim Strong, although he wasn't that far behind us. Jan and I began to plot how we could pull a Dennis and make a break for it.

At the finish line with Champaign and balloons. These moments made the tough race across Alaska worth everything.

We decided the perfect place to make our move was at White Mountain, just seventy-seven miles from Nome. The three of us pulled in there together. We fed our dogs and enjoyed the hospitality of the checker. All the while, we made an elaborate pretense of getting ready to spend the night. Jan and I wandered out the door and down to the river under the guise of crawling into our sleeping bags for the night. In the dark, we rapidly hitched our dogs and packed our sleds except for Jan's sleeping bag.

Jan then instructed me, "Turn on your headlight," which I did. In the light of my headlight, Jan began an elaborate act of pulling his sleeping bag out of its stuff sack. He shook it out, fluffed it up and carefully spread it out on top of his sled load.

He then crawled inside, zipped it up and whispered loudly, "Turn off de light!" When I did he leaped out of his sleeping bag, jammed it into his sled and away we went. By then the dogs had joined our excitement and we were making rapid progress away from White Mountain toward Safety and

Nome, chuckling gleefully down the trail. I doubt if Jim even knew what we were doing, but it sure was fun.

The miles faded behind us as we mushed along through the night. Finally, day-light began to glow in the early morning sky. In the half-light of early morning, Jan missed the trail to Nome and headed off down a side trail to a shelter cabin on Topkok Hill. We soon discovered our error and began swinging our teams around to go back and pick up the correct trail. Instead of waiting for me to get my dogs turned around, Jan mushed on by and I mistakenly thought his sled ran over one of my dogs' feet.

In the fatigue of mushing all day and then all night, I became furious at what I thought was Jan's act of carelessness. I shouted a warning at him, which he ignored. I was hotfooting along behind him in a rage when he mushed right on by the fork in the trail that would have taken him to the finish line. He continued back down the trail we'd just come in on without noticing the trail that he'd missed.

Aha, revenge would be sweet. I directed my team onto the correct route, toward the summit of Topkok Hill and beyond that, Nome. Turning back occasionally, I watched Jan become smaller and smaller as he mushed the wrong direction down the trail toward whence we'd come.

Eventually, Jan looked around and became aware of his mistake. He turned his team around and began furiously attempting to catch up. His team was fast and powerful and he gained on me at an alarming rate. He caught me as we crested Topkok Hill. As we began our steep descent toward the ocean, he called out, demanding trail. This meant I should stop and let him go by. I refused to yield to him, shouting that I couldn't stop my team going down this steep hill with my heavily loaded sled. Actually, I didn't try too hard. I was angry over his apparent carelessness in striking one of my dogs, an act he had no idea he'd committed. With his instantaneous flashpoint, he was soon more furious than I was. He thought my refusal to let him by was just a callous attempt to let him mush off in the wrong direction and then cheat him out of his attempt to regain the lead. Jan was screaming at the top of his lungs, making one threat after another, each one more fearsome than the last.

"Burt, got dammit! You stop and let me by! You're breaking de rooles!"

The louder he screamed, the more excited our dogs became until we were careening madly down the mountain at a high speed. Applying the brakes with all my might did little more than keep things mildly under control.

Jan first threatened to pass me on the run and then threatened to knock me off my sled as he went by. Careening down the mountain as we were, he simply wasn't able to draw abreast. He next threatened to report me to the officials who would surely disqualify me from the race. By then the whole thing was becoming slightly funny and I yelled back at him that I was sure the officials would give a lot of attention to two mushers fighting over last place.

Joe Redington Sr. greets Burt at the Finish line in Nome, 1984. The conversation always drifted to trail conditions and the dogs.

He screamed, "I have a camera! I have a camera! Look at me, turn around and look at de camera. I have proof to have you thrown out of dis race. You vil be vorbidden to ever race again." His thick Czech accent was cracking me up.

I yelled back, "Take a picture of this," and made an obscene gesture.

He screamed bloody murder.

By then the whole affair became so ridiculous that I couldn't help laughing. He interpreted this as ridicule, which threw him into renewed fits of anger and frustration. He threatened to beat me to within an inch of my life as soon as we stopped. I don't know why I didn't take him seriously since I had no idea what kind of physique lay hidden beneath those mounds of arctic clothing, but somehow the whole affair seemed even funnier.

The more I laughed, the wilder he became. He threatened to shoot me right off my sled if I didn't stop this clear violation of the rules. I turned and thought I saw Jan holding a gun. My mood went sober in the blink of an eye. I'd only known Jan for a few days and had no idea what he was capable of. But one thing was certain, I wasn't going to stop and deal with it until I had to. With all this shouting, the dogs were still in a panic thinking it was all directed at them. There was no hope of stopping my team with the dogs so excited and upset over Jan's shouting.

We finally reached the bottom of the hill and turned along the beach toward Nome. Still excited, the dogs raced madly along the ice-covered lagoons that lie just inland of the beach. I eventually came to my senses and realized that if I dared stop, this guy might be fully capable of carrying out his threats. He continued to holler for trail, which I continued to refuse to yield. I was afraid that if he got ahead of me, or even beside me, he would stop and we would have a violent confrontation. I needed to buy enough time to let him calm down a bit.

Although his team appeared to be faster than mine, he couldn't get the dogs to pass, probably because all of the shouting back and forth had made them wary of getting close to me. We continued to mush along for another hour or so. The time to snack our dogs and give them a brief rest came and went. I hoped he would stop his team, giving me time to gain a little space so I could snack my dogs and avoid the confrontation that was sure to come. There was no way, however, that Jan was going to allow this. By then he was absolutely determined not to let me out of his sight.

After another twenty minutes or so, I decided, the hell with it. I just wasn't going to mush my dogs beyond the rest they'd earned. I picked a spot, braked the team to a halt, set my snow hook as firmly as possible, and tipped my sled over on it so there was no way the dogs could get away. I then whirled around to face my assailant. When Jan saw me brake to a stop, he hurriedly accomplished the same thing. As I spun around, he began sprinting rapidly toward me. He threw his hat to the ground and his long hair stuck out wildly in all directions. With a crazy look in his eyes and with all those clothes on, he looked imposing! He screamed a tirade of Czech cuss words at the top of his lungs.

I got set for the fight of my life and figured to nail him at least once or twice before he really got set. As he got to me, I reared back to hit him, when to my great surprise, he stuck out his hand and hollered, "Burt, we can't do this, we're friends! It was the coffee! It was the caffeine! It was the long hours with no sleep! It was the strain! We're not ourselves! We're angry with each other for no reason! We're friends and we must stay friends! We can't fight like this! I'll apologize with you if you'll apologize with me!"

I was dumbfounded. All of my pent-up adrenaline and energy were immediately deflated.

Burt at the finish line with the halfway prize and a bottle of Champaign to celebrate. Jim Fuhrer, a faithful friend, always painted a banner to hang on the burled arch when Burt finished. Jim's wife, Sherry, organized her sorority friends, at Epsilon Sigma Alpha, to sew hundreds of booties to protect the dogs' feet on the long journey to Nome.

"Well, for crying out loud," I said. "I thought you were going to kill me."

"I was going to kill you, but now I'm not!"

I shook his hand and we stood there hugging and banging each other on the back. Moments passed. We snacked our dogs, gave them a few minutes' rest, and then mushed off toward the finish line.

I finished thirty-two, next to last. Jan beat me to Nome, but our pal Jim Strong crossed the finish line last and won the red lantern. He told us later that he'd been planning for days to beat us out of the Red Lantern award.

Alaska radio stations always showed up at the finish line to interview mushers. Iditarod board member Tom Bush, center, is announcing for KNOM radio.

Chapter Five
Trail Hazards and Other Yarns

Late in the 1983 training season, we were extending our runs out from camp fifty miles. My handler that winter was a young woman named Kathy Turko, who was a wildlife biologist. We had mushed north and then east across the Kahiltna River along what I called the Joe May Highway. This trail was a part of famed Iditarod musher Joe May's trapline. Although we rarely met other teams, we often saw tracks where other teams had gone. They came from far away in the opposite direction.

On this day, we'd driven our teams across the Kahiltna River and were approaching one of Joe May's trapline cabins. Our dogs' ears perked up as we drew nearer, a sure sign that somebody was at the cabin. When we mushed by, we saw teams belonging to Vern Halter, Mark May (Joe's son) and Bill Hayes parked there. A friendly curl of smoke rose from the chimney. We normally didn't like to stop at cabins or roadhouses on the outbound leg of a training run since it's good discipline to drive the dogs on by. Otherwise, the leaders sometimes develop the bad habit of pulling into any cabin you approach, hoping for a little rest and a snack.

We often stopped, however, on the return trip as the dogs were then eager to get home anyway and it didn't teach them bad habits. With this in mind, we continued past the cabin another ten miles to our turnaround and then mushed on back, figuring to stop for a break and a visit with the other drivers at the cabin. A spruce tree approximately six inches through had leaned across the trail under the weight of heavy snows, stopping about four feet above the trail. We had cut through so much brush and scrub timber that we had become quite

casual about these obstructions. We saw it coming and ducked under it as we went by and never really thought about it. We'd gone under this one on the way out, continued to the turnaround and were coming back.

In those days we dragged a logging chain to help give the dogs something to pull against and develop some muscle. We dragged it all the way out and then loaded it into a milk basket for the return trip to give the dogs a chance to stretch their legs and pick up the pace a little. We'd reached the turnaround, loaded the chains into baskets in our sleds and were gliding silently along the trail toward home. As I approached the "leaner" tree, one end of my chain slipped through a gap in the basket and started clattering itself free. I instinctively bent down to grab the chain, gathered it into a ball, and stood up to toss it back into the basket just as we reached the tree.

Burt drives his team up off the Kahiltna River along one of Joe May's trapline trails that Burt had labeled the Joe May Highway. The banks of the Kahiltna River were steep along this stretch so Joe had cut a side hill trail to make the river crossing accessible.

I couldn't believe I had been so dumb. As I stood, the tree caught me alongside my head and wrenched me violently from the sled. I heard a crack in my neck that was certain evidence that it was broken and I would probably be paralyzed for life. Stunned, I lay in the trail knowing that Kathy would be along soon and hoping she could get her team stopped before it ran over me. I felt like I didn't dare move for fear of injuring myself further. I tried wiggling my toes and my fingers and found that things seemed to be working well. I staggered to my feet just as Kathy came mushing up and I was able to collapse into her sled for the ride home. After a few miles, we reached Joe's trapline cabin, where I found my team. They had recognized a rest stop with the company of other dogs and just pulled in.

Burt was distracted as his sled glided under this sweeper and he was knocked off his sled. Burt's team ran off and left him lying in the trail. Handler Kathy Turko was close behind and gave Burt a ride until he recovered his team. Kathy's sled is stopped under the deadfall. Note the trailing log chain used to add drag.

The guys were anchoring my sled and stretching out my team, figuring that something must have gone wrong back up the trail. Kathy and I came driving in, anchored her team and wandered in for a cup of coffee. It's kind of embarrassing to have to admit you got knocked off your sled. Fortunately, it's happened to most everyone at one time or another so nobody ever says too much. But it better not happen often. If it did, there'd better be a good excuse, and you sure didn't want it to happen during a race . . . like it already had to me.

NEIGHBORS

We had neighbors. One was a bachelor/hermit named Gordon B. McWilliams, aka Mac, who lived in a small cabin across the lake. The others were the Meyers family, consisting of Mike, his thirteen-year-old son, Mikie, his wife, and his three daughters. Before long Mike, Mac, and Mikie had each developed a mad crush on Kathy. In the beginning, their visits had been occasional. Now, they began showing up every morning. At first, they arrived for their morning cup of coffee just as we were finishing breakfast so we would take an extra half hour to chat. We began to get up earlier and earlier to be gone when they arrived, but that worked only part of the time. I finally asked them to come after we'd finished our runs so we could get our work done. After that, they kept their eyes peeled and showed up as soon as we drove our last teams back into the yard.

Burt's driverless team traveled several miles without him and then pulled into Joe May's trapline cabin where Joe's son, Mark, and Bill Hayes were taking a break. Kathy visited with Mark and Bill while Burt untangled his team and lined them out for the run home. Bill Hayes was training an Iditarod team under Joe's tutelage. This tiny cabin was a cozy place to hole up in any weather and is typical of trap line cabins throughout Alaska.

We finally limited their visits to a couple of times a week, which assured us time to get our training done along with our other chores. They took these limited visitation rights with good grace, which I appreciated, until I realized what was really happening.

I normally spent three or four days a week in camp training dogs and would then fly home and spend two or three days catching up on business and family matters. I returned to camp to train dogs and repeat the cycle. I noticed as I was roaring off down the lake to fly back to Anchorage, that Mac and Mike, along with Mikie, would emerge from the trees on their side of the lake and begin trudging toward our camp. Apparently, they heard my airplane engine warming up, and immediately began pulling on their coats and boots. By the time I was airborne, they were on their way over for some uninterrupted visiting with Kathy.

Often, I saw them trudging back toward home as I made my final approach onto the lake several days later. They had apparently heard my airplane coming and split in a hurry. All of this visiting, of course, was perfectly harmless and was okay with me as long as it didn't get on Kathy's nerves. I told her more than once that if it did, she needed to solve it herself or let me know and I'd help her with it. But she said she didn't mind, particularly when she was there alone.

The problem solved itself. Apparently, Mike had heard my engine warming up one morning as I was preparing to head to Anchorage. Telling his wife, Shirley, he was going to check his trapline, he and young Mikie pulled on their coats and boots and trudged across the lake to our cabin for a visit. They must have been so carried away that they lost track of time and didn't head for home until that evening. All would have been okay, except young Mike told his mother that they'd been visiting Kathy all day. She knew I'd headed for town that morning. Just about everything hit the fan that could have! The end result was that she put both Mikes on restriction for a week.

VISITORS

We loved company, though. That was probably a combination of the isolation and a love for the people we knew out in the bush. They were all interesting and fun to be around.

One day we heard a commotion outside and looked out to see four teams coming across the lake. We donned our coats and boots and went out to greet our visitors. It was Dewey Halverson and his entourage. First came Dewey and then his beautiful ladies, Jane and Chris, followed by his beautiful Swedish handler. Dewey loves women and they love him. Two girlfriends. Lots of bachelor mushers and probably a few married ones in the Trapper Creek country were envious of Dewey and his two ladies.

We helped them get the dogs anchored down on the lake on beds of spruce boughs. Dog food was cooked and we retired to the cabin for coffee, lunch and hours of visiting. Dewey had such ability with dogs. I would sit and listen to him for hours talking anything from training schedules to food drops. We ate dinner and talked long into the night.

The only time I ever saw our neighbor, Mike, speechless was one afternoon when Ted English mushed into our yard. The guys had come over for their twice-weekly coffee and hot chocolate when our dogs started barking, announcing the arrival of a visitor. We looked out the window and saw a dog team mushing across the lake toward our cabin. As was the custom, we all went out to greet him and help him secure his dogs before inviting him in for coffee and a snack. Ted had been training down in the Trapper Creek country approximately fifty miles away and had mushed up into our area for a little camping trip. His camp was about ten miles away on the other side of the Kahiltna River. It included a derelict automobile that he slept in which he'd dragged in there somehow.

We poured coffee all around and sat down to visit. Of course, the neighbors carried the ball and made sure that no awkward silences developed. But I'd heard all their stories a hundred times. Ted was a world-class BS'er, but even he had trouble getting a word in edgewise.

Our visitor had *new* gossip and news so I broke in and said, "Well, guys, let's give Ted here a chance to tell us all the latest." It was like putting a cork in a bottle of green home brew. The place calmed down momentarily, but you had the distinct feeling it would all explode before long. The guys just couldn't keep still. Ted and I began trading dog stories and soon he was asking me about several dogs I had in my team.

Out of the blue he asked, "How is Kentucky doing?"

Kentucky was one of the dogs I had bought from Joe Redington. "Fine," I said, "but I gave him to the neighbors across the lake. How do you know Kentucky?"

"He was one of my favorite dogs," Ted drawled in his thick southern accent. "I raised that dog from a pup. He was like one of the family. We let him in the house. Not much of a sled dog but he sure was nice to have around."

Then Ted asked how some of his other dogs were doing. As he named off the dogs, all were dogs I'd bought from Joe Redington Sr. after the 1982 Iditarod.

Since all the dogs had been too slow to make my team, I had culled them and passed them along to Mike for his trapline team. This included Kentucky. I had hoped Kentucky would help round out his trapline team. We were two-thirds of the way through our training season at the time so Kentucky's physical condition was superb. He was a powerful, eager, aggressive dog and, in fact, was far stronger than any of Mike's other dogs, none of which had been in nearly as strenuous a training program as ours. Our problem was that he was just a little slow.

When Mike had taken Kentucky home that day, he had fastened the dog's collar to a chain and had gone into the house for dinner. In the excitement of being in a new home, and likely hearing his buddies barking across the lake, Kentucky began lunging at his chain. It was worn and rusty and wasn't near stout enough to hold him. He broke free and headed straight for Meyers' chicken house where he began doing what came naturally. The chickens must have been terrorized by the sight of that big husky and began flapping and squawking all over the chicken house, which drove Kentucky into a frenzy of excitement! He careened pell-mell around the chicken house chasing chickens and dispatching them with alarming effectiveness.

Hearing the racket, Mike thought there must be a fox or coyote in his chicken house. He grabbed his gun and sprinted outdoors. He ran to the chicken coop, and threw open the door. The chicken house was a disaster, with blood and feathers everywhere—he shot Kentucky dead in his tracks. It wasn't until several weeks later, when I inquired how Kentucky was fitting into the team, that Mike had the nerve to tell me the story. There wasn't much I could do as it appeared they felt terrible about the whole episode. I just admonished them to use a heavier chain next time and let it go at that.

Anyway, our conversation had rolled merrily along until Ted started asking about those dogs, with special attention to Kentucky. Ted kept asking about Kentucky and then related a long story about how he'd raised the dog from a pup, what an outstanding dog he had been, being out of Redington's famed Tennessee stock, and so on, and so on.

Ted was from Alabama and had a deep southern accent. Like other southerners, he could use that southern accent to make anything sound like the best there ever was, be it food, women or dogs. I once worked for a Texan named Cosby, who could make me so hungry I'd eat the upholstery in five minutes listening to him describe how his mother used to fix catfish. Ted was every bit as full of "it" as Cosby, and soon had us believing Kentucky was not only the most beloved sled dog he'd ever owned but a member of the family as well. This was in spite of the fact that Kentucky hadn't even made Ted's team.

The longer he talked, the more Mac and the Meyers fidgeted until finally Ted asked me again how Kentucky was doing. I figured I might as well prolong the agony as long as possible so I slowly got up, asked everybody if they would like another cup of coffee or hot chocolate and then went to the stove. By the time I got done freshening everyone's cup and passing a plate of cookies around, Mike looked like he was going to jump right out of his skin. I'm sure he felt like he'd shot someone's kid and was about to be discovered. I slowly sat down, and said as convincingly as I could that the dog was fine.

The sigh of relief that followed could have blown the door off its hinges.

I still didn't get it. How did Joe get Ted's dogs? I asked Ted to tell me the story. Ted said that he sold Joe his culls before the 1982 race. Ted said he had kept the best twenty dogs from his yard and had sold the rest. They just weren't fast enough for his team. Ted said he had sold the remaining forty slower dogs in the yard to Joe for $2,600 and that Joe had kept the best ones and then sold off the remaining dogs that were the slowest of the slow to me.

I chewed on that for a while and it didn't taste that great. Joe had bought forty of Ted's culls for $2,600. He had then cherry-picked the best of those for his own use and sold seven of the remaining slowest culls to me for $4,900.

Here's the story. We were in Nome after the 1982 Iditarod. I had asked Rick Swenson if he'd sell me seven dogs out of his 1982 finishing team. Rick had won so I figured that any dog that finished in his team had to be a top-sled dog.

He said, "Sure, $1,000 each."

"Rick, are they cheaper by the dozen?"

Rick pondered that for a minute and then said, "sure, $700 each if you take seven of them."

"Right out of your finishing team?"

"Yup."

"Deal, you pick 'em out and ship them right from here to Anchorage if you want. I'll write you a check now."

I then approached Joe Sr. who by then had become a close friend. I asked him if he was interested in the same deal that I'd made with Rick. I added the caveat that I wanted the dogs out of his "Redington" bloodlines, since Joe had finished seventeenth compared to Rick's win. In my view, the dogs weren't worth quite as much without the bloodline thing. I had told Joe that Rick sold me seven dogs out of his finishing team for $700 apiece for a total of $4,900. Joe agreed to the same terms and said all the dogs in his finishing team were his own bloodlines. I wrote him a check. I took delivery of Joe's dogs at his yard in Knik when we got back from the Nome finish.

Now here I was with this story from Ted English. I'd been puzzled over Joe's dogs not being fast enough. Joe was a competitive musher and had been breeding dogs for years. There's no way his dogs would not be able to keep up with my team. When I checked the tapes of the race, I couldn't find any of the dogs he'd sold me in his team at the finish line. When I asked him about it, he said, "Well, they were my dogs, my breed, and they all finished."

I insisted, "Joe, I couldn't find any of those dogs in the pictures of your team at the finish. The deal was that they would be out of *your* finishing team."

"Well, they were mine and they all finished."

So I asked Joe about it again telling him that Ted English said they were all out of his yard and bred by him. I repeated Ted's story about the dogs being just culls from his team. I went on that if the dogs had made my team, I'd have let it go, but none of them had so I was out the whole sum of money. I'd given all seven dogs to the neighbors.

Joe's reply was that the dogs were his dogs. Although they had been leased out to several other mushers who finished, they were still his and all had finished the Iditarod. And they had to be from of his bloodlines, because Ted had handled for him a few years earlier and everyone knew that handlers stole breeding all the time. So these dogs had to be Joe's bloodlines. "And they were all from dogs I owned that finished."

Then he said, "They're guaranteed, Burt, just bring them back and try another seven. I've got five hundred dogs in the yard and you can keep trying them until you find seven you like."

There was no way was I going to start sorting through Joe's dog yard for replacements for those seven dogs. With five hundred dogs out there, it could take years. We remained the best of friends, but I figured Joe had given me a valuable lesson.

I think of this as my MS degree in dog buying and the $4,900 was tuition, since I had already earned my BS in dog buying from Lloyd.

Things haven't changed a bit since I was a kid and used to go along with my uncles when they were buying horses and mules. It was all among friends, but you had to be shrewd. Once you figured it out, it was part of the challenge, part of what made the whole thing so much fun.

MOOSE

Moose were the most common animals—and the most dangerous—that we ran into when mushing dogs. We began driving dogs as soon as the snow fell and continued mushing most of the winter. Because of that, the snow along our trails was always well packed and firm, making it a nice place for dog teams to travel and also for wild creatures. During early winter, before snow became deep, wild animals traveled almost anywhere without difficulty. As winter advanced, however, and snow became deeper, it became more and more difficult for animals to venture forth in their search for food. Snow depths could reach five or six feet, making it extremely difficult for even the lordly moose to make his way. It didn't take them long to find our well-packed dog team trails and they were soon using our highways as if they were their own.

Moose and dog teams just don't mix. A moose can weigh up to three quarters of a ton and stand as much as seven feet high at the shoulder. An awesome creature indeed with their long legs and great agility, they can wreak havoc in the middle of a dog team.

One of the predators moose most fear in winter is wolves. Wolves can corner a moose in deep snow where their lighter weight permits them to move around with relative ease on top of the snow while the moose get mired. The wolves double team a moose and are able to tire and eventually kill it. The similarity between a team of dogs moving briskly along a trail and a pack of wolves is quite obvious. A moose instantly identifies a dog team with a pack of wolves and then proceeds in a natural fashion. The moose feels cornered. It attacks instantly unless it feels it has enough room to get away, in which case it will often attempt to flee. Many of the experiences we had with moose along the trail seemed to reflect this moose-wolf relationship.

Sometimes the contact was so quick that it was over almost before you knew it, leaving you and your dogs with an adrenaline surge of intense proportions.

One of our trails out of the Kahiltna country led along Oilwell Road, a winter trail down to the Yentna River. Most of our larger rivers have their own trail systems that serve as highways for the residents living along them. The Yentna is no exception. We would drive our teams down to the Yentna trail system, whence we could literally mush back to Anchorage or out along the Iditarod Trail to Nome with hundreds of miles of trails branching out in all directions. The snow got deeper and deeper as winter progressed, and moose would collect in the vicinity of the Yentna River to enjoy eating the large supply of willow brush that grew there. Also, it was easier traveling for them along the many trails in the area.

A huge bull moose lived in the area. We met him at least every other time we were out. He had a belligerent attitude and a white muzzle that made him look much like a mule. We named him Francis.

We first met Francis on a bright, sunny day approximately a mile from where Oilwell Road intersects the Yentna River trail. I was in the lead with my handler, Jeff, following about a hundred yards behind. I first spotted Francis nearly two miles ahead.

It was a gorgeous day for driving dogs. It had snowed about four inches the night before, so everything was white and beautiful. The birch and spruce trees along the trail had a fresh dusting of snow that almost looked like frosting. The dogs quickened their pace as they became aware of Francis in the trail ahead. We continued until we were within about a quarter mile of Francis hoping that he would yield the right of way as he became aware of the team's rapid approach. He did nothing of the kind. By then it was clear that he was walking right toward us and that he figured if anyone was going to yield the trail, it wasn't going to be him. We continued until we were within 200 yards of him, all the while hollering and yelling, hoping it would scare him off the trail. No reaction.

Kathy retrieves dog snacks from her sled during a rest stop north of the Kahiltna cabin. Many of our rest stops were more to train the dogs to relax and eat on the trail than to actually rest them.

I stopped the team and anchored it firmly by setting the snow hook and then tipping the sled over, putting its hundred pounds of ballast on top of the snow hook. This held the hook in place so it wouldn't pop loose. It made the sled a whole lot harder to drag. By this time, Francis had stopped to study us. With that white muzzle, he did look like a big mule but a lot more formidable. Jeff stopped his team a hundred feet behind mine and I told him to be ready to swing his team around in the trail and head the other way if Francis decided to charge. In the meantime, I walked up ahead of my leaders and started yelling and whistling and waving my arms. Again, no reaction. Then suddenly Francis started plodding up the trail toward us again, but not in any big hurry. It was obvious that this was the direction he'd decided to come and he wasn't going to give ground.

Turning a team of twelve or fourteen huskies around in the middle of a narrow trail in deep snow is a difficult thing to accomplish in a hurry. Dogs are social animals and they like to sniff and nuzzle one another when they're close. When you bring your leaders around and start bringing them back along the team to turn around, the nuzzling and sniffing slows things down considerably. Because of the tight conditions, dogs often try to thread themselves between one another, causing terrible tangles. Obviously, we didn't want this to happen when we needed to swap ends and retreat in a hurry.

In spite of my yelling and arm-waving, Francis kept coming. I didn't want to turn the teams around if we didn't have to. I knew it would result in a tangle and we would then be forced to drive the dogs past my cabin and on to other trails to get our miles, which was upsetting to the dogs. They liked to think that if they were on their way home they were going to go home. Much like children, they became sulky when they didn't get the snacks and petting that always followed our return to the dog lot.

In addition, our destination that day was Skwentna Roadhouse, a favorite stopover of ours owned by John and Joyce Logan. I'd known John for twenty-five years, since the early sixties when we had both worked for the Alaska State Department of Highways in Juneau. It was always a pleasure to reminisce over a cup of Joyce's coffee and one of her famous Roadhouse dinners.

I decided I had to make one more try at discouraging Francis before turning around, so I un-holstered my .357 Magnum handgun and fired a round over Francis's head. Francis must have been stone deaf because he didn't even twitch as he continued plodding toward us. The commotion that occurred behind me, however, was instantaneous. Magnum pistols make a lot of racket. Sled dogs have supersensitive hearing and aren't trained to tolerate the noise the way hunting dogs are. Although it happened too fast for me to watch, the dogs in both teams must have all just swapped ends and headed in the other direction. They were piled up in a huge ball on top of my sled as they tried to get around it on their mad dash to get away from me and that gun.

Jeff's team was in an equally big mess even though he was a hundred feet behind me when I touched off the round. I ran back and furiously started untangling dogs, meanwhile glancing back over my shoulder trying to see how Francis was doing. He kept coming closer and closer as I methodically untangled first one dog, then another, trying to get them strung out behind the sled. Francis had cut the distance in half by the time I got the dogs again lined out in some semblance of a dog team.

Meanwhile, my sled was still facing the wrong way. With its load of ballast, it weighed nearly 175 pounds and was nine feet long from the tip of the brush bow back to the trailing ends of the runners. Our trail was two feet wide with its packed surface a foot and a half below that of the surrounding snow, which was loose and fluffy and nearly three feet deep.

I wallowed out into the deep snow as I dragged the front of the sled around. I was in a near panic. Francis had closed the gap to about fifty yards. I hoped he wouldn't try to assert himself by just galloping right through us. Meanwhile the dogs, half-crazy with the scent of that moose, were barking at the top of their lungs and straining at the tugs. It wasn't that they were afraid so much as the scent of a wild animal tends to excite them even more when they are already excited. They just want to run; it doesn't matter where. The instant the sled was in the trail heading in the right direction, the snow hook pulled loose and we departed at a frantic, mad gallop. Francis was within twenty-five feet of the sled, still plodding along like a determined retired prizefighter who had been through the wars and knows just what to do if anything gets in his way. I was glad to have that gun along.

We never again confronted Francis. He was easy to spot with his mule-like appearance at a distance. Whenever we knew it was him on the trail, we just stopped, turned the teams around and took our journey elsewhere.

MOTHER NATURE CAN BE CRUEL

Critters continued to be a big part of our daily lives. Standing on a dogsled as it silently glides across Alaska's winter landscape provides a view into all of nature's moods. Sometimes the mood was bright and cheery and other times it was dark.

Mother Nature has no feelings in the way she governs her wild creatures. The side of nature that most of us saw was the happy side. We saw wild fowl in their annual migrations north and south, and watched squirrels and other animals in our backyards. We missed much of the cruel, ruthless reality that goes on out in the wilds far from view.

One day Jeff and I mushed the teams down Oilwell Road and up the Yentna River to Skwentna Roadhouse. We spent an hour there, snacking our dogs, enjoying a hot cup of coffee and having a nice visit with the Logans. Skwentna Roadhouse was always one of our favorite places to take a break. On the way back down the river, we noticed a cow moose in the distance with a half-grown calf making her way through the snow on the river. The river here was quite broad and the cow would wander through the deep snow, first to one side then the other in her search for tender willow brush to eat. Her calf was trying gamely to follow her, but the snow was nearly five feet deep, well up on the chest of the mother. The calf was obviously having a terrible time making its way through that deep snow.

We stopped our teams a half a mile away so as not to push the moose to any greater exertion. Even an adult cow needs to conserve energy during Alaska's bitter cold winters. We anchored our teams, pulled out a thermos of hot coffee and sat on our sleds to relax and visit a bit. Meanwhile, the cow and calf made it up onto the main trail which was well packed. The calf began slowly wobbling down the trail toward us. It then keeled over with a thud. It hit so hard that its limp body and legs bounced when it hit the hard surface of the trail. We didn't know if the calf had fainted or died. Its mother walked over and sniffed it and then plunged into the deep snow as she made her way to a stand of willows near the west bank. It was going to be a long wait before that calf woke up, if it did. We didn't want to disturb it if it was still alive, so we might have to wait before going on home where we would feed the dogs and have our own dinner. Even the cow looked weak and tired. I was determined not to cause them one bit of exertion if I could help it.

Hours later we were still sitting there. It was obvious by then that the calf had died. We normally left our snowshoes at home when training on well-traveled trails. Most of the time, there was really no need to break trail. After several hours sitting there in the evening chill, Jeff decided to see if he couldn't break a trail out to the far side of the river to our left and then try to bypass the calf. Without snowshoes, he immediately sank up to his chest. Since this was going to involve breaking out at least half a mile of new trail, it just didn't seem practical to wade through the chest-deep snow. So we sat back down on our sleds.

As dusk settled, we knew that the calf moose hadn't moved a muscle since it lay down; it had most likely died. We decided that we'd better mush our teams on up closer in hopes of making the cow move down the trail to avoid having a problem after dark. We mushed up to within a hundred yards of the calf, which brought the cow thundering from her willow patch. She stood over the fallen calf, defying us to come any closer.

Still the calf didn't move and we were certain that the poor thing had died. It was big enough to have been weaned so it needed willow brush for energy, the same as its mother. Deep snow had made the job of foraging too difficult. During the weeks preceding that day, the young moose must have grown progressively more tired and undernourished. Each snowfall made its job more difficult until he didn't have the energy to continue.

The mother, in her own efforts to survive, didn't realize the burden placed on her young offspring and, in fact, probably didn't know that it had died.

When we stopped advancing toward the moose, she wandered back to her willow patch and ate for a while and then lay down out of sight in the deep snow. We waited until we were sure she was sound asleep, and then made our plan. We decided that we would make a mad dash past the fallen calf and, hopefully, get by it before the angry cow could again come rumbling from her willow patch to stand guard. Jeff would have his .44 Magnum pistol out and ready to fire, so if I got by and he was in danger of being cut off, he could fire his gun in the air. This would, theoretically, stop the cow and spur his team on to greater speed. It might give us both a better chance of getting by. I didn't intend to shoot my gun for fear it would panic his team into stopping next to the irate mother moose.

After having been stopped for so long, the dogs were more than eager to go. They knew that dinner and a warm bed waited at home. I didn't even have to command them to go. When I released the snow hook, they took off like a shot, which I hoped would give us a moment of surprise over the sleeping cow.

No such luck. She stood, her hackles went up, her ears lay back, and she came thundering at us. She charged through the chest-deep snow as though across an open field. It was obvious that she was going to win this mad race. Fearing that she might charge us when she hit the trail, I stopped the dogs and rushed forward to turn the team around as quickly as possible. I signaled Jeff to do the same. We both turned our teams around and mushed back before turning around to see what was happening. The cow had again reached the trail and was standing protectively over the dead calf. We mushed back down the trail a ways and stopped to reconnoiter. Our options were diminishing as darkness approached.

I told Jeff to stand by the teams so they couldn't get away and I took my handgun back closer to the cow. I intended to fire a shot in the air to see if we couldn't move her off the trail. If that didn't work, we would again discuss things. Wandering back to the point where I had stopped my team before turning around, I fired my gun in the air with no reaction from the moose. It was obvious that nothing would change and we would have to find an alternative. As I turned to go back to the teams, I noticed twelve yellow spots in the snowy surface, exactly where I had stopped the team. They must have been as frightened as I had been at that charging moose and reacted in typical fashion. Every dog had peed his pants. Now that's a scary situation.

Our choices had now reduced themselves to returning to the Skwentna Roadhouse for the night or pushing through deep snow on foot to break an alternative trail around the moose. Jeff was young and strong, and he volunteered to perform the task of breaking a trail for us. It was after dark when he completed the bypass trail, and when he did we mushed on home. It was a sad night in dog camp thinking about that poor calf and wondering how many other calves were struggling out there in the frozen wilderness.

Chapter Six
Head Games

We left Shaktoolik before daybreak to begin our trek across the ice of Norton Bay to Koyuk during the 1983 Iditarod race. The dogs moved briskly during the cool early morning. Weather was perfect—no wind and a clear sky. Six of us—John Barron, Dave Olson, Neil Eklund, Emmitt Peters, Bruce Denton and I—had been traveling in a loose pack since the Yukon River, sort of leapfrogging along. First one stopped for a rest and then another. I had somehow managed to delude myself into thinking that I could pass any of them any time I wanted to and walk off and leave them. This kind of thinking was always a mistake. For one thing, they may have been letting me pass them, making me think I was faster than they were. I think I probably was faster than all, save Dave Olson and Bruce.

We were mushing across the ice as dawn broke and a really marvelous day unfolded before us. There was little snow on the Arctic ice. What little there was turned hard as rock. The ceaseless winds caused the snow to settle into itself and pack tightly, so tightly you needed an axe to cut it. At times we traversed areas of ice covered with a thin layer of hard-packed snow and at other times went for miles over glare ice, polished to a slippery sheen by the Arctic wind. At other times the ice appeared rough and frothy, the result of its freezing while the wind blew.

As we mushed along, the outline of the shore behind us faded until it was no longer visible. We still couldn't see the shore ahead of us. We were so far out on the ice that land had disappeared ahead and behind. Sky and ice blended in a way that blurred the horizon. This condition was referred to as a whiteout. The result was that we felt almost suspended in space. Flying in these conditions had been the demise of many Arctic pilots. Without a visible horizon, it was difficult to control an airplane unless the pilot was skilled in instrument flying.

We began to pick up the low ridge of land off to our left and ahead and slowly but surely made our approach to Koyuk. Our loose-knit little pack made no effort to travel together. We weren't even in sight of one another most of the time. We traveled together if there was a purpose such as safety in a bad storm or cooperating to gain an advantage. It was seldom for the company.

It's Joe Redington Sr.'s turn to lead. It took the strain off the leaders to follow another team. You could usually trust your good buddies . . . but not always. One needed to keep a little skepticism just to make sure you weren't getting side-tracked.

We stopped to rest halfway across Norton Bay, as the sun's rays grew warmer. Neil Eklund, Emmitt Peters, and I snacked our dogs and then took a half hour's snooze before continuing. Neil and Emmitt left ahead of me by about ten minutes. I soon caught them and passed them and after several hours arrived at Koyuk. As my team hurried up the bank, I looked back and could not see any teams. This meant that I had made considerably better time during the last few hours than either Emmitt or Neil. I was becoming more secure in my knowledge that neither of them had a chance of beating me to Nome. At least my dogs wouldn't be the problem.

I directed my team to the checkpoint at the Koyuk National Guard Armory. After checking my equipment with the checker, I pulled my team out of the way on the far side of the armory. We attempted to get our teams as far away from the commotion as possible to help them rest during our stay at the checkpoint. I prepared their food, fed them, and then went inside to fix something for myself. I'd finished eating my standard checkpoint dinner of New York steak and chili when Emmitt Peters came in. We chatted for a little while and then he motioned me over to a point out of earshot of the other mushers. He asked me if I'd like to sneak out with him at about eight o'clock that evening.

Emmitt, a Native from Ruby, was an Iditarod legend, an Iditarod champion. Boy, did I feel privileged. Speaking of being both green *and* dumb, I said, "Sure, that'd be great."

Emmitt went on, "Burt, I think we could get a head start on those guys. Even a small lead this close to Nome would really help. And those guys would have to start playing catch-up and maybe get their dogs all tired out."

We'd arrived in Koyuk sometime shortly after noon, so this downtime would leave our dogs well rested for a night run to Elim. We would arrive in Elim sometime before the heat of the day tomorrow, spend a few hours and then leave for a late run to Golovin and the White Mountain.

Emmitt's nickname was "The Yukon Fox." He lived on the banks of the Yukon River at Ruby. The Fox part spoke for itself. He was known in mushing circles as being one sly, slippery fellow. One of his favorite tricks was to announce loudly that he was going outside to feed his dogs and then sneak away, leaving all the other mushers holding the bag. One time we were standing outside the checkpoint at Ophir, feeding our dogs, when Emmitt stepped on his sled, hollered to everybody that he'd see us in Cripple, and away he went. Fifteen minutes later, he came walking back to camp looking sheepish. He'd just mushed his team around the corner and anchored it there hoping to get everyone else to pack and give chase. When we didn't follow, he just came back. It would have upset everybody else's routine but wouldn't do him any harm. He was already done feeding his dogs and just parked them around the corner where things were a little quieter. Seeing through his treachery, we had just waved good-bye to him and had gone on about our business.

It was a different story in Koyuk, however. I knew I was faster than Emmitt and really didn't fear him upsetting my plans. Also, the timing he suggested fit my schedule pretty well. I thought it would be nice to have someone to travel with. We could trade lead and give each other's leaders a break. And after all, who could pass up an invitation to a "sneak" from the famed Yukon River Fox? It was something I just had to do.

Emmitt and I moseyed outside approximately five minutes apart so as not to arouse suspicion. Soon his dogs were hurrying silently out of town and back onto the ice of Norton Bay for the trip to Elim. Five minutes later, I too left and followed Emmitt. It was pitch black. As we sped through the narrow streets of Koyuk, only the occasional house lights showed that other humans were nearby. My headlight was turned off so as not to arouse the attention of anyone who might warn other mushers in Koyuk that we were on the move. After all, a sneak was a sneak.

Once on the ice and away from town, I could see the pencil-thin beam from Emmitt's headlight knifing back and forth as he searched for markers to show him the trail toward Elim. I caught up with him after twenty minutes or so and he stopped to let me by.

I could hear him behind me encouraging his team to stay with me. On we went until we followed the markers to our right and left the ice. We were once again mushing through scattered trees on the overland trail to Elim. On we went, two night riders hoping the other teams were resting peacefully in Koyuk as we put mile after mile between us. I'd slept little the night before and had only a brief nap during the day. I was becoming more tired as the miles went by and a feeling of deep fatigue settled over me.

Although a good lead dog would usually stay on the trail, a musher must be alert or he could easily become derailed and find himself lost in the dark, especially if that leader was a little devious. The lead dog uses all of its senses in its attempt to follow the correct trail. Even in the dark, dogs can see where other teams have been. They could also smell the scent that remained after a team had passed. In addition, the lead dog could tell by how the trail feels whether or not he's in the right place. But the musher was the coach. If the leader makes a mistake, the musher must command the leader back onto the correct route at once.

When we left the ice and went onto the land, the trail became more difficult. Since my team was breaking trail, Emmitt was easily able to keep up with me. My eyes were becoming heavy as I became more and more tired. The boredom of having only the thin view granted by my narrow headlight beam did nothing to help keep me awake. I began thinking that if I could only close my eyes for just a few moments, they would quit feeling so heavy. Maybe then I would feel a little better.

The fatigue from my heavy eyelids alone was making it more and more difficult to keep them open. I decided that when I passed the next marker I would close my eyes. I stood on the runners, hanging onto the hand bow with my eyes closed and suddenly felt like a new man. After a couple of minutes, I opened my eyes and waited for the next marker. When we passed it, I again closed my eyes and rested for a few minutes. Sweet ecstasy! It made such a difference. Soon I had a routine established; my eyes open for a while and closed for a while. Mile after mile I became more and more tired and it became almost impossible for me to keep my head up.

"Emmitt, you've got to take the lead here. I'm so tired I can't stay awake. I'm going to get us lost."

"Burt, my leaders are burned out. They won't lead any more. The only way I can go is to follow you."

Well, I thought, I could rest my chin on my chest and give my head a little rest while I was resting my eyelids.

I wished I'd been able to sleep at Koyuk, but the checkpoint was so busy and noisy. People had rushed in and out, and kids played all around us, making sleep impossible. Meanwhile, my dogs had rested well in their hideaway out behind the checkpoint. They were clipping along at an eager pace.

I was getting so much benefit from closing my eyes and resting my head on my chest that I decided to try bending over the hand bow and lying on the sled bag for a while to rest my back. Whew, did that feel good. Lower back problems seem to be the most common plague afflicting mushers and I'm no exception. Standing on that sled hour after hour, especially without sleep, creates a fatigue factor. By leaning over my hand bow, it helped to at least partially alleviate that.

Soon I was into a routine of closing my eyes, resting my chin on my chest and bending over my hand bow every time I passed a marker. It really did help except I was becoming more and more tired as the miles went by until I was *really* having trouble staying awake. It was hard to believe that a person in such a miserable posture could even begin to fall asleep, but it was becoming nearly impossible for me to stay awake. I became more and more relaxed each time I went through the routine until after a while I was finding myself being jerked awake by some inner mechanism that was warning me to keep watching for those trail markers. I was literally falling asleep each time I saw a marker.

I knew if my dogs took the wrong trail, we could get seriously lost. "Emmitt, you've got to take the lead. I'm so damned tired I don't know which way is up. Get your damned dogs up here and take the lead!"

"Burt, my leaders won't go without you to follow, keep going."

After a while I wasn't really sure how many markers had gone by before I would wake up and see the next one. Fall asleep; wake up; spot a marker. Fall asleep; wake up; spot a marker; fall asleep; wake up; spot a marker; and fall asleep. The routine went on and on until all of a sudden there was no marker. I could see where teams had gone ahead of me so I assumed that a marker would soon show up and I would then have the reassurance of knowing that I was still on the trail.

Burt and Joe Redington Sr. making plans to outfox other teams. Some of the plots were downright hilarious, although they didn't always fool anybody. *Jeff Schultz Photo*

Time went by and still no markers. Now I was alarmed enough to stay awake with my headlight sweeping back and forth, looking for the marker that would tell me that I was where I should be. On we went for seven or eight minutes. I knew by then that I should have seen a marker if I'd been on the right trail.

I stopped and yelled back at Emmitt, "I'm swinging my team around since we're obviously on the wrong trail. I want to go back until I find a marker and make sure we're not lost."

He hollered back that all the trails in this area headed for Elim and we should continue. We would soon pick up the correct trail.

We continued for a couple of miles until I again told him, "I think the smart thing to do is to stop and turn around to make sure we aren't lost."

He hollered back, "I've been through here lots of times. All trails lead to Elim."

"Emmitt, if you've been through here lots of time, you take the lead."

"Can't, Burt, my leaders just won't go—burned out."

We mushed along this way until we had gone at least fifteen miles. By then it just wasn't practical to turn around and retrace our steps. A dim trail was still visible ahead but it was less and less traveled and was hard to follow.

After a while we became aware of a flashing light ahead of us and to the left, which had to be the Moses Point beacon. We followed the next fork in the trail that headed in that direction and soon were back on the Iditarod Trail. I hoped the only thing lost was whatever extra energy my team had expended in breaking trail and that I'd expended in worrying. Several teams had been on the trail we were on so it wasn't an unbroken trail. Many more teams had been on the actual race trail, however, making it much smoother and easier to follow.

As we continued, a dim light began to glow behind us in the eastern sky and soon daylight was upon us. We mushed past Moses Point, then out onto the ice for the remaining few miles to Elim. The shore approaching Elim was a beautiful rocky bluff, an unmistakable and welcome sight. Soon we came to a sign, which had been put up by the Elim high school kids, welcoming Iditarod mushers to Elim. We parked our teams on the beach below the village, fed the dogs and adjourned to our host families for a brief rest. My host in Elim had always been Tommy. He was so friendly and hospitable that I really hated to leave Elim to finish the race.

This was my second race and I wanted to finish in the money, which meant finishing in the top twenty. I was exhausted from the trip across the ice and the run from Koyuk to Elim. I desperately needed a good nap but was afraid that the teams behind us would keep right on going if I slept at Tommy's house. The thing to do would be to visit Tommy for a half hour or so and then return to snooze on my sled. If other teams came, I would know it.

When I finished with my dogs and went up to Tommy's, he had a wonderful breakfast for me and I sat down to eat with great gusto. Tommy's dad was there, so we began a nice visit as we ate breakfast. The combination of a nice warm house, good company and good food took its toll almost instantly as exhaustion suddenly overwhelmed me. I was chewing my fourth or fifth bite when my eyes started to droop. Three or four more bites and my head began slowly sinking to my chest. I was telling Tommy's dad something about the race when I heard a loud snore. It was with some shock that I realized it was *my* snore. I shook myself awake, but had the same problem again. I couldn't stay awake to eat breakfast or even visit. Tommy's dad had a concerned look on his face as he told me, "Burt, you've got to go lie down for an hour or two or you'll never make it to Nome."

I told him that I knew I had to take a nap but wanted to take it on my sled so I could keep track of the other teams. I finally finished breakfast, picked up my gear, thanked everyone for their kind hospitality and wandered back down to my sled.

Emmitt was just getting his things together to go take a nap at his friend's house as I laid down on my sled.

"Burt, wake me up when it was time to leave."

I said I would and fell almost instantly asleep. I awoke an hour later to the clatter of sleds and the sound of a dog's bark. I awoke to see Neil Eklund and John Barron mushing their teams out of Elim. I had not heard them arrive so I'd no idea how long they'd been there, but I knew that we couldn't let them get too far ahead so close to Nome. My gear was already packed so I asked a friend to wake Emmitt because teams were getting ahead of us.

I said, "Tell Emmitt I'll wait for him."

After fifteen minutes or so Emmitt arrived, hurriedly threw his gear in his sled and away we went. The trail out of Elim traversed open ice that provided a hard, fast trail for a dog team. Once again Emmitt was dropping back. About ten miles out of town, I noticed two of my dogs weren't pulling. There was a slight sag in their tug lines indicating that they were just coasting along. One was a dog named Fawcet, which I had bought from Rick Swenson, and the other was Rick Swenson's famous lead dog, Old Buddy, otherwise known as OB, which Rick had loaned me. I had needed a leader—OB still loved to run lead, and OB wasn't quite fast enough for Rick anymore. Win-win for OB and me.

The dogs weren't neck-lining or hanging back at all; they just weren't pulling. In my fatigue, I began worrying that they might be too tired. We must climb through a small range of hills before Golovin Bay and the next checkpoint. I worried that I might have to carry the dogs on my sled through those hills, putting an extra burden on the other dogs. I should have realized that all they were doing was coasting along catching a little rest much the same as I had done with my eyes-closed and head-on-chest routine earlier.

I became more and more concerned and decided I'd better check with my partner, Emmitt, to see what he thought. I stopped my team and waited nearly fifteen minutes for him to catch up. When he came up behind me, I hollered back at him that I had two dogs that weren't pulling and wondered if he had any suggestions.

"Burt, I believe I'd turn around and take those dogs back to Elim."

I swung my team around and headed back for Elim. I looked over my shoulder to see Emmitt's leaders forging ahead toward Nome. They sure didn't look burned out to me.

After four or five miles, I met Dave Olsen and Bruce Denton who were heading toward Nome. They asked me what the heck I was doing. I replied I had two dogs that weren't pulling and was taking them back to Elim to drop them.

Dave said, "Burt, don't do that unless one of them is injured. Let them trot to the next checkpoint and reevaluate it there. If they can't make it, you can always put 'em in the sled. Then give them a free ride and not waste any more time than you're wasting going back to Elim. You're really hurting yourself going backwards."

I replied, "I talked it over with Emmitt and he told me that best thing to do was to take Fawcett and OB to Elim."

I kept heading back towards Elim. It didn't dawn on me that I'd been snookered until I was almost back to Elim. *Emmitt had just eliminated one competitor from his race.*

Mushers liked to visit after the chores were done. Burt and Joe Redington, Sr. trade information and misinformation with other mushers at Rohn checkpoint. The temperature could vary considerably from high ground to creek bottoms as a team mushed along, so Joe attached a thermometer to the rear of his sled bag to help him pick his camping spots. *Jeff Schultz photo.*

I had just learned one of my most difficult lessons in Iditarod racing. Many village mushers are ruthless when they race and have no sympathy for some dumb city boy. Emmitt was a good pal, but it wasn't fun to reflect on what he'd just done to me. First, he got me to break trail for him most of the way from Koyuk to Elim, putting pressure on my leaders and taking it off his. Then he got me to *wake* him up and *wait* for him so I could *lead* him out of Elim taking the load off his leaders and delaying my departure. Then he sent me on a fool's errand back along the trail, which demoralized me and my dogs, and wasted more time.

Now I knew why they called him the Yukon Fox. *I learned it the hard way.* For a while, I was a babe in the woods among those slippery mushers. Later, I learned to chuckle with glee over this chicanery; however, in my earlier races I was unbelievably naïve, most likely because of my life before Iditarod. While I did learn to watch out for myself, I was never able to practice chicanery on anyone. I just couldn't do it.

I quickly turned my team around and began a mad chase to catch up with the teams ahead of me. Instead of catching and passing John Barron and Bruce Denton, which I should have been able to do with my faster team, I was now behind all five. Furthermore, my backtracking had caused my dogs to run a greater distance, tiring them.

I left the ice, finally, and headed up into the long, treeless hills before Golovin. I ran behind the sled up all those hills in an attempt to help my dogs in every way I could. It didn't help that I felt like a moron for letting Emmitt manipulate me like a puppet.

Turning a team around during a race causes an adverse psychological effect. Dogs are perceptive; they figure out when a driver doesn't know what he is doing. When I turned my team around for the second time to head back to Nome, the effect was to demoralize them. They weren't nearly as eager mentally as they had been before I'd stopped them the first time. I was trying to cheer them up by talking happily to them and whistling but with limited success. I finally caught sight of teams ahead of me, so I knew I was gaining. Finally, the mushers ahead stopped and I joined them as they rested and snacked their teams. I quickly snacked mine so I would be ready to leave when they were, hoping to maintain position with them until I might possibly draw away.

We continued to White Mountain, but the shenanigans had taken something out of my team that I couldn't seem to put back. I could keep up with the other teams, but I couldn't pass them. I finished out of the money in twenty-second place.

After a good night's sleep in Nome, I sat down and thought about my race from Koyuk to the finish line. My position in Koyuk had been good with a well-rested team. I don't know if I could have stayed ahead of the other teams, but I was confident that if I hadn't made any mistakes I would have at least finished in the money.

What went wrong? I had been gullible was what went wrong. By conspiring with me to sneak out on the other teams, Emmitt had put me just where he wanted me. He knew I would catch him shortly out of Koyuk and that he wouldn't be able to stay ahead of me. It would be logical for him to suggest that I go on ahead so he wouldn't be holding me back. This put me ahead of him, giving his team something to chase and be excited about. A slower team actually moved quicker with less fatigue when following a faster team. When we lost the trail, I broke trail, which was more work than following another team.

In Koyuk, I had made the mistake of thinking that Emmitt and I were racing the other teams instead of each other. This caused me to quit seeing Emmitt as a competitor. Instead, I saw him as a teammate; after all, didn't we sneak out of Koyuk together?

And, of course, the final straw was asking *him* to coach my team. I had to have been so tired and rummy at that point that I probably deserved what I got. After I'd been in Nome a day or two, I bumped into Emmitt and told him that it wasn't too nice a trick to pull on me after I'd helped him break trail and had him awakened so he wouldn't be left behind.

Emmitt just laughed and said, "You do what you have to do toward the end of the race when you're fighting over those last paying positions."

Emmitt had given me a hell of an education and I decided then that I was going to take a smarter more subtle approach next time. As in many things, it's sometimes difficult to strike a balance between when to trust and when not to. We need to be careful because the possibility of getting suckered is always there in life and on the Iditarod Trail. On the other hand, we don't want to become so paranoid that we miss out on the camaraderie and companionship that was the heart of the race in those days.

MORE SHENANIGANS, 1984 RACE

I made a mental note of Emmitt's lesson as I began the 1984 race to be just a little more cautious than I had been in the past and then set out to run the best race I could. Joe Redington Sr. and I traveled together off and on during the first part of the 1984 race. We took turns breaking trail over Rainy Pass, first one team in the lead and then the other, arriving in Rohn River checkpoint as darkness fell. Our teams were in good shape, so we didn't need to take our mandatory twenty-four-hour stop yet.

Temperatures had been high during the day but then fell at evening time to below freezing. This combination usually produced a trail that was damaging to dogs' feet. As the surface of the trail refroze, crystallized ice formed, which could be as sharp as razor blades. The remedy for this was to put booties on the dogs' feet to protect their pads from cuts.

Joe hated to use booties and rarely did. He bragged about breeding his dogs for tough feet. "You don't have to boot dogs if their feet are right." He'd boot them if he had to but would do anything to avoid it.

Actually, it was not that big a problem to boot up the dogs, but we learned of an additional problem when talking to the checkers at Rohn. They told us there was a great deal of overflow on the lakes we would be crossing between Rohn and the next checkpoint at Nikolai. Running a team through this water in below freezing temperatures froze the dogs' booties solid after you left the water. You often had to remove the wet booties and replace them with dry fresh ones each time you went through overflow. It could be a lot of trouble and effort when done several times in one stretch.

We decided to feed the dogs, jump in our sleeping bags for eight hours then wake and test the snow conditions. If the snow appeared granular and sharp, we would roll over, go back to sleep, take our mandatory twenty-four-hour rest stop there and hope for better conditions the following evening.

On the other hand, we would get about as much good from our rest stop after eight hours as we were going to by staying, so we wanted to leave then and get moving if possible. We could then save our twenty-four-hour stop for later when it could be put to better use, like waiting for sick dogs to get well or to allow a weather situation to move on.

I woke up at four o'clock, pulled my boots on and went over to Joe's sled for a conference. After shouting several times at the top of my lungs, I shook his sled to wake him up. Joe had taken his hearing aids out and was deaf as a post. I shouted at him, "IT'S TIME TO CHECK SNOW CONDITIONS."

He stuck just the tip of his nose out of his sleeping bag and hollered, "WHAT?"

I repeated, "It's time to check snow conditions."

First his hand and then his arm reached out. He grabbed a handful of snow beside the sled, felt it, scrunched it around, and then announced, "It's going to be too icy. We should stay for twenty-four and leave tomorrow night."

His hand zipped back into his sleeping bag, his nose disappeared, and that was that.

As long as I was up, I wandered through camp with my bucket, heading for the water hole so I could feed my dogs. While I'd slept, I thought I had heard a team clatter by and, sure enough, Rick Swenson's team was missing. He'd left in the still of the night while the rest of us slept.

Doctor Terry Adkins and Joe Redington Sr. paused to palaver in front of the cozy log cabin at Rohn checkpoint. The checkpoint is located at a guide's hunting camp and is served by a small bush airstrip during hunting season. Checkers and race officials occupy the cabin while the Iditarod teams are present.

When a musher leaves early, especially a champion like Rick Swenson, it was always smart to reevaluate your own position. I reflected on the discussion Joe and I'd had in reaching our decision to stay. I decided that it still seemed like the sound thing to do. We would waste at least a couple of hours out there changing booties, while if it did warm up by tomorrow there might be no need.

I continued toward the water hole and bumped into Susan Butcher. She'd heard Rick leave and was agitated. She was wondering aloud whether to follow him out now or continue with her twenty-four-hour stay. I told her that Joe and I had decided to stay, but she wasn't so sure we'd made the right decision. If Rick got out there far enough and bad weather developed here in the mountains at Rohn, he might be able to get far enough ahead to gain an insurmountable lead. I shrugged, filled my bucket and returned to my sled.

Several other mushers were now pacing around camp trying to figure out what to do. I put my water on to boil and fixed myself an early-morning snack. The dogs and I were soon fed and I was back in my sleeping bag sound asleep. Not long after, I heard a sled clattering by and then several more as teams began to leave without finishing their twenty-four-hour layovers. They had decided to leave Rohn early in their chase after Rick. By then, these teams had fourteen or fifteen hours invested in their twenty-four-hour stop. I thought, my gosh, it had worked. Rick had managed to flush them out after all. In only nine or ten more hours, they would have been done with their mandatory twenty-four-hour stop and had it out of the way.

We learned later that Rick had driven his team twenty miles out of Rohn and camped, hoping to upset the rhythm of the other teams. Sure enough, it worked. The amazing thing about it was that he accomplished it without saying a word to anyone. It was a measure of how driven Susan was that she was able to overcome this early handicap and still finish second behind Dean Osmar at the finish line in Nome.

Joe and I waited out our twenty-four-hour mandatory stop and mushed out of Rohn into the darkness. We'd been traveling along together. He would lead out of one checkpoint, and then I would lead out of the next. It was my turn to lead. I was ready to leave a few minutes before Joe, so I traveled alone along a trail that was dark and icy. As mentioned earlier, the first few miles of trail out of Rohn is called the Buffalo Tunnel. The trail is narrow and twisting with a side hill to the right for most of it. This area normally doesn't get a lot of snow and this year it was basically bare ground. There was a lot of glaciation and with no snow; the ice was bare. My headlight picked up the shiny surface of ice on the trail ahead of my leaders as we clattered along. We skidded and slid wildly on the slick, uneven surface, sometimes striking a protruding rock or root in a glancing sideways blow that would nearly knock me from the runners. I wondered how much of that abuse the sled would take before it cracked into pieces.

As the team started up a glaciered side hill, a large twisted stump appeared in the middle of the trail. Firmly frozen in the ice, it was covered with sharp, protruding sticks and roots. A musher could usually maneuver his sled around this kind of obstacle but not on that icy side hill. It was a handful just to keep things upright. The dogs dodged around the stump with no problem but the sled didn't make it. The gang line just ahead of the sled caught a protruding root and led the sled right into the nasty obstruction. We hit the stump with a resounding crunch. The sled caught the snag at the brush bow with a savage glancing blow and then snagged the karabiner that holds the gang line, sled and snow hook together.

Then we were free of it and cruising up the trail again, apparently unscathed. All of a sudden, my snow hook, which had been attached to my hand bow, jerked loose and skidded down my sled bag as the sled slowed to a halt. As I stood on the motionless sled, the snow hook clanged off down the trail after my team. The dogs quickly realized that their job had just become a whole lot easier. With no loaded sled and no heavy musher to pull, the well-rested dogs could really boogie. I leaped off the runners and hotfooted it up the trail at a rapid pace. Most people who have ever seen me run would tell you that I don't run; I lumber. But for a few minutes, there was no faster man in the world. It was another seventy miles to Nikolai and I had no intention of walking it.

Burt's team at Rohn checkpoint where a lot of the strategy was planned. The dogs were usually tired from the trip over the mountains when they arrived at Rohn, but Burt wanted them well rested before they began the long trip across the Farewell Burn to Nikolai. It was a challenge extricating the dogs from among the trees when they were rested and wild to go.

However, the team quickly faded into the darkness, snow hook clanging along behind. Fresh from their twenty-four-hour rest stop, they were ready to roll. My sprint soon turned to a lumber as I huffed and puffed after my now unseen pals.

As I continued, I began to see points of light flashing ahead. It was my head-light reflecting the dogs' eyes, with the team stopped dead in their tracks and lunging eagerly against their traces. Between lunges, they looked back at me with huge, slobbery grins. As I approached closer, I saw what had stopped them. The snow hook had miraculously caught an exposed spruce root no bigger than my little finger. With each lunge, the tiny root threatened to give up its hold and turn my dogs loose for another wild run toward the burn and Nikolai.

Making calming noises, I sneaked up on the snow hook and pounced on it like a cat on a mouse. But now what? If it came loose, there would be no way I could stop them. If the hook pulled loose, I would skitter along behind like some kind of trail drag until gravity and fatigue, or another frozen snag, loosened my grip and the dogs once again bounded off down the trail.

As I lay there searching for an idea, some of my dogs looked back. A quick glance over my shoulder saw a headlight bobbing up the trail toward us. In a moment, Joe Sr. drove up. As I lay there in the trail with my death grip on the snow hook, he asked what the heck I was doing lying there. I hurriedly told him the story and asked him if he would come and hold the snow hook while I went back and pushed my sled up and reconnected it.

He took one look at the hook and its tenuous hold on the tiny spruce root and said, "Burt, I wouldn't touch that for a million bucks. Wait here and I'll go back for the sled!"

Moments later he was back and we soon had me back together and heading down the trail. Sometimes it is nice to have a friend around to lend a helping hand. I was glad it wasn't Emmitt this time.

We banged along through the Buffalo Tunnel and reached Farewell Lake. The trail went right to the edge of the lake and into water. The wind was brisk out of the north and whitecaps lapped against the shore. We could see stakes out on the lake, so we figured we might as well plunge in and see what happened. Joe's dogs balked at the frothy water so I went around seeing if my dogs would go. I'd driven the dogs through many open creeks during fall training, so the dogs plunged in when I asked. We splashed along as though this was normal.

Before long, the stakes played out and we had nothing to guide us to the trail at the far side of the lake. The wind and whitecaps made north easy to determine so we just continued. As we approached the far shore, we started sweeping our headlamps back and forth through the trees looking for a reflector. None appeared. Then we turned along the shore looking for tracks that would indicate the trail. We found it and again headed north. As I flashed by a tree, I saw a white metal tag nailed to a birch tree. It was a reflector installed backwards with the reflector nailed against the tree. Every reflector from there to Nikolai had been nailed to the trees backward. Birch trees were white so the reflectors were nearly impossible to see.

SULATNA CROSSING

We continued into the Kuskokwim Valley and then across the long run past Cripple Creek towards Ruby. A number of us were camped at Sulatna Crossing when Rick ambled over to visit. "Burt, your team looks great. How do you keep that team fast when they're so fat? I don't know how you keep up with us with those dogs looking like pigs."

I was about to load them up with a huge meal of mutton and fat. "Woops, maybe this was not such a good idea." I wandered over to talk to a couple of other mushers and the talk turned to dogs. "Guys, tell me what you think. If a dog team is keeping up, is it better to have them a little heavy or a little light at this point?"

Both responded that a little heavy was better through here because it could get terribly cold on the Yukon and the dogs would do a whole lot better with some extra cushion. I told them about Rick's comment and everybody burst out laughing. "Consider the source. No one is better at screwing with your head than Rick. He can pay you a compliment that'll derail you for days."

NULATO

My team that year was as good a team as I'd had. I went into Ruby on the Yukon River in fifth position. Ruby was more than halfway to Nome, so my team was really doing well. The Yukon River out of Ruby was extremely rough with steep drifts from the tireless wind. Because of that, the trail followed a series of sloughs along the south side of the river. The sloughs were protected from the wind so were nice and smooth. Willow brush abounded and was full of ptarmigan, a small north-country grouse. Small coveys of ptarmigan flushed often as we mushed along. Ravens flew overhead, following the trail looking for goodies much as they follow our highways looking for scraps tossed from autos.

Each time a covey flushed, the dogs would pick up the pace. It was nice to have something to break the monotony. I became aware of a dark shape moving much faster than the ravens and looked up to see a gyrfalcon making a power dive at something in the trail about fifty yards ahead of my leaders. A covey of ptarmigan flushed and the falcon slammed into one of them with a cloud of white feathers. The falcon swooped up and back down in an airborne loop, and landed on the dead ptarmigan as the remainder of the small covey clattered off.

The falcon stood momentarily on its prey in the middle of the trail and then, with the leaders only feet away, took off with powerful wing beats. As my sled carried me by, only the marks from the falcon's wing tips and a couple drops of blood remained in the snow to mark the story of that death in the Alaska wilderness. Now, years later, I've earned the classification of Master Falconer, inspired by that brief but powerful drama. Morticia, my peals peregrine falcon, rests in her weathering yard as I write this.

We continued through Galena and then halfway to Nulato, where I again caught up with Rick Swenson and Terry Adkins. They had stopped to rest and feed their dogs. I stopped, too, and then continued, arriving in Nulato with Swenson. Terry was close behind.

The cabin at Rohn made you feel like you were truly back in old-time Alaska. While trapline cabins were often tiny with barely enough room to move around, hunting cabins usually had more room to house and feed hunters and guides. A hunting cabin needed some horns to set the mood and assure hunters that they were truly in hunting country. The propeller is likely the result of a pilot misjudging his ability to lift off the short bush strip with a heavy load. It likely gave the hunters something to think about as they took off to go home. The wind blew hard out of Rainy Pass carrying silt and seeds that collected on the cabin roof. A garden of grass and spruce trees eventually grew on the roof.

We were at the checkpoint and I was opening my food bags and getting my cooking equipment out when Rick strolled over and visited for a few minutes. He told me that he'd decided to stay just two hours and then leave for Kaltag. He figured the lead teams would still be there giving their dogs a long rest before the ninety-mile push over the portage to Unalakleet on the coast. That would put him about where he wanted to be for a good effort at the finish.

We chatted for a few more minutes and then I continued feeding my dogs. His plan sounded good, so I fed my dogs and then settled down for a brief nap in the Nulato community hall. When I heard Rick stirring, I got up and made ready to leave. I wanted to leave right behind Rick, as I knew my dogs would be tired and would be a little more eager to go if they had another team to chase.

The team was well rested and eager to run as Burt led several teams out of Rohn toward Nikolai. When teams were traveling close together, it was usually better to be the following team to save on your leaders, but the tracks showed several teams ahead of Burt.

When my sled was packed, I took one more moment for a trip to the outhouse. While there, I heard Rick directing his team out of town. I was annoyed with myself for not being ready to go when he was. When I got back to my sled and lined my team out, they gave me a look I hadn't seen before. It was clearly a mutinous look, but then they headed through town and down onto the frozen surface of the Yukon River. A hundred yards further, my leader stopped to do what I'd taken time to do a few minutes earlier. This stopped the team. Racing dogs are trained to do their business on the run. Their stopping was clear evidence of their lack of enthusiasm and poor attitude.

When they finished, I told them to get going. They refused. The attitude progressed through the entire team within moments and several of them sat down. I again commanded them to go as sternly as I could but with no results. I proceeded to the head of my team and began leading them down the trail hoping that if they were all standing up and moving it might make a difference. When I let go of the leaders and walked back to the team, they all sat down again. After five minutes of this, it was clear that I was getting nowhere.

After seven more hours, I tried again, but still my team didn't want to go. They'd obviously figured out that I was a softie. If they refused to go, there was no way I could make them go. By now, we'd been in Nulato nine hours, which was more than plenty of rest for the dogs. I knew that what was happening was the result of my not being more insistent when we first left Nulato.

Burt, on the right, chats with Emmitt Peters (the Yukon Fox) and Rick Swenson near Rick's team at the start in Anchorage on Fourth Avenue. These are two of the cagiest Iditarod mushers ever. Emmitt could convince you that he was your best friend and you should travel and work together . . . until he decided it was time to make his move. Rick didn't even have to say anything to send the best teams in the race on a wild goose chase. Head games were a fun but serious part of the race and everybody remained good friends when it was over.

I rearranged things in my sled, walked up to the leaders and started walking. If my leaders wouldn't pull us to Nome, I'd pull them to Nome. This I did for about a mile and a half. Then I decided this was ridiculous. There was no way I was going to lead them all the way to Nome.

I walked along until we came abreast of a trail marker. It was a spruce tree about eight feet high that had been planted in the river's ice to show travelers between the villages where the trail was during bad weather. People living along the river had frozen these trees into the ice approximately a quarter mile apart so travelers wouldn't get lost during winter blizzards. I broke a limb off the tree and started walking up and down my team swatting my pant leg and talking to them as angrily as I could, up one side of the team and down the other. When I'd stopped leading the team, they'd all sat down. When I broke the limb off, they all stood up. When I started swatting my leg and swearing at them, they began to look alert and eager. By the time I'd walked up and down the team three or four times, they looked as rested and eager as they had at the start in Anchorage.

Tossing the switch aside, I stepped on the runners, said, "Get up," and away we went. When we arrived in Kaltag, we found all of the front-runners, including Rick, still there but preparing to leave.

My team ultimately finished twelfth in Nome, which I thought was quite good. Later on I was telling Susan how much I'd enjoyed the trip and how helpful Rick had been at Nulato. I told her that most mushers would have sneaked out on me and left me sitting there. Rick was nice enough to tell me what his plans were so that I could follow along if I wanted to.

"Don't you see what he did to you, Burt? He knew that his team would do anything he told them to. If he told them to leave Nulato after two hours and head for Kaltag, that's what they'd do. He also knew this would give him seven or eight hours of good rest in Kaltag. He figured that your team wouldn't be ready to go after only two hours but that you might try to leave in order to stay up with him. If it didn't work and your team became balky, he might succeed in sticking you out on the trail, away from the checkpoint, and get you out of his race. That is exactly what happened."

The measure of Rick's finesse was that I still don't know whether he was sincerely trying to help me or whether he actually did pull me out of Nulato prematurely and effectively put me out of the race for seven hours.

Head trips are a big part of the Iditarod Trail Sled Dog Race. They make it interesting and keep you on your toes. Am I mad at the guys? Heck no. It was part of my Iditarod experience and my own danged fault.

Chapter Seven
A Dog Named Tiger

Tiger was more than a dog; Tiger was a friend. It was a bit puzzling why he was a friend, since our relationship was far from perfect. He let me down several times and I know I let him down. Although we occasionally failed each other, we each got so much from our friendship that our momentary lapses only seemed to emphasize our compatibility. What made this kind of friend, or in this case, dog, that you'd stick by through thick and thin? The kind of individual that came along only a few times during your life? What made the kind of a friend whose faults you'd overlook no matter how obnoxious or painful you found them? Well, Tiger was that rare dog.

He was one of the dogs in the string that I had bought from Duke during 1980. Duke had told me that Tiger was a leader he'd bought from Don Honea during the 1978 Iditarod Race. I used Tiger in lead during training for the '81 race but wasn't impressed. If he knew anything about gee or haw, you couldn't prove it by me. He was independent to the point of being obnoxious about it. He would lift his leg on every other bush we passed and if his bowels needed to move, he'd put on the brakes with enough force to stop the entire team rather than do it on the run. This had disastrous results when he was up front, since the entire team would ball up sometimes before I could get the sled stopped. He was a feisty dog and would fight anything that moved if it challenged him. This included me until we reached an understanding. He knew a rookie musher when he saw one.

Now this may not sound like the basis for a relationship. I spent the first year of training and the first Iditarod race trying to minimize the effect of his obnoxious personality. I would run him toward the back of the team, so the rest of the team could drag him down the trail when he lifted his leg or stopped to poop. This also meant he was one of the last dogs hitched, so he usually didn't have time to pick a fight. He generally pulled well with me breathing down his neck from the sled just behind him. As my experience as a musher grew, I began to realize that moving him around was just a cop-out on my part. I was taking the easy way out, which only gave him slack to become more and more obnoxious. And by not demanding that he shape up, I was turning him more and more into an arrogant, spoiled brat.

Burt and Tiger waiting their turn for the lead dog ceremony at the start of the 1981 race. Tiger was referred to as a village dog, one that came from the strain of dogs that had been developed over centuries by Native mushers. He was a tough, fast, intelligent dog from Don Honea's breed at Ruby on the Yukon River.

Dogs are like people. They need guidance and reasonable discipline during their growing-up years, and continuing through their working years. It assures them of a happy, productive life. Tiger hadn't gotten that lately; because of my inexperience, I wasn't giving him the guidance and discipline he needed. The result was a dog that became more obnoxious and less productive as the months went by.

Later on, I learned that many of his idiosyncrasies were the manifestation of an undisciplined dominant male personality. His leg lifting was his way of marking his territory and his feistiness was the way he protected it. His occasional growls at me when I got too rough with him were his way of establishing his ground. His indifference to his tasks as a leader was his way of testing. When he became lackadaisical and was moved back in the team, I was actually teaching him that if he didn't perform he would be moved to a position of less pressure and responsibility.

Tiger and I were definitely becoming acquainted during our first year together, but it wasn't a healthy relationship. He had me buffaloed and he knew it. Until then my contact with dogs had always been with the neighborhood pets. Those dogs were for companionship. They were never disciplined because nothing more than a wag of the tail was ever really expected. During my first year training sled dogs, I honestly felt that anything more severe than raising my voice at one of my dogs was cruel and something I just wouldn't do. Anything more than swatting one of them was a lot more than I would do.

In spite of all this, we were beginning to enjoy each other more and more. Many racing sled dogs have hyper personalities. They are bred for a number of characteristics, including a high level of natural energy. Because of this, most sled dogs will go berserk when they see you coming to them in the yard. Their normal sphere of activity is a circle twelve to fifteen feet in diameter determined by the length of their chain. Although they are surrounded by other sled dogs, the bright spots in their lives happens when their master is in their midst. Either they are going to be fed or they are going to be hitched and run.

There's a bit of psychology involved in handling the dogs so they want to run. If you take a dog that has been running loose, put a harness on him and then hitch him to a sled, he is going to feel restricted because he doesn't have the freedom that he had before. Restrict his freedom and he has no fun.

If you take a dog that's been tethered in the yard, however, and put a harness on him, hitch him to a sled and take off out of the yard, he feels wild abandon. That is essentially the same as turning him loose, and he will eagerly look forward to the times you show up with a harness. Then he is free of his restrictive, limited chain.

Most sled dogs get so eager and crazy at the sight of their musher that the whole dog lot literally erupts when the musher comes into view. Dogs run at great speed around the stakes at the end of their chains while hopping up and down off their doghouses, or leaping into the air, barking frantically.

Some dogs just stand there and look at you. Tiger was one of those, as were several other seasoned leaders. When I came into view, Tiger immediately fixed me with his gaze and never took his eyes off me as I made my way through the dog lot. Sometimes I wandered through the yard just petting each dog and saying a few words to them to further cement my bond with them. Most of them literally climbed my frame in eagerness to be petted. Many stood on their hind legs, grabbed me with their front legs, and hugged me in an effort to keep me from leaving them. It was a touching thing to have them bestow so much love and affection, yet it created one hell of an obligation on my part.

Tiger never went crazy when I came into view. His gaze followed me as I worked my way toward him and then he stood perfectly still with his head stretched as far as he could toward me waiting to be petted. As I stood there, petting, and talking to him, his eyes would look into mine as though he understood every word I said. I'm sure that in his primitive mind, he was making an effort to communicate and his stillness was an indication of the intensity and focus with which he was attuned to my every move and sound.

He reacted to the inflections of my voice with an expression as clear as that on any child's face. If I was in a happy mood, he grinned back and wagged his tail. If I was in a quiet mood, his expression was tranquil with his tail perfectly still. If my mind was burdened with heavy thoughts, I sometimes voiced them aloud as I wandered through the dog lot. It was amazing how almost any of the dogs would pick up on my more somber tone, but Tiger was particularly sensitive. When I was in a serious or stern mood, he would get an almost guilty look on his face as though hoping that he wasn't really the cause of my displeasure.

Now to someone who had known animals only as pets or had never even had a pet, I'm sure this all sounds ridiculous, but so help me, it is true. Tiger and a few other dogs I've known were almost human in their responses. Of all of them, Tiger was probably my favorite.

Although he was beginning to treat me with a little more respect from an "attitude" standpoint, he was much too feisty among other dominant male dogs. I was still letting him do his leg lifting during runs and he was slowing to poop at will rather than stopping. With that uncertainty, I never put him in lead if it was critical. For example, he was back in the team when we began the 1983 race on Fourth Avenue. I did not want him jamming my team into a mess by stopping to poop in the middle of Fourth Avenue in front of all those people. We didn't need a tangle on race day.

Burt with Tiger, Iditarod president Al Crane and announcer, Orville Lake. Al was an Iditarod musher and board member who did more than most to shape the race during the early days. Al is among a handful of men, nearly forgotten, who received little recognition for their incredible impact on making The Iditarod Trail Sled Dog Race the institution it is today. Earl was a famed sprint musher and well-known race personality, always ready to entertain when you put a mike in his hands.

As time went on, he led with more intensity, although he still refused to acknowledge that my commands existed. In spite of his annoying habits, Tiger was always willing to run ahead of the team, so he was spending more and more time as a leader.

It was during the 1983 Iditarod. All mushers were required to take a four-hour mandatory stop at White Mountain. While we were there, Dave Olson and I were invited to the checker's house for dinner. What a great home-cooked meal we enjoyed. Roast beef with mashed potatoes and gravy with all the trimmings. What a change from trail food. The entire family joined us, including kids and grandkids.

The checker was telling us about Terry Adkins having to be airlifted off Topkok Hill because his dogs had stopped and refused to go. Terry was one of the most experienced mushers actively competing in the Iditarod Race. For something like that to happen to a trail-wise musher like Terry gave a second-year compet-itor like me a lot to think about. Why would a team quit like that? Had it been pushed too hard during the race or was it the result of a training error before the race even started?

Dave felt that dog teams reached an extremely critical phase at this stage of the race. "By now," he said, "the dogs are tired and probably bored. The miles have probably begun to look much the same and the food tastes the same. Now the whole thing has become a job."

The situation isn't a whole lot different from the one many working people find themselves in after a few years on the job. The need to put food on the table keeps us in harness; however, the dogs have no such motivation. The dogs in a well-trained team are doing it because they really aren't aware of having a choice.

Dave continued, "It is crucial that we not push our dogs too hard at this point because they might just quit the same as Terry's did, leaving us less than a hundred miles from the finish like some stranded hitchhiker whose car has run out of gas."

I'd made several mistakes after leaving Koyuk and I'd about convinced myself I was going to finish out of the money. I left White Mountain in low spirits and my dogs, as usual, read me like a book. They noticed my discouragement almost instantly and began acting discouraged themselves. Half of them weren't pulling and the other half looked like they were about to quit. Four or five times my leaders ducked under a tree or ducked off the trail and stopped. I was probably feeling a little bit sorry for myself and for my dogs. Too much darkness and too little sleep leads to some weird, uncharacteristic bouts of depression.

The conversation at dinner in White Mountain began to play tricks on my mind. The more bummed I became, the more bummed they became. And vice versa. As we approached the emergency shelter cabin on Topkok Hill, I concluded that the best thing for us to do was stop and camp for six hours. Roxy Woods, a well-known sprint musher in Alaska, was the next team back of me and I knew she was hours behind.

We pulled up to the cabin under clear skies with temperatures at around ten below zero with blowing snow. I fed the dogs and then went inside to spread my bedroll out. There was a stove but no fuel, so I prepared to snuggle down in my sleeping bag. I got to thinking that if those dogs were half as miserable as I was, they might enjoy coming inside for a change, so I opened the door and called them in. They bolted through the door, sled and all, and began eagerly sniffing around the cabin, wagging their tails. They were super-energetic and really didn't look nearly as bad as I thought they should under the circumstances.

I closed the door behind us and crawled into my sleeping bag. The dogs calmed down and within moments we were all sleeping soundly. My pal Tiger even grabbed a corner of my sleeping bag to lie down on. After a good nap, I woke up, fed the dogs, had a snack myself and brought the dogs outside. Dawn was breaking and temperatures were still below zero. The snow was quite granular, so the dogs would need to be booted before heading for Nome. As I strung the team out and anchored the sled, I thought I saw open water only a hundred yards ahead of us. I wandered over to take a look and found approximately an inch of water flowing over the ice of a small creek. If I booted the dogs at the cabin and ran them through the water, the booties would freeze and become uncomfortable for the dogs. The easy solution was to drive the dogs through the creek first, run them another two or three hundred yards to shake the water off their feet, and then boot them.

I drove the team through the water and booted them up. I stepped back on the sled and commanded the dogs to go. They didn't move. As I shouted another command, Tiger, who was in lead, turned around and looked at me and then sat down. I shook the sled and again hollered, "Get up." Tiger didn't even bother to turn around. Two or three other dogs sat down with him. Within a minute, every dog in the team was either sitting or lying down. To say I became "alarmed" is probably an understatement. I could only think of Terry Adkins and his helicopter, and I realized with horror that this was the spot where his misfortune had occurred.

Burt shuffles dogs around during a training run north of the Kahiltna cabin. Each dog got a chance at every position in the team to be sure we best used his talents. Some dogs loved to lead and out race their teammates while others became insecure and balked at the challenge. Like people, some dogs had the talent to lead while others were happy to follow.

I walked to the head of my team, took hold of Tiger's harness and led the team, trotting, down the trail toward Nome, hollering "get up" as we went. After a hundred feet or so, I stopped and ran back to the sled hoping that their momentum would carry them forward and we would be on our way. The instant I let go, the entire team stopped and by the time I got back to the sled, they were again all lying down. I tried this technique three or four more times with the same results. I was never as disappointed in any living thing in my life as I was in Tiger for betraying me in such a cruel fashion. Not to mention the disappointment I felt in myself for not being the alpha male that a musher needed to be.

By now, I was ready to try anything. I felt like the dogs and I hadn't been communicating too well. I knew that much of what was happening here resulted from the mood I'd been in the night before. I went forward and knelt down beside Tiger to have a little visit. In firm, persuasive tones I reminded him how we'd worked together for two whole seasons and how we'd come to know each other so much better. I reminded him that we had already run three thousand miles this year and had only fifty miles left to complete our winter with honor. I talked about how humiliating it would be to arrive in Nome by helicopter and about how proud we would be to enter Nome with class and style under our own power.

I talked about how the year before, my wife and family and friends had met us in Nome, giving us our first big Iditarod finish. They'd hosed us liberally with cheap champagne and had magnums of the expensive stuff chilled and ready to be consumed the moment we crossed under the famous Iditarod arch. I had quite a conversation with Tiger. Believing that I'd convinced him that honor was the only thing we had left, I walked back to the sled, gave it a shake, and hollered, "Get up." Tiger didn't even turn around.

About that time, an elderly Eskimo couple drove up on a snowmachine and asked if I needed any help. There was nothing in the world I wanted less than to have anyone else know of my predicament. However, I told them my plight and asked the old gentleman if he would mind leading my leaders ahead while I stood on the sled hollering "get up." I told him that as soon as they were moving forward he could step aside and I'd be on my way to Nome. He agreed to give it a try and we soon had the dogs in motion. He stepped aside and the dogs stopped to lie down.

It almost began to look as though the dogs were interested in my efforts. They could hardly wait to see what I'd try next. I tried the trick with the Eskimo man two or three more times with similar results. Then he told me that he really did have to go to Nome and wondered if I minded if he and his wife just got on their snowmachine and left. I told him to go ahead and I'd figure something out.

I sat down on my sled and began to think. Dave had told me not to push the dogs too hard or they might quit. Well, they had been frisky at the cabin, so I didn't think I'd pushed them too hard. And, after all, some teams were already in Nome, so they'd been pushed a lot harder than mine. Besides, mine had already quit so things couldn't really get any worse.

Three hours had passed since I'd booted these dogs and they hadn't moved one foot under their own power since. I've often felt the ghosts of the past breathing down my neck as I mushed my dogs along Alaska's winter trails. I don't know that I ever felt it stronger than I did right then. I had the uncanny feeling that Leonard Seppala and Scotty Alan were standing there, shaking their heads over the ineffectiveness of this greenhorn dog driver. I could picture them laughing and telling each other they could walk over here, step on the sled, and drive those dogs to Nome in a minute if it were their team. It was obvious to me that if a *real* dog driver were driving this team, he'd have been on his way to Nome long ago.

We'd been stopped for nine hours now, including the time we'd slept in that cabin. There was no doubt that the dogs were physically as well rested as they'd been at any time during the race. The problem was in their minds and in mine, not our bodies. Tiger had decided it was his turn to be the boss. He was now the alpha male, not me, and we were going to do this on his terms. This had been communicated through the rest of the team and they were all perfectly willing to follow his lead.

I was absolutely convinced that Leonard Seppala could drive this team to Nome. If Leonard Seppala could drive this team to Nome, I'd better dang well figure out how to do it, too.

As I sat there attempting to sort things out, it became more and more clear that Tiger had tested me and I'd failed the test. He was more stubborn than I and he'd gained control. The only way for me to get it back was to dominate him, to make it more painful for him to lie around like a lazy bum than to get on with the job at hand. He needed a good licking.

I left the team and searched the surrounding area for the biggest willow tree I could find in that high Arctic hillside. I'd break off a limb and use it for a switch. I saw a tree off in the distance that looked about ten feet tall. I walked over to it, but when I got there, I saw that the entire tree was about as big around as my little finger and no more than eighteen inches tall. This subarctic tundra created a strange perspective.

Tiger and Jade leading Burt toward the Alaska Range out of Finger Lake. By now, the dogs
are in the routine of travel away from home and have settled into a
gait we called the Iditarod trot.

I cut off the eighteen-inch tree. I anchored the sled firmly so the dogs wouldn't run off to Nome without me. I took Tiger out of the team and led him back behind the sled where I gave him a good switching without having the team panic into a tangle trying to get away from my anger. At every swat, I yelled at him for being such a lazy, arrogant son of a bitch. After the first swat, the other dogs leaped to attention.

I led Tiger back up to his position in lead. Then I marched up and down the line of dogs giving them all a good chewing out while I swatted my pant leg with that switch. By now, they were all looking as eager as they had been at the starting line in Anchorage. The dogs were looking at me as if to ask why we were standing around here talking and why didn't we just get going. Tiger was literally jumping forward in his harness in an effort to get the heck out of there before he got another swat with that switch. I walked back to the sled, told the dogs to get up and away we went, looking every bit as fresh as we had at the start.

I stopped several times between Topkok and Nome to give the dogs a brief rest and a snack. When we stopped, their tails wagged as they eagerly awaited their treats. As long as my leadership was firm and fair and my attitude was good, the dogs were happy. When my attitude faltered, theirs faltered. They became lazy and unhappy. Somewhere along the way many years back, I'd come to believe that physical punishment was inhumane. Too much is inhumane, but switching and a good stern word is sometimes needed to maintain your alpha male status. You ought to see what an alpha wolf does to maintain its dominance.

Alpha domination, male or female, is what keeps pack animals behaving as a pack. In the wild, that domination is not established and maintained during committee meetings and reasoned discussions. Intimidation is occasionally necessary. Punishment must of course be moderate and the result of a reasoned decision rather than anger. It must never be cruel or risk injuring the animal, but it is occasionally justified if we are to work together in a productive relationship with a team of dogs.

My experience on Topkok Hill was a giant step forward in cementing my relationship with Tiger and in my becoming a competent musher. I began to realize that the strength of character, which kept him in lead when many of my other leaders gave up, was the same strength of character that occasionally caused him to challenge my authority. I promise you, Dear Reader, that Tiger and the other dogs were a lot happier once they knew where the boundaries were.

After the incident at Topkok, Tiger never defied me again, but he never showed any fear of me either. He did, however, have a way of communicating his feelings. We had just left the Rabbit Lake checkpoint during the 1984 race when the trail took a sharp left, which Tiger followed. When the sled got to the point where Tiger had jumped left, I could see that he had hit a fork in the trail. At least one team had gone straight ahead, but another team had obviously made that turn to the left. The snow was deep, so there was really no way to turn the team around. I decided to follow the trail he was on, hoping that it would loop back onto the correct trail.

There were only one or two teams ahead of us on the detour. It was obvious that someone's leaders had made a mistake or revolted. My dogs were simply following along. Within fifty yards or so, the trail we were on began veering sharply to the left, making it obvious that whoever had made this mistake had realized it and had looped his team back to pick up the correct trail. We were almost back where we had left the trail when Tiger disappeared over a shallow bank and down onto a creek bed. He swung down the creek in a direction that would intersect the correct trail.

As my sled went over the bank onto the creek, Tiger fell through the soft snow into overflow approximately a foot deep. He stumbled and went down soaking himself thoroughly. I stopped the team to give him time to regain his balance, which he did, but then he couldn't continue. He was trapped in the water with snow too soft and deep to climb out of. I hurriedly put my snowshoes on, ran up, and pulled him out of his predicament. I packed a trail with my snowshoes in the direction of the correct trail and then went back to the sled.

I commanded Tiger to "get up," which he did but with the most pathetic look imaginable. I drove him forward to the main trail, but he kept looking back over his shoulder in obvious misery. That drenching had taken the starch out of him and he just didn't want to have to be up there leading the team. His looks told me as eloquently as any words that he needed a chance to get himself back together. I moved another leader forward and moved Tiger well back in the team. This gave him no responsibilities other than to keep up with the other dogs.

Once the weight of command had been lifted from his shoulders, he bent to the task of pulling his share of the load and was soon trotting along in that mile-eating Iditarod gait. The exercise was good for him as it warmed him up and helped shake the water out of his coat. I left him back in the team for another two hundred miles until it was obvious he was becoming bored with the mundane duties of being a team dog. When I moved him back to lead, he was once again the good leader, but I never forgot the pleading look he gave me when he needed relief from that extra burden.

Tiger and Jade waiting patiently to leave Nikolai. These dogs were professionals who didn't waste a lot of energy when it wasn't needed. They were tough and fast on the trail. I liked putting Tiger with one of his girlfriend's so he wouldn't get territorial and feisty when I needed him. *Jeff Schultz photo.*

140

We became closer and I depended upon him more as time went on. He was so reliable that I used him as leader in the teams my handlers were training. I never really had my handlers train dogs in the strict sense of the word *train*. Instead, they served as exercisers, driving a team that followed mine. That way I could set the pace, govern the rest breaks and be there to catch their teams if they should lose them. With Tiger leading their teams, I knew they were not far behind me and that Tiger would never pull any shenanigans. The first time handlers were allowed to drive Tiger, I lectured them first that he was the most important living creature in camp besides me. That meant he was more important to me than the handlers were. If anything happened to Tiger, the handler was done.

I was particular about keeping Tiger safe if trail conditions were bad. If moose began punching holes in our trails or other hazards developed, I would automatically put Tiger back into my team, so I could be certain that the possibility of an injury was minimized.

Midway through training for the 1985 race, I decided that Tiger's importance to me and his advancing age made it desirable that I be the only one to drive him. I had two handlers that year as we were training nearly fifty dogs, counting puppies. We had plenty of leaders, however, so I shuffled them around a bit in my team. The less talented leaders were assigned to my handlers while I took the ones that had the most potential. This was both handlers' first year, so they were in as much of a training mode as the pups.

I was a lot happier once I decided that Tiger would remain in my team. He was so dependable and at the same time, personable, that having him there always made things more enjoyable. He was by then about eight years old and had dropped most of his earlier bad habits. He wasn't even as feisty as he'd been, although he still had a hate on for a big dog named Wayne that he had disliked since the beginning of the '83 season. Dogs that don't like one another sometimes expand their animosity in the yard, even while on the chain. They'll argue back and forth until pent-up rage becomes a factor. Put them together in a team when this develops and they're likely to attack each other with fury. I'd put them at opposite ends of the yard, but they'd sit on their doghouses and stare across the yard at each other.

Wayne, too, was a dominant male and was literally the biggest dog I'd ever owned. He was as agile as a wolf and didn't have the clumsy gait associated with many large huskies. Instead, he ran like a wild animal, snaking through the brush, dodging moose holes and leaping low obstructions on the trail.

Wayne and Tiger were both fighters and had tangled with each other several times. I had always managed to get them apart. At first it was Tiger who initiated the conflicts, but their dislike grew to the point where neither was willing to get along. Since Wayne was so big, I almost always ran him in wheel just ahead of the sled. That way the dogs ahead of him kept the gang line tight so he was stretched between them and the sled. I would then put females beside him and ahead of him so he didn't feel like he had to protect his territory from any other males and, of course, I kept him well separated from Tiger. No one else ever drove Wayne.

I'd been in town working for two days and was scheduled to return to dog camp on Wednesday, January 2, 1985. My work had taken longer than I had planned, so instead of leaving in the morning, it was eight o'clock that evening. By the time I drove to Moose Creek and then snowmachined the remaining ten miles to camp, it was nearly midnight. I was feeling good and since my handlers had had several days off, I decided to make a twenty-five-mile run before we went to bed. We could sleep in the next morning, make a short run the next afternoon and then be back on schedule. Although we were all a little bit tired, I felt it was important not to lose a day's training.

I drew up diagrams for the teams my two handlers would drive and told them to begin hitching. I wanted to get underway as soon as possible. I would unload the groceries from the snowmachine sled so they wouldn't freeze while we were gone. Then I would hitch my team and follow. I hitched Ivor and Tiger in lead with ten dogs hitched in pairs behind them. Wayne was with Kelly just ahead of wheel, with Sonic and Jewel just ahead of them.

Ninety-nine percent of the time, Ivor was one of my best leaders. But sometimes he was an erratic goofball. On rare occasions, he'd jump off the trail under a bush or attempt to mate with the male dog hitched next to him. I can't explain it; it just happened. The events of the next twelve hours are almost too painful for me to describe. I would prefer to put the memories of that terrible night out of my mind forever, but I mustn't. Few people are able to experience the dog mushing life, so I need to tell the pain as well as the joy.

We left the yard at a rapid pace and the cares of a long day were left quickly behind. The dogs had been off for several days so were well rested. The dogs in my team were either the dogs with problems or the best dogs, the ones that don't like another team ahead of them. They normally would do anything to catch another team and get past it. A well-trained dog team provides a tremendous amount of power, so we were quickly leaving the miles behind us as we chased the other two teams.

It was midnight and cold and the moon was full, giving the countryside a beautiful dark silvery glow. I turned my headlight off to enjoy the night. The trees left shadows, as did the rapidly trotting dogs. We'd gone ten miles or so when the dogs quickened their pace, indicating that one of my handlers was on his way back from the turnaround and we would soon meet.

Tiger and Timber leading Burt's beautiful dog team along the Yukon River out of Ruby. On clear warm sunny days, I could get by with a light parka and gloves but nightfall meant plunging temperature that required beaver mitts and a heavy parka. *Jeff Schultz photo*

In a few moments I saw his headlight approaching. As our teams passed head-on, on the narrow trail, Ivor swapped ends and started following the homeward-bound team, right behind the other sled. It was a stupid thing for him to do and he knew better. In his excitement, though, he had instinctively taken the expedient way of catching that team. When Ivor swapped ends, he dragged Tiger with him so both were instantly heading in the opposite direction and were running backwards alongside the other dogs in my team.

In an instant Tiger spotted Wayne and went after him. Before I could anchor the team in the deep snow and get to them, they were locked in a savage brawl with other dogs attempting to join in. I set the snow hook and turned the sled over on its side hoping to be able to spread the team out enough to separate the dogs. Hollering and yelling as I worked, I ran forward and tried to pull the dogs apart. So frenzied had it become that one of them bit me in the finger through my mitt without even realizing what he'd done. Wayne was anchored by the sled, so I grabbed Tiger and attempted to pull him back. Wayne had hold of him by the lip and wouldn't let go.

I can't think of many excuses for kicking a dog, but I kicked Wayne in the head half a dozen times in a frantic attempt to loosen his grip on Tiger but with no effect. Meanwhile, Ivor and a male named Dancer kept trying to join the battle. I kept throwing them aside as I hung on to Tiger in a frantic attempt to save him from Wayne's powerful jaws. Both dogs were so savage it occurred to me that both had been saving this up for two and a half years and for some incomprehensible reason had picked this time to have it out.

As this deadlock continued, Ivor and Dancer jumped in, always going after Tiger as though realizing he was the underdog. The frenzied battle resembled the eye of a tornado. Each time I grabbed a dog, it instinctively swapped ends and tried savagely to bite me. In their minds, anything that grabbed could be an attacking dog so their instinct was to defend. I grabbed my whip. It was a popper whip, one that would crack like a bullet when snapped. Its butt was loaded with buckshot, heavy but flexible. I banged Wayne on the head with the heavy shot-loaded butt repeatedly trying to loosen his deadly grip. He had to have seen stars but he wouldn't let go.

Each time I let go of Tiger to fend off another dog or pound on Wayne, Wayne reset his grip and reeled Tiger in another notch. Each time, Wayne was able to get a firmer, more deadly grip until Tiger was seriously injured. After several minutes, my other handler arrived and the two of us separated the dogs and lined them out toward home. I unhitched Tiger and set him gently on the sled, fearful that his injuries might be fatal.

I walked up the line of dogs still hitched, checking to see that no others were injured. Wayne stepped out in front of me as he usually did so I couldn't get by without giving him some attention. He wagged his tail and gave me his big wolf grin expecting to be petted. I could hardly believe it—he didn't have the faintest idea that he'd done anything wrong. What he'd done in defending his territory was so natural for him that it was already forgotten.

Tiger was faithful from start to finish. Here, he leads the team toward the finish line on Front Street in Nome. You could always count on Tiger to get the job done.

I pushed past him, made Tiger as comfortable as possible and mushed backed to camp. I transferred him to a snowmachine at camp and then into my truck at Moose Creek for the long drive home. We were at Dr. Sept's office at eight o'clock the following morning. Bob operated on Tiger until noon, attempting to patch him back together. As I stood there helping, I remembered how much Tiger and I had given each other during the past four or five years. Although we'd occasionally failed each other, we'd both grown so much from our relationship. We'd occasionally tested each other and we'd had hundreds of happy moments.

Together, we'd lived a life of adventure and excitement that he quite obviously appreciated. He'd loved those many silent runs through our beautiful Alaska wilderness and raised holy hell when he occasionally was left behind. With rare exceptions, he knew when it was important to be professional. He led us past countless moose with never a sideways glance when it could have meant disaster

145

had he given chase. He'd led us through all kinds of overflow with little objection and once dove in over his head to lead across a narrow creek outside of Ophir.

Tiger died on the operating table. When I think of that awful night, sadness comes over me. I try to shake it off and think of the countless wonderful days we spent working together. I feel lucky for what Tiger brought into my life. I guess the valleys so low made the peaks so high.

Chapter Eight
Ghosts

We were in the holding area on Fourth Avenue in Anchorage for the start of Iditarod on the first Saturday of March 1984. I parked the big dog truck in our assigned spot and shut it off. Later, with just a half hour until the start, we pulled the dogs down and harnessed them. With ten minutes left, I hitched them all to the gang line in readiness.

An official gave us the high sign and I commanded my dogs forward to the starting line a couple of blocks down Fourth Avenue. They surged eagerly, a handler holding the gang line next to nearly every dog to hold the powerful animals back and keep the pace at a walk. We didn't want any out-of-control disasters happening now.

We brought the dogs to a stop at the starting line and official handlers grabbed the sled to hold it in place. My handlers stepped back, still ready to help if needed but far away enough not to be a distraction for the dogs. I wanted the dogs focused on the trail ahead down Fourth Avenue.

I walked up the line of dogs checking to be sure that all dogs were in place and no one had tangled. Timing was everything as I strolled along chatting with my dogs and giving each one a little pat. I walked back on the other side of the team, looking nonchalant as though oblivious to the timer's count. I stopped to pat a dog and shake hands with a friend. I stopped to chat again, always keenly aware of the timer's count. With just seconds to go, I strolled toward the race marshal as though to shake his hand. He gave me a concerned look as though to get my attention and chastise me for my indifference. I smiled and glanced away as I continued forward.

By now, my crew was going nuts trying to get my attention. They frantically tried to alert me to the few seconds remaining. I pretended I didn't hear them or the timer counting down. At the last moment, I veered to my sled, grabbed the hand bow and stepped on the brake, just as the official said, ". . . two, one, GO!" The idea was always to appear cool and to scare the bejeebers out of my crew and the officials. I hope I succeeded.

It took a lot of effort to hold a fresh, powerful team back as it headed for the starting line on
Fourth Avenue. Burt's mind was already thinking ahead to
Nome and the adventures to come.

We took off with a tremendous surge of power, as I chuckled to myself at giving my gang their collective heart attack. I began my race through Anchorage, down a series of streets, bike trails, and neighborhoods to the Alaska Sled Dog Racing Association (ASDRA) trails south of Tudor Road. Throngs of people lined the route, many sitting in chairs tending their barbecues just like a giant tailgate party. Cries of, "Yea, Burt! Go, Burt!" "Go get 'em, Burt!" and "Good luck, Burt!" made me feel like a star until I realize that the field was listed in starting order in the morning paper. They didn't really know me, but I didn't care. It felt wonderful to have those cheering people giving me warm wishes. That warmth would help sustain me on the long, cold trail across Alaska to Nome.

We reached the ASDRA track and entered several miles of good, groomed racing trail. Sprint mushers who didn't like distance mushers on their turf maintained this section of trail. We tend to use our brakes too much, leaving grooves that might injure a faster sprint dog. The trail veered south up a power line, then took a sharp left turn and we headed off the well-groomed trail. We traveled through the Fort Richardson military reserve to the checkpoint at the VFW in Eagle River.

For some reason that section of trail was always a little bit unpredictable. It could be a smooth run or one could find himself wrapped around a tree. It depended a lot on who had groomed the trail. Snowmachine trailbreakers sometimes forgot that a dog team moved in a serpentine fashion, which must flow along a trail in a series of S curves. Hard right angles in the trail tend to pull the inside dogs toward the inside of the turn, banging dogs and sled into obstructions, often a tree.

This part of the race was more ceremonial than competitive, since most of us held our teams back to avoid injuries. The beauty of the Anchorage start was that it gave thousands of fans a chance to get a close look at the teams and to enjoy the hoopla of race day. This was the part of the race most people saw firsthand and a part that got a lot of media play. It seemed commercial and flashy to many people. When critics complained that the race was too commercial and had lost its roots, it was most likely because they'd seen the start but had no a clue what it was like once the mushers left Knik, the last checkpoint accessible by road.

After checking in at Eagle River, we trucked our dogs to Wasilla for the restart of the race. Previously, this was all done on the same day, but by 1984, the race to Eagle River was made on the first Saturday of March, while the restart at Wasilla was held the following day. Crowds still gathered for the first few miles out of Wasilla and a large group of fans could always be found at Knik, the tiny community on the north shore of Knik Arm.

Knik was really the jumping-off place for the race. Pockets of fans still gathered by snowmachine along the trail, but from Knik we entered the wilderness of Alaska. Civilization had crowded the trail in spots, causing the trail to make a sharp turn here or there to avoid someone's private property. But, for the most part, we were alone in the wilderness. The trail wound through forests of stunted black spruce and then out onto lakes or meadows and back into the forest.

I'm a hopeless romantic when it comes to Alaska. A hundred years ago, Alaska had character. Authentic characters were everywhere. In those days, they weren't even considered characters—they were just everyday Alaskans. Those kinds of people still populate the Iditarod. When I was still a small boy in grade school, my dreams were filled with pioneers, gold miners, bush pilots, dog mushers, and trappers. Mom would shake her head and tell the women in the Ladies Aid, "Burt was born one hundred years too late; the world he was born for is gone."

How she figured that out when I was so young, I'll never know, but she was an extremely intuitive mother. Even as I studied to be an engineer and followed my career path, something deep down inside me was not settled. I was intuitively searching for something, and somehow knew I'd finally picked up the trail. I hadn't found it yet but I was close. Something deep down made me leave the comfort and luxury of corporate life to live in a small cabin deep in bush Alaska with a dog team parked out front and friends who more closely resembled adventurers and early explorers than they did today's urban dwellers.

My dogs settled into their quick, steady, mile-eating trot and the beauty of this great wilderness surrounded us. In a few moments, I was transported back as though by time machine to the Alaska I believed was pure and genuine. Gone were the trappings of modern civilization. Back were the true sourdoughs.

Tales of gold rush Alaska flooded my thoughts as they had during my grade-school days back in the Dakotas. An Alaska loaded with dog mushers, bush pilots, and trappers filled my dreams back then as they do today. As I mushed along in the early hours of this Iditarod Race, civilization and all that went with it faded quickly from my mind. The flash and glitz of the Anchorage start had nothing to do with this great race once it left Knik. Now we would face the cold winter trail and all its challenges. Our companions and friends along the trail would be much the same as travelers found a century ago. My hope was always that the press had enough sensitivity to find the traditional Alaska that still exists in the Iditarod Race. Some did.

Author's note: As I review my notes to write this, the year is 2012. Sadly, the race has changed. Many of the great personalities that made Iditarod what it was are still with us but no longer race. Native mushers like Gerald Riley, Don Honea, and Emmitt Peters, and sourdoughs like Bud Smyth, Gene Leonard, Dean Osmar, Larry Smith, and Roger Nordlum. What great characters they are and how they are missed. It's always great to see them come race time!

The miles passed quickly as the trail continued across Fish Creek and then to Flathorn Lake. Flathorn Lake was always a good place to stop and snack the dogs while giving them a break.

Bill Firmin, rest his soul, lived at Flathorn Lake with his wife, Sue. He always broke out some side trails with his snowmachine for mushers to drive their teams off the main trail and park for a snack and a bit of rest. If I stopped and was lucky, Bill would come by for a visit while I snacked my dogs. I liked to find out the latest news from Flathorn Lake.

Burt never missed a chance to park the dogs at abandoned roadhouses to rest and cook for the dogs. Here the team rests at the ancient Farewell Roadhouse outside Rohn checkpoint. Once a busy place, it was fun to think of what life must have been like a century ago. Family's, kids, good times and bad, visitors and solitude, all were once a part of these abandoned old camps. Ghosts still populated these spots.

That year I chose not to stop there. I drove the dogs past Flathorn, through the trees at the north end of the lake and out onto Four-Mile Slough. We continued out along the treeless frozen marsh until almost the end. A brisk north wind hinted of the cold night to come. Now I stopped where I had a view of several miles of trail behind us so we could keep track of the competition. No one appeared on the trail, so we stopped and I set the hook for a brief stop. Rummaging quickly in my sled bag, I retrieved a bag of thawed liver and doled out a half-pound snack to each dog. A sled dog will always gulp down thawed beef liver. Some mushers believe the best way to resuscitate an expired dog is to drag a piece of raw liver past his nose. He'll rise from the dead to eat a piece of raw liver. Who knows? Hope I never have to try it.

The point of the quickness of the stop and the liver was to make the stop just a momentary pause. I didn't want the dogs to settle in and think we were going to take a rest break. That would throw them off their pace and slow them down. My theory was that I needed to be with the front of the pack by Skwentna. Then, if the dogs and I had trained enough, we might maintain a pace that would keep us with the front pack and develop a bit of a lead over the main pack. The lead could then be expanded as the lesser teams tired.

There were other reasons for mushing at the head of the pack. The section of trail from the Susitna River through to Rabbit Lake and then to Skwentna didn't see that much traffic. Trappers and the rare snowmachiners used it occasionally, but the area was uninhabited. When the trailbreakers on snowmachines came through for the race, they tended to go fast and float along on top of the snow. This packed the top foot or so but left a considerable depth of soft powdery snow underneath.

As the dog teams followed one another over this portion of trail, the firm top portion cracked and punched through. Each later team was confronted with a softer, more bottomless trail than the team ahead. I figured it was better to cut the rest short now and get ahead of the teams coming along later. My dogs might be a little tired from the short rest, but not nearly as tired as they'd be wallowing through deep snow. The trail conditions would be harder on the dogs than the lack of rest.

We continued to Skwentna and pulled up to the checkpoint, which was manned by Joe Delia. He showed us where to park down on the river below his wilderness log home. Joe and the other sourdoughs and natives we'd meet between here and Nome were a lot of what this race was all about for me. Joe was the postmaster for Skwentna, a small group of homes on the Skwentna River just upstream from its confluence with the Yentna River. Joe was also a trapper who generally had a cache full of prime pelts, including beaver, marten and an occasional wolf. Joe loved to tell tales of his life in the bush making this the first place along the trail for mushers, fans, and the press to get into the authentic flavor of the race.

Joe's traplines ran for miles in all directions. He'd been there so long that he had priority over most any other trappers around. With this advantage of seniority, Joe had nearly tied up the trapping along the upper Yentna and Skwentna drainages. Traplines were held by seniority, strength, and force of will. Pilgrims came along regularly, trying to push into someone else's trap-line. It said a lot for how tough Joe was that he had one of the most extensive traplines in Alaska. In fact, it ran clear to Gene Leonard's trapline off to the west near Finger Lake. Rumors were that these two formidable giants had their arguments about just where one's trapline ended and the other's began. I'm curious about their confrontations, but they're both dear friends so I've never dared ask.

"Burt, how are you doing tonight? Is the trail okay?" Joe asked.

"The trail isn't that bad, Joe. And I saw no moose along the way." Joe broke out this portion of the trail and it was always good through here. I always complimented Joe since it was volunteer work and the only pay he got was our thanks.

Dad, Burt and son Brad, visiting Dad who was still hale and hearty at 101 years old. After he could no longer make the trip to Alaska, he loved to have Burt come to Iowa and regale him with tales of the trail.

I found a place to park my dogs 100 yards down along the riverbank that would be out of the way of the commotion that would follow when more teams began to arrive. The first order of business was to bail four gallons of water out of the water hole that Joe had chopped through the river ice for us. My Coleman stove was stoked up and water set on to boil. I found my bag that was number one of several and retrieved a bag of beef hamburger, which I then cooked.

The dogs ate ravenously, licking up every last bit of slurp and then looked at me for more. Now that they all had a nice warm meal in them, I tossed them some frozen snacks of lamb and beaver to fill their little tummies until they were ready to burst. I don't normally like to feed them frozen chunks on an empty stomach, but this way seems okay. Then the dogs would get a good rest on full bellies. They'd be strong when we began our assent up the trail toward Finger Lake and the mountains of the Alaska Range.

Now it was my turn. I grabbed some of my own snacks and headed for Joe's cabin for some food and good conversation. Delia's always put out a spread for the mushers and volunteers but one likes to contribute. Call it Bush ethics. As I came in, Joe motioned towards a chair at the table and we began to talk.

Again, Joe asked, "How was the trail, Burt?"

Something odd flashed through my mind as we talked. We could have been visiting a hundred years earlier, transported back by some eerie time machine. The topics were the same: dogs, weather, and trail. That image of my mother saying I'd been born a hundred years too late came and went.

"Well, Joe, the trail's not that bad. It was well packed out of Knik all the way to the Susitna River."

That section of trail was used all winter by dog teams and snowmachines so it had a good bottom to it. With all that traffic, each succeeding new snowfall was packed down, making the base of the trail hard, clear to the ground. It had also been good on through to Rabbit Lake and then to here, but the following teams would probably punch it through before long. I didn't envy them.

"And how are the dogs looking?"

"They're not that bad." My best seven dogs were right out of Rick Swenson's 1982 team. All made it to Nome in 1982 and were as good as I'd had.

Aside from a dog I had bought from Libby Riddles, much of the rest of my team were out of Susan Butcher's yard. Every dog that Susan sold me was top-notch. One time she sold me a leader that I didn't like. When I mentioned it to her, she said to send it back and she'd refund my money. I'll bet I got the check back before she got the dog. My relationship with Susan cooled over the years, but I would tell the world that my dog deals with her were honest and above-board. And she was one hell of a musher.

So, the dogs were good enough and it was up to me.

"Joe, what kind of year did you have trapping?"

"I had a good year. My cache is full of fur. Those boys from the press corps love it. It gives great photo opportunities and something to write about." That full cache would also help fatten Joe's wallet when the fur buyers came through.

Breakfast in a warm cabin and some good conversation after running dogs all night soon took effect. I trundled upstairs to look for a space on the floor to spread my sleeping bag and dozed off instantly.

It was time to rise and shine all too soon. I snacked the dogs and enjoyed a quick meal of rich, thick stew and a cup of hot black coffee. I lined the dogs out and the hook was pulled to release them for another ran, this time to Gene Leonard's place at Finger Lake. The trail wound its way westerly up the

Skwentna River for a mile or so and then jumped onto the south bank and onto the swamps to the southwest.

We crossed swamps and meadows for several miles and then mushed across the Skwentna River near the Old Skwentna Roadhouse on the far bank. The Roadhouse had been built to serve dog teams traveling to the goldfields a hundred years before and the buildings still stood. Today the ghosts of pioneers and sourdoughs occupy them. Who knows how many dog teams had driven this same trail and stayed at this roadhouse through the years?

I know those ghosts watched our passing and I couldn't help but wonder if they approved of the dog drivers and teams that would pass this way now. The answer was clear to me—of course, they would approve. Dog men haven't changed that much and Alaskans have always thrown out the welcome mat for a stranger.

Burt living his dream caring for the dogs at Anvik on the Yukon River. The great wilderness of Alaska often feels like a different world, even in the villages. *Jeff Schultz photo.*

We bounced up onto the bank and mushed past the tumbledown buildings as a couple of ghost teams from gold rush days fell in behind. They were waiting for someone to come along and break trail for them and I was their choice. Anyway, I was happy for the company and looked forward to sharing tales around the campfire with them later. After all, I didn't just show up. I'd been on a path leading here since the day I was born.

Don't tell me it was my imagination! If you don't believe in spirits, they'll never come around to keep you company. My mom taught me that the first time I ever questioned Santa. "Burt, if you don't believe in him, he'll never come." I still believe and I'm in my seventies.

The trail continued uphill. We were beginning the gradual ascent into the foothills of the Alaska Range. The trail along the southern edge of the Shell Hills would lead us to Gene Leonard's place at Finger Lake. Upward we traveled through mixed spruce and birch. This was a beautiful wooded trail that jogged left and right where trailbreakers had found the best going. There's nothing easy about this trail, uphill stretches followed by miles of windblown swamps. It was the kind of mushing that typifies the romantic vision of Alaska, the Alaska that Robert Service and Jack London described so well.

Not many teams were ahead of us, but I had no idea how many. After a few hours, we burst into the sunshine and open meadows south of Shell Lake. The folks who lived on the lake and people from Anchorage who had cabins out here always showed up for a party. We used to call them summer cabins, but by 1984, with snowmachines and ski planes, the cabins were occupied as much in winter as in summer. A roaring fire had already burned itself four feet into the snow. The hole was melted six feet across, the hole so wide that people could sit on the edge and warm their legs and feet.

I pulled the team off to the side and snacked the dogs. My pal, Nelson Defendorf, told me I was the first team to arrive and offered me a sandwich and a beer. His airplane was parked a little ways off. We visited and enjoyed the warm rays of the afternoon sun for a bit. Most of the people were city folks, but the kind that were equally at home in the wilderness. They were bush pilots and snowmachiners along with a few dog mushers. Many worked in town, but their reason for being in Alaska was this great Alaska bush country. Soon it was time to rouse the dogs and be on our way. We were closer to the mountains now, which began to loom to the south and west of us.

The trail traversed more meadows and lakes interspersed with belts of timber. I've occasionally hunted moose in this country, but that was years earlier. By 1984, we usually flew over to our cabin on the Stony River. There is less traffic out there, although I'm sure there's more moose right here in this valley.

As darkness settled, we approached the sharp knob of a hill that we'd pass just before we reached Finger Lake. Moments later, we glided out onto Finger Lake and heard Gene's sled dogs announce our arrival. The lights of Gene's cabin provided a beacon across the lake, and my dogs eagerly quickened the pace. We passed a couple of airplanes parked on the lake and the dogs trotted briskly up the steep bank to the Leonard's yard.

Gene stood there, clipboard in hand, big grin on his face and a giant paw of a hand stuck out in greeting. I grabbed it and we shook hands like old pals do. Gene was a former member of New York City's finest and had also been a heavyweight boxer. He'd been ranked tenth in the world at one point. None of his formidable presence and strength was missing in spite of his years. Now that he was here, he guided big-game hunters and mushed his dog team along his trapline trails.

Gene needed to check my gear, so we rummaged through my things looking for items mushers were required to carry, including an axe, a sleeping bag, plenty of booties for the dogs' feet, and a Coleman stove and a cook pot. We also carried some mail that had been postmarked in Anchorage and would also be postmarked in Nome when we arrived.

Gene then led my dogs off in the direction of his generator shed and told me to make myself at home. I grabbed one of my food drop bags on the way to where I'd parked the team. The dogs were fed and I found a place for my sleeping bag in the generator shed. The steady thumping of that diesel generator put me to sleep before my head hit the pillow. With Gene's warm hospitality, it was difficult to venture forth into the cold Arctic night after my nap, but it was now time for our trip through the Alaska Range.

Thus, it went through one checkpoint after another. Although I made my living as an engineer and surveyor building roads, pipelines, and docks, my dreams of Alaska had always been this. I loved the vision of a simpler time gone by. Those ghost drivers from the ancient Skwentna Roadhouse were still behind me. It looked like they'd follow me all the way to Iditarod. I hoped so.

The miles slid by as we made our way across the great interior of Alaska. By the time we reached Kaltag on the Yukon River, I'd traveled hundreds of solitary miles with my dogs. It was fun rubbing elbows with miners, trappers, Native Alaskans, and mushers who were every bit as colorful as the ones described by Jack London and Robert Service. Although rest stops were filled with intense activity, taking care of dogs and self, the solitary miles left hours and hours for my mind to wander far and wide. It was fun to compare tales of the *Malamute Kid* and the *Cremation of Sam McGee* to my own experiences in the great North Country.

Those ghost teams that joined me at the roadhouse were good company. They were taking care of their dogs while I cared for mine. Before long, dreams blended with reality to the point where I felt as though I was living in bygone days. This was the beauty of the Iditarod Trail Sled Dog Race for me.

It was in this frame of mind that I left Kaltag in the early morning hours to begin my trek over the ninety-mile portage to Unalakleet on the Bering Sea. For a few moments, the dogs loped down the path between the small village homes. Then we ran across the airport and into the wilderness heading west.

The trail was well packed through the scattered spruce forest. The trail's surface was nearly a foot and half below the snow's natural level, indicating a good hard trail. Village snowmachine traffic between Unalakleet and Kaltag kept the trail packed all winter.

Our route wound gently upward. The portage traversed a broad pass with low hills on either side. Vegetation consisted of small spruce trees, mostly scattered, but with some dense thickets. Dawn broke and the sun rose behind me as we crossed one ridge after another. Slowly, we made our way to the low summit. The terrain was so gentle it was difficult to tell when one stopped ascending and started mushing down the western side toward Unalakleet and the Gold Coast . of Norton Sound. I was so in love with this country that I would later establish "The Gold Coast Trophy" to be awarded to the first team to arrive in Unalakleet during each year's Iditarod. I commissioned an artist to sculpt a beautiful bronze statue of a dog team to serve as the permanent trophy. It is now displayed at Iditarod headquarters.

Eight hours out of Kaltag, the trail dropped into a small creek bed that wound in tight curves for a couple hundred yards. The trail then jumped up onto the bank where I mushed directly into the site of the historic Old Woman Roadhouse. Mark Boily and Terry "Doc" Adkins had arrived there earlier and were already doing their chores. Mark was a construction worker from Fairbanks and Doc was a veterinarian from Montana. Tough guys. Doc Adkins had been the first official Iditarod race veterinarian in 1972. At heart, he was a dog man and a cowboy. Once hooked on mushing, he raced Iditarod many times.

The ruins of the ancient roadhouse were still there, with log walls partly standing. Most travelers now used a plywood shelter cabin several miles farther along, but I preferred to stop here at this warm, friendly place. The new cabin further on was built near a spring that remained open all winter, so cooking was easier. For me, it just wasn't as friendly a place. I liked this tumbledown roadhouse where the early mail drivers had stayed. I drove my team off the trail into the deep snow to the right of the trail to give the dogs a rest.

Before beginning my chores, I paused for a moment and reflected on what stories the roadhouse could have told. Then I bent to the task of unhooking the dogs' tugs and removing booties from some of their feet. The dogs were made comfortable, and the pot of snow began to melt on the stove. It took about a half hour to melt enough snow for the dog food. While the snow melted, I ate my own lunch and boiled a pot of tea.

Mark, Doc, and I gathered around their fire, sipping tea and talking quietly of the stuff mushers talk about. Talk drifted to the trail behind and the trail ahead,

Dad loved the outdoors his entire life. His pals would kid him about dressing up to go fishing, but the truth was he didn't even take time to change out of his suit after church to go fishing.

the weather, and our dogs. And we spoke of other mushers, both the ones we knew and had been racing against and the ones we knew of from bygone days. Scotty Allen, Ironman Johnson, Leonard Seppala and others must have stopped a thousand times at Old Woman Roadhouse.

But for a leap in time, they must have had the same conversations with only the names of the people and dogs having changed. In a world of advancing technology where complexity and tension are the order of the day, it was a beautiful journey back through time.

Although it wasn't much past midday, the sun was low to the south. It glistened off the fresh, soft snow like a million diamonds lying on a white, velvet cloth. The timber nearby and the weathered logs of the roadhouse behind me created an overwhelming feeling of timelessness. I couldn't help but wonder if some of the ghosts of those old-time mushers had their teams parked by the roadhouse across the clearing. Maybe they, too, were boiling a pot of tea and telling their stories, commenting on the trail and their dogs. Then I *knew* that they had picked up their tea and wandered over to our fire to listen to our stories and tell a few of their own. Why was I so comfortable in this crowd?

I was telling Mark and Doc about an old Native man I had met on the trail between Nulato and Kaltag when we heard the rustle of traces and the soft scrape of runners on snow as Cowboy Smith, of the Yukon Territory, mushed up the bank and into our midst. He quickly took care of his dogs, put his water on to boil, and joined us.

I began again telling them about the elderly gentleman I'd met back this side of Nulato that afternoon. He was driving a dog team and stopped to let me by. I stopped to chat for a few moments and he was telling me about the teams ahead of me and how far ahead they were. We admired each other's dogs. All the while we visited, he kept looking at me with a quizzical stare. I was forty-seven years old, but my hair was gray. My whiskers were white and there were plenty of them after a week or so on the trail. I looked as though I had aged from forty-seven to about eighty just that quickly. Finally, he paused and asked me just how the hell old I was, anyway. When I told him, he said, "Boy, you must be one tough white man!"

I responded, "Why, thanks." After working in an office for twenty-five years, it was the kindest compliment anyone could give me. Coming from him made it special.

With a sudden urgency, he said, "Don't thank me, Burt, you're just wasting time! You've gotta get going! Those teams ahead of you are moving all the time and you're getting farther behind! You've gotta get going and catch them! And those teams behind are coming closer every minute. If you don't leave now, they'll catch you. You gotta get going now and don't be stopping for anything!" So I bade him good-bye and mushed off down the trail wishing I'd thought to ask him his name, but the warmth of the conversation and his encouragement stayed with me.

All of this filled my head as I again bent to the task of caring for my dogs. I mixed the food, fed the dogs and laid down on my sled for a short nap. As I dozed off, the image of ghost teams parked all around us was as vivid and tangible as anything could be. In this spiritual state just under the level of consciousness, I began to visit with the ghosts that haunted this decaying roadhouse. Mushers from a distant past began to wander up to join the conversation. Soon a dozen mushers gathered round my sled, some visiting animatedly while others just sat smoking their pipes, sipping tea, and occasionally nodding in agreement over some comment.

Their presence pleased me. It seemed to indicate an acceptance that was important, as though I was one of them. Some had names I recognized, others must have been from among hundreds of dog drivers who had carried mail all over Alaska before airplanes and snowmachines interrupted the stillness. Others might have just been people who had lived here. As we visited, I knew that while some things change for the worse, some *good* things never change.

The ghosts of the people who joined me were of all types, the good and the bad, the friendly and the hostile. It did not feel like all was sweetness and light.

Burt picked up the outdoor bug early. He'd seen a fish mounted at somebody's house so he caught a bluegill that he mounted himself. He placed it over a radiator behind the couch to dry and his aunt found it by following her nose.

But overshadowing everything was a feeling that true values, the good things in life, friends and family, a love for animals and the outdoors would always live in my heart. And the good times could be recaptured to a striking degree if one searched in the right places, maybe in books, maybe in a conversation with some old-timer, maybe by just doing something rewarding.

It was at that moment, I realized what my mom had seen and tried to express years ago. Again, I remembered that she had told the Ladies Aid Society, "Burt was born a hundred years too late; the world he was born for is gone." It was a truth that occasionally entered my mind and took me decades to understand. It was a truth that defined who I am and must have been transmitted to my soul through some form of collective memory.

I had first learned of collective memory in junior high when the game warden brought an orphaned baby raccoon by the house. The warden was my dad's fishing buddy and asked if I'd like to raise the raccoon until it was mature enough to be released. It would need to be bottle-fed to begin with. Of course, I said yes. Months later, my pal and I were going down to the creek to play. The raccoon followed right on our heels. As we approached the creek, we could hear the sound of rushing water. The raccoon raced ahead of us into the water where he began to search under rocks with his tiny paws. In seconds, he pulled out a crawdad and expertly shucked and ate it. He continued from rock to rock until his little belly was bulging fit to burst. He knew what was in that creek and what to do with it without ever having seen a creek or anything like it before. The collective memory of his ancestors occupied him to the core and he knew just where he was and what he should do.

Later, after the race was over, I found a couple of photos that illustrated the point. The pictures were of my dad when he was a boy and of me when I was a boy. Years apart, we were each proudly holding a fish we'd caught. I could imagine that my ancestors had been outdoorsmen since time began.

I realized then that my whole life had led to this place. If it hadn't been Iditarod, it would have been some place where traditional values ruled and adventure was the key. It wasn't the race—it was the life that surrounded it. The life made Iditarod the perfect place.

When I awoke, the other teams were gone and so were the ghosts and the dreams. I hurriedly repacked my sled and directed my team back onto the trail. I told myself that now it was time to start chasing my competitors to the finish line in Nome instead of chasing fantasies around the clearing at Old Woman Roadhouse.

I've always believed in ghosts. I haven't always been quick to admit it, but I do believe they exist. You don't believe it? The following summer I flew my daughter and three of her friends sightseeing across the Kenai Peninsula and then headed to the airport at Kenai for lunch. We parked the Cessna 206 and walked across the tarmac to the terminal, where the café still served a good burger. Halfway there, someone called my name.

It was Harold Barr, a friend and fellow pilot. He and his wife, Chici, had operated Spenard Television Repair in Anchorage for years. He asked me how last winter's race had treated me. I told him I'd finished twelfth and was happy about it.

We visited a bit and then he asked if I'd met the ghost at Old Woman. Now until this moment, no one had ever mentioned anything about ghosts at Old Woman to me.

I said I had but didn't know if I should admit it. Nobody would believe it anyway.

He said, "You'd better believe it, because it is true."

Harold continued, "My dad was a Finlander who was brought over to Unalakleet to herd reindeer near the turn of the century. He married my mother, a local girl from Unalakleet. When the reindeer were turned over to the Eskimos, my dad became a mail driver. Dad drove a dog team carrying the mail from Unalakleet, to Kaltag on the Yukon River, and then on to Nulato. He would then make the run back to Unalakleet. My mother loved his company and would often accompany Dad on his dogsled. She especially loved making the mail runs with him as it gave her a chance to visit with friends and relatives along the way."

Harold continued, "There were roadhouses located every twenty miles along the route. In those days, twenty miles was a good day's run for a dog team. One of the roadhouses along the trail was Old Woman Roadhouse." (The site was originally established as a telegraph station by the United States Army Signal Corps, in 1903. Later, it became a roadhouse, serving travelers.)

He said that the name Old Woman Roadhouse had come from a tragedy. During a severe winter blizzard, an old woman at the roadhouse went to use the outhouse. There was a line from roadhouse to outhouse to assure that no one would get lost during those blinding subarctic blizzards.

Somehow, she let go of the line and got lost. As the wind and snow battered the roadhouse, the woman never returned. Searching for her that night was futile in those terrible conditions. The following spring, her body was found miles away near a lone mountain that was then named Old Woman Mountain. The roadhouse was referred to as Old Woman Roadhouse from that day forward.

It was believed by many that the ghost of the woman haunted the roadhouse and traveled the area from that day until now. It was thought that she was hostile to travelers passing through *her* space and would do them harm if given the chance. There were incidents when guests would be awakened from a deep sleep by the sound of a door slamming. In the morning, there would be puddles across the floor where someone had tracked snow in during the night. The trail of puddles was from the door to the kitchen table and back but it did not extend to the sleeping areas, certain proof in some minds that a ghost had come in during the night. Also, everyone there denied that the tracks were theirs.

Harold continued that his mother believed so strongly in the power of the ghost that she refused to spend the night at the roadhouse. Instead, she and Harold's dad would eat at the roadhouse, visit with the staff and other travelers, and then drive another mile down the trail and set up camp for the night. I told Harold of my strong feelings about ghosts being present at the roadhouse and that I certainly felt their presence. He wasn't surprised.

The story gets even weirder. Years later during the 1992 Iditarod, I was mushing along in the middle of the pack. I'd been too busy with business issues to train properly, so my team and I were not in top form. I left Kaltag on the Yukon River, arguing with myself as to whether to shoot straight on through to Unalakleet or stop to rest halfway at Old Woman. It was obvious we wouldn't finish in the money, so I decided to relax and just play tourist the rest of the way into Nome.

We began the gentle climb to the portage, first through sparse timber and then out into the open of the high tundra. I could see for miles to the low hills on the north and south, which defined the portage. The dogs trotted briskly, by now half bored with the job of getting us to Nome. To them, the trail had become monotonous. It wasn't in them to enjoy the country we passed through and they were all too familiar with the many scents of dogs already having passed this way.

A couple of the bitches had gone into heat, which was a special pain to deal with during a race. I kept those two at the back of the team hoping to keep them from distracting the males. I fantasized about putting one of the "in heat" females up front, so the males would hurry to catch up with her and maybe speed things up a little. In reality, it just didn't work that way. Put a female in heat up front and she'll continually slow down and even stop to get back to the males. Bitches have no shame.

We hurried along with only the gentle rustle of the dogs' traces breaking the stillness. Then we dropped down into the creek bottom that precedes the historic Old Woman Roadhouse. We followed the series of sharp S curves before bouncing up onto the bank and into the yard. Off to the right were the aging remains of the early log roadhouse.

I debated briefly on whether to stop here. If I did, it would involve melting snow for watering the dogs and then napping on my sled, a cold prospect that somehow wasn't as inviting as usual. I loved this spot but just wasn't in the mood to deal with it. I elected to continue to the shelter cabin five or six miles further down the trail. Water would be easier to come by and I could nap on a bunk in the unheated cabin. So we went on. The dogs didn't care; all they had to do was trot, eat, and nap. The chores were mine.

Less than an hour later, we pulled into the yard at the plywood shelter cabin. It was much more functional but didn't have near the romance and history. I lined the team out beside the cabin, bailed water from the creek, and cranked up my alcohol stove. I anchored the sled and tied the leaders to a tree with a spare tug so the males and bitches that were in heat couldn't connect. The dogs were soon fed and snuggled in for a couple of hours. I pulled my sleeping bag out of my sled and went inside. I was soon fast asleep on my comfortable bed, feeling a little guilty for sacrificing my usual journey through history to creature comforts.

Was it guilt or was I uneasy over something else? Alone in the cabin, I began to feel like I had company—company I didn't really like. I was uneasy and dozed fitfully. Finally, I decided to retrieve my .357 Magnum pistol from the sled, maybe then I'd sleep better. The task of unzipping my sleeping bag was almost more than I could handle. I tugged and tugged, and then realized the zipper was just inches from where it had been. I was weak and seemed to have no stamina at all. The zipper wasn't stuck, just *really* hard to pull.

Finally, the bag was open enough for me to crawl out. Pulling my mukluks on was a chore, as was attempting to stand.

At a pre-race party before the start of the 1981 race, Burt's mom tells his daughter Jill that he was fascinated with pioneer tales when he was still a small boy.

Taking baby steps toward the door, I had to steady myself, first on the bunk then on the cabin wall. As I leaned against the doorjamb, gaining strength to walk the thirty feet to my sled, I noticed that one of the leaders had chewed the tug fastening him to the tree and he was back with one of the bitches, all snuggled and cozy. I didn't have the energy to line them back out, so I rationalized that the damage was already done.

The dog yard at Willow. Gravel was taken right out of the pit leaving rocks of all sizes in the dog yard. Big rocks in the yard gave the dogs agility and made their feet and ankles tough.

I staggered to my sled and retrieved my pistol, used the outhouse, and went back to bed. We'd now been there a couple of hours. Far from rested, I was more exhausted than when we had arrived. I crawled back into my sleeping bag, still uneasy over some unseen hostile presence, but secure that I could handle it. I was armed.

Someone clumped into the cabin and asked if I was okay.

I told him, "I don't feel that great. Something happened to me after I pulled in. Not sure what. Feel like something isn't right. Do you see anything weird?"

"No, Burt, you look like hell, but I don't see anything else. Gotta get going."

I awoke again in a couple of hours, still feeling weak and sick and still paranoid over someone near who meant me harm.

I made the decision to get the hell out of there. I wasn't getting any rest and wasn't feeling any better. Again, getting out of my sleeping bag was a huge, tiring chore. The dogs were still where they'd been, in a tangled mess. At least they weren't fighting. I slowly packed the sled and untangled the dogs. It took forty-five minutes to complete this ten-minute chore. I worried that in my weakened state I might lose the team but hung on for dear life as the dogs surged into motion. They were obviously well rested.

Mile after mile, I felt better and better. In an hour, I was myself again. We arrived in Unalakleet without further problems. I anchored the team in the designated corral, fed them, ate a snack, and crawled into my sleeping bag for a short nap.

"Burt, wake up! I've got to talk to you. Wake up!" I was roused from my deep sleep by violent shaking. My eyes opened to see a friend, Tia Wilson, poking me and talking in concerned, determined tones.

"Burt, we heard you stopped at Old Woman! You can't *ever* stop at Old Woman! Ever. Nobody stops there. The ghost of that woman is the most evil thing out there. You must keep on going. If you stop, and she gets you, you might never leave there, okay? Don't ever do that again."

Tia gave me a serious lecture, one I would never forget.

Later on, I saw a prominent musher being interviewed on television. He was talking in conspiratorial tones about the ghost at Old Woman. He spoke with a smug look and an "I've got a secret" expression about how he had left a candy bar for her when he passed through to stay on her good side. He'd obviously heard the legend.

I thought, "You poor lamb; you haven't a clue." No way was anyone getting off the hook with a candy bar.

Are there really ghosts? Was there a ghost at Old Woman who actually existed? Could she harm you? I know what I think. I'll let you be the judge, but don't say you weren't warned.

Chapter Nine
Moving to Petersville, October 1984

W e started training for the 1985 Iditarod race on Tuesday, October 9, 1984. We moved twenty dogs to our training camp at Petersville, Alaska, by truck and made our first run of the season the same day.

We hitched three teams to a three-wheeler and ran them down Schulin Lake Trail for a couple of miles. There was no snow and the warm sun had thawed the frozen surface of the narrow dirt road. We were soon spattered with mud and then covered with the thick, gooey slime. The dogs were mud-soaked like a bunch of pigs. It seemed ridiculous, something dog mushers shouldn't be doing. But it did the trick and the dogs were more than eager to race off down the trail, mud flying in all directions. We needed to get on with our training or we'd have a team with no bottom (depth of strength and endurance) come race day.

The next day we trucked another load of dogs to Petersville giving us a total of fifty. Some were too young for this year's race but not too young to begin training. We ran all the dogs again on that muddy trail with similar results. The dogs loved it, but rinsing and drying the harnesses and gang lines in the old galvanized wash tub with all that mud was a mess.

To avoid the mud, we decided to get up early the next morning before the ground thawed to see if we could keep things a little cleaner. We got up early and hitched a ten-dog team while the ground was still frozen. The freeze-thaw cycle had resulted in lots of ice crystals on the trail surface. I worried about the dogs' feet but felt we had to try it this once to see how it worked. Not good. We had some minor abrasions and Felix nearly lost a three-eighths-inch piece from one of his pads. It was still attached with a narrow tag of skin. Live and learn. We decided it was better to tolerate the mud, so we held off until later in the day to run the rest of the dogs.

While we waited, I took some Super Glue and reattached Felix's torn pad, a trick I had learned from Rick Swenson. Caught soon enough, the pad would heal as good as new. Then we built a nice big lean-to so our dog food-cooking operation wouldn't be snowed in. Petersville had a reputation for huge snow dumps. It often reached clear to the cabin roof, so it was easy to lose tools under the snow that wouldn't be seen again until spring. While we were at it, we also built a frame of spruce poles and covered it with a large blue nylon tarp to store dog food. Before long, our dog food and cooking gear were under cover, safe from the snow that would soon come.

The cabin at Petersville was accessible by road in the summer, a huge improvement over the Kahiltna cabin that was miles off the road system. Burt and Jack Felton hauled dog food in the fall, which was much safer and easier than by airplane, sometimes in bad weather.

We continued using the three-wheeler to train through Saturday, October 20. After that, we had enough snow for the sleds. Enough snow meant it was deep enough to use the brake without busting it off on the hard frozen ground below. It also meant enough snow to set your snow hook deeply into it.

That day was a red-letter day for us in many ways. Joee Redington Jr. had called me the previous summer while I was in Iowa visiting relatives. He had two dogs he thought I might like. One was a big dog named Stinker, and the other a tiny leader named Puddin. Each was aptly named. Puddin was the color of butterscotch pudding and as sweet and attentive a dog as ever lived. She would later become the finest leader I ever owned. The other dog's name speaks for itself. No matter what his diet, he produced more gas than the North Slope.

While I'd made the deal with Joee the previous summer, he lived in Manley on the Yukon River. That's a fairly out-of-the-way place. I hadn't been able to get up there all summer and now I needed the dogs. Rick Swenson called and a solution to the transportation problem resulted. He had made a dog deal with Joe Redington Sr., Joee's father. The deal was that Joe Sr. would loan Rick Swenson two top bitches. Rick would breed them to his males. They would then split the litters and Joe Sr. would get the bitches back.

Joe was supposed to have picked up his half of the pups when they were weaned and now they were half-grown. Joe had a lot going on and picking up those dogs wasn't high on his priority list.

Rick knew that Joe and I were mushing buddies and neighbors and spent a lot of time together at Petersville. Joe didn't have a phone and Rick wanted me to get a message to him. Rick was angry over having the extra dogs underfoot and with the mounting food bill. The message from Rick was simple. Either Joe Sr. would meet Rick in Nenana by Sunday to take the dogs or Rick would shoot the bitches and Joe's half of the pups.

I asked Rick if he really wanted me to say all of that and he said, "Hell, yes!" Rick was known to be more than blunt at times. That was okay with me. I would just deliver the message, then sit back, and enjoy the entertainment.

I wasn't disappointed. When I went to Joe's and delivered the message, he went through the roof. "If Rick does that, I'll sue the bastard for everything he has! That cheap son of a bitch! If he can't afford a little dog food, what a sorry excuse for a champion! If I was a four-time champion, I'd have $100,000 in sponsors," blah . . . blah . . . blah. It went on for a while.

Joe eventually calmed down, but continued to stomp around his wall-tent cursing under his breath. When I figured I'd milked all of the entertainment value I could, I told Joe that I'd be happy to drive my truck to Nenana and pick up all the dogs if he'd come along and keep me company. Joee could bring my new dogs, Puddin and Stinker, to Fairbanks and deliver them to Rick. Rick could then drive to Nenana with Joe's bitches and pups, and my two dogs, and hand them over to us. We'd all be happy. Joe agreed so we made plans for the trip. We would drive directly from Petersville to Nenana and return in one long but enjoyable day.

I drove on up to get the dogs but somehow Joe slipped out of going along. I wasn't surprised.

My wife rode along and it was a nice trip. Mount McKinley stood out in all her glory and we were soon in Nenana where we found Rick waiting. After lunch and a nice visit, Rick began unloading dogs. I was anxious to see Stinker and Puddin. When he got to the pups from the Redington/Swenson breeding, I could hardly believe they were sled dogs. They were the scruffiest looking bunch of mongrels I'd ever seen. One of them looked like a poodle while another looked more like a mongrel border collie. I stood there laughing while Rick tried to explain.

Although the parents were out of top racing stock, Alaska racing huskies are a mixed breed. Sometimes you just get the wrong combination and throwbacks result. Joe couldn't believe it when I dropped them off at his place. "Burt, I've never seen a worse-looking bunch of mutts in my life. Did you ask Rick what the hell was going on? Did he actually carry out his threat and shoot my share of these litters and then replace them with strays he found on the street?"

"No, Joe. We both know that Rick would never do that. He may be a little cranky, but everyone knows Rick's a straight shooter."

"Well, I think I've been had."

"Joe, join the club." *I guess he'd forgotten about the bath he gave me after the 1982 race.*

I don't know what Joe did with those dogs, but I never saw them in a racing team. When Joee called me later to see how Puddin and Stinker were doing, he laughed about the pups. He'd seen them when he stopped by Swenson's to drop off Stinker and Puddin. He asked me if his dad had accused me of stopping by the pound on the way from Nenana to pick up some mutts to pull a switch so I could keep Joe's share of the top breed pups for myself. I told him no but that Joe was pretty disgusted.

Stinker turned out to be a big strong dog that pulled hard. You couldn't hitch him at the back of the team near the sled or his air pollution issues would knock you right off the runners! I liked Puddin from the first run. I ran her in the team for a few days to let her get acquainted with me and her teammates and then ran her in lead for the first time on October 24, 1984. She had an intense personality and was quite small for an Iditarod dog.

By then we had thirty-eight dogs in training, including some yearlings. The adults were strong and fast while the yearlings didn't have the stamina to hang in there on the longer runs. I divided the dogs into three teams so that I drove the main team most of the time while my handlers, Mark and Nina, drove the rest.

Mark generally drove the young dogs. He seemed to have a mellow personality, which worked well with the younger dogs. Nina and I drove the adult dogs. Nina Hotvedt was eighteen years old and from Norway. She had a competitive personality, which worked well with the racing dogs.

The dogs ate tons of dog food during the winter. This pile of dog food in camp reduced the workload and the stress level for the entire winter. The new cabin at Petersville was heated by fuel oil eliminating the chore of chopping a winter supply of wood. These two conveniences reduced the work load tremendously.

It was during this early period that we began seriously sorting out the dogs. Fawcet was just a tad slower than the other dogs. Ivor, a leader I'd bought from Susan, had a tendency to bolt. Sonic, Babs, and Dancer were neckline chewers. Roger didn't like running alone and Rabbit had terrible feet that would get nicks and cuts on the best of soft trails. Jewel loved to lead some days and refused on other days. Tiger was still with me in the team I was driving, so when Jewel balked, I'd put Tiger in lead to replace her. Tiger was getting older but was always ready to go.

By early November, we were making fifteen-mile runs. That's not far but the dogs had a lot to learn and I still had a lot of sorting to do. Short runs with short teams worked well early in the season because it was easier to judge who was pulling well and who was not. With a six-dog team, any dog that isn't pulling is obvious. And it is easier to work with leaders. It is easier to stop and anchor the less powerful team if you need to stop, discipline and continue with a minimum of lost time.

On November 5, we woke up to a five-inch dusting of new snow. This was perfect for training the team. It was important for them to plow through fresh snow as routine business. Racing trails were usually packed well, but you still needed to have dogs that would take what came. It could get rugged out on the Iditarod Trail. Babs was such a pain in lead that I put her back for another day.

We often met Joe Redington and his handlers on the trail. Oncoming passes took a little practice, so the more practice the better during training. These passes went okay, but Wayne was a little too curious. He could be aggressive so I never let anyone else drive him, and I always watched extra carefully when strange dog teams were around. But all teams passed well and we were on our way.

Joe always trained his dogs to pass with a minimum of noise and fuss. Neither he nor I said anything to our dogs but a quiet "go ahead." The teams just glided by. This was in contrast to many drivers who yelled and hollered at the top of their lungs, "ON BY, ON BY, ON BY, GO AHEAD!" My dogs would just about jump off the trail from all the commotion when we met one of them.

It was nice to have other teams in the neighborhood so all the dogs and drivers got used to other dogs and to passing and being passed. Things proceeded much more easily during races when the dogs had been exposed to everything beforehand.

November 8 broke clear and cold with a north wind. We headed north into one of the most beautiful Alaskan panoramas imaginable. Snow-drenched trees, blue skies, and a fast-moving dog team, Mount McKinley towering above us, and the silence of the wilderness as we headed north into the foothills. I couldn't help but think of how often we look back on something and remember how great it was but how seldom we appreciate things as they are happening. This was one of those days when the world was right. Even the dogs' shadows created fascinating, ever-changing patterns as we hot-footed along.

Our last run of the day was after dark and was even more spectacular than during daylight. A full moon lit up the landscape. Everything in the moon's bright light was silvery while shadows were the darkest black. The dogs' shadows formed crinkly, Picasso-like patterns on the snow and seemed to move even faster than during the day. The dogs noticed our euphoria so the run was especially happy and quick. It was during times like these that I believed I'd found what I was searching for.

My days began before dawn with a half-hour of sit-ups and push-ups and riding the exercise bike while the handlers watered the dogs. As the handlers were finishing their chores, I'd fix a huge breakfast of pancakes and bacon or ham and eggs. The teams were then organized on paper and I'd check the schedule for mileage goals for the day. We selected a trail that was about right for miles, grabbed a bundle of harnesses and started hitching dogs. This was followed by hours spent gliding through the woods behind our teams of fast-moving huskies.

There was time to reflect, time to plan, time to sort through the weeds in one's life and time to judge if we were getting any closer to the real thing.

By mid-November, we were extending our miles and expanding the team's experience. We would turn the dogs off the trail and run several miles through trackless swamps before returning to the trail. Sometimes we reached an area where the snow had drifted and dogs found themselves up to their chests in soft powder. I was proud of the way the leaders lunged through the deep snow, guiding their teammates in near-perfect straight lines without hesitation. We practiced turning the team with commands of gee and haw. The intensity of the command and the repetition told the leaders how far to turn in these trackless meadows before again heading straight. Even a well-broken race trail is snowed in sometimes and the dogs must learn to proceed where you guide them.

On November 18, we headed north but had trouble getting the dogs to go past the Forks Roadhouse, a sign the dogs were getting a little tired and bored with the routine. We made a point of never using the dogs for transportation to the Roadhouse for just this reason. That's how bad habits develop. Later on, when training had really become long and boring, the dogs would look for any excuse to stop and rest. If they were used to stopping somewhere that you'd liked to have coffee, you'd made a perfect excuse for them to take matters into their own paws. Although we hadn't been stopping there, the veterans in the team had plenty of experience stopping at checkpoints during races. I guess they thought the Forks Roadhouse would do.

The Peters Hills are in an area of heavy winter snowfall. On the Kahiltna, we could often break trail with the teams after a fresh snowfall. At Petersville, the snow fall was so heavy that we often had to wait days after a heavy snowfall to allow the snow to settle before we broke the trails out with the snow machines. Otherwise, the machines just buried themselves.

It didn't take much to cure them of that.

On Saturday, November 24, we awoke to twenty degrees and a foot of fresh snow. I took the snowmachine out to break trail but didn't need to. The weekend snowmachiners from Anchorage who had broken the stillness all night had already made tracks everywhere. We passed a number of snowmachines during our runs and for the first time found some of them unfriendly. Normally, snowmachiners pull off the trail and shut off their engines to give the dogs a chance to get by without spooking them. These guys just raced on by, some nearly hitting the dogs.

The cool weather and new snow created a perfect situation for snowballs in the dogs' feet. Small, pill-like ice balls develop and collect on the hair between the dogs' toes. These balls rub the tender skin between the toes creating painful burn-like sores. We clipped the hair between the toes so the ice didn't have anything to cling to but didn't remove all of it because it served a purpose in protecting the dogs' feet. We stopped five or six times during each run to clean the ice balls out. The alternative was to put booties on all the dogs' feet before we left the yard, something we would have done had we realized how much time we would lose without them. Trapline dogs that are stopped often for longer periods while their musher sets and resets traps learn to bite the ice balls out during their stops.

On November 26, we made our first forty-mile run. I broke the trail out the night before with my snowmachine so it had firmed up nicely. We booted the dogs to avoid ice balls that were sure to develop with fresh snow and low temperatures. The materials used in booties today as I write this are far superior to the ones we used then. We had both trigger cloth and pile booties. The trigger cloth booties wore through quickly while the pile booties soaked up a lot of water.

Lil had a weird thing happen to her. When I checked her booties, one bootie seemed frozen to the bottom of her foot. When I went to remove it, I discovered that the bootie had worn through and some snow and a small ice ball had come in through the hole. I was extremely worried that she might have a frost-bitten foot.

We had mushed out of camp heading south under gray leaden skies. Snow was sifting down gently as we mushed out of our yard, across the swamp and onto Shulin Lake Trail. It was later in the season so the dogs weren't quite as crazy to go as they had been early in the season. By now, we had a few long days behind us and dogs learned to save a little something after they'd made a few long runs.

The dogs were trotting along at their mile-eating Iditarod pace, averaging ten miles an hour as we climbed and descended the low ridges. I had measured five mile increments down Schulin Lake Trail with my snowmachine and put up little mileage signs on trees to mark the spots both coming and going. I carried a stopwatch so I could accurately calculate our speeds in my head as we mushed along. It gave us another clue regarding the dogs' condition as the season advanced.

Ten miles from camp, the dogs quickened their pace. Since we were in heavy moose country, it was obvious that a moose was somewhere nearby and I glanced up along the trail and then back to the dogs. We mushed on for a hundred yards at the faster pace when the loudest roar I'd ever heard blasted right in my ear. It was so loud and frightening that the dogs instantly erupted into a full gallop that put my heart right in my mouth. My heart was beating so loud I could actually hear it pounding in my head. I grabbed my gun and glanced over my shoulder and saw a huge cow moose and calf standing within twenty feet of the trail. The hackles on both were standing straight up and their ears were laid back. The calf was wheeling to run in the other direction and the cow was stepping between it and us as we fled down the trail. They must have been lying down and we had startled them as we mushed quietly along in the falling snow. The cow had reacted instantly. Her instinct was to challenge her potential attacker, and she had done that.

The trails surrounding the cabin at Petersville traversed some of the most beautiful areas of Alaska wilderness. A musher was kept busy scanning the dogs for anything unusual in their behavior, watching for hazards such as moose and downed trees across the trail and then taking a moment to enjoy the incredible beauty.

At this point, my team and I were obviously safe, but my handler with the other half of the dogs would be no more than a quarter of a mile behind and approaching fast. I regained control of the team within a hundred yards and brought them to a stop. I began yelling at the top of my lungs, hoping that the cow would begin moving her calf out of the area.

Within moments, my handler came into view and stopped her team behind me. I asked her if she'd had any problems and she said, "Nope, everything was routine." The moose had apparently moved off by the time she got there. I didn't bother to tell her of my near miss until we were back in camp putting our dogs away.

Our forty-mile trail ran south to a turnaround we'd made along a section of the Joe May Highway. Joe Redington and I liked to meet there for a break when our training schedules coincided. We'd stop for three or four hours and build a campfire. It allowed the dogs an opportunity to have a snack and snooze in the woods away from home while Joe and I, and our handlers, enjoyed a campfire and a pot of tea. Joe always brought honey along to share. It made the tea a special treat.

As we pulled into the turnaround for a short break and a snack, I reminisced about a stop Joe and I had made there the year before. It was a midnight run and we'd camped in the woods at the turnaround for four hours.

Moose were always a threat as we mushed along, especially at night. They are nocturnal and find the firmly packed dog trails much easier going than the deep snow on either side. As I explained earlier, our problems with moose resulted from the similarity between our dogs and a pack of wolves. When confronted by what appeared to be a large wolf pack, the moose had little choice but to stand and face the dogs, and the dogs naturally wanted to chase the moose. Although I always tried to keep the teams small enough to stop if we encountered a moose, the possibility of one charging after you'd stopped or blindsiding you from off the trail always existed.

I always carried a .357 Magnum pistol for defense, but Joe thought he had a better idea. Actually, everybody thought they had a better idea. Anyway, Joe suggested that we each buy a twelve-gauge flare pistol to keep in the sled bag. If we encountered an irate moose, we would grab the flare gun, aim at the moose, and fire. The bang and sparks and singed hair if you hit it would scare the moose away. We would then proceed down the trail without having to salvage the meat. I thought it was worth a try, so I bought a flare gun and had it along that night.

My handler was an athletic young woman named Donna, eager but without a lot of wilderness experience. Donna and I had started ahead of Joe and reached the turnaround first. We anchored the teams and started gathering wood for a fire. Donna had never built a fire before, so she asked if she could do it while I took a break. I said sure and finished snacking my dogs. I then decided to try out the new flare gun. I figured that if I shot it straight up in the air, Joe would see it and know we'd arrived, and I would get an idea of how the thing worked.

I pulled it out and let one fly. It shot several hundred feet in the air and exploded with a bang and a shower of sparks. After our eyes once again became accustomed to the dark, I checked to see how the dogs enjoyed the show. They were nowhere to be found. The only thing visible was the gang line leading from the sled off into the brush. By following tug lines, I found first one dog, then another, each burrowed as far beneath snow and bushes as their tugs would permit. It took a half hour of petting and coaxing to get everybody back in the open and reasonably happy.

Meanwhile, Donna gathered up a pile of twigs and broken branches and soon had a cheery but feeble blaze going. I figured the best way to help her learn was to just stay out of the way and let her work on it. While she nursed the campfire, I found a comfortable place to lie down and take a nap.

I was still chuckling over the experiment with the new moose medicine. In my imagination, the scenario that came to mind was a moose in our path as we mushed around a blind corner. We would manage to stop the frenzied huskies in time to avoid hitting the moose. But the moose would be angry, hackles up, ears back, pawing the snow. I would reach for the flare gun, pull back the hammer, and fire. The flaming ball would zoom along, just over the dogs' heads, burning all the hair off their tails as it went. The flare would graze the moose, and continue over its back, setting its hair on fire and land on the far side where it would explode with a loud bang and a shower of sparks. Frightened out of its wits, the panicked moose, hair afire, would run full tilt away from the explosion toward us, through the dogs and over me, destroying everything in its path. When it was all over and the smoke had cleared, the hairless huskies would be nowhere to be found, scared witless by the exploding flare and the smell of burning hair. I decided to put the flare gun in my airplane with my survival gear, where it resides today.

Our dogs raised their heads and woofed as Joe and his handler approached. We helped them anchor their sleds and they began snacking their dogs in readiness for a nice interlude around the campfire. When the chores were done, Joe took one look at Donna's campfire and told her to "stand back." He dug into his sled and, to my surprise, pulled out a chain saw and cranked it up. Headlight ablaze, he headed for the woods in search of a tree.

He found a nice dead spruce tree, which he felled and cut into three-foot lengths. Ordering the handlers to haul his firewood, he arranged the logs log-cabin style. Before long Joe had a fire big enough to drive the shadows back into the woods and spread warmth in a large circle of the cold winter's night. We boiled a pot of tea and each of us pulled up a handy log to sit on.

Trading stories with Joe Redington around a campfire in the middle of the night with dog teams tethered nearby was just about as good as it got. God bless Joe for those wonderful memories. And God bless him for being human. People painted him as a perfect, saintly icon. The fact was that Joe had lived a challenging life. He rode the rails with his dad and lived with gypsies. In Alaska, he lived a subsistence lifestyle in the wilderness and raised a family out there. Things weren't easy and he had to live by his wits. He was perfectly capable of a little chicanery now and then. What made Joe a giant who rose above many others were his sense of destiny, his imagination and his grit. He developed great ideas and could mobilize an army to bring those ideas to reality.

I contemplated how Joe Sr. had affected my life. He didn't bring me into dogs, because I was committed to mushing before we ever met. In fact, we met at Dick Tozier's when I was Dick's handler and already into dogs. I was already an adventurer, and well into all things Alaska—bush flying, hunting, fishing and a love for bush Alaska. What Joe did that affected my entire life was establish the Iditarod race, which in turn provided me the perfect world in which to live my dreams. Of course, he didn't do it for me. The lives of the entire Iditarod family, from mushers to staff to fans, were changed in some way by Joe's Iditarod race.

It was impossible to say no to him. We were sitting by a campfire at his camp on Carpentiers Lake the night before the Knik International 200 one year when Joe asked me if I would sponsor it. I said, "No, I really am not interested in sponsoring races. I am spending too much just feeding my own dog habit." But he wouldn't let up and an hour later, I gave him a check for two thousand dollars.

That same year, I loaned Joe my new Polaris wide-track snowmachine to break trail if he was snowed in during training. I gave him one condition, "Don't let anyone else drive it. It's a new machine and I don't want some careless idiot wrecking it." At the Junior Iditarod banquet, the trailbreakers thanked Joe for furnishing the snowmachine for breaking the race trail. They told a story of how their machine broke down and they had to use "Joe's" machine to tow the broken-down wreck miles back to civilization. After the banquet, I said, "Joe, that was my machine. I told you not to let anyone else drive it."

He said, "Burt, what could I do? It was for the kids."

Of course, he was right.

I never minded helping him. It was usually for a worthy cause that I felt good about.

Conditions were ever changing during a race, from the weather, to the trail conditions or the competition. Burt and Joe Sr. loved to discuss strategy out on the trail. Notice their bare hands! It's a measure of how tough you become spending winters outdoors in Alaska

Joe accomplished a lot in his lifetime, and it was important to him that people knew about it. His legacy was important to him and he protected it. He wanted credit for what he did and didn't want to be wrong. One time he told me he had never made a mistake. As one who makes mistakes every day, I told him that was pretty danged good.

He had developed a collar that he claimed no dog could escape. One day we were standing in his yard as he showed me the collar. He handed it to me to use as a pattern and told me he'd never had a loose dog since he invented that collar. As we spoke, two of his dogs prowled the far side of the yard. I pointed this out and asked him to explain it. He responded, "Those aren't dogs, they're bitches." Dog men differentiate males and females as dogs and bitches. A little bit of a stretch there.

As I work here, I can't help but wonder if Joe is sitting around some ghostly campfire, dogs tethered nearby, with other old-timers like Leonard Seppala and Scotty Allen, maybe even Herby, trading stories and tossing logs on the fire.

I've known few people from humble beginnings who had such an impact. Joe Redington and his Iditarod Trail Sled Dog Race have done more for this great sport and for Alaska than anything else I know.

We woke the dogs, booted them up and lined them out. I checked Lil's foot and saw no sign of a problem. What a relief. We kicked a little snow on the fire and then made good time heading home. We still weren't a smooth-functioning team. Bill and Lil seemed slower than the rest when we really honked. I got on Bill, and that helped some, but the reality was that he just didn't have the fast trot that the rest of the dogs did. I didn't hassle Lil because of her foot problem, so I didn't know yet if she was a little lazy or just not as fast. Roger, King, and Cisco were all a little goofy at times. Jade was a sweetheart. Suzie and Charger were each somewhat tentative in lead, but it was early in the season. Most of those problems disappeared as the miles went by and running became routine. It wasn't long before we were back in the yard putting the dogs away. While the handlers fed the dogs, I prepared a big meal of my favorite moose steaks, mashed potatoes, and asparagus. Those handlers loved asparagus!

Sleep came quickly in dog camp.

During our trips up into the Peters Hills, we noticed that a small pack of wolves had been hanging around. Every day when we mushed up through a saddle in the hills, we found where they had hunted and traveled. It was fun to try to figure out what the wolves were like from the size of their tracks and what they'd been up to. The wolves stayed in an area about twenty-five miles long. They moved on later when the moose in the hills became spookier and harder to deal with. We kept the knowledge of those wolves to ourselves in the hopes of getting to enjoy them as long as possible.

Then one day as we mushed through the saddle between the Peters Hills and Little Peters Hills, we found fresh wolf tracks heading in our direction. A couple of miles further, we spotted three big moose a quarter mile ahead acting aggressively. When they spotted us, they made a couple of false charges and pranced and bucked like wild horses. It was an awesome sight and a bit intimidating. The trail veered to the right before we got to them, which avoided a confrontation.

A couple of miles further along, we pulled off the main trail and headed west across unbroken snow and found a sheltered spot to spend a couple of hours. We parked the teams and then hunkered down behind a drift and built a campfire. We snacked the dogs and were eating our picnic lunch when the wolves began howling a few hundred yards away. That explained the spooky moose. Then our dogs began to howl back. I stood up to watch the dogs and had to chuckle. The bitches were all sitting up on their haunches howling their hearts out, trying to make some new friends. What a chorus. The males were all hunkered down with their chins on the snow, obviously hoping not to be noticed by some big alpha male wolf. It reminded me of a bunch of college kids on a picnic when the bikers come riding in, girls excited and boys nervous. I kept my gun handy.

The time we spent with the dogs out on the trail was great, and camp life was also enjoyable. I especially enjoyed living in that log cabin up in the hills south of Mount McKinley. Dusty Rhodes lived at Trapper Creek and built log cabins. He and his kids had erected the logs for me. A dear friend, Jack Felton, had helped me with the interior. The logs were cove-fitted one upon the next so the walls were tight and warm. I'd varnished them to the luster of fine furniture. It had a loft and a nice front porch and was surrounded by fireweed in summer. Joe Redington admired it and said it was like the Alaska trapper cabins of long ago, cozy and functional.

I loved to snuggle under my goose-down comforter after a cold day on the trail. It reminded me of my childhood. Whether in our own drafty house or staying with cousins on the farm, those early Iowa and South Dakota houses were cold at night, but there was always a goose-down comforter to keep us warm. The bed in the cabin was simply a thick foam mattress resting on plywood but, with that comforter, it had to be the most comfortable bed in Alaska. I loved to climb into it after a cold, rigorous day on the trail. I installed a propane lamp just above the head of the bed so I could read in bed for a half hour or so, a favorite pastime. When that light went out, it was only seconds before I was fast asleep. I would wake up to the sound of the alarm and just let it ring as I gazed around at the beautiful log walls and the rough-hewn ceiling.

I almost hated to cover the walls with pictures and tapestries, but I had such nifty stuff to hang that I couldn't resist. I had a large Machetanz color lithograph of a dog team coming head-on hanging just above my bed. Also above the bed was a montage of family pictures that my daughter, Jill, had given me for Christmas. There were pictures of all kinds of family holidays and outings and parties. There were pictures of everyone in our family doing just about everything we enjoy doing. That helped keep things from getting too lonely. Over the door hung a huge tapestry of a dog team mushing romantically through the Alaskan wilderness. This particular tapestry had great significance. Some friends of ours had gone with us to celebrate on the night I signed up for my first Iditarod Trail Sled Dog Race. We were having a beer at the Peanut Farm when a vendor came by asking if we would like to buy fine Alaskan tapestries. I told him to shake one out and let me look and sure enough, it was of a dog team. It was too much of a coincidence to be anything but good luck, so I handed the guy his twenty-five dollars and took the *fine* tapestry. Actually, it was just a print on blue denim but from a distance, it didn't really look all that bad. Later, my pal, Shannon, laughingly told me the lead dog looked like it had stopped to take a dump. It was still my lucky tapestry.

The warmth from a wood-burning stove did a marvelous job of heating the cabin. I would open the vents when I got up in the morning and within twenty minutes the cabin was nice and warm. I turned it back down in the evening and the lower levels of the cabin where my bed was would become cool. Mark preferred it a little warmer, which was perfect since it was always warmer up in the loft.

This is the sled that Joe Redington, Sr. drove in the inaugural parade for President Reagan. He donated it to Iditarod to be auctioned at a fundraiser. Burt bought the sled that Joe Sr. used and donated it to the Anchorage Museum.

I would arise in the morning, pull on my fleece boots and head for the stove to put on a pot of coffee. When that was going, I hollered for Mark that it was time to get up and, thus, our day began. We had a quick cup of coffee, then

Mark woke up Nina, the other handler, who slept in a tent, and they went out and watered the dogs while I fixed breakfast.

I fixed a pitcher of orange juice and mixed up a batch of pancakes. There's something so cheery about fixing pancakes and bacon in a log cabin. We always use "Krusteaz" because it is so easy and the hotcakes are always so good. A half pound of bacon and we were all set for a hearty breakfast. When my willpower was under control, I'd settle for a bowl of shredded wheat with a banana on top, but usually pancakes and bacon were too hard to resist. It was especially nice if a light snow was falling outside as the slowly settling flakes added to the peace and solitude of our remote camp. As scarce as snow seemed to be down at our Kahiltna camp, it was always snowing in Petersville. The snow reached clear to the cabin's eaves the first winter we occupied that cabin.

After breakfast I took yesterday's team lineups, and rearranged them slightly to establish the new lineups. We then donned our heavy winter clothes, grabbed a bundle of harnesses, and began hitching dogs. During the earlier part of the season, we hitched shorter teams since they were easier to control with the rowdy leaders. Early-season runs were shorter so we had time to make more of them. Once our training runs reached twenty-five miles, however, we doubled the size of the teams to about ten or twelve dogs so we didn't have to make so many runs in a day. There just wasn't time.

We loaded the sleds as heavily as we could without being too hard on the sleds. This helped the dogs develop their muscles and prepared them for the lighter loads pulled during the race. Rick Swenson once told me that he wanted training to be so rugged that the dogs thought things had become easier during the race.

At the end of the day, we ate, got the dishes done and then played a game of backgammon.

Even out in the woods, there was quite a social life. We occasionally invited the neighbors over for dinner or I took my handlers over to the Forks Roadhouse a couple of miles away for hamburgers. Although rare, these were always pleasant experiences. Occasionally, we invited Joe Redington Sr. and his two handlers, Tony and Robin, over for dinner. Joe often refused to come if there were going to be too many people, but when he did come, it was a treat. He came this particular night, and I served steaks from a moose that my buddy, Sandy Williams, and I had shot that fall at our hunting camp on the Stony River. The steaks were delicious with new potatoes, asparagus, garlic toast, and a fresh salad. What a feast.

The conversation was terrific. Joe Sr. had thousands of stories to tell, as did everyone else in the cabin that night. One of his handlers, Robin, and her husband, Bucky, lived in the mountains. He was a guide at Rainy Pass Lodge, a hunting camp up in the Alaska Range. It was the site of Rainy Pass checkpoint. Needless to say, her experiences at that hunting camp were interesting. Joe's handler, Tony, was an Italian, who along with one of my handlers, Nina Hotvedt, from Norway, rounded out this interesting group. We jabbered on after dinner until nearly midnight when finally Joe and his gang trudged the quarter mile back to their camp to prepare for another busy day.

The contrast between this simple bush lifestyle and the corporate executive lifestyle that I'd left behind was dramatic. The engineering surveying business in Alaska had been extremely competitive. It was full of the pressure and tension that was common to corporate life everywhere. I'd enjoyed it a lot and earned great success, but ultimately was ready for a break. Mushing was giving me that, and the dogs were every bit as rich and rewarding to be with as friends from my business life.

Chapter Ten
Forks Roadhouse Race, 1984

We were excited! Joe and Vera Duhl at the Forks Roadhouse came through. I'd approached them a couple of days earlier to see if they'd help put on a race. I'd said, "Joe, if you'll furnish the posters and put on the mushers' banquet, I'll help with the prizes. I'll furnish trophies, a bag of dog food and fifty pounds of frozen meat for prizes."

The Forks was just a couple of miles up the trail from our cabin, so it would be a neighborhood event. What a treat and what great people the Duhls were. Joe and Vera were typical old-time Alaska bush folks. In their seventies, they welcomed one and all to the Forks Roadhouse at Petersville.

Joe and Vera actually made most of their money off snowmachiners from Anchorage, so it was a special favor for them to sponsor a mushing event. Their snowmachine costumers came ready to spend money and party most every weekend during the winter.

I'd stopped by earlier for a burger and found Joe polishing glasses behind the bar. The scene could have taken place a hundred years earlier. A sourdough bartender polishing glasses in an ancient log roadhouse, with walls covered with knick-knacks and photos from a time long past. The first dollar earned had been thumb-tacked to the wall behind the bar.

"I'll have a burger, Joe." That was my excuse for being there. I didn't want to look like I was bugging him over the race idea. Of course he knew, but there was a protocol.

Joe went to the rear and gave Vera the order.

Petersville was accessible by road in the summer; however, the snowplow stopped 15 miles away at Moose Creek. Occasionally, somebody waited a little too long in the fall to get their vehicle out and got snowed in. Then a dozer would be brought in to plow the road and get them out before it really began to snow.

When he got back, Joe asked, "Burt, you know the difference between snowmachiners and dog mushers? A snowmachiner would spend three hours driving up from Anchorage towing an expensive snowmachine. He would rent a room and run up a $200 bar tab. He'd buy some fuel for his machine, maybe some two-cycle oil and some spark plugs, maybe even a spare belt. When he left, there would be no sign he was ever here except for tracks in the snow and the extra money in the roadhouse safe.

"On the other hand," he continued, "most mushers are like Fred." Fred Agree was a musher and a mutual friend who lived with Vickie down in Trapper Creek, twenty miles away on Petersville Road.

"Fred mushed his dog team up from Trapper Creek the other day and tethered his team right in front of the Roadhouse door. He walked into the Roadhouse, tracking snow off his boots on Vera's newly mopped floor. There were puddles all the way to the lunch counter where he ordered a fifty-cent cup of hot chocolate. When he was done, he searched his pockets and had no money. Said he had left his money at home. So Fred asked Vera to put it on his tab, and he tromped back out leaving a new trail of puddles on the floor as he went."

Joe continued, "As she mopped the floor again, one of the snowmachiners strolled outside and saw that half of Fred's dogs had left piles of fresh poop in front of the door. The customer was grossed out at the sight and the smell and came gagging back in to report."

Joe continued, "I figured somebody might step in it and track it in. So I had to get up, go out and shovel up that stinking mess." Joe chuckled as he related the story, obviously enjoying the telling as much as I enjoyed listening. Knowing both Joe and Fred, I suspect the story was fiction, but I wondered if Joe was setting me up for a "no" on the sponsorship issue.

Then Joe said, "Burt, in spite of the differences, we love having mushers come to the Forks. The reason we stay out here in this wilderness is that we like the time-honored ways. Those dog teams that come mushing in here are the finishing touch for us. We'd love to sponsor the race. Let's talk details."

You can see why we mushers appreciated Joe and Vera's sponsoring the race. Dog mushers really weren't their best customers but, just like in the early days, everybody was welcome so long as they checked their guns with the bartender. The sign at the door still demands this one concession.

The Forks was built in the 1930s to serve gold miners in the area. I first visited the Roadhouse in 1965 when I went fishing in the area with an attorney friend named George Dickson. Access to Petersville Road at that time was by boat across the Susitna River from Talkeetna, or by dog team or snowmachine from the same place in winter. The Parks Highway had just been extended north to Trapper Creek and a new bridge across the Susitna River had just been constructed. The bridge and road from there north weren't open to the public yet; however, I worked for the State Highway Department, so I knew where the key to the gate was hidden.

When George and I visited the Forks Roadhouse in 1965, it was essentially abandoned. The original owner/builder had become sick and I believe just walked away to get medical attention, leaving the roadhouse wide open. We walked through the building and found it fascinating. It looked as though time had stopped in the 1930s. The bar was still set up with glasses, bottles of booze and all the trimmings. Vintage posters and pictures hung on the walls. There was a kitchen and a stairway leading upstairs to a sleeping dorm. A tack room attached to the north side of the roadhouse held saddles, bridles, halters, and packsaddles, all in readiness to pack up and go. Out back was a fully equipped shop with a huge, ancient Witte generator that still ran like a Swiss watch under Joe's gentle touch. Everything remained as it must have been when the owner left, obviously intending to come back and take up right where he'd left off.

Touching nothing, we closed the doors behind us and left, our minds busy imagining what must have gone on here before the turn of the century and even just thirty years ago. Gold miners, pack trains, and dog teams. For me, *that* was the real thing. We pictured gold miners with maybe just a partner or two, mucking for gold, not the big multi-million-dollar operations that have replaced the romance of the early sourdoughs. We thought of the pack trains hauling supplies in and payloads out over miles of steep rocky trail . . . and strong, fast freight dogs able to pull heavy loads for miles through Alaska's wilderness.

Now here we were in my cabin nearly twenty years after that first visit with a yard full of sled dogs eager to go. The place was alive, not just with ghosts of the past but once again with true Alaskans. And dog teams, teams bred and trained for long-distance mushing through any conditions Alaska could dish out. And, hopefully, we dog drivers would be equal to the task.

And we were going to have a race! The race was to be a tad more than fifty miles and was scheduled for Sunday, December 16, 1984. We would travel in a circle, first heading north from the Forks to Petersville, along the steep cliff, over a low ridge, and down along Cache Creek to a picturesque mining camp. There, we'd begin the steep ascent up Spruce Creek, and over the saddle to the ridge above Black Creek. We'd follow that low ridge above Black Creek all the way down to where we started at the Forks. The trail was challenging—just what we wanted.

The next couple of weeks of training would be important. We would condition the dogs for all the challenges of that varied trail, while bringing them to a mini-peak just at race time. All of this had to be done without adversely affecting our Iditarod race, still months away. This race would be exciting as well as important to us from a training point of view. For the first time, my dogs would get to pull up to a starting line and hear the race marshal give us the countdown to go. Hopefully, some new teams would show up for training and we might get to practice a little passing. We sure didn't want to give anyone else practice passing us.

We wrote the rules for this race to require that mushers carry all the mandatory gear required by the Iditarod Trail Committee during the Iditarod. This would give us a chance to get everything together to see how it fit in the sleds. We really didn't think we'd need all that equipment for a fifty-mile race, but it was good practice.

The best part? We would get to hang with our mushing buddies for a day or so, first along the race trail, and then at the awards banquet after the finish.

We awoke Monday, December 3, with a new eagerness. Three inches of fresh snow had fallen and the temperature was right at the freezing level. With these conditions, it would be slow going. We had rested the dogs for three days, so they would be raring to go, but it would be hard going—just what we wanted right now.

The cabin and surrounding woods were unbelievably beautiful after a fresh snow. The branches were heavy with the purest white, fluffy snow imaginable.

I had finished my push-ups and sit-ups by the time the handlers had finished watering the dogs. Having suffered a broken back while still a teenager, I needed to keep my torso strong. It was the only way to avoid excruciating pain after hours on the sled, particularly during races. We had fed the dogs their heavy meal the night before so they could sleep on it, but they needed water before the training runs. Not heavy food because it made running difficult, just enough to keep them hydrated.

The dogs have been fed and Burt brews a pot of coffee before crawling into the sled for a nap. We camped out a few times during training to get the dogs used to living away from their doghouses and to give us a chance to get our equipment in order.

After a few moments, the handlers were back inside, shaking the snow off their parkas and taking off their boots and I fixed breakfast. Spending most of the day outside working hard in Alaska's cold winter burned calories rapidly. My metabolism was extremely efficient, so I had to really watch it when working in the office and not getting as much exercise.

Then it was on with our parkas and boots and off to the dog yard. This time we headed west across Peters Creek and into the hills. We were mushing along the race trail, but in the opposite direction the race would follow. We ran past the roadhouse and up along Black Creek, hoping for some wind in the saddle to go with the fresh snowfall.

We liked to have most of the runs nice and quick so the dogs developed a race pace rather than getting into the habit of slogging along, but we did need regular sessions of hard going to get the dogs used to breaking trail. Iditarod could throw most any condition at you, so you needed to be prepared for whatever came. The best time for teaching the dogs to break trail in fresh snow is after they have had a good rest. If not, they might become discouraged and learn to hate running in fresh snow.

With Dancer in lead, the dogs moved quickly along as we drove north up Schulin Lake trail and then picked up Petersville Road to the Forks Roadhouse. We proceeded past the Roadhouse with a wave to Vera and Joe as we drove by, and then began gaining altitude. The first part of the trail was fairly steep, but it became more gradual after a mile or two. Onward and upward, the dogs pulled us. With too much of a load for them to lope, they maintained a fast trot as the miles flew by. The snow got deeper as we gained altitude, reaching six to eight inches as we neared the top.

It was then that we broke into the open of the big meadows north of the Little Peters Hills. I commanded Dancer off the trail into the trackless snowfields to the southwest. He seriously needed to get used to the idea of charging off into unbroken country upon command. Dancer just couldn't get the idea of going where no trail existed. No matter what I tried, he would bail out or lie down. I put Noise up with him, which helped a lot. Noise knew what I wanted when I gave him a command.

Deep down, though, Noise really didn't like the exercise. Fresh snow and high temperatures combined for the worst kind of mushing. Best was a cold hard trail. We drove for a couple of miles with no trail but then found it just as we reached the high point in the saddle separating the Little Peters Hills from the main Peters Hills range. It was never a good idea to push the dogs to the point where they quit or disobeyed. Once they did that, the idea was grooved in their minds and you never knew when they might do it again. If they did, you could bet it would be when the going was formidable and you needed another problem like a hole in the head.

After we picked up the main trail, we angled the dogs back toward home. The downgrade, coupled with the fact that we were heading back toward home and hearth, helped the dogs pick up the pace and the trail was soon flying by. We entered the yard with a clatter of sleds and the rustle of harnesses, a sound that to this day brings back the fondest of memories.

By the time we were ready to feed the dogs, some were exhibiting soreness and stiffness. Rigorous training could do that. The stiffness didn't go away for a couple of days, so we rested until we all got our enthusiasm back. Warm wet snow was no fun, but you had to train for it sometimes or you'd really slow down if you saw it during a race.

We never met snowmachines on our trails down in the Kahiltna country—too inaccessible, but they invaded the Peters Hills on weekends. The drivers were usually polite and would pull over and stop their machines to avoid scaring the dogs. Occasionally, machines would go ripping past a team leaving us muttering under our breath. Usually, we liked to see them, though, because they saved us having to start up our own machines to break trails for the dogs.

The Forks Race was on our minds. It was great to have something to look forward to, something that would happen soon, not in a couple of months.

The skies cleared after the snowfall and temperatures dropped to near zero. During the coming days, our runs were along hard, fast trails. The residual loose snow from the earlier fresh snowfall had caused lots of ice balls between the dogs' feet, and the dogs' attitudes began to sour a little. Don't ever believe that dogs don't communicate among themselves. One dog's attitude gets bad and soon the whole team is slogging along like a bunch of spoiled brats. No person can give you an accusing, disapproving look like a dog that believes he's been put upon and decides to pout.

Some mushers deliberately push their dogs a little harder about this time during training, just to get them to go a little sour. Then if they disobey, you have an excuse to show them who is boss. The theory is that you get it over with and the dogs learn that you are in charge. The dogs must see the musher as the alpha male in the pack and this is one way to establish that fact. I'm not much for deliberately causing a mutiny because I like to have fun and want my dogs to enjoy it, too. Sometimes it just happened, and when it did, I dealt with it the best way I could. You could keep on driving them in hopes that you'd get through it or you could back off a little until the dogs were again eager to go. I prefer the latter. Sled dogs just naturally want to run and pull a sled. If you back off a bit, they'll sometimes get a little bored on the chain and want to go, thus regaining their enthusiasm.

In any case, I wanted the dogs eager to go on race day so we backed it off a little. We had lots to do preparing for the race, so time off the trail was well spent. Also, I hadn't taken time to do much visiting, so I decided to spend some time with my neighbors.

I loved spending those winters training dogs at Petersville. It was great to visit Joe and Vera Duhl at the Forks. Vilma and Bob Anderson lived a mile away and Joe Redington lived about a quarter mile up the trail. Shannon mushed up to visit from down near Trapper Creek and we stopped down to visit her and Eric.

Joe Redington would stop over occasionally but he preferred to have me drop by his place where it was quieter. He was willing to work with novices and give advice all day long but, when he wanted to just sit and visit, he became impatient with too many dumb questions and too much hero worship. The level of adulation got a little thick by hero-worshiping handlers, sometimes, who would sit at his feet and say, "Please, Joe, tell us another story" or, "Joe, when did you learn to mush dogs" or, "Joe, why do you still say 'mush?'" Joe was a little hard of hearing, so he liked it better if the two of us just yelled back and forth over at his place.

With that, I'd often slip out after things quieted down and my camp was asleep and visit Joe or the Duhls. Vera Duhl and I would sit over a cup of coffee or tea while she'd talk about her experiences all over Alaska. She must have been in her seventies by then but was still full of it. She cooked and kept house at the Roadhouse while Joe tended bar, did repairs, and hauled firewood. Some sled dogs were still tethered outside. They belonged to their daughter-in-law, Shannon Chase Pool, a noted Alaskan artist and dog musher. Shannon was married to Vera's son, Eric, also a dog musher, who operated heavy equipment for the Department of Transportation.

Conversations with Joe Redington could be about anything from training to equipment to the dogs themselves. We often discussed Iditarod business since both of us served on the Iditarod board of directors. I must say, though, that the fun part of Iditarod was mushing dogs, not serving on the board. Iditarod politics were brutal beyond anything the public saw on the surface. Some of the most enjoyable times talking Iditarod board business was during those sessions at Joe's cabin, not in board meetings.

I'd usually rap on the door and Joe would appear, ready for company. Clean-shaven, hair combed and dressed no matter what time of night. I could arrive at midnight and find him up and ready to visit. Years later I learned that he had difficulty sleeping lying down so he slept sitting up in his recliner. Joe had an acid reflux problem that ultimately may have caused the cancer that led to his death.

Also, Joe believed that an Iditarod musher had to be able to operate on a schedule that was no schedule, so he probably would have slept sitting up even without the physical problem. Joe did what he wanted anytime of the day or night and expected his close friends to do the same.

When I arrived, he would put the teapot on and we compared notes on our teams. Then we'd talk about the competition and who was the team to fear. Rick Swenson was always at the top of the list, followed by guys like Herby, Sonny Lindner, Vern Halter, Rick Mackey, Dewey Halverson, and John Cooper. Of course, we always put ourselves fairly high on the list, too—heck, it *was* our list.

Joe had lots of friends, as well as his sons, who were all dog mushers and were scattered across Alaska. That along with the friends that I was talking to formed quite a mukluk telegraph for keeping track of the competition.

We'd often experiment with equipment, which was always fun. Iditarod mushers were required to take certain items in their sleds during the race, such as snowshoes, an axe, booties for

There was always plenty of snow at Petersville, a pleasant change of pace from our Kahiltna trails that could be full of big ruts and dirt clumps.

the dogs, an arctic sleeping bag, and some promotional material. Other items were also needed, of course, to traverse Alaska in winter, so the list could be about as long as a musher wanted it to be. Joe liked to go first class so his sled was usually bulging with stuff. After my first race in 1981, I made a list of the things I didn't need during the race, and from then on, that stuff was left behind.

No more trying to be prepared for any possible emergency that the frigid Arctic might throw at us. I just took the necessities and then was prepared to innovate when I needed to.

Considering that the only stuff you'd have was what would fit in your sled, it was a wonder how much time you could spend fiddling with its contents before the race. Weight and functionality were paramount considerations. Ounces counted when you knew you were going to have to drag every bit of it all the way to Nome. We weighed everything from the sleeping bag to the pistol.

Stoves were a good example. In those days, we used Coleman stoves—not just any Coleman stove. We would juice them up by adding extra fuel tanks, one for each burner rather than one tank to serve all burners. The tanks operated under pressure so the more tanks you could add, the more fuel flow was generated. You needed two or three stoves to make one Iditarod stove. We would drill out the jets for more fuel and take the burner elements off one stove, stacking them on top of each other, attempting to get more flame on the second stove. Then we spent hours out in Joe's yard or my garage back in town, timing how long it took to reduce a bucket of snow to a bucket of boiling water with each variation. It was lucky we didn't blow ourselves up.

Eventually, Gene Leonard invented an alcohol stove that all Iditarod stoves are modeled after today. Gene was my buddy at Finger Lake near the entrance to Rainy Pass. We had suffered so much frustration with the Coleman stove idea that Gene began experimenting at his Finger Lake home. He'd seen alcohol used for everything from fondue pots to small army stoves, and an idea was born. Why it didn't occur to the rest of us, I don't know. Anyway, Gene put a roll of toilet paper in the bottom of a bucket, poured a couple of inches of alcohol in and set it ablaze. He then set his cook pot down into the bucket, resting the handles on the topsides of the bucket. The rest was history. The alcohol provided a lot more heat and the bucket formed a heat jacket around the pot, and it was cheaper. We traded two $30 Coleman stoves for one $6 metal paint bucket. Here's to Gene Leonard!

Headlights were another matter. We fiddled endlessly with our headlights, altering the reflectors, experimenting with dozens of different bulbs, altering the battery boxes, changing to Arctic-grade wire so the insulation wouldn't break in the cold. We would connect a couple of battery boxes together so we had eight D-cell batteries instead of only four to get more volts and more life out of our system. I only took the two-box idea to a race once and then junked it because of the added weight on my belt. Joe, however, continued to like that arrangement.

He had to wear suspenders just to hold all those batteries up so they didn't pull his pants down.

Lithium cells became the rage. There is nothing worse than racing along on a moonless night on a poorly marked trail, dead tired, when your headlight is so dim you can hardly see your wheel dogs, much less your leaders. I'm sure Joe and I weren't the only guys tinkering with our headlights, so God bless all those other guys who helped and came up with the lights we use today.

One night when we were visiting, I asked Joe why he came all the way to Petersville to train when his home in Knik was virtually on the Iditarod Trail. He replied there were a number of reasons that made sense from a training point of view. Petersville was known for its huge dumps of snow so there was never a shortage of snow like there was almost anywhere else. We had our choice of hills or flats to run on, depending on what we were trying to accomplish at a given time. There were high winds and open spaces, which helped a lot when we reached the coast. And there just wasn't a lot of traffic except for snowmachiners on the weekends.

Aside from that, he had to train away from home to get away from the distractions. Everybody and his brother stopped by at Knik to see the Father of the Iditarod, so it was difficult to get anything done. Joe didn't know how to say no, so people he hardly knew would trap him for hours.

Although Joe was a master mechanic, his mind was on dogs. His wife, Vi, was a resourceful woman and could be counted on to keep things running at home while Joe was gone. But if he were at home, he'd have to fix everything that went wrong. This might include anything from faulty wiring to a frozen pipe. He said he didn't even like to call home when he was in heavy training because of what he might learn. It just gave him more to worry about.

Joe told me that he had called home once and a man had answered the phone. Joe asked, "Who the hell is this?"

The guy responded, "This is Bill." Joe wanted to know what the hell he was doing there.

Bill responded that he was there to fix the furnace.

Joe asked where Vi was.

Bill said she was in the bedroom with Frank. Joe wanted to know who the hell Frank was.

Bill said Frank was trying to fix a water heater pipe in the bedroom that had broken when the furnace went out.

Joe told Bill to tell Vi to pick up the phone in the bedroom.

Bill hollered into the bedroom and a man answered the phone.

Burt and Raymie Redington entered many of the same races and always had fun. Raymie was tenacious on the trail and demanded everything his dogs could give him. Even after his last Iditarod, he is always there to support his sons, Ray, Jr. and Ryan, who carry on the family tradition.

Joe wanted to know who in hell THIS was.

The guy responded, "Frank."

Joe yelled, "Well, where in the hell is Vi?"

"In the shower with George."

"WHO IN THE HELL IS GEORGE AND WHAT IS HE DOING IN THE SHOWER WITH VI?!"

"He's my partner. They're trying to fix a broken water pipe in the shower that froze and broke when the furnace went out."

With that, Joe muttered, "Just tell her I called," and hung up. He was careful about calling home after that.

After an hour or two of visiting or experimenting, I'd head on back to my cabin. Many times, I would no more than lay my head on the pillow and I would hear the dogs bark. Checking out the window to see what was up, I would see a headlight moving steadily along the lake trail to the south. It was Joe making a late night run.

I treasure the hours spent with Joe and the miles of trail we traveled together, and I still haven't come to grips with his untimely death in the summer of '99. Yes, it was untimely to me even though he was eighty-two. I visit his son, Raymie, and wife, Barb, frequently at Knik, but there's definitely an empty spot at Petersville without him.

The dogs loved to run at night and so did I. It was cooler and the dogs just naturally picked up the pace. Between a few night runs, I took a day, went to town and bought two trophies for the big Forks race. And I decided to buy a big Alpine snowmachine after all these years. With my bad back, wrestling my smaller machine around was killing me. Jerking any stuck snowmachine out of deep snow was more than I really wanted to handle. An Alpine is a big double-track machine with lots of power and lots of flotation for packing trails in deep snow. The only problem is that if you did get one stuck, you'd be there for a while getting it unstuck. Standard gear included a shovel, a come-along, and car bumper jack.

We made a few more short night runs on fast trails. We put booties on the dogs most every night to protect their feet from those pesky ice balls.

Then one evening, Leeda and Timber balked going out of the chute, causing the swing dogs to run over them. This earned them both a good swat, since leaders just couldn't be pulling that stuff. We headed south in the direction of the forty-mile turnaround. As we journeyed south, we were about to mush past a small hill located twelve miles out that we sometimes used as a turnaround to get headed back home. We called it the twenty-five-mile turnaround since down there and back gave us close to a twenty-five-mile run. As we neared the turn-off, Leeda tried to head around the hill rather than continue on to the forty-mile turnaround. She was apparently fed up with the training and decided to take things into her own paws again. This also earned her a swat and a good cussing out, after which she picked up the pace and gave us an excellent run.

When we got home and began unhitching the dogs, Sambo yelped when I touched him. Actually, I thought he yelped just before I touched him. An examination turned up no sign of any injury or even stiffness, so he might just have been nervous after watching Tiger and Leeda catch heck. He had a doormat personality, which is hard for me to stomach from a sled dog. We liked to have them eager and aggressive. A mutt that just naturally slinked and flinched when you raised your voice, and cried before he was hurt, didn't earn a lot of respect. Other than that, the team was outstanding.

Thursday, December 13, was to be our last run before the big race at the Forks. We started first thing in the morning for what was intended to be a short, happy run. The dogs set a nice pace and we were heading back home when we passed Mark coming toward us head-on. Tiger and Dancer tried to turn around and follow Mark back to the cabin and got into a fight in the process. While I was breaking up their fight, Ivor, a male, got back to Sonic, a female, who was hitched with Leeda because she was in heat. In a flash, Ivor connected with Sonic. It was double trouble. It took them forty minutes to disconnect and I didn't need a pregnant race dog.

Long after they parked their dog sleds for the last time, Burt and Norm loved to get together and reminisce. Here they meet in the Iditarod holding area on 4th Avenue in Anchorage

It was a dismal experience for the last run before the big race.

Thursday afternoon we cranked up the snowmachines and tried to break out the race trail for the second time. We had trouble finding the trail in the higher country where it crossed long open stretches, so I asked Joe Duhl to help us. He'd operated the Roadhouse so long that he knew the country like the back of his hand. When Joe came along, he found the trail so overgrown with alders that he couldn't find it either. Later on, the snow would get deep enough that it would cover most of the alders, making travel a lot easier.

I needed to head for town, so Mark and Joe gave it another try on Friday and got the job done by traversing the trail backwards. Why this helped, I'm not sure except that when you're in heavy brush, it sometimes helps to look at things from a different angle.

We awoke at the crack of dawn on Sunday, December 16, 1984. It was race day! We entered two teams with me driving one and Mark driving the other. I had to promise to let Nina enter the upcoming Knik 200 race or she would have taken Mark's team away from him. That Norwegian was one competitive young lady.

A number of good friends showed up for the race. Shannon Pool, the daughter-in-law of Joe and Vera, came up from Trapper Creek. A good pal, Shannon often mushed her team up to our cabin and joined us for dinner. We always liked company, so it was a special treat when she stopped by. The handlers would throw on their coats and run out to tether her team and give the dogs a snack. When company stopped by, we tried to fix something special. Then we'd all have a good visit and get caught up on all the latest gossip. After dinner, Shannon would put on her boots, string out her dogs and disappear into the darkness.

Lavon and his son, Lance, came up from Wasilla to race. Lavon ran a print shop and sat on the Iditarod Trail Committee along with Joe Sr. and me and several others. His son Lance helped him in the print shop and was a top Junior Iditarod racer. They each planned to enter a team.

Raymie Redington, Joe Sr.'s youngest son, came up from Knik. Raymie had been a pal of mine since we met in Anchorage in the late 1960s. My handler Mark rounded out the field. Raymie and Lavon were both top Iditarod contenders, so it would be a good test of our teams. We'd have liked to have more teams enter, but this was a local race and six was enough to have a great time. All were good friends whom I see a lot of to this day.

My leaders were Noise and Ivor. I bought Noise from Rick Swenson when he was about six months old. Rick promised me he'd make a nice leader and he was right. Noise became a flawless gee-haw leader. Ivor came from Susan Butcher's yard. He was one fast dog. Until he knew who was boss, he would test my resolve by deliberately trying to take the shortest route home or by taking a wrong command. No problem. He was an asset to the team and helped a lot. You just couldn't trust him to get you home safely in a blinding snowstorm because you never knew when he'd decide to do things his own way.

Dancer and Timber were in swing. Dancer was a little like Ivor for being bull-headed. Again, this was not a serious problem. When I could see where we were going, he'd usually do what I told him. Snowstorms with poor visibility were another story. Timber came from Joe Redington's yard. When I bought him, Joe told me he was the most beautiful husky in his yard. No doubt about it, Timber was beautiful. He was a good leader, too, and was excellent in swing because he always followed the dog ahead of him. This was important for swing dogs because the leaders need all the support they can get. You want swing dogs that will help pull the team along where the leaders want them to go, so the leaders only have to worry about leading.

Leeda, Sonic, Sambo, Lil, Fuzz, and Tiger filled in behind them. All had their own stories and reminded me a lot of a class of kindergartners. Bill and Stinker rounded out the team in wheel, just ahead of the sled. I really didn't want Stinker that close to me, but he was a big dog, so he could handle the heavy sled behind him. I would just have to endure Stinker's unholy gas problem. Bill was in wheel so I could deal with him more easily when he goofed up.

I felt bad not having Puddin in lead. She was such a sweet little leader that every run was more fun if she was along. She had developed a slight limp on our last run, so I didn't dare take a chance of aggravating it on fifty miles of fast, rough trail.

Mark drove the other dogs from my racing team. Charger and Jade were his leaders with Fawcett, Jewel, Felix, Daiquiri, Sonny, Wayne, and Kelly rounding out his team. Mark was at a disadvantage in this race. Everyone wanted to do their best, but Mark had strict orders not to push it. I couldn't take a chance on him pushing the dogs too hard because of his inexperience and the resulting possibility that he might hurt one of the dogs. Also, I didn't want him in a race situation with Wayne in his team. Too much aggression so better to be behind all the other teams.

We booted all the dogs because of the strong possibility of poor trail. All the conditions were right for a punchy trail and for the dogs to develop snowballs between their toes.

Burt modified five Coleman stoves in different configurations, one year, and then tested them in his garage to see which could boil water faster. The buckets were taken out and filled with snow from the plowed snow at the side of the street. Whichever stove first reduced a bucket of snow to a bucket of boiling water won the contest and got to go along on the race.

We started out number three. The race marshal counted us down and we burst from the chute, heading north toward Petersville. The dogs set a nice pace. They naturally wanted to lope because of the excitement of the strange dogs and all the strange people. They had plenty of energy because we'd rested them for several days before the race. I dragged my heels for a while to slow the dogs down a bit until they settled into a nice quick trot. After a couple of miles, Tiger began limping. Where that came from, I have no idea, but Tiger was too valuable to run fifty miles on an injury. I loaded him into the sled and continued. It didn't occur to me to turn around and head back. I thought we might still do okay and at least we weren't hurting anything. I knew I would have to work a lot harder on the uphill sections to make up for his added weight and probably wouldn't do that well carrying an extra fifty pounds of dog in the sled.

The race was to be a tad over fifty miles long. We continued north along a trail that made this one of the most interesting and challenging fifty-mile races I'd ever entered. We continued towards the gold camps at Petersville, eleven miles away, located right at the beginnings of gold country. An active mine still existed there and we passed a white frame house that went back to the early days of mining in this area. The house sat on the ridge above Peters Creek and held a commanding view of the placer digs along the gravel bars far below.

From there we traversed a narrow ledge along a cliff several hundred feet high above Peters Creek. In summer, the trail was wide enough to drive a car on, but now, when the winter snows were deep, and drifted, it was but a sled width wide and sloped eerily downward toward the edge. One couldn't help but suck it up a bit. You didn't want your sled to slip off this icy narrow perch. There was nothing to grab if the sled slid off.

The team and I then crossed some high, open country. A brisk south wind blew wisps of loose snow along with the team. I passed the team ahead of me so that Raymie and I began sharing the lead. We traveled together for a while, first one in lead and then the other. We still had miles to go, so we preferred to cooperate by trading lead to help keep our leaders happy. I was ahead of Raymie when Noise and Ivor suddenly took us down a steep plunging descent into Cache Creek in the heart of the old Cache Creek Mining District. We wound our way along the creek bottom, first on one side, then the other, crossing ice bridges above the rushing creek.

For some reason Ivor's tug was slack. I wasn't sure if he was slower than the rest of the dogs or if he just wasn't himself. Maybe it was the excitement of race day. In any case, I didn't need him in lead slowing things down. I stopped to move him back and put Timber in lead. The dogs immediately picked up the pace and held it. We continued to glide along and saw several groups of moose lying up in the willows. We were always glad to see them off to the side rather than on the trail, where they were likely to challenge the dogs. We were all armed but just didn't need the drama, especially during a race.

After several miles, we saw the picturesque mining camp at the mouth of Spruce Creek and began the long steep grind up Spruce Creek Canyon. We'd been doing well until now and it looked like we might have a chance for a good finish, but the weight of Tiger in the sled was a serious handicap grinding up this steep canyon. I stopped the dogs and quickly hitched Tiger back in the traces. While I switched dogs, Raymie pulled around us and out of sight going up the hill. I had hopes of catching him as we crested the hill but needed to be careful to keep the race in perspective. Any time we raced, the adrenaline started to flow, but these preliminary events were still just training runs for the main event that was Iditarod.

As soon as we reached the top, I put Tiger back in the sled and gave him a free ride home. By now, Raymie was nowhere in sight. He was seasoned and lightweight, built like a jockey, and was an outstanding competitor. Raymie had grown up in the bush out at Flathorn Lake, which was just across Knik Arm from Anchorage but way off the road system. It might as well have been deep in the Alaska wilderness. Raymie's dad, Joe Sr., raised the boys on a subsistence lifestyle with trapping, hunting, fishing, and dog mushing as a way of life. Raymie was as authentic an Alaskan as any sourdough that may have lived here a hundred years ago, and every bit as interesting. We still visit Raymie and his wife, Barb, every chance we get.

From the head of Spruce Creek, we traversed the saddle between the main range that was the Peters Hills and Little Peters Hills. As we mushed along the open country on top, we picked up the trail of a small wolf pack. The tracks paralleled the race trail for several miles. Tracks left a record of the wolves' activity as clear as any newspaper. Always hunting, the wolves veered off the trail to follow a fresh moose track but soon returned. Then we found a loose pile of white feathers with a few spatters of fresh blood on the snow. A ptarmigan hadn't been quick enough to escape from under a low berry bush. Eventually, the tracks headed off to the north into the shallow valley where Black Creek meandered alternately through swamps and alder patches.

Our trail dropped quickly along the ridge south of Black Creek to the finish line at the roadhouse on the banks of Peters Creek. I did manage to catch Raymie but couldn't get past him. No one else caught me so I finished second, even with Tiger in my sled most of the way. What an interesting drive through history that was. If you believe in ghosts, this was a heck of a trip. We enjoyed one of those rare magic moments that I'd dreamed of for years, where I managed to live my dream of mushing a dog team through Alaska and its historic backcountry. I again felt alive with the ghosts of sourdoughs, trappers, hunters, gold miners, and Alaska's Native people.

Joe Sr. loved to tinker with equipment. There's no telling how many stoves he rebuilt and experimented with. His work area was full of projects from the sled propped up and ready for new runners to the old refrigerator he'd turned into a smokehouse. The camper trailers housed handlers and stored "good stuff." These Coleman stoves went away when Gene Leonard came up with the alcohol stove that was much simpler and cheaper. It consisted of a five gallon metal paint bucket with a roll of toilet paper in the bottom to serve as a wick. Alcohol was poured in and lit, and the smaller bucket of snow set inside.

That Forks Roadhouse race was a lot of fun, but things don't always run smoothly in a dog team. Lil never pulled during the entire race. Leeda didn't begin to pull until we started up the steep grade out of Cache Creek. All the other dogs did well except that Ivor wasn't sharp.

When you were racing with Raymie, you always had a good time, even if he beat you. He had a wry sense of humor that left me in stitches. He always showed up with a hot team, especially for the middle-distance races and was always at the front of the pack. Raymie liked to push his dogs along and you could often hear him coming up behind you because he talked to his dogs so much. His language was salty enough to turn the air blue.

Shannon finished right behind me. She and I entered many of the same races and always seemed to finish next to each other or, at least, close. I won occasionally, like today, but Shannon probably won more often. Lance, Lavon, and finally, Mark, followed us across the finish line.

Chapter Eleven
Don's Iditarod 200, 1984

After the Forks Roadhouse race, we all felt tired and lazy—the dogs, the handlers and I. There had been a lot to deal with in getting ready for that first race of the season. We'd had to rummage for mandatory gear items that hadn't seen the light of day since the last Iditarod. I hated leaving things to the last minute, so sleds had to be packed several days in advance. There was nothing worse than entering a race exhausted because you had been up all night trying to find some item you hadn't seen in a year and couldn't do without. After all the preparation, the race, and the excitement afterward at the banquet, we were tired. So we took a couple of days off to rest and to allow any pains and strains to heal. When we all felt good and rested, we ran ten miles on a fast trail to the south. The dogs were healthy and eager.

On Thursday, December 20, my daughter, Jill, brought a friend, Deana, home from college and brought her out to our training camp. Jill was an extremely athletic woman and had been an all-American swimmer while attending Dimond High School in Anchorage. Like all our kids, she loved the outdoors and grew up on a diet of hiking, camping trips, hunting, skiing, fishing, dog teams and airplanes. It was always a delight to see her.

Deana was new to the north country, so we spent the rest of the afternoon showing her the dogs and our camp. That evening we regaled her with stories of Alaska and life on the trail. We dug out some spare insulated clothing to be sure she'd be comfortable and safe the next day, and then we all hit the sack.

The next morning, we packed a picnic lunch and headed for the hills with my dog handlers, Nina Hotvedt and Mark, each driving a team. Jill was in my sled,

Deana in Mark's, and the picnic lunch was in Nina's sled. We drove the teams to a favorite spot out of the wind at the headwaters of Spruce Creek and parked the teams. The scene could have been out of a Robert Service poem, with dog teams resting quietly in the trees. We built a roaring fire and enjoyed a picnic lunch under the towering majesty of Mount McKinley. The entire Alaska Range occupied the horizon to the north, west, and south. We had a wonderful visit while basking in the fire's warm glow.

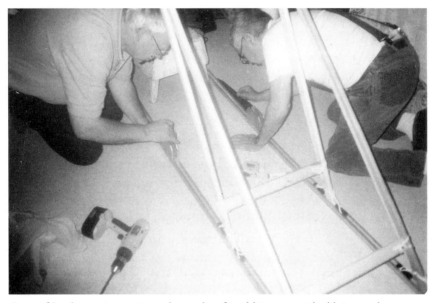

Some of Burt's most interesting and rewarding friendships were with old timers who were so important in bringing a flavor and personality that was truly Alaskan. Jerry Riley taught Burt the art of building a toboggan sled at Jerry's home in Nenana.

After a couple of hours, relishing our own private little patch of Alaska, we reluctantly loaded passengers and gear and drove the teams back along the route we'd come out on. Our journey out had been slow, uphill over the unbroken trail, but the return trip was brisk and fun. Any time the dogs went out slow and returned fast, it could be a sign that they were somewhat reluctant to leave their nice straw beds, and that they might be a little burned out. Even with the easier homeward trail, the quick trip home told us that they were physically all right but maybe a little tired mentally.

While the handlers and the girls put the dogs up and fed them, I once again prepared my favorite dinner for company. Our tales of the great bush Alaska had far more meaning for Deana this night after experiencing Alaska firsthand by dog sled into the wilderness.

We retraced our steps the next day with the whole gang in the sleds and then gave the dogs a day off while we caught up on chores around the cabin. We ran the generator to recharge the batteries for the twelve-volt system and fill the water pressure tank. Those two things gave us most of the comforts of home with lights at the flick of a switch, and running water.

That evening we hitched the teams and drove the girls ten miles to the parking lot, so they could make the three-and-a-half-hour drive back to our home in Anchorage.

On December 23, we awoke to a stiff, cold breeze out of the north. We looked for these days because they gave us a chance to drive the dogs into the biting wind. This would test the dogs' mettle and be good training for the windy conditions we were sure to find out on the west coast of Alaska during the Iditarod race. We left late in the day so that much of the run would be after dark. The trail I chose was the same one we had followed during the Forks Roadhouse race. We had decided to make it a night run to make it especially difficult with the blowing snow.

We left the yard and headed north towards Petersville, directly into the bitter north wind. By taking this route, we would have the steep climb out of Cache Creek on the way home and would have to cross the saddle between Peters Hills and Little Peters Hills on the last leg. A strong north wind at the cabin and the trail north from the Forks would translate into a grueling, blinding ground blizzard for about six miles through the saddle as we returned home. We all needed the practice, both mushers and dogs. I particularly needed to know what my leaders would do under difficult conditions. When the blizzard was so bad that I couldn't see anything, and the dogs weren't having any fun, they might decide to take things into their own hands. A dangerous situation could result so I needed to know if I could trust them to do the right thing and get us to our destination. You could trust some dogs with your life under horrendous conditions. Other dogs couldn't be trusted and could take a team from a bad situation into a deadly one in a heartbeat. We wanted to find these things out close to home, not out in the middle of the wilderness in a howling blizzard.

I'd put Dancer and Noise in lead with Ivor, Timber, Puddin, Sonic, Tiger, Fuzz, Koyuk, Suxie, Bill and Stinker behind them in the team. I was still putting Puddin back in the team most of the time, as I wanted to bring her along slowly as a leader. Mark would follow me with Nina behind him.

It was a formidable run. We drove into a fierce wind with blowing snow right from the start heading north towards Petersville. The trail was partially blown in making especially rough going for the leaders, who had to break trail for the rest of the team in the fresh snow. As we made our way along the cliff north of Petersville, the swirling snow became thick because of the wind gusting down over the cliff above us. The light from our headlights reflected off the driven snow, making everything look opaque and featureless. The trail was nearly impossible to see and the wind had blown the trail almost completely away. We could only guess how far the fall would be for anyone whose sled slid off the trail. Once here, there was no way to turn the dogs back on the narrow treacherous trail. We were committed.

It became even more difficult as we made our way across the Peters Creek Bridge and began working our way up into open country before the drop into Cache Creek. The leaders, of course, knew the way from their experience earlier during the race. The question was whether they would do the right thing when they figured out that I really had no control because of the lack of visibility. It was then that they might decide they'd had enough and turn downwind away from the unpleasant blinding snow. If they pulled that trick in these conditions, it wouldn't take much to get us hopelessly lost. Also, the drop into the creek bottom along here was too steep to negotiate safely, even when we could see.

We continued across open alpine tundra and, before long, we were hurtling down the steep hill into Spruce Creek. So far Dancer and Noise were right on track, but the worst was yet to come. No matter how bad it was heading north toward Peters Creek, it would be much worse mushing across the saddle in the hills on the way home.

We continued down Cache Creek without incident, crossing and re-crossing the creek, sometimes on ice bridges and sometimes splashing through the creek itself, all good training for the difficulties we would encounter during the Iditarod race. It was much easier to see here out of the wind. It actually wasn't snowing too hard down here, which meant that most of the blowing snow was the result of a ground blizzard, just snow that had already fallen and was being blown along the surface.

We were still doing well as we proceeded up the steep hill along Spruce Creek; however, once on top, we were again picking up a strong wind. The trail was generally southerly after it first topped out so the wind was at our back. The gusts pushed the sled so strongly from behind that, at times, it forced the sled almost into the dogs.

As we approached the saddle, we began to veer to the east and started catching a strong quartering crosswind from our left. Then the wind suddenly caught us with all its force, pushing the sled sideways almost off the trail. We were all wearing heavy winter gear, including beaver mitts, goggles and heavy parkas. Even then, the cold seeped through. All my faith was in my leaders. Visibility was zero and I hadn't a clue where the trail was. The ground blizzard reflected the beam from my headlight, literally blinding me. I could actually see better without the light on. When I looked south, I could see the glow of the lights of Anchorage one hundred miles to the south, but the furiously driven snow totally obliterated the trail.

When winter came, the dogs were already in great shape and their feet were incredibly tough from the gravel. Jeff Prawley stops to rest the dogs north of Kahiltna. Jeff had been a competitive junior musher and still had the competitive spirit.

I was beginning to see a struggle developing between my leaders, with Dancer pulling off to the south away from the wind, while Noise seemed to want to go ahead. The fact that the two were acting at cross-purposes was not good. One of them was right and the other wrong and I couldn't tell which. Dancer won and the team veered off to the south, downwind and downhill. I had no choice but to hang on and hope he was right. Suddenly a patch of alders appeared in front of us and Dancer dove right into the middle of it. The wrong leader had won. Noise, bless his heart, had known what was right, but he had been overpowered

213

by his larger teammate. I plowed after Dancer into that alder patch and strongly reminded him that his maneuver was more than wrong; it could easily have placed us in a life-threatening situation.

For now, this wasn't really dangerous; we could just hunker down and wait for daylight if we had to. Then I could find the way back to the trail. But the point of training is to develop skills necessary to sort out these situations when far from home during race conditions when you needed to keep moving forward. So I untangled the dogs and started leading them on foot back into the wind in the direction I knew the trail to be. The wind was directly out of the north so I could keep my bearings by heading into it. That allowed me to keep my eyes on the ground searching for the trail. I hoped to find it without going across it or before my handlers came along and followed Dancer's path into nowhere. Then we'd all be lost.

Some of the trail followed old seismic trails cleared during oil exploration and mining activity. Here we take a moment to check the dogs' feet to see if they should be booted up.

As I trudged into the cold, harsh wind, I glanced up and saw a faint glimmer of a headlight passing by from left to right. It had to be Mark with his leaders Charger and Jade following the race trail and ignoring the scent of Dancer's detour. What a break! I ran back to the sled and commanded the dogs forward. Never taking my eyes off Mark's headlight, I was able to guide the dogs back to the trail from where we easily made our way home. Not a really fun night but definitely an education. I knew then that I would never be able to trust Dancer when the chips were down.

As we entered the yard, I noticed that Koyuk had a slight limp. That, coupled with Dancer's attempt to duck out, showed that I'd probably been pushing the dogs a little too hard. Dogs were no different from any other athletes. Top athletes need to train hard, of course, but if you train too hard, stress injuries and stress ailments occur because fatigue destroys agility and lowers resistance. This puts the athlete temporarily out of action, so training time is lost and the whole program suffers. Better not to let it happen in the first place. When symptoms begin to show, it is good to just back off. I wrote a note to myself in my diary that evening that said, "Back off! I mean it!"

It was the Christmas season so the timing was perfect. We let the dogs have a five-day break over Christmas while we took one ourselves. I headed home to be with my family and left Mark and Nina to spend Christmas with the gang at Petersville. Petersville in those days was a close-knit community of interesting Alaskans. Mark and Nina would have a great time.

I've always loved my Alaskan city friends because of the "can do" spirit and the excitement most seem to have by just being here. But out here in the hills south of Mount McKinley, the characters were true and authentic old-time Alaskans. The road was plowed to within about fifteen miles of the cabin, so we were isolated through much of the winter. Even most villages have regular air service and a general store. We had none of that. The troopers were hours away if we needed help and could even get a message to them. Fire protection was a distant memory of another life. One had to be self-sufficient to love this life the way we did.

As I made my way back to Christmas in Anchorage, I reflected on what great friends these neighbors were. At the top of the list, my all-time favorites were Joe Redington Sr. and Norman Vaughan. Norm had dropped out of Harvard at eighteen to be Admiral Byrd's chief dog handler on his expedition to the South Pole in 1926. A couple of years later, I would sell this cabin to Norm and his wife, Carolyn, and I would build a new one next door. We lived across the meadow from each other for years, where I could see the warm glow of the cabin window in the evening.

The cabin deal with Norm and Carolyn began like this. I was lying in bed in the cabin reading my book by the light of a gas lamp. It was during December 1986. At about midnight, the dogs barked indicating a visitor. It could have been a moose, wolves, a stray dog from the neighbors or a friend. I arose, opened the door and flashed my spotlight into the darkness. The eyes of a dog team reflected in the powerful beam when Norm's booming voice rang out. "Burt, it's Norman Vaughan and we can only stay thirty minutes!"

Translated from the language of the Alaska Bush into plain English he really meant: "It's Norman. I'm not alone. I'm not going to violate protocol by asking for a place to stay on such short notice, but what the hell. It's midnight and there's no way Burt will throw us out in thirty minutes without feeding us this time of night in the cold of an Alaska winter."

I responded, "Norm, come on in. We'll put the coffee pot on."

Translated into plain English this meant: "We're super glad to see you. We've got plenty of room for you and your pals. You couldn't possible have eaten so we'll put the feed bag on and we're looking forward to some good conversation, and I'll have the handlers put your dogs up while you come in and get warm. And what is this BS about thirty minutes—you can't get your boots off and on in thirty minutes."

Norm, along with Carolyn Muegge and a reporter from Yankee Magazine, stomped the snow off their boots and came on in. I fixed leftovers from dinner that evening, and we visited for hours. Carolyn Muegge, Norm's friend, was an adventurous woman from Atlanta. Of course, they stayed the night. We visited until the wee hours of the morning, all of us hanging on Norm's every word. Seasoned, crusty coot that he was, Norm slept out in a snow-bank, as did Carolyn, while the writer from back east was happy to bunk in the loft. I was privileged to perform Norm and Carolyn's wedding ceremony on New Year's Day, 1987, and they later bought the cabin.

The stories I heard from Joe and Norm over the years were priceless. What lives they'd lived.

Those two along with my dad were my greatest inspiration. All shared the same credo—no matter your age, keep doing just what you want to do as though age and health are not factors. Even if you occasionally fail, your life will be a whole lot more fulfilled and you will probably live a heck of a lot longer. *Dream as if you'll live forever—live as if you'll die today!* It seemed to work. My dad lived to be a hundred and two, and several newspapers in Iowa still published his column after he was a hundred. Norm lived to be a hundred, and climbed Mount Vaughan in Antarctica when he was nearly ninety. Even with cancer, Joe was still planning his next Iditarod when he died at eighty-two.

It brings a smile to my face every time I think of those guys. Before Norm found Carolyn, he and Jan Masek had been pals for years. They were both single and had no one to worry about but themselves. They reminded me of a couple of college kids who were full of adventure. They both had endured plenty of

216

responsibility and hard work in the past and were now free to enjoy this great Alaskan adventure. Both had worked with horses and dogs all their lives and loved it.

The wedding of Col. Norman Vaughan to Carolyn Muegge was the social event of the season at the Forks Roadhouse in the Peters Hills country south of Mount McKinley. Burt officiated at the wedding with guests coming from near and far by dog team, snowmachine, helicopter, airplane, and snowshoes. Lt. to Rt.: Skip Winfrey, Best Man; Norman; Erik Muegge, Carolyn's son; Carolyn; Judy Jacobson, the Brides Maid; and Burt.

I recalled going up the hillside east of Anchorage to see Jan Masek about something one afternoon in the summer of 1983, and found him with Norm exercising their dogs. They had borrowed a horse walker from Diamond H horse ranch. It looked like a merry-go-round and was designed to lead horses in a circle. I'd seen horses exercised this way but never dogs.

Jan explained that his family had used horse walkers in Prague to exercise their competitive horses and Norm had used the same rig to train his polo ponies back in Massachusetts. They figured it would work just as well for their racing dogs during the off-season. That sounded good to me, so when they were done with it, I bought the rig from Diamond H and used it to exercise my dogs until I dropped out of mushing.

Joe Redington had let me keep my dogs at his yard in Knik during the off-season in the 1980s, so I wouldn't have to drive clear to Petersville to care for them. He pointed out an area in his lower yard and told me to make myself at home. I hired a dozer to clear and level off a spot and had Matanuska Electric bring in power. I moved the training wheel there and wired it up. I had a small camper trailer that I also moved there and hooked up to power. I would hitch the dogs to the training wheel most every evening and then sit in my little camper. I'd read my book and drink tea as the dogs racked up the miles going in a circle.

Carolyn, the glowing bride ready to toss the bridal bouquet. The surrounding trees were fading from view in the falling snow, while fur coats and Carharts were the dress code of the day.

Occasionally, mushing pals, some well known, would stop by and tease me about my dog "carnival ride" and the fact that you couldn't train sled dogs to pull a sled without hitching them to a sled. I'd explain that I didn't want the dogs to mistake this for pulling a sled. This was just exercise. Marathoners run long slow miles in the off-season to keep their muscles toned and their hearts and lungs strong. That is what this does. It's not intended to train them to race—it's intended to keep them fit. Besides, if you run them fast, you'll wear out their pads. The idea is to get the job done while making it seem like play. For them it's play. When the dogs see me crank up the wheel and begin hooking dogs up, the whole yard goes nuts.

Later, when I set a record winning the 1988 Knik International 200 Sled Dog Race, I credited all those off season miles on the horse walker for keeping the dogs fit all summer.

One evening as I sat in my camper reading *Gold, Men and Dogs*, a book by famed Nome Sweepstakes musher Scotty Allan, I read the following passage:[1]

> Another good plan [for exercising racing sled dogs] is to erect a "Russian merry-go-round" with four or more arms, to each of which a dog is chained. This will give them all the exercise they want. If there are more than two dogs, it very often happens (especially with the young ones) that they never all want to lie down at the same time. It is very amusing to watch them jerk the lazy one to his feet and start pulling him around when he does not want to go. The more he pulls back and growls, the more the others seem to delight in keeping him on the jump.

The three-tiered wedding cake and bouquets of beautiful flowers were all brought in by dog team. They made a beautiful picture against the ancient log walls of the old roadhouse.

Before then, I believed that this was the first time anyone had ever used this method to exercise sled dogs in Alaska. Now I saw there was nothing new about the idea at all, but Jan and Norm were the first mushers I knew of to use it lately. I learned later that they use these devices to train racing greyhounds in the Lower 48, so I just wasn't that informed. Things have progressed and many mushers use

---

[1] <u>Gold, Men and Dogs</u>, A. A. (Scotty) Allan, 1931, G. P. Putnam's Sons, New York, Page 277

various exercise devices now. These include not only exercise wheels but squirrel cages and treadmills.

I returned after Christmas and we began training again on December 26 with a short, brisk ten-mile run. Koyuk was still limping so we left him home. I put Puddin in lead. What a wonderful little dog. She weighed about forty-five pounds and seemed a bit fragile. I would have to pay especially close attention to her conditioning to be sure she was as hardy as possible. She did great, as did the rest of the team.

Norman Vaughan greeting wedding guests. Norm, the seasoned explorer, and his guests hardly noticed the snow and cold of Alaska winter at the Forks. He charmed all in attendance. Like other early explorers, the Colonel was equally at home in the quiet solitude of the most remote wilderness and in the midst of a crowd, whether it was here or on the dais in the banquet hall at the Explorers Club in New York City.

We ran twenty-five miles with short teams on December 27. The trail was hard and fast. I put Dancer in single lead to place him where he was completely responsible. The point was to give him practice in lead where the trail was clear. I wanted to minimize the bad experience from the other night and put it behind us. Dancer did well, as he always did when he knew I was in control. The short team would be easy to stop and hook down, and Dancer knew it.

Puddin was put back in the team to continue her easy orientation program. She had diarrhea, possibly from the rigorous training earlier. Everyone else did fine and all appeared eager. I hoped that the slump was behind us. The dogs collected many snowballs between their toes, always an irritation. Dancer stayed out front and followed commands flawlessly. I still was optimistic for him as a leader when no danger threatened but continued to have a nagging worry about what he might do when the chips were down and I needed him to do the right thing.

Burt's Kahiltna dog camp was remote, making it impossible to train dogs during the summer while working in town. Joe kindly gave Burt an area below his dog yard at Knik so he could still train the dogs all summer. Burt moved right in, bringing his dogs, his training wheel, and a small camper to make a comfortable camp closer to home. Joe would often stop by to visit Burt and enjoy a cup of tea with honey while the dogs made endless circles on the training wheel.

Dogs like Dancer, who had a tendency to let you down when you needed them most, reminded me of a couple of alcoholics who had worked for me years earlier. They would do an excellent job most of the time, but when the going was tough and discouraging, and you really needed them, that is when they'd let you down.

We ran ten fast miles on December 28, with all the dogs happy. Koyuk was still limping, so we continued to leave him home and give him rest and relaxation in his doghouse. He had a nice straw bed and got many ear rubs. Koyuk was a beautiful sled dog, but years later, it dawned on me that Koyuk had never made it all the way to Nome during Iditarod, even with all the trouble we went to during training. He always came up lame about halfway there.

We ran twenty-five miles south on December 29. It was snowing lightly, the temperature was fifteen degrees and the dogs picked up lots of ice balls. Puddin still had mild diarrhea during the run. I didn't know if it was stress or a bug, but I always considered it a symptom that it was time to back off a little, at least where she was concerned. We would make a short run in the morning and then lay off for the 200-mile race the following week.

That night it snowed heavily. We got up and mushed the ten-mile trail we had scheduled to be the last run before the big race next week. That run could only be described as s-l-o-w. Three and a half hours to go ten miles. We took many rest breaks in the deep snow so as not to exhaust the dogs. Tired was okay; exhausted was not.

Don's Iditarod 200 Sled Dog Race had been scheduled for January 6 and 7 but was canceled due to the heavy snow and poor trail conditions. This was especially disappointing because I'd finished second in the 1984 Knik 200 the year before, with my handler finishing third, both of us behind Harry Sutherland. This was the same race that had been renamed for this year's sponsor, Don's Iditarod Café in Wasilla. Most any sled dog race is fun; that's why we do them. But that Knik 200 was more fun than most, largely because we did well. Two teams from the same kennel taking second and third in a major middle-distance race is something to be proud of.

I'd told Jeff, my handler, that I was going to be racing, but he wasn't. For him it would be a training run. This was much the same thing I always told my handlers. I hadn't wanted them causing any injuries or finishing with bummed-out dogs because they ran them too hard. I'd been especially emphatic with Jeff, because he was young and had been a Junior Iditarod musher. He was at an age when he felt competitive and thought he knew everything. If you've ever had teenage children, you'll know what I mean.

Sometimes when Jeff became especially aggressive during a training run, I'd give him a subtle lesson. I usually had him follow me, so I'd be first to encounter any trail problems such as a moose on the trail. We normally set a pace that was quick but reasonable so he could stay with me. That way, I knew what he was doing. When we got within a few miles of home at the end of a run, sometimes I'd call the dogs up with my special signal and go off and leave him. I'd watch him back there kicking for all he was worth and hear him hollering at the dogs for more speed, but it was no trick for me to just go off and leave him. He would come into camp in a sweat and ask what I did to make the dogs pick up the pace that way. I always shrugged and told him it came with experience.

I finally taught Jeff how to do it but probably shouldn't have, considering how he ran that particular Knik 200. His job was to make it a training run. I told him to take a two-hour rest at Flathorn Lake going out, then a couple of hours at Yentna Station, and finally four hours at the Skwentna turnaround. I started behind him, so I found him at Flathorn as expected. I spoke to him as my team passed and told him I appreciated his resting the dogs. The moment I got past him, he pulled his team out onto the trail and fell in right behind me. He stayed there until Yentna Station. At Yentna, I reminded him of the race plan. He said, "Oh, yah. Okay."

Burt leaving the starting line of Don's Iditarod 200. Preliminary races served a real purpose in training the mushers and dogs to race, and in giving mushers a chance to see how they compared to other teams.

My plan was to hustle right on through but he was to stay and rest. I was again surprised to find him hot on my tail. His response when we reached Skwentna was that the dogs were so eager to go that he couldn't hold them. We're talking about a big strapping young man who grew up in a gold camp. Couldn't hold the dogs, my foot!

We had arrived at Skwentna about the same time as Joe Redington, so after Jeff and I finished feeding our dogs, Joe and I visited for a bit. He suggested that we leave Skwentna at the same time and travel along together. It is always nice to travel with friends when you're racing, because you can switch off breaking trail and share other work if the situation warrants. The main thing is that you don't want to do all the trail breaking. Breaking trail can be hard on leaders, so the idea is to trade off to make things as easy as possible. Also, we planned to travel along together during Iditarod, so it would be good practice.

We set a time to leave, and I found a nice quiet place to take a nap. At the appointed time, Jeff and I hitched the dogs and I stopped over to let Joe know we were leaving. He wasn't ready to go, so I told him we'd just putt along until he caught up with us. We left and were running down the Skwentna Airport about a half mile out of the checkpoint when Joe caught up with us and hollered for trail. Joe was pushing hard and my handler wanted to know what to do. The runway was gravel and plowed bare making it difficult to stop. Also, we were in danger of busting our brakes off or at least taking the points off on the frozen gravel of the runway. Joe was obviously irate, so I told Jeff to get his team stopped and let Joe by. Joe was on a tear. He seemed angry that we hadn't waited for him, and obviously wanted to show us who was boss.

Joe passed us both easily and began gaining distance as the three of us wound our way down the Skwentna River toward its confluence with the Yentna River. His yelling got his dogs attention so they speeded up and, of course, scared our dogs so they backed off a little. The trail forked where the two rivers converged. The race trail back to Knik made a hard right turn down the Yentna River, while the trail that the locals used proceeded across the Yentna and up into a creek bottom where a bunch of cabins were. I'm not sure what got into Joe's dogs that made them go that way instead of taking the trail home. Sled dogs usually head for home and hearth but that was a long way off. Maybe they just didn't like all the commotion and were trying to escape. Maybe they heard the dogs barking near the cabins over there and wanted to go visiting or saw another chance to rest.

In any case, off they went in the wrong direction, with Joe vigorously urging them onward. Jeff and I flashed our headlights on and off in their direction and shouted until we were hoarse trying to get Joe's attention, but he continued in that direction until he was out of sight. Joe liked to remove his hearing aids when he didn't think he'd need them, so he probably had them in his pocket and couldn't hear us.

We continued, passing one team after another until we caught up with Harry Sutherland about halfway between Flathorn Lake and the finish. Both Jeff and I managed to pass Harry and I held the lead for a bit. Harry was motivated though, and definitely knew what to do. He passed us both before we reached the finish line. I wanted to win but had to keep in mind that this race was really just a training run for the main event, Iditarod '84. Many times, dogs have just one good race in them each season and you don't want it to be a preliminary event. Anyway, I was tickled to death that both of my teams finished as well as they did. I even forgave Jeff for his failure to follow orders. I finished second and Jeff finished third. This was good for two teams out of the same kennel, considering the competition.

It was always a thrill driving a tough, hard charging dog team. The dogs had been exercised on the training wheel all summer and we were anxious to see the results and were determined to do well.

Needless to say, I'd been anxious to repeat the performance again this year while training for the 1985 Iditarod. I did have a little chat with Jeff about the importance of following the race plan but he just sat there and grinned. He knew sometimes it's better to ask forgiveness than permission. I told Joe, later, that we yelled and flashed our lights to get his attention when he left the trail and headed across the river just out of Skwentna. He may have questioned our sincerity; after all, with him derailed, we had one less team to worry about.

A few days later, the dogs were full of energy, so we decided to run the fifty-mile loop around the Petersville Hills race trail. It had snowed, so I had to break the trail out before I could run it. At least it was easy to find because the Forks race trail was still visible, even after it snowed. We would run it in reverse.

It took all day and was dark when I finished breaking out the trail, but it was a great night for running. The sky was clear and the temperature was twenty degrees above zero. As I mushed the team past the mouth of Spruce Creek onto Cache Creek, I saw a headlight coming toward me. I couldn't believe it. I'd spent the entire day breaking out that trail and here was a musher on it before I was.

Mushing toward the Susitna River during Don's Iditarod 200. The race was run on the Iditarod trail so we became familiar with the Iditarod race trail all the way to Skwentna. At least the first day of Iditarod would hold few surprises

It turned out to be Frank Bettine. He had heard there were good trails at Petersville, so he drove his truck full of dogs to the end of the road and hitched his team. He left his truck after dark and just kind of followed his leaders. Without a clue, they took him on a fifty-mile loop that constituted one of the nicest trails we had. Anyway, it was nice to see another musher out in that lonesome wilderness. As I write this, that country is a mass of snowmachiners and very few dog teams. I liked it better then.

We ran the same trail again on Monday at a bit slower pace because of higher temperatures and the long run the night before. We had to cross open water in a number of places along Cache Creek, the first being just inches deep and not wide. The next open water was about ten feet across and a foot to a foot and a half deep. The dogs hesitated for a moment and then charged in and lunged across. We met several teams with relatively smooth passes except Wayne wanted to bite dogs in the oncoming teams. He would knock it off when I yelled at him, but it was always worrisome to have an aggressive dog in your team. It was a cardinal sin to have your dog attack a dog in another team, especially if an injury resulted. I'd always been a stickler about dogs fighting. A dog that got nipped by another team often became shy about approaching other teams in a race. It could make it nearly impossible to pass if the dog happened to be a leader or swing dog. This was a lousy thing to do to another man's dog.

We drove into strong winds for six or seven miles as we moved across the saddle and then came on home. When I checked the dogs after our return, I found that Leeda had severe harness burns because one of the handlers had put a harness on her that was too small. The long run gave it plenty of time to chafe. I couldn't believe it. Already short of dogs and then an experienced handler pulls a stunt like that. For the next few weeks, we put Leeda in Nina's team without a harness, just a neckline to give things a chance to heal.

On January 9, we drove up north past the Roadhouse into blowing snow in the high open areas toward Mount McKinley. This was excellent training for the ascent of Rainy Pass during Iditarod. Blown-in trails, gritty blowing snow and whiteouts were common in the Alaska Range and it was essential that the dogs have some practice in dealing with it. I'd put Timber in lead, but he just didn't seem to get it. He had a dickens of a time following the snowed-in trail. While the trail was blown in and soft, there was a solid base below from being broken out and driven over earlier. An experienced leader would unerringly stay on that firm base, making progress easier. Some leaders never figured it out and kept wandering off the solid base. When they did, they found themselves wallowing in snow that could be over their heads. Eventually, we came down out of the high country, but this run showed that we needed more training in blowing snow and whiteout conditions.

We continued our training runs with noticeable improvement every week. Consistent demands for the same thing every run made the dogs sharper as the season progressed. Puddin was a joy to drive. She was committed to doing it right and had great concentration and determination. If she knew what I wanted, she would do it. If conditions made it impossible for me to see, she knew what was right and *always* came through if at all possible.

We had a great run on January 19. Puddin was in lead. We passed five teams and a half dozen snowmachines. She never hesitated, just looked for the hole and went for it without a glance at whatever we were passing. There was no doubt she was a dog that would pull you through when conditions were bad.

Don's Iditarod 200 race was never meant to be, but a good substitute came along. On the weekend of January 26 and 27, 1985, we finally had a race to run—the first annual Knik International 200 Sled Dog Race from Knik to Skwentna and back. It covered the same trail as other years but with a different sponsor. Temperatures were reaching forty degrees during the heat of the day. We had mixed rain and snow and then it cleared. The trail going out was good but the return trail was wet and icy. I used Noise in lead with most of the first string making up my team, fifteen dogs in all. Nina drove ten dogs with Charger in lead. My dogs were heavily muscled, which I believed would be good for Iditarod, but it certainly wasn't good for this kind of a race. The dogs were too heavy for the temperatures, so they became a little dehydrated by the time we reached Skwentna. The serious problem, however, was our dog food. We both carried a cooler full of hot food. We mixed the concoction at the start and just let it soak until we fed it at Yentna Station. I was using quite an array of vitamin supplements that year, including brewer's yeast that Joe Sr. had recommended.

The team came through and our training season was a success. Burt accepts the trophy for finishing second in Don's Iditarod 200 from the sponsor and owner of Don's Iditarod Café.

By the time food had soaked all the way to Yentna, it was fermenting like a vat full of beer. I'm sure that it made the dogs sick. It wasn't Joe's fault. I should have figured out what yeast would do over a period of hours. On top of the spoiled food, the dogs developed some kennel cough during the race. They must have had the bug before the race and the stress of temperature and spoiled food probably triggered the symptoms.

When all was said and done, the dogs were tough and finished well even under the worst conditions. We didn't do as well as I'd hoped but did finish fifth, which was in the money. This was our last preliminary race prior to Iditarod '85. The dogs that did well were the same ones who later finished well in Iditarod.

Chapter Twelve
1985 Race to Finger Lake, 1985 Iditarod

The 1985 training season was over. A glance out the window indicated improving weather as I rolled out of bed and pulled on my socks. It was Tuesday before the start of Iditarod. Today we would move the race team and all the gear from our cabin in the hills south of Mount McKinley to my home in Anchorage.

Heavy snows the past few days had left our trails covered with a deep powdery deposit. The task of driving the dogs fifteen miles to the truck at Moose Creek would not be easy, especially with heavily laden sleds. Weekend snowmachiners usually kept the trail along Petersville Road well packed. Unfortunately, they had all left before the heavy snow stopped, so the trail was covered with several feet of unpacked powder.

I cooked a batch of pancakes to celebrate our last day at the cabin. The secret of my light, fluffy pancakes was something my mother taught me as a little boy. Mine filled the whole plate and were smothered with butter and maple syrup. It makes my mouth water to think about it. We were going to savor these pancakes. I wouldn't be back until the race ended in Nome and there'd be few pleasures like this between now and then.

A slow but uneventful slog through deep unbroken snow brought us to the truck. We loaded twenty tired sled dogs into their individual holes in the big dog box. Sleds were stowed atop the box and gear was jammed into the boxes' inner compartments. It was five days until the start of the race, so the dogs would be well rested come race day.

Once home, we staked the dogs alongside the house at Campbell Lake and began unloading sleds and gear to be sorted and arranged for the race. Gear would be placed on the living room floor, sleds and all. It would take hours, so I might as well be comfortable.

It's important to be ready for a cold night on the trail. All cold weather gear was already on before the re-start, even though it was warm in the afternoon sun. Clear skies meant plunging temperatures when night fell and you didn't want fast moving teams crowding you while you tried to dig a parka out of your sled.

I took the dogs in for their vet check as required by race rules. Iditarod has always done everything possible to assure the best possible care of the dogs. The vet check was part of the process. A veterinarian examined each dog from stem to stern assuring sound lungs and heart and good muscle tone. While I was at the vet's, the handlers were sent to the freight company to send spare sleds to McGrath and Shaktoolik. The spare at McGrath was in case I got busted up traversing Happy River Gorge or the Dalzell Gorge. Even the Farewell Burn could be rough on sleds if conditions were right.

As I sorted through my things, Bob Snider, a pal and hunting buddy called. "Burt, I'm coming to Nome to cheer you across the finish line, but don't be messing around out there. I'm not going to waste time hanging around Nome if you're sitting on your butt out on the trail. Now when are you going to get there?"

Bob was a genuine Alaskan and one of my best friends. We'd hunted and flown together for years. We would fly miles through steep mountain passes and across open ocean in our tiny floatplanes to hunt elk and deer on Afognak Island and sheep in the Alaska Range. We were sheep hunting one time and saw a band of rams on a cliff high up the mountain above us.

"Let's go get 'em, Burt."

"I don't think we can climb those cliffs, Bob."

"Burt, we can go anywhere those sheep can go."

"Maybe you can, Bob, but I can't."

Bob took off up the mountain leaving me feeling a little wimpy. A couple of hours later, I watched Bob inching along that cliff, a couple thousand feet above me on the mountainside. Yah, Bob's a tough guy. He got the sheep.

I told Bob I intended to arrive in Nome with the lead teams, so he shouldn't waste any time getting there.

The sled we were sending to Shaktoolik was a lightweight racing sled that I would switch to if weather was good, and I might be competitive. If the weather were bad, I'd keep the bigger sled that I could crawl into in case I needed shelter from a storm between Shaktoolik and Nome.

Two sleds were needed here in Anchorage. The first was a slower, heavier, sturdier sled that I would use to leave the starting line on Fourth Avenue. The trail to Eagle River was notoriously rough, snaking tightly around trees that could snag the sled. Occasionally, we even banged over discarded washing machines and boulders. I didn't want to wreck my expensive racing sled trying to negotiate that obstacle course.

Burt stepped on the sled just as the announcer counted 4-3-2-1-GO! It drove race official's nuts. All teams were required to take a handler along out of the start and re-start. Here, Big Joe Daugherty rides Burt's sled, although he could have elected to ride a trailing sled.

From Eagle River, we would truck the dogs to Wasilla where we would hitch the dogs and mush across Knik Lake and on to Nome. Knik Lake was the jumping-off place into the great Alaska wilderness. It was there I would need my racing sled packed with everything I'd need out along the trail, which extended 1,137 miles to Nome. My buddy, Jack Felton, and a group of friends would be waiting for me at Knik Lake. They would lead me off to the side, where we would unhook the team from the clunker starting sled and re-hitch to the faster racing sled.

Now still at home, I would be adding gear to the racing sled during the next couple of days. I wouldn't be satisfied until everything that was needed was in place. It wasn't that smart to wait until the last minute to pack. Any forgotten items would be near impossible to replace once out on the trail.

The weather was actually fairly decent when I awoke Thursday morning. This would be one of the busiest days of the year. We would start with the mushers' meeting and end with the banquet to draw starting positions that night.

The mushers' meeting was always a highlight. Race officials would explain the rules while staff and volunteers told us what to expect out on the trail during the race. Most of the presentation was much the same as in other years until the race marshal discussed the recent heavy snowfall. Officials had flown the trail and found that many moose were congregated along the trail. They emphasized the importance of carrying a gun. A moose in the trail would usually hear a dog team coming and do one of two things: flee if it could or stay and fight. Deep snow made travel difficult, even for our giant moose, so they were not likely to get out of the way.

As I've said before, it was obvious that moose often mistook a dog team for a pack of wolves, so they weren't likely to turn their backs. They were often willing to fight to the death. In harness, the dogs were vulnerable since they are tied to the gang line with a neck line and a tug line. They cannot escape so the musher must avoid the moose, defend the team from attack with a gun, or screw up his courage and enter the fray to cut the dogs loose with a knife. Most mushers prefer a gun if they can't avoid the situation all together. Knowing all of this, few experienced mushers proceeded into moose country after a heavy snow-fall unarmed. Truth is most of us distance mushers won't step on the runners unarmed, ever.

At the banquet that night, I bumped into Joe Redington. "Burt," he asked, "would you like to fly out in the morning to see how things look along the trail?"

"Sure, Joe," I told him. "I'll drop into Knik Lake first thing in the morning and we can go from there. I'll put the heater in the airplane tonight so it'll be ready to go."

Joe showed up at the sound of my airplane and we took off from the snowy surface of Knik Lake. We picked up the trail right off the lake and began looking. We saw a few moose as we flew toward the Yentna River and then the numbers increased. The Susitna River Valley had always been moose country, so it wasn't at all surprising to see the numbers. Actually, our reconnaissance didn't really do anything but satisfy our curiosity. Neither one of us ever mushed our dogs without a gun. We landed back at Knik Lake and enjoyed a cup of tea and a visit with Vi, Joe's wife, and then I flew home. I spent the rest of the day going over the sled's contents one more time.

The start of Iditarod was always exciting and this one was no exception. Things went as planned and I found myself moving fast near the front of the pack as we crossed the Susitna River. Only Susan Butcher, Dewey Halverson, Glen Findlay, Rick Swenson and Jerry Austin were ahead of me. I caught occasional glimpses of Jerry's headlight flashing in the trees as we mushed silently along. The rustle of the dogs' traces softly interrupted the silence.

I stopped and quickly snacked the dogs as we neared Rabbit Lake.

The dogs had occasionally picked up the pace signaling the presence of moose nearby. None was visible but the dogs knew and their excitement was evident. Their acute sense of hearing, sight, and smell told the tale as their ears perked up and they looked intently into the darkness. After each time, they settled back into their mile-eating race pace.

Suddenly, I could see Jerry's headlight beam just ahead of me and then saw Jerry's team stopped in the trail. My team stopped behind him. I hurried up to Jerry and asked what was going on.

"Susan ran into a moose and Dewey's gone up to help her out. It'll be a while." That's all he knew.

I could see teams parked ahead of Jerry in the powerful beam of my headlight, but no Dewey.

A handler is required to accompany the team out of the start at Settlers Bay to Knik where the trail headed into the bush and at the restart. Here, big Joe Daugherty was riding the sled out of the restart. Joe was one tough guy and would often ride the sled without hat or parka in the coldest temperatures. Here, he just kicked back and enjoyed the ride.

I assumed that Susan had shot a moose in her team and that Dewey had gone up to finish the job. It was legal to kill an attacking animal in Alaska, even outside hunting season. State law and race rules required that if you shot a moose that attacked your team, you must gut it out so race personnel could salvage it later. Until that process was complete, all following mushers had to wait in line with no passing.

I walked forward and visited with Jerry until the trail was clear. We whistled up our teams and mushed forward. I could see the dead moose lying in the trail ahead of us as we approached. The dogs never hesitated as we bounced across the legs of the dead moose. A large area was stomped down to bare ground and trashed bushes and blood were everywhere.

We arrived at the Rabbit Lake checkpoint and the checker signed us in and went through our gear. As she worked, she said that Susan had run into a moose that had injured and even killed some of her dogs before it was killed. I could see Susan being interviewed by the television reporters.

I fed my dogs while people stopped by and the story began to emerge. Dewey had come upon Susan and found her in the middle of a fierce moose attack. The moose was wildly kicking out at anything that moved. Dewey had anchored his own team to keep them out of the melee and then had run forward into serious peril and killed the enraged moose with his handgun. Susan had moved out of the way but could have also been seriously injured if not killed had it not been for Dewey Halverson's heroic action.

As I fed my dogs, a camera crew from Anchorage Channel 2, an NBC affiliate, approached. The reporter was talking about Susan running into the moose. He put a microphone in front of me and asked for a comment.

I said I felt bad for Susan at the loss of her dogs and told the reporter that it could happen to anyone, and that it had to be an awesome ordeal. I told the reporter that I'd met many moose on the trail but had always managed to get the dogs out of the way and had never had one in my team. There is really nothing you can do once one attacks other than do your best to defend your dogs. You'd hope the moose would run off, but if it didn't, you'd have to kill it to protect your dogs. I told the reporter that I felt it shouldn't reflect on Iditarod because it was an accident, like any other. I went on to say I was a great fan of Susan's and that I'd bought dogs from her. I said it happens and it is sad when it does. I didn't really have anything else to say.

It was a sad place to be as I fed my dogs and rested for a couple of hours. I couldn't wait to line out the dogs and mush away from Rabbit Lake toward Skwentna. I wanted out of this sad place.

Weeks later, after the race was over, a group of friends were watching the post race Iditarod program on Channel 2 television at my home. Susan's moose encounter was being discussed and Susan said, "Conservatively, the moose had to be in my team at least twenty minutes."

Then Dewey was interviewed. He stated that when he approached her, Susan asked him if he had a gun. He told her he did. Dewey then described getting as close to her team as he dared. He described the moose kicking the dickens out of those dogs. Dewey shot the moose four times with the last shot putting it down.

Dewey said the moose was still attacking the dogs even after he'd put a couple of bullets into it.

That was the end of the incident. None of us thought about it until several years later when Susan commented on difficulties experienced by the Northwest Passage sled-dog expedition and urged sponsors to bail out. Craig Medred added an interesting perspective to the two incidents in an editorial in the Anchorage Daily News on December 23, 1991[2]. See Appendix A, for the entire editorial. Until his opinion piece, we didn't realize she wasn't armed.

As we glided along the trail out of Finger Lake, it felt good to get away from the crowd and the sadness of Susan's experience. The trail through here was especially beautiful and soon all bad feelings evaporated. The wilderness was pure and white with little sign of human activity. Not many people came here except during Iditarod. Heavy timber surrounded the trail.

We were within three or four miles of Skwentna, only one hundred miles from Anchorage, when my serenity was interrupted. I crested a low rise and saw Lavon stopped ahead with his team. There was a moose approximately a hundred yards beyond and facing him. I pulled up to within a hundred feet of his team, firmly anchored mine and walked up to see what was going on. The moose was about three-fourths grown and was standing in the trail facing in our direction. Its hackles were up and its ears were laid back, a sure sign of aggression. Lavon was holding a small Hudson Bay axe in his hand as I walked alongside his team to discuss the matter. Being in a race, there was, of course, no way we were going to turn our teams around and start heading back to Anchorage.

"Lavon, why don't you snowshoe a trail off to the side around the moose?"

"Why don't you?"

"I just got here. What happened? Why are you just hanging around?"

He had been traveling with Tim Osmar when they confronted the moose. Tim was eighteen years old and in his first Iditarod Trail Sled Dog Race. He was an outstanding young musher, having won the Junior Iditarod Race three years in a row. Apparently, these young dudes were a little gutsier than we older guys, because Tim had just mushed right on by the moose, startling it to the point that it jumped momentarily off the trail. After Tim passed, the moose walked back onto the trail and refused to budge.

As I walked up, Lavon asked me if I had a gun along.

I told him, "Yah, but I'm not going to shoot that damned moose. I don't intend to spend the rest of the day trying to get it gutted and out of the way." I

[2] APPENDIX A, The Anchorage Times, December 23, 1991

continued, "Lavon, neither one of us can get out of here until you get out of the way. Get your snowshoes on and start walking."

"Burt, if I go, and my team breaks free, it'll be right in the middle of that moose. You go and I'll make sure your team doesn't get past me until you're back on your sled."

Full of energy and with the thrill of the crowds, the dogs loved to lope out of the start. Realty would eventually set in and they would slow down to a mile-eating Iditarod trot.

"Lavon, you're first in line here. Put on your snowshoes and break out a trail. I'll hold our teams until you get back."

Lavon wouldn't budge. He just wasn't going to get down on that swamp with that moose. Lavon had been waiting there nearly an hour, trying to screw up his courage to snowshoe past the moose. It was obvious that he wasn't armed and had no intention of being out on that swamp where the moose might get agitated and charge him.

As I dug out my snowshoes, I said, "Lavon, I'm only doing this under one condition. You promise that you will not move until I finish and am back on my sled with these snowshoes stowed and I'm ready to go. I don't want you to mush down *my* detour to the far side of the moose and spook it back here to where it cuts me off from *my* trail."

"Burt, I give you my word. I will wait here until you get back to your sled with your stuff stowed and you give me the signal."

There was no choice. If we were ever going to get moving, I'd have to snowshoe around the moose and let it have its little section of trail all to itself. I strapped my snowshoes on and began the slow trip around the moose. The snow was deep and soft, causing the tips of my snowshoes to catch and bury themselves at every step. Meanwhile, the moose pivoted slowly, always facing me with his hackles up and his ears back, a sure sign that he was every bit as uptight as I was about the whole thing. Lavon kept assuring me there was no way the moose was going to attack me through that deep snow, but I kept thinking otherwise. I'd seen too many big moose gallop cross county through deep snow. It was still obvious that Lavon didn't want to be out there in the swamp with the moose.

I trudged through the deep snow on those heavy snowshoes until I had made the trail clear enough to get safely past. Then I retraced my steps back toward Lavon.

As I went by him, Lavon had a shifty, nervous look about him. "Damn it," I said as I moved past Lavon. "Don't you dare move until I'm ready."

Meanwhile, several teams had pulled up behind us. They stayed back a hundred yards wanting to allow us room to retreat if the moose should charge. That turned out to be a mistake for them.

I was hurrying to my sled just past Lavon when I heard him signal his dogs to go. I lumbered frantically one hundred feet along the soft trail to my sled, as my dogs barked and lunged forward trying to break loose and follow Lavon's team. I tossed the snowshoes into the sled bag and looked up to see that Lavon was already well down the detour and abeam the startled moose. As Lavon continued, the moose spun around and began to gallop away from Lavon and back toward me. I whistled urgently at my dogs for them to speed as fast as they could go toward the advancing moose and the beginning of the detour. It appeared she might win the frantic race and block off the entrance to my detour before we got there. This would cut us off and possibly put her right in my team. I prayed the dogs would obey my command and turn onto the detour rather than try to attack her. The gap between us shortened at an unbelievable pace as we raced forward. This had become a race against death as the galloping moose charged us.

The moose came faster as she forgot Lavon and focused on my dogs. The distance closed. The dogs surged. With her nostrils flared, her ears laid back close against her neck and her hackles up, she seemed to focus her bloodshot eyes on Puddin, my tiny faithful leader. God bless Puddin. She was at the cutoff and turned instantly onto the detour at my command, guiding her partner, Noise, right along with her. Would the rest of the team and I make it safely out of her way? Dog after dog made the turn out of harm's way. After what seemed like an eternity, the sled and I made the turn, skidding wildly, almost into the deep snow. I could have reached out and touched that moose, she was that close as my sled whipped onto the detour and out of danger. I was busy doing everything in my power to keep that sled upright through the turn. The last thing I wanted was to be upside down under the sled with that moose stomping my dogs and me.

Past the moose, the dogs hot-footed it down on to the swamp and then back onto the trail to Skwentna. Their hearts must have been thumping as hard as mine was, considering the quick pace they set all the way into the checkpoint.

A dog's tail straight up is referred to as "flagging," a dead give-away that the dog isn't pulling. This is one of several ways a musher can tell if his dogs are pulling or just moving along. Several dogs are wearing booties to protect cuts or abrasions and give them time to heal. When trails were hard on feet, all the dogs wore booties. *Jeff Schultz Photo*

Once out on the swamp, I turned to see that the moose had continued southward toward the other teams and had blocked them off from the beginning of our bypass trail. We heard later that they ended up having to snowshoe their own bypass trail before continuing after us.

Joe Delia met us down on the river below his house and checked us in. I'd forgotten the moose as the dogs were fed and I dragged my sleeping bag up to the loft in Joe's cabin for a quick nap and then back down to the river to load my sled for the trip to Finger Lake. I couldn't wait to get to Finger Lake to see my pal Gene Leonard. We'd become friends during Iditarod and now I flew my airplane to Finger Lake several times each summer to visit. The lake was remote and accessible only by plane in summer and dog team or snowmachine in winter. I usually tossed some dog food and fresh vegetables into the airplane to drop off as both were hard to come by in the bush because of the isolation.

Gene made us all park up on the low ridge above the lake near his cabin rather than down on the lake. The Leonards got their drinking water from the lake and didn't want a thousand dogs befouling the supply.

Rick Swenson and Emmitt Peters were parked side by side and I pulled in next to Emmitt. Gene and I chatted briefly as he checked me in and told me that when I was ready to go sleep I could bunk in his generator shack. I began cooking for my dogs. Gene left to check another team and I fed my dogs, ate a snack, and nestled into my sleeping bag. The steady thump of the Witte generator drowned out all sound and soon lulled me to sleep.

I got a great rest for the generator made it impossible to hear the sounds of barking dogs and drivers shouting commands as they parked their teams at the checkpoint. Something told me to wake up and I wandered back to my dogs to see what was going on. I returned to hear a hundred dogs barking frantically and saw that a male in Rick's team had hooked up with one of Emmitt's females. Every dog in sight was telling on them. Some of the other dogs in their teams were becoming aggressive, so I went to find the guys. Emmitt was a little grumpy over Rick's dog breeding one of his leaders. I told him he'd be lucky if Rick didn't charge him a stud fee.

Emmitt chuckled and responded, "Hey, maybe I'll get some good dogs out of this!"

The dogs were well rested, fed, and eager to be off. It was time to leave Finger Lake after our six-hour stop. We made good time as we wound our way through the spruce forest. The trail climbed gently as we made our way through the foothills approaching the magnificent mountains of the Alaska Range. This was heavy snow country with a large population of moose.

As I mushed along, I thought of the trail ahead to Rainy Pass, which had some notoriously hairy stretches. The descent into Happy River Valley was extremely steep with several switchbacks. From there on into Rainy Pass, the trail followed a steep side hill. I'd been there before, three times, but nothing had prepared me for the hair-raising trip I was about to experience.

Chapter Thirteen
Finger Lake to Rohn Checkpoint, 1985

I t normally takes about an hour and a half to get from Finger Lake to the bluffs over Happy River. I liked to get there near the front of the pack before too many teams had made the descent down into Happy River Valley. Team after team, with their brakes digging, creates a deep trench down the center of the trail. At times, one runner on the sled drops into the trench, tipping the sled on its side as you plummet wildly down the treacherous, steep canyon. It is hard to keep things under control on a steep, winding descent with your sled on its side and brakes out of reach and unusable.

As I got closer and closer to Happy River, I began to think I was seeing things. I would catch a bit of movement out of the corner of my eye, but when I tried to see what it was, ghostlike, there was nothing there. It happened three or four times, and each time I instinctively thought there was a moose up ahead. I never did get a look at it though, and soon I was within a quarter of a mile of the descent down those bluffs into the valley.

Every time I got close to those bluffs, I was glad I had gained the experience that I did during my first year of training with those awful trails in the Kahiltna country. I'd been thrown from my sled many times that year because of hazardous trails. After that experience, I never really confronted any stretch of trail during the Iditarod race that was much of a problem. Nothing really compared.

It was a wild ride down those Happy River bluffs, though, and if you ever did lose control, you were in for one hell of a rough time. The trail ran steeply down the bluffs (referred to as "side-hilling") so if the sled ever slipped off the trail or began to roll, there was no telling when it would stop. Giant spruce trees lived

The Iditarod Trail out of Finger Lake in the foot hills of the Alaska Range, crosses several lakes as we get closer to the Alaska Range. Joe Redington pauses to watch Burt approach where he has stopped to take a break beside the trail.

on both sides of the trail so sleds could crash into them or wrap around them. Even though I'd never had any of these problems, it definitely was a thrill going through there and my adrenaline began to shoot in anticipation.

As I thought of the excitement sure to come in just a few minutes, my lead dogs literally disappeared from sight. Then my swing dogs disappeared and next the first pair of team dogs. I'd seen dog tracks ahead of the leaders where my team headed, but it was freaky to have the dogs dropping so quickly out of sight.

I slammed on the brakes as hard as I could, and stopped the team. Half of my dogs were still in sight. I set my snow hook and stomped it into the trail as hard as I could. Then, I tipped the loaded sled over on top of the hook to hold everything securely while I went up to take a look. I worked my way up along the gang line hand over hand, holding things as steady as possible.

When I got up midway through the team, I couldn't believe what I saw. The leaders had literally dived off the top of a cliff with the Happy River looking at least 1,000 feet below us. My leaders were in contact with the face of the cliff but were literally hanging in their traces with the swing dogs and the first pair of team dogs in the same predicament.

I called for Noise and Ivor, my leaders, to come back up. They managed to get their feet on something firm and got themselves turned around. They scrambled back up the steep slope onto reasonably level ground.

I swear, each of those front six dogs had a look on his face that said "what in the hell was that?"

Years later, Mitch Albom, award-winning columnist for the Detroit Free Press, was discussing the rigors of the Iditarod Trail Race and had this to say, "What happened to Burt Bomhoff? Six years ago, his team was behind the Iditarod race leader when the leader took a wrong turn, off the trail. Realizing his mistake, the leader turned his dogs around. Burt Bomhoff wasn't so quick. And the next thing he knew, his lead dogs disappeared over a cliff. They were dangling help-lessly 1,000 feet above a river, like something from an Indiana Jones movie. Bomhoff locked his sled in place, crawled to the edge, pulled on the ropes, and managed to save them from death.

A few more feet, and they would have been pulling him out of the water.[3]

I held them there for a moment while I looked around to see where the trail actually went. It had made such a hard turn to the left around a small spruce tree that the dogs had overshot the turn and continued out over the bluff.

Lavon's team had started to do the same thing before, which accounted for the tracks I'd seen ahead of us, but he had seen it in time and commanded his dogs to haw down the correct trail. My dogs had seen his dogs' tracks, smelled their scent, and assumed the trail simply went straight ahead.

One way to lure company to stop for a visit during a race was to prepare a nice place to pull out. Joe Sr. stomped out a trail to make a parking spot for Burt's dogs off the side of the trail. Teams are required to rest off the trail so as not to block the trail and be in the way of other teams.

After I got the dogs straightened out and heading in the right direction, I again tipped the sled over on the snow hook and started chopping limbs off a spruce tree to make a barrier fence across the false trail. I made a good thick fence of spruce boughs stuck in the snow around the outside of the curve to assure that no other teams would go the wrong way and possibly plummet over into the

---

[3] Anchorage Daily News, March 5, 1991

Happy River far below. A musher dopey from lack of sleep might not be alert enough to get his dogs stopped in time. We continued on our way.

As I approached the lip of the bluff, my lead dog suddenly made a hard turn to the right around a big spruce tree and then disappeared out of sight to the left over the Happy River canyon rim. I began pedaling furiously with one foot in an effort to push the sled forward to keep up with the dogs and minimize the sled's drag on the team. This helped to avoid dragging the dogs to the inside of the curve and that big spruce tree, thereby minimizing the possibility of an injury to one of them. It also helped to keep the sled from banging violently into the tree, ricocheting out into space and out of control.

As I neared the tree, I tipped the sled halfway over toward the outside of the curve in an effort to steer it away from the tree. The dogs all managed to avoid the tree; however, the sled slammed into it with a resounding thud, knocking it to the right and nearly tipping it over. Before I could right the sled, we were hurtling nearly straight down the first of a series of near vertical drops. Plummeting straight down, we dropped quickly with the dogs at full gallop and the sled half out of control. The sled settled down onto both runners and I stood on the brake with both feet in an effort to control our plummeting descent. I didn't envy the teams farther back after the trail got chewed up.

The most I could hope for was to keep the sled upright and slow its descent with the brake enough to keep it from overrunning the wheel dogs. This was accomplished and in a few moments we were safely at the bottom of that first run. The trail took a hard turn to the left at the bottom of the first descent. My sled snapped over on its side as the dogs took up the slack, snapping the sled hard to the left.

Righting the sled, we continued through a series of similar, near-vertical descents. Halfway down one of these, a sled ahead of me had slipped off the edge of the trail and tumbled down to the right, where it had hung up against a huge spruce tree. I thought as I went by that the musher of that outfit must have had an awful time getting the loaded sled back up around that tree and onto the trail. Perhaps the ghostly images I'd seen earlier weren't really a moose but this phantom musher gliding silently ahead of me. The descent down Happy River and a couple of other areas could be downright hair-raising, but the old-timers did it; it made the race challenging for us and added a lot of excitement for the fans. We wouldn't want the ghosts of mushers past, much less our fans, thinking we were wienies!

After a few minutes, we were safely down onto the frozen surface of Happy River. We mushed downstream for a quarter mile or so to where Happy River joins the Skwentna River. From there the trail ascended to the bluffs on the other side of the canyon and continued toward Rainy Pass.

It was there that we caught up with the team driven by young Tim Osmar. He must have been the one who rolled his sled off that steep trail. His father, Dean, had won the Iditarod Trail Sled Dog Race the year before. I knew he had quite a dog team, so I was pleasantly surprised to see us gaining steadily on him as we climbed the steep ridge out of Happy River Valley. We caught up with him at the crest of the ridge, where both of us stopped our teams for a brief rest and a snack. I then went on by and continued toward Rainy Pass. I gradually increased the distance between us until Tim was no longer in sight. As we mushed forward, it occurred to me that it had taken one heck of a man to wrestle his sled from around that big spruce tree with his team pulling hard down the steep trail ahead.

By the time a dog team reaches Nome on the coast of the Bering Sea, it will have traversed just about every terrain feature that Alaska has to offer. The Iditarod trail winds through a forest of scattered spruce out of Finger Lake on the way to the Happy River Steps.
Jeff Schultz Photo

The trail made one last steep descent down onto the surface of Long Lake and I hoped the worst was behind us. Rick Swenson and Jerry Austin had pulled their teams off to the side of the lake to rest and snack their dogs. I drove my team just beyond theirs and then stopped to visit for a moment and give the dogs a light snack.

Rick asked me if I had a first aid kit, which, unfortunately, I didn't. Jerry Austin had broken his hand on that rough section of trail and was in considerable pain. How he made it through that rough area with a broken hand I'll never know. It was an indication of his grit and his skill as a musher that he went on to finish the race in a respectably competitive position. Since I'd already rested the team above Happy River, I stayed but a moment and then continued with only Lavon Barve's team ahead of me. I expected the trail the rest of the way to Rainy Pass to be routine, but little did I know.

The trail climbed steadily through this area with much of it located along the top of the ridge above Happy River. At times, I caught a glimpse of the river far below us as we continued our silent trek toward Rainy Pass. One of the biggest problems with that trail was the extreme right-angle turns around trees. A dog team travels in a serpentine fashion so the curves in the trail must be gradual. It is important that everything flow.

These right-angle turns were hard to deal with. At one point, we started angling down a hill and then took a hard downhill turn to the right around a tree. The sled barely missed slamming into the tree and I worried for the teams that would come behind after the trail had worked its way farther down the hill and closer to that tree. At one point, I made such a sharp turn around the low branches of a tree that it knocked my hat off. I managed to get the team stopped even though it was heading downhill. I went back and retrieved my hat before the dogs ran off and left me in the middle of nowhere.

During the 1984 race, a group of snowmachiners had decided to put on a snowmachine race from Anchorage to Nome. There had been a lot of concern over what impact their race would have on the Iditarod Trail Sled Dog Race. Snowmachine racers travel at speeds up around 80 to 100 miles per hour. We feared that if they began their race within two or three weeks after the start of our race, there might be snowmachines tearing through the slower teams at the back of our race pack. We felt this would be hazardous. We were also concerned that if the snowmachines left ahead of us, their passage through areas of little snowfall might result in a trail that would be hazardous to the dogs. Both sides of the controversy were well intended, though arguments erupted at times.

The snowmachiners and dog mushers, in an effort to get along with each other, decided to share trail-breaking duties for the 1985 race. Because of that, we had snowmachine trailbreakers who were unfamiliar with dog mushing doing the work. This team of trailbreakers, led by John Arnold and Eric Halverson, were highly qualified professional snowmachiners. Unfortunately, the Iditarod race manager had not bothered to tell them the difference between a snowmachine race trail and a dog team race trail. As mentioned earlier, a dog team travels in a serpentine fashion, especially with the large dog teams used in races then; whereas, snowmachines can make right-angle turns.

Many teams consisted of eighteen or twenty dogs back then, which was an extremely long, powerful group of animals. They are not capable of making

When the teams were rested, it was Burt's turn to lead with Joe Sr. following. Teams ran with either one leader or double leaders, depending on the dogs. Some leaders preferred to go it alone while others felt more secure with company to help share the load.

right-angle turns. The lead dogs can make the turns okay, but each succeeding pair of dogs is pulled across the corner until the middle of the team and rear dogs along with the sled are dragged across the corner through deep snow. If a tree is standing on the inside of the curve, dogs and eventually the sled can all be hammered by it. This is extremely hazardous for the animals and, with all that power, the sled can literally be beaten apart. At the end of this "crack the whip" scenario is the musher hanging onto his sled.

Side-hilling is especially difficult. A snowmachine can hold itself on a side hill simply by turning its skis uphill to offset the machine's natural tendency to slide downhill. Dog sleds have no such advantage and tend to skid sideways downhill, each sled pushing the trail a little farther down the hill. Because of this, the dog team race trail must always skim along the downhill side of a tree rather than the uphill side. Then the trail is edging downhill away from the tree.

While we used snowmachines to break out the race trail just prior to the race, the trails were actually better a century ago because they were kept packed by teams constantly using them from the first snowfall on. Because of that, they were firm all the way from the snowy surface down to the ground.

Since much of the Iditarod Trail is no longer used except for racing, many feet of unpacked snow covers the trail by race time. Without snowmachines to break trail, the racers would have to snowshoe a trail, an impossible task that would have teams mired in snow rather than racing. The use of snowmachines to break the trails out ahead of the teams provides a trail much like the ones used many years ago during the gold rush, except that it isn't firm underneath. Sometimes there is no bottom.

We continued this mad side-hill ride, arriving at Rainy Pass about mid-morning. No dogs were injured and the sled and I were both intact. The trip from Finger Lake to Rainy Pass had been a rough one.

I anchored my team at a spot next to the horse corral so I would only have following teams parked on one side of me. I headed the dogs toward the outgoing trail since I hoped to be there only a few hours before going on. Awhile later, Joe Sr. mushed in and parked next to me. It was fun having him close to visit with. Little did we know that it would be three long days before we would finally leave. Severe weather and failure to deliver our food to the Rohn River checkpoint prompted the race marshal to freeze the race at Rainy Pass. This meant that the teams were frozen in place and could not advance until she unfroze it.

The Iditarod Sled Dog Race is much like other major sporting events such as marathons, the Indianapolis 500 and the Kentucky Derby. Although we mushers might enter other preliminary races during the winter, we had all year to focus on this one event. We were so keyed up by the time the race finally arrived that anything resembling a delay made us extremely hyper. We trained our dogs in such a manner that they too would peak at race time. This meant that we attempted to bring the dogs and ourselves to a peak of attitude and physical conditioning right at the starting line. One could imagine our state of hyperactivity after even the first day spent lounging around Rainy Pass checkpoint. We were eager to go, but the race manager hadn't gotten the food drops delivered at Rohn and now a howling blizzard up in the pass made staying the only sensible thing to do.

As soon as we were settled in, I stopped over to visit Lavon for a minute. "Lavon, did your dogs almost dive over the cliff above Happy Canyon?"

"Yah, that was a close one. Got them stopped just in time."

"Lavon, your tracks headed right to the edge of that cliff. My whole team just about lost it there."

"Yah, I figured somebody might get in trouble there."

"Well, don't worry about it. I took my axe and snicked off a bunch of spruce bows and made a fence around the outside of the curve. I was afraid somebody might get some dogs killed."

"Yah, I thought about that."

Lavon was a buddy, so I figured I'd said enough. The camaraderie that developed among mushers in the race was one of its most enjoyable aspects. It was nice to visit with one another in the checkpoints while stopped. I wasn't going to wreck it by being too picky. As the hours went by, I spent most of the daylight hours out by my team taking care of my dogs, rearranging my gear, repairing equipment, and just snoozing on my sled.

Lavon Barve and I had a conference that first evening and decided that one of us should stay and watch the teams at all times to ensure they didn't get into trouble, while the other took a break. Our fear was that a dog might get loose and get into a fight or that a dog might chew the gang line in half, thus allowing the team to telescope together. This might result in a fight or an accidental breeding, neither of which was desirable. As the dogs got more and more rest, they became more aggressive and the potential for a problem grew. We agreed that we would take four-hour shifts, one watching the dogs while the other slept. We would then trade places during the night.

That first night, Lavon headed for the cabin for his four-hour snooze at about ten o'clock while I lounged on top of my zipped-up sled bag hammock-style. I was half-dozing but alert to what was happening with the dogs. The dogs slept peacefully for four hours, at which time I grabbed my sleeping bag, wandered over to the cabin and awoke Lavon so that he could go out and watch the dogs. Four hours later, we traded again and then again, even though by then daylight was upon us. It worked really well and we had no problems with the dogs.

We spent the second day lounging around, visiting, drinking coffee here and there and generally enjoying ourselves. Robin Winkley, who with her husband Bucky managed the lodge, invited me for lunch that second day. What a pleasant two hours that was. She and Bucky and I, as well as two of their camp helpers, had a nice lunch in front of their big bay window overlooking the lake. I'd met Robin earlier in the winter at Joe Redington's camp where she had worked as a handler to gain experience as a dog musher. Bucky was a talented artist, doing bronze sculptures of all manner of Alaskan subjects. His works included Alaskan animals and people performing various outdoor tasks. He was also a cinematographer and a big-game guide.

I then wandered back to feed my dogs and take stock of my dwindling food supplies. Once the dogs were fed and my food and equipment rearranged, I wandered into the cabin that had been set aside for the mushers to visit with my fellow competitors. It was an enjoyable pastime. It seemed like when we were training, we were too busy to really have a chance to visit and when we were racing, of course, we were so busy caring for our dogs and trying to catch a nap, we didn't get near the sociability we craved. There was a lot of camaraderie, but it was often all too brief.

We visited for a while with approximately thirty drivers in the cabin when somebody suggested that we take up a collection to pay the Winkleys for any cleanup expenses that resulted from our stay. We also had a discussion about keeping things picked up since sixty mushers in a three-bedroom cabin had quite an impact. Also, it was pointed out that the outhouse hole was rapidly filling and we would need to pay the Winkleys something so their helpers could dig a new hole come spring.

It was nice being there and having a chance to visit with some great Alaskans and arguably the finest dog mushers in the world, champions! Four-time winner Rick Swenson, as well as Emmitt Peters, Rick Mackey, and top-notch drivers like Roger Nordlum, Sonny Lindner, Dewey Halverson, Jerry Austin, Terry Adkins, Libby Riddles, Herbie Nayokpuk, Lavon Barve, and Joe Redington were all there.

We were beginning to wonder just how long we'd be there and made attempts to have food sent in should our stay outlast the food. I wandered back over to Winkley's and told Robin I'd like to ask her a favor. "Nope," she said, "I'm not selling you one of those horses."

I said, "What do you mean, sell me one of those horses?"

"Half the mushers in this camp have approached me already wanting to buy one of those horses for dog food and we aren't selling them for that."

I told her I wasn't about to feed one of her pet horses to my dogs. What I needed to know was if there was a radiophone in camp so I could call Anchorage and see about having some food shipped in for me.

She said, "Sure," and showed me where the phone was.

I called home and asked my wife to have the boys put together a load of meat and dog food and see if somebody could get it up here between snow squalls. She said she'd try. Later, I discovered we were running out of white gas for our cook stoves, so I made another call and ordered up a few gallons of white gas. For some strange reason the white gas arrived right away but the dog food didn't arrive until I was about ready to leave on the third day. No harm done, though, as the food supply did last.

Eventually, the sun shown, the food drops were delivered to Rohn checkpoint and the trail breakers broke out a fresh trail. Burt and the other teams were finally allowed to leave Rainy Pass.
Jeff Schultz photo.

After the telephone calls, I wandered back to my sled, fed the dogs and made myself a dinner of New York steak and chili. By then the dogs were so hyper they rarely laid down. They just stood or walked around in a tight little circle around their neckline, eyeing one another and sniffing and licking. Some of the more aggressive dogs growled whenever another moved, so I knew we were on the verge of developing some problems. Dogs don't always understand the concept of "play nice."

Lavon and I again decided to share "night watch" duties, so at about ten o'clock he wandered into the cabin for a snooze. He had been visiting the campfire of Rick Swenson and Sonny Lindner before he hit the sack. I could hear laughter coming from over there, so I wandered over to chat for an hour or so. Swenson, Lindner, Austin, and Adkins were around the campfire doing chores and telling jokes. Terry Adkins, a veterinarian from Montana, told the raunchiest, funniest jokes I ever heard. I don't know if it was his military background or what, but he was a really funny fellow to have along on a camping trip.

I remember one joke in particular. Terry was a veterinarian and a cowboy back in Montana. He told about some cowboys in camp who had an arrangement about who would cook. They drew cards for who would be the first cook. That person would cook until somebody complained about the food, at which time the complainer would become the cook. After a couple of days, the first cook began to think he might be stuck with the job for the duration. He decided he had to do something to make the guys complain. He went out to the corral and picked up a horse turd to stir into the stew.

The cowboys sat down to eat and immediately began to squirm and make faces, but none complained. They continued to eat but still no one complained.

Finally, one of them said, "This stew tastes like horse manure!" Then, after a pause, "But it is GOOD!"

As we sat around the campfire, it was good to be reminded of why we did this because there were plenty of reasons not to. Anyone who made it to the finish line in Nome had probably spent the winter away from home unless he lived in bush Alaska. The money went the wrong way—out, not in. Workdays began before daylight and ended after dark. Things were generally safe but could be deadly for the careless and ignorant. Only the top of the field made enough off the race to pay for the habit through winnings and sponsors. It took a lot to feed a yard full of dogs, and if that wasn't bad enough, just wait until the vet showed up. I had learned to give shots, diagnose ailments and dose antibiotics early on to save on vet bills.

Nevertheless, the love of Alaska and sled dogs and the romance of a life that had all but disappeared a century ago outweighed all the challenges. This great North Country life might have been pretty much destroyed by advancing civilization, but it lived on in the cold, deep woods of the Alaska wilderness. Finally, if you came from a high-stress job like mine, there was something priceless about waking up each morning knowing that whatever problems arose during the day would be resolved before you laid your head on the pillow that night.

It was hard to leave that cheery blaze, but eventually I wandered back to check on the teams and lay down on top of my sled. As I became drowsier, it seemed to me that Lavon's team was moving around when it should have been stationary with the sled firmly anchored and the lead dog's end of the gang line firmly tied to a bush. I walked over to find that one of his dogs had chewed the gang line in two behind his swing dogs. The front end of his team had joined the back end of his team and they were all bunched together. Fortunately, his dogs were friendly, so none of them was inclined to fight; however, one of the males found a female in heat.

I stood by patiently for a half hour or so until they disconnected and then spliced his gang line back together again for him. When I woke him up, I told him he had a chewer in his team that had gnawed the gang line in two but didn't bother to tell him that two of his dogs had had a passionate affair as a result. I figured—why make him worry?

When it was my turn to sleep, I grabbed my sleeping bag and headed for the cabin. The front bedroom was full of mushers, as were the living room and the bathroom. Beds, floors, couches, everything was full of bodies. I wandered into one of the back bedrooms and found room for about half a sleeping bag on the floor. I wandered into the other back bedroom and found about the same situation. It seemed to me that the other bedroom looked a little better, so I dragged my sleeping bag back over there, but it just looked too full. I dragged my sleeping bag back to the other one again and then back and then back again. I suddenly realized how rummy I'd become wandering back and forth between bedrooms time after time trying to decide which one had one square foot more room on the floor than the other. Like a dog circling his bed, repeatedly trying to get it just right, this was carrying things a bit far.

I decided the heck with it and just wandered into the last bedroom. It was obvious I could get half my sleeping bag on the floor inside the room and the other half would just have to stick out in the hall. There was a pile of four or five pillows at the foot of the bed nearest the door. I tossed all the pillows but one aside and rolled my sleeping bag out with my head right at the foot of the bed. Libby Riddles was sleeping on the bed and muttered something about that loud snoring as I crawled into my bag. Ron Robbins was sleeping on one of the other beds and was snoring louder than anybody I'd ever heard in my life. It was the most abrasive, loud, raucous racket imaginable and how anybody else in that bedroom could sleep was beyond me. Libby hollered at him to be quiet, which shut him up for a moment, but he was soon at it again. I've had more complaints about my snoring than I care to remember, some of them angry. It felt good to see someone else catching heck.

Although I'm normally a light sleeper, I was soon sound asleep, flat on my back. Perhaps the fact that it was two o'clock in the morning had something to do with it. I'd slept for an hour or so when an owl swooped down out of the sky and landed on my face grabbing me and pulling with all of its might with its talons. It absolutely scared the daylights out of me and I let out a yell and grabbed it with a fierce grip. The owl tried to let go of my face but by then I had it firmly in my grasp.

Climbing the broad saddle before entering Rainy Pass was easy going on a nice sunny day. The beauty of the snow-covered range was unsurpassed but rough and dangerous during a blizzard because there is nothing to stop the wind and nothing to seek shelter behind. In rough going in poor visibility, the team could get hopelessly lost if the leaders veered just a few feet off the trail. *Jeff Schultz Photo*

Libby let out a frightened shriek that woke me up. I asked her what was going on. Apparently, Ron's loud snoring had kept her awake to the point where she was totally annoyed and, remembering the pile of pillows at the foot of her bed, she had reached over to grab one to throw at him. Instead of a pillow, she'd grabbed my face, scaring the daylights out of both of us. How ol' Ron managed to sleep through this, I'll never know, but he kept snoring faithfully through the entire episode. When Libby and I got ourselves calmed down, Libby grabbed one of those pillows and threw it at him again as hard as she could, and hollered at him to shut up. He did for a little while but was soon at it again. The next time I was aware of anything was when Lavon woke me at six o'clock in the morning to take the early-morning shift with the dogs.

About that time the race marshal asked Bucky Winkley if she could hire him to take a couple of snowmachines up into the pass and see what the weather was doing with the possibility in mind of breaking a trail out through the pass to Hell's Gate and down the south fork of the Kuskokwim to the Rohn River checkpoint. The mushers all rejoiced over the possibility of getting out of there and eagerly watched Bucky making his preparations. After an hour or so, he took off with two snowmachines, one pulling a sled loaded with fuel and the other pulling a sled loaded with trail markers consisting of laths with flags tied to them. He disappeared instantly into the swirling blizzard. We decided we'd wait an hour or two and then maybe try to follow him.

Approximately twenty minutes later, however, he came back covered with snow from head to toe. He said there was such a dense whiteout up there in that blowing snow that he literally couldn't see where he was going. There was no definition so you couldn't tell whether you were going uphill or down or whether you were driving into a creek bottom or over a bluff. It was just too dangerous to stay out there so he'd come back. With that sobering news, the rest of us just settled in as comfortably as we could for a long wait.

That night at ten o'clock the race marshal unfroze the race, which meant we could leave anytime we wished; however, travel was impossible. There were still no trail markers for the first thirty miles up in that high country and there was no trail. The wind was still blowing, creating a fierce ground blizzard, so travel was impossible until morning. The race manager had finally gotten food hauled into Rohn River, up the trail, so there was technically no reason to hold the teams any longer.

By now our dogs were so frisky and wild that leaving them alone even for a few moments was too hazardous. With the race unfrozen, Lavon wanted the option of leaving anytime he wanted to without having to wake me up. Because of these two factors, we both slept in our sleds that night to be handy if problems arose. Four times during the night, dogfights developed in my team. I didn't have any dogs along that were fighters but these circumstances were different. This was similar to having a group of children confined in a house for too long. They had far too much energy and had been prancing and dancing and pulling and teasing one another for days. Some of the older dogs had become irritable.

I awakened to the sounds of a savage fight, leaped out of my sleeping bag with a roar, and headed for the dogs. Normally, just my yelling at them was enough to make them stop and back off. I shuffled dogs around to separate the two that were in a row. It was Fuzz, an older dog from up north, and Jack, an eighteen-month-old pup. The battle didn't last long enough to even seem serious. Later, there was some growling and a little tussle and that was it. As soon as I heard the noise, I yelled from inside my sleeping bag as I struggled to get out and the fight stopped. I went over and moved Jack away from Fuzz, figuring it was probably Fuzz that had caused the problem.

Even the flat stretches coming down the Dalzell Gorge could be a challenge. Note the top of the dog's head being carried in the sled. She had become tired climbing the mountain to the pass and Burt was giving her a rest to see if she couldn't regain her energy and continue on to Nome. A dog that was rested would usually refuse to accept a ride, but an exhausted dog was more than happy to lie down on Burt's parka and enjoy the ride in comfort. *Jeff Schultz photo.*

As I led Jack away, I noticed he was limping. On closer examination, I found where Fuzz had bit him hard on his right foot, creating a number of severe puncture wounds. I made Jack comfortable for the night and crawled back into my sleeping bag. Come morning, I had the vet examine Jack. Fortunately, no lasting damage had been done, but he was definitely in no condition to continue. I left him tied in the dropped-dog area with an ample supply of food to last until he could be taken back to Anchorage by airplane.

It was time to get ready for our final push through the Alaska Range. By then we knew that Rainy Pass was too dangerous and that we would be directed to take the long way through Ptarmigan Valley and Hell's Gate. We expected this route to be eighty miles or so, which was a long trek through the mountains. Because of this and the gale-force winds that were still blowing in the high country, I took a huge pile of food along for the dogs in case we were pinned down back in those mountains.

I cooked the final meal for them in Rainy Pass, ate a good meal myself and was ready to go. John Arnold and Eric Halverson had finally made it through from the other side and were on their way back toward Rohn when I left. It turned out to be a gorgeous day for a trip through the mountains. Although the wind was blowing thirty miles an hour, still the sun was shining and the mountains and valley were beautiful covered with fresh snow. The dogs were well rested and eager for a quick trip.

Most of us pushed to have the race marshal time us out of the checkpoint in the same order and spacing as we'd arrived. After all, those of us up front had worked hard to gain a position at the front and didn't think it was fair to make us restart in a group. She disagreed and I left Rainy Pass in twenty-sixth position in a mass start. I had arrived in Rohn in sixth place after passing twenty teams along the way. I felt like my team was as good as any in the race except for maybe three or four others, so I expected an exciting race in the days to come.

There might be heavy snow through the Susitna Valley and on the trail to Rainy Pass, and totally different conditions on the other side of the mountains. The Farewell Burn out of Rohn checkpoint was often devoid of snow making it rough on sleds, dogs and mushers. A couple of the dogs turned around to look at Burt as if to say, "Hey Boss, are you sure we're on the right trail here?"

Chapter Fourteen
Nikolai to Iditarod, Freight Train, 1985

My trip out of Rohn was routine, but the run from Nikolai to McGrath was difficult. Temperatures were high when I left Nikolai after an eight-hour rest. Dogs move more slowly when temperatures are warm or if the trail is a little soft. In addition, they don't seem to move quite as quickly during daylight as they do in the dark. All of these factors played a part since the run was made in the daylight with a soft, punchy trail. Not only was the trail punchy but snow had fallen all day. The good work of the teams ahead of me breaking trail was neutralized by continuing heavy snows. At one time, it was snowing so hard that I literally couldn't see more than a hundred feet ahead. Rick Swenson was behind me and yelled he didn't think he had ever seen it snow that hard in his whole life.

Even with these factors, it seemed that my dogs were moving more slowly than usual. Rick trailed along behind me for a while, although I offered to yield the trail to him a couple of times. I wasn't really sure why he was staying behind me, since I was sure his team was faster than mine. He was the premier long-distance musher in Alaska, having won the Iditarod Trail Dog Sled Race four times—more than any other musher.

After a while, I stopped my team and motioned him on by, being curious to see just what the difference in our teams was. He went past and disappeared into the distance so fast that I was a little disheartened. I began to worry that maybe my dogs had become sick or that I had taken too much out of them on the run from Rohn to Nikolai. It was obvious that Rick had been coasting along behind me resting his dogs. When he figured I'd broken enough trail, he just blasted by me and disappeared.

Part of the fun during Iditarod is the hoopla and excitement brought to Alaska by press from all over the world. Here, the press interviews Burt at the start of the 2004 Iditarod race.

I arrived at McGrath after dark feeling a little blue. Dick and DeeDee were there when I checked in and told me that my team looked great, stronger than any team that had arrived so far. They suggested that I feed the dogs and just keep on toward Takotna. It was tempting with Takotna only twenty-three miles down the trail, but memories of slogging along during the day were still fresh in my mind, so I expressed my appreciation and decided to keep on my schedule and stay for five or six hours.

I was directed to the home of a family that had volunteered to host some mushers. I found a good place to park my dogs, fed them, then went inside to eat and get some rest. The television was on and Lavon was being interviewed. The announcer asked him about his moose encounter out of Rabbit Lake. "Yup," Lavon said. "I was coming over a low ridge out of Rabbit Lake when I came upon a moose out in the middle of a swamp. I just put on my snowshoes and broke a trail out around her. No problem."

I just shook my head and crawled into my sleeping bag.

Five hours after arriving in McGrath, I awoke from a deep sleep, hitched my dogs and drove them out of town. I hadn't seen a soul since I checked in and had no idea who might be out ahead of me. The trail was hard and fast and the dogs seemed to enjoy the run. With all the snowmachine traffic between McGrath and Takotna, the trail had been well packed all winter so the trail always had a good hard bottom.

We popped up on the bank at Takotna and could see the lights of the checkpoint a short distance ahead. A team was parked near the checkpoint, so I pulled my team beyond it for a quick getaway.

I went inside to check in and found Tim Osmar relaxing.

The Takotna checkpoint always had great food for the mushers.

"Burt, get over here and have a piece of pie. While you're at it, you can sign these annuals."

"I'd love to take the time, but if I spend more than five minutes here, my dogs will settle in and won't want to move. I'd better keep moving."

"Burt, you aren't going anywhere until you *eat* a piece of pie and *sign* those damned annuals!"

I obediently sat down, ate the pie and signed the annuals.

When I walked out the door, Tim was so close behind me that I thought he was attached.

"You in a hurry, Tim?"

"Nah, just getting ready to leave."

I hiked up my team with Tim's lead dog's nose literally pressed against my leg. Tim stayed right there all the way to Ophir. We arrived and Audra Forsgren checked us in.

I had led the race into Ophir with Tim right behind me. The checker for some reason checked Tim in first, indicating in the records that he was leading the race at that point. I didn't really mind since Tim was a nice young man in his first Iditarod and was doing well.

Audra told us that Dick Mackey, the race manager, still didn't have all the food drops delivered to Iditarod, the next check point, which was the ghost town the race was named after. Tim asked Audra if the race was frozen. She was vague in responding and Tim pushed the issue until she said yes, the race was frozen until food drops were delivered to Iditarod. What a danged smart question for a young man, eighteen years old to push. I've respected Tim for his acuity ever since. He is a fine musher and a fine young man.

As long as no one told the mushers that the race was frozen, the clock kept ticking. Once the race was frozen, we hoped that all teams would be held and released in the order and time that they had arrived at the checkpoint. We felt that the race marshal was unfair when she put off freezing the race as long as possible to allow the later teams to catch up with the front-runners. We had worked hard to stay up front and she intended to erase our advantage for the sake of convenience. She wanted to get the race over with and didn't want to have to drag it out any longer than necessary. According to Audra, the marshal had *told* the checkers to announce the freeze only if someone asked.

A timed start required spacing the teams out of the checkpoints, which would take more time and effort and would spread the pack out, but it was the fair thing to do. When we did restart after the freeze, the marshal started Tim and me fifty minutes later than our timing warranted. A reporter noticed it and chastised the race marshal in the press for the unfairness.[4] A reporter for the Anchorage Daily News explained the scenario in detail (See Appendix D).

Problems persisted and many of the mushers were pretty disgusted. The level of frustration among the mushers was clear when famed Iditarod musher, Rick Swenson, said at Koyuk, "Whatever happens, I'm not running this race again. I'm just not going to put up with the crap they (race organizers) put you through. They can find some other sucker."[5] See Appendix C for the entire article. Whether at the front of the pack or the back, every musher was *racing*. Each had invested everything for an entire year to do the best they could. Many had dreamed for years of the time they would be part of this great event. Mushers expect Alaska to throw everything it has at them on the way to Nome. We are tough and will endure any agony that nature bestows, but we become irate when not treated fairly. Small wonder resentment ran deep when the race manager failed to deliver and the race marshal issued peculiar rulings that impacted the outcome of the race. Most mushers appreciated Rick speaking out for them.

Of course, Rick's heart was with Iditarod and he continued to race.

As the freeze continued, we used the time in Ophir to doctor the dogs' feet, feed them huge amounts of good rich food and visit with our buddies as they arrived.

While we were resting the dogs and feeding them at Ophir, the press and a number of fans showed up. Normally, the press rarely came to Ophir because of the difficulty of getting there, the lack of accommodations, and because they liked the hoopla of covering the first teams into Iditarod, the halfway point in the race. Nobody wanted to get stuck in Ophir and miss the excitement at the halfway point. This time, however, the weather was so bad up ahead toward Iditarod that planes couldn't get there with the press and officials. Ophir was their next choice.

Eventually we got word that the race would restart and we would be leaving in the same order and timing in which we had arrived. A good pal, Tony Oney, stopped by to visit as I fed my dogs and prepared to leave Ophir. Tony was one of the finest bush pilots in Alaska and was flying the television crew along the race. He was a famed Dall sheep guide as well as one of Alaska's old-time polar bear guides. In fact, we'd met while polar bear hunting years earlier.

---

[4] Anchorage Daily News, March 14, 1985

[5] Bill Sherwonit Article, Anchorage Times, August 4, 1985

As we talked, he asked if I thought I could win the halfway prize at Iditarod. The halfway trophy would be a great thing to set on the mantle, and the winner received $2,000 worth of silver ingots from Alascom, our local long-distance carrier. I told him that I probably could but the important race was to Nome, not Iditarod. It was still snowing and I didn't want to break trail all the way to Iditarod and take something out of the dogs that would slow them down for the rest of the race.

Burt checking the records of other teams with the checker at Ophir. It was good to get a feel for the other teams to help with your own strategy. *Jeff Schultz photo.*

"Too bad," he said. "I bet on you to win the halfway prize." I told him sorry, but no way could I do that if I hoped to keep things together all the way to Nome. I told him how much I appreciated his loyalty, but I had the best team I'd ever had and so far hadn't had much of a problem staying up front. If I didn't goof something up, I should have a top-five finish, and even had dreams of winning.

As we visited, I asked him what the stakes were. A jug of whisky, he replied. Well, I figured I could buy him dinner and some drinks when we got to Nome to make up for the lost jug. I appreciated him for being a good buddy and having faith in me. I asked him whom he bet with.

"Doctor Bob Sept."

"*Doctor Bob Sept?*" I repeated in disbelief.

Bob was *my* veterinarian and a good friend. I couldn't believe he would bet against me. He'd taken care of my dogs for a couple of years and didn't have any more faith in me and my team than that? It is hard to describe how disgusted I was. Some friend. Those things seem to be magnified when we're tired.

I told Tony, "You don't have to worry about winning that jug. I'll go win it for you."

What fools men can be.

Soon the dogs were fed and the official signaled us that it was time to go. Tim and I had a discussion about who would lead. I reminded him that I'd led all the way to Ophir and it was his turn. We weren't going anywhere until he got going. While we were discussing it, the checker reminded us that she had checked Tim in first so he should leave first. I was more than happy to have him break trail for a while.

We had cruised on for a mile or so when Tim stopped to tell me that his leaders wouldn't go. I'd heard that story before, and it was obvious that his dogs were doing just fine. We argued for a few minutes and then Tim continued. It didn't take much to figure things out. Dean Osmar, Tim's dad, a former Iditarod champion and good friend of mine, had coached him well. Being the first team takes a lot out of the dogs whether there's fresh snow on the trail or not. It is always easier on the dogs to follow another team. It lifts their spirits and gives them something to chase.

Tim knew this and was doing whatever he could to get me out front. But I'd led him from Takotna to Ophir and was ready to do whatever I could to keep him out front until I figured he'd done his share.

The trail wasn't too bad and in about an hour and a half we broke clear of the timber and started out onto the open tundra. It was still daylight but beginning to get dim. As soon as we got to the open country, Tim insisted that his leaders just wouldn't go without a good trail to follow and he pulled them over. I went on ahead, determined that if he wouldn't take his turn in lead, I'd try to ditch him somewhere along the way. He was just too danged good to do any favors for, eighteen years old or not. I believe he'd won every Junior Iditarod race he was ever in and looked to do exceptionally well in the bigger race.

We drove on across open tundra to Don's cabin, affectionately known as the "lettuce crate." They called it that because the cabin was so dilapidated that the slats forming the siding on the walls had spaces between them just like a lettuce crate. You could see daylight from inside through all the holes in the walls—drafty but nice for a musher traveling the long, cold trail to Nome.

We parked our teams and I got out the snacks for my dogs. Tim asked me how long I intended to stay and I told him about four hours. He unloaded his sled and soon had gear scattered all over the place. There were pots, pans, cooking gear, a sleeping bag, axe, booties, spare clothes, bags of meat and whatever else he had. Soon I could see fire from his stove and figured he was as spread out as he was going to get.

I quietly loaded my sled, lined out my dogs, pulled my snow hook and eased on out of there.

I'd gone about fifty feet when Tim shouted, "Hey, where are you going?"

I yelled back that I was out of there and I'd see him later.

I had to chuckle as I looked back and saw him throwing everything back into the sled. My little trick

Burt leaves Ophir on the way to Don's cabin. It's a warm sunny afternoon so both parkas are unzipped, but he's wearing everything in anticipation of a bitter cold night after the sun sets. Jeff Schultz photo.

hadn't worked as well as I'd hoped, though. Tim was soon hot on my tail. I drove on a couple of miles and then stopped to give my dogs a little better break than I'd given them at Don's cabin. I figured that if I couldn't shake Tim, there was no sense making it hard on the dogs. I'd just watch my chances and try to shake him again somewhere else down the trail. Eventually, I could see the glow of headlights in the distance behind us and knew that some teams had arrived at Don's cabin and were stopping to feed and rest their dogs. I didn't want to break trail for them, too, so I pulled up and left again with Tim right behind.

It began snowing and the trail was becoming difficult to find. As we mushed along a side hill, I thought I saw a depression in the snow heading off to the right up the hill. The dogs trotted past it so fast that I couldn't be sure at that instant just what had happened. With no teams ahead of us, the dogs had no scent to follow and were going by sight and feel. The dogs began to wallow in the deeper snow. It was apparent that my leaders had zipped right past the trail and we were heading down toward a creek bottom and a mass of alders, bushes and deep snow. This was the perfect spot to try to ditch Tim.

I yelled back to Tim that I wasn't certain of the trail and thought we ought to split up to improve our chances of finding it. I asked him which way he'd like to go: downhill along the path we were going or back up hill. He chose down as I hoped he would and went by me in the direction we'd been heading. I swung my team around and made my way back to where the trail had veered off up the hill. I gave the command for my leaders to "haw" and we were back on the trail to Iditarod. As soon as I was sure of the trail, I turned off my headlight and moved quietly up the hill and out of sight on the other side. What the heck, if I was going to break trail for Tim all the way to Iditarod, I didn't need him in my back pocket. Besides, these shenanigans were half the fun.

It continued to snow all of the way to Iditarod, making going difficult and slow. I turned my headlight off going uphill so I wouldn't be seen from behind and turned it back on going down the other side to make sure I was still on the right trail.

About an hour out of Iditarod, a snowmachine approached me from ahead. When the driver saw me, he spun the machine around and headed back to Iditarod. The loose, fresh snow on the trail was six to eight inches deep, so the snowmachine track packed the trail and really helped. A few minutes later, I heard the sounds of an airplane. I'd been concerned that the officials and press wouldn't arrive because of the blizzard and I wouldn't get to hear those immortal words, "You go for the gold in Nome, but you race for the silver halfway."

I didn't see Tim again until he reached Iditarod fifteen minutes behind me. He'd seen me cresting every ridge after daylight but was never able to gain. It made me proud of my dogs to be able to stay ahead of him while breaking trail. The Osmar boys always had good teams.

I had broken trail all the way from Ophir to Iditarod except for the first hour and a half. The trip took all night and into the next day. I knew that the gold miners who journeyed to Iditarod decades earlier had more challenges than I was having even with the slow trail so we had no reason to complain. The *Dictionary of Alaska Place Names* shows Iditarod located on the bank of the Iditarod River. Iditarod had become the supply and commercial center of the Innoko-Iditarod placer district shortly after its founding in June 1920. It was on the summer water route and winter sled trail. In those days, Iditarod had a population of about 600 or 700 people. A post office was maintained from 1919 to 1929. It's abandoned now.

Approaching Don's cabin, known as the lettuce crate because it was so rickety you could see daylight through the slats in the walls. Rich Swenson and Sunny Lindner went out one summer and made a project out of repairing the old cabin and making it weather tight. Gold miners still mine this historic area. *Jeff Schultz photo.*

As we approached Iditarod, the prospect of being awarded the Alascom halfway prize became exciting. The first teams into Iditarod were always greeted by a huge contingency of race officials, members of the press, and Alascom company officials waiting to present the trophy and the silver ingots. *Except for 1985, the year I won it.* The storm was so bad and snowfall so heavy that no aircraft with officials and press could make it into Iditarod. That airplane I'd heard had lost visibility and turned back toward McGrath.

But the ghost town had more than just ghosts. A giant of a man named Freight Train was standing there! In his thirties, he had a smile as big as himself.

Sulatna Crossing checkpoint. Mushers meeting at a remote Alaska wilderness camp in winter brought visions of a time long past. Burt fills his thermos while the dogs rest. These moments are hard to find in today's civilized world. *Jeff Schultz photo.*

"Welcome to Iditarod. While you take care of your dogs, I'll fix you something to eat."

I parked my dogs on the outgoing trail so I could leave quickly and bailed some water out of the river. My gosh that water was muddy! I boiled it for the dogs but melted snow for my own drinks.

When I was done with the dogs, I went inside and Freight Train invited me to sit down for a dinner of what he said was buffalo. He was kidding. It turned out to be moose roast with all the trimmings, including vegetables, mashed potatoes, gravy and coffee. Freight Train and several of his buddies mined gold over in Flat several miles away. They'd come over to watch the teams come through and took over checkpoint duties when nobody showed up. What a guy he was. Big, boisterous, and happy. His pals seemed to worship him and I figured I'd found some true Alaskans. Those guys will never be forgotten.

Freight Train made such an impression on me that I have to take you forward several years to a sad day in my life. On that morning, sadness hit me when I read the obituaries like one does in his sixty-fifth year. I saw the familiar face, and my heart sank. The obituary said that Darrell Raymond "Freight Train" Olson, forty-three, died on December 15, 2000, at his home in Seward. It went on to say that simultaneous potlatches would be held at four o'clock in the afternoon. Saturday in Palmer and Seward.

As I read the obituary, my mind raced back to when Freight Train and I had met at Iditarod, deep in the Alaska bush. I remembered how the 1985 Iditarod Trail Sled Dog Race had been a series of hurry-up-and-wait situations, how those heavy storms had made it a challenge to move food drops and officials along the trail ahead of the teams. It was amazing how Freight Train had saved the day for me. I'd looked forward to the greeting by the press and the officials, and being awarded the halfway prize and was disappointed when it didn't happen, but the minute I met Freight Train, all of that became unimportant. He was so hospitable and gregarious and just plain fun that nothing else mattered.

I'd promised myself for years that I would fly out to Flat one day and get to know Freight Train better and make sure he knew how much his actions had meant to me. I've always had an airplane, so could have flown to Flat most any time. But I'd been busy and kept putting it off until it was too late. Now I'd never get to see him. It is surprising how an acquaintance of but a few hours can have such a strong impact on you for the rest of your days.

Back to Iditarod—after jawboning with Freight Train for an hour or so over dinner, he showed me to a tent frame set aside for the mushers. It consisted of a wooden floor with a framework over which a wall tent had been stretched. I rolled out my sleeping bag and fell asleep listening to the howl of that furious blizzard.

I'd slept for several hours when a volunteer came and yelled at me through the door. "Burt, Libby has left and Rick is getting ready to go. You need to get up and get out of here."

I explained from the depths of my sleeping bag, "Thanks for the info, but there's no way I'm leaving Iditarod in the middle of the night in this howling blizzard. There are a hundred ridges to cross between here and Shageluk. The trail across those ridges will drift full in two minutes after a musher has passed. I broke trail most of the way from Ophir. I'll rest the dogs 'til daylight and maybe the wind will die down some. I am comfortable in this tent, but it won't be fun if I get pinned down out there on one of those ridges."

I left later with Dewey. All the teams that had left the previous night during the blizzard were camped along the trail as we mushed by.

As we mushed toward Shageluk, the dogs dropped down into a creek bottom and made a hard right turn up the creek. There stood Rick Swenson—not a dog in sight. "What the hell happened to you?"

"I dropped my camera when I came down into the creek bottom. I thought my team was anchored, but when I stepped behind the sled to retrieve it, the dogs got away. Would you mind anchoring them when you catch them? The hook is dangling so it should catch on something before long."

"Rick, you better get on my sled and ride along with me. We'll see if we can find the dogs together. You don't know how far they've gone and you might be hiking all day before you catch them."

"Okay, thanks, Burt."

Rick got on the runners with me and we did find his dogs. The snow hook had caught on a stump and stopped the dogs dead in their tracks.

"Thanks, Burt. See you up the trail."

Hitting the trail out of Sulatna Crossing after a good rest for Burt and the dogs. This wilderness camp with its wall tent and smoke from the wood stove was a cozy, unforgettable image. The contrast between the warmth here and the bitter cold night to come out on the trail was part of what made the memories so rich. *Jeff Schultz photo.*

Chapter Fifteen
A Musher's Bond with His Dogs, Thoughts Out of Iditarod

As we mushed along toward Shageluk, my mind drifted back to when we had trained for this race. I'd learned so much since I'd begun training sled dogs and had developed so many great relationships with my dogs. I'd learned that my dogs had personalities nearly as varied and interesting as my human friends. Well, not quite as interesting. I'd come a long way since I handled for Dick when I could hardly tell one dog from another. Back then, they all looked alike. Now they were individuals. I believe part of the reason I never really got lonely out in the bush was my love for the dogs.

It was my personal goal to treat my dogs with as much love and attention as I could. That won for me the coveted Leonard Seppala Humanitarian Award for the best care of a competitive dog team during the 1984 Iditarod Race. A clipping from the Anchorage Daily News dated March 20, 1984 under the headline "Bomhoff Wins Award for Treatment of Dogs" read:

Iditarod musher Burt Bomhoff had rested his team a while in Nulato then harnessed them to head for Kaltag, 42 miles down the Yukon River.

But instead of the Last Great Race on Earth, his dogs had something else on their agenda—a nap on the frozen river in the sun.

Many a musher would have wrung his hands in despair, or taken his leader aside for a little meeting of the minds. Not Bomhoff. He left them to their nap, and after a quick chat with Larry "Cowboy" Smith at the Nulato checkpoint, he joined them, snoozing on his sled in the afternoon sun.

Few would call that racing strategy, but it worked well for Bomhoff, a 48-year-old Anchorage engineer. He finished twelfth in Nome, high enough to take home some prize money. He also was awarded the Leonhard Seppala Award for the most humane treatment and care of his team.

The 16 race veterinarians stationed along the 1,131-mile trail from Anchorage to Nome each voted for the five mushers they thought showed the best care and treatment of their team. The musher with the most votes won the award, a lead-crystal cup with an illuminated wooden base. It was presented Monday evening at the Iditarod Trail Sled Dog Race awards banquet in Nome.

Del Carter, chief veterinarian for the race, said Bomhoff was chosen because he kept a written history on all of his dogs, and the condition of their feet. All along the trail, he could be seen scratching notes into a tattered little notebook he kept in his breast pocket.[6]

I was proud to receive the award, and a certain day during training came to mind as we mushed along. It had been our day off. The dogs and I had earned a break. I sat on Lil's doghouse in the middle of the yard and surveyed my dogs. I felt like a teacher surveying his classroom or a coach his team. Lil loved it when I sat on her house. She would politely but warmly lay her head on my lap and slowly wag her tail. She would bask in the closeness, almost afraid to move for fear I'd notice and move away.

I'd had dogs before, pet dogs and hunting dogs. But those were dogs that hung around looking for a friendly pat or lunch. Even the hunting dogs were primarily companions except for a month or so during hunting season. Between work and family, even hunting season wasn't too intense.

---

[6] Anchorage Daily News, March 20, 1984

Mushing was different. We were in constant contact, twelve hours a day, seven days a week. I was either hitching them or driving them or unhitching them. Lots of physical contact. On the handler's day off, I fed them, although feeding and shoveling poop was normally the handler's job. As I sat with my team, I spoke to them, one after another, giving each dog some attention. It wasn't necessary to call out, just a soft greeting by name and the farthest dog perked up his ears. Just like people, each dog reacted a little differently. Some actually smiled; others gave me a glance that said, "Hey, boss, it's my day off. How about a little space here?" Some came alive and danced all over the place as if to say they needed far more than a simple greeting . . . they needed some quality time.

Burt and Joe Daugherty let the dogs out to stretch at the restart of the race. Everything is done to assure the dogs comfort, including straw bedding. Always supportive, Burt's daughter Jill and son Brad are to the right of the picture.

As I mushed along, a conversation I'd had years earlier came to mind. I'd been sitting in Joe Degnan's roadhouse in McGrath one evening visiting. Joe and I were the only people there, he behind the bar polishing a glass and me on a stool sipping a Crown on ice. Joe was a man who'd been out in this Alaska mining country for decades. He had partnered with pioneer miner Toivo Rosander in placer mining for gold in the creeks west of McGrath. He had mushed dogs in the early days throughout the Kuskokwim River country. Now he ran the roadhouse. I did a lot of engineering work in the villages along the Yukon and

Kuskokwim Rivers back then and never missed a chance to spend time with the old-timers.

Degnan's Roadhouse, with its bar, restaurant and rooms, was a favorite place for sourdoughs traveling the country. Sourdoughs included miners, trappers, bush pilots, and mushers from the outlying area. These guys were loners, used to plying their trade in Alaska's most remote and lonesome places.

Puddin, one of Burt's favorite leaders, enjoyed a little reassurance. She seemed almost human in her responses. A tiny dog, she had a huge heart and lead Burt through some of the worst blizzards he had ever encountered. Burt crouches beside the leaders, not in front of them so they never lose focus on where they're heading at this important moment. Famed furrier, Perry Green, made the parka ruff for Burt out of wolverine and white wolf.
Jeff Schultz photo.

We were talking sled dogs when Joe commented on the bond that develops between a musher and his dogs. These aren't just animals that you put up when you are done for the night. They are your friends and workmates. You care for each one personally. It is a bond that a non-musher probably wouldn't ever really understand. The relationship between man and a working dog isn't the same as the relationship between man and pet, no matter how many tricks a pet may learn. It is just not the same as working together. Joe's eyes turned misty as he talked about mushing a dog team for so many miles across the quiet wilderness Alaska. That life was hard but satisfying. Those were years when you traveled by dog team in the winter or you didn't travel at all. Many used snowshoes but it was a hard way to travel. Dick Berg and I regularly traveled a twelve-mile circuit on snowshoes, hunting goats in southeast Alaska during the early sixties, so I knew it was rough.

The dogs were always fed first then the musher. Burt snicks ground beef patties apart with his axe so they'll thaw quicker once the water has boiled. The patties are pre-cut before the race to make it easier, but they still freeze together. The Coleman stove has been replaced by Gene Leonard's alcohol burner, which simply consists of two buckets, one larger than the other and with air vents. This was much faster, hotter, cheaper and easier than keeping a Coleman stove operating in extreme cold. *Schultz photo.*

Sled dogs have individual personalities much like people do, with some of them being absolute characters. A pecking order seems to establish itself much as you find in an office or at a construction job site. Some dogs are extremely affectionate and others are aloof. Some are dominant and almost go looking for a fight, but others won't fight even with another dog on top of them. Some seem to be extremely intelligent, playing with a stick or a food pan in creative ways, whereas others act dumb with almost no personality at all.

I've told you something about Puddin before. She was my favorite leader of all time and weighed about forty-five pounds. She was purchased from Joee Redington in the fall of 1984.

We had started this race with Noise, my fastest dog, in the lead, but he just didn't like the pressure of being up there alone. Leaders have a way of letting you know when they are feeling too much pressure and Noise was doing everything he could to tell me. First looking back over his shoulder occasionally, then more and more until he was looking at me almost constantly, imploring me to either give him some help or put him back in the team. In a race you have to solve your problems fairly quickly, so I moved Puddin up next to him.

Noise was a little temperamental and didn't really like sleeping with the team. Burt tied him to the sled to give him a little space but then awakened from his nap to find Noise had made himself comfortable. It was amazing how cozy one could be in the Alaska winter, with warm gear and a soft place to lie down. *Anchorage Daily News Photo.*

Fatigue lines Burt's face after a week of little sleep, as he takes a break at Ophir. His gear is hung up to dry at the left behind him. One can almost fall asleep sitting up. The dogs are the priority so it's up to the musher to keep them happy and healthy at whatever cost to himself.
Jeff Schultz photo.

From that moment on Puddin did a super job, but Noise just never really got with it again during the race. He would run okay for a little while and then start looking back over his shoulder and slowing things down. I stopped again to move him back in the team and let Puddin do it on her own. From that moment until we crossed the finish line, we never again had any problem with speed or control. Puddin streaked along as fast as she could go and never needed a command. She was following the scent of the teams ahead of us. She never hesitated as she followed the course, first over the Iditarod Trail to the Susitna River, then up the Susitna and Yentna rivers to Skwentna.

But, more about that later. We had enough to do making our way to Shageluk and on to the Yukon River in the aftermath of that devastating blizzard.

Chapter Sixteen
Cold on the Yukon River

The weather improved as we mushed through Shageluk and then on to the Yukon River at Anvik and up-river to Grayling. I arrived at Grayling in second place behind John Cooper and then spent ten hours visiting friends and taking a nap. I gave my dogs a good rest. Then I drove my team out of Grayling onto the Yukon River ice at mid-afternoon under clear skies and high temperatures. It was the kind of glorious day that makes dog sled travel such a wonderful experience. Clear skies often make daylight hours warm and pleasant, but the lack of clouds frequently causes nighttime temperatures to plummet, sometimes right off the bottom of the thermometer. It was to be that kind of night.

My plan was to snack the dogs briefly somewhere along the way, and then run all the way to Kaltag. As the sun dipped lower on the horizon, the temperature dropped and the cold began to settle down on the Yukon River. It got colder and colder until it reached fifty-two degrees below zero. Traveling alone up the Yukon with only my dogs for company was pleasant and the miles drifted by. The northern lights came out and flashed brilliantly ahead of us. Even with a heavy parka and insulated pants, the cold slowly penetrated to my body. Mukluks and beaver mitts kept my hands and feet fairly warm, and a face mask protected my nose and cheeks.

Beaver mitts are one item of winter gear that technology has not managed to improve. They hold residual heat like nothing else. Take them off to do chores until your hands are nearly frozen, put them back on and your hands are instantly warm.

The dogs sped along a well-packed trail while the Northern Lights continued to shoot their fiery curtains across the sky with different patterns and colors coming and going all the time. Sometimes a ribbon of light shot across the sky in an irregular path and then the entire bottom seemed to drop out of it, falling like a curtain toward the earth, only to disappear and reform in another pattern. It was evenings like this when I would put the seat out on my sled, pour a cup of hot chocolate from the thermos, turn off my headlight and enjoy the wonder of winter in Alaska.

Ready to face extreme cold weather with the right gear, including ruff made with wolverine and white wolf, Native beaver mitts and heavy parka. Beaver mitts held residual heat so you could work bare-handed and then warm your hands immediately by simply putting them back on. The dark fur in the ruff was wolverine. It was sewed next to your face because it didn't collect frost like most other furs.

Aside from occasionally feeling a slight chill, the only sign of the numbing low temperature is the frost rising above the dogs as they trot quickly along. Your eyes occasionally freeze shut when you blink. When this happens, you don't try to pick the ice away or you are likely to pull your eyelashes out. Instead, you take off your mitt for a moment and lay your finger over your eye to thaw the ice and then try not to blink again. You don't want to be taking off your mitts any more than necessary.

I looked back and saw a trail of ice fog behind us over our path. This was formed by the dogs' breath coupled with the extreme low temperatures, which created our own smog, our own natural contrail.

I continued up the Yukon River, enjoying the night

and occasionally stopping to rest and feed the dogs. They burned up a great deal more energy when the temperature was extremely low, so it was necessary to stop more often and feed them more fatty foods. The dogs' snacks were kept on top of the sled, so no time was wasted when it came time to feed. Soon we were at Blackburn, two-thirds of the way to Eagle Island. I stopped to quickly snack the dogs and saw that five or six teams had already arrived and were apparently asleep in the cabin.

Just then, Libby drove in and quickly snacked her dogs. Then she commanded them to go. In moments, her dogs had settled in for a nap and didn't want to get up and go. With all due respect to Libby, whom I admire and respect, I had never heard such language in my life! I had worked my entire career from the time I was sixteen in and around construction and thought I'd heard everything. I was amazed. So were her dogs. They got up and hiked up the trail toward Kaltag like it was their idea.

If I'd had a brain in my head, I'd have followed her.

In one of the dumbest moves I've ever made, I decided to go on up and say hello. Several guys were sitting at the table drinking coffee and offered me a cup. I accepted it and sat down to visit. The warmth of the cabin enveloped my body and I decided to take a nap. One thing led to another and I slept until dawn, landing myself right back in the pack. Had I left, I'd have led into Kaltag and had a shot at winning.

Not long after I left Blackburn, the sun was rising in the east. By mid-morning I had arrived at the checkpoint called Eagle Island. Even with the sun having been up for several hours, the temperature was still thirty-five degrees below zero Fahrenheit. I parked the dogs close to the riverbank, hoping that the sun's rays might somehow reflect on the dogs and give them a little more warmth.

It took two hours to melt snow into boiling water and begin soaking my dog food. In my befuddled state, I didn't realize that within twenty minutes the water was as hot as it was going to get. The heat escaping from the sides of my bucket into the extreme cold equaled the heat produced by the stove. Blazo stoves don't work well at extremely low temperatures. More time wasted. By the time the dogs and I ate, four hours had gone by. I was obviously tired and the low temperatures probably had something to do with drawing my energy down. I should have been more efficient than I was and should have been thinking a little more clearly.

It was about then that I decided to rearrange my sled. I spent a couple of hours emptying everything out onto a tarp, re-sorting it and repacking it onto the sled. By the time I went up to the cabin, I must have been in the checkpoint eight hours and still hadn't rested. When you find yourself wasting time to that extent, you ought to realize it is time to hit the sack and take a nap, which is what I did. The upshot of the whole affair was that I spent fifteen hours at Eagle Island and allowed many teams to leave ahead of me.

After twelve hours mushing on the Yukon River at 56 below zero, everything is frosty including the wolverine ruff. It has to be cold for that to happen, yet Burt was comfortable with the right gear. The two coldest nights Burt spent mushing included a night on the Kuskokwim River at 60 below zero and a night on the Yukon at 56 below zero. With experience and the right gear, travel is possible during these conditions, but can be extremely dangerous for the cheechako (a person newly arrived in Alaska).
Jeff Schultz photo.

I was lulled into relaxing since Rick Swenson was still at the checkpoint and I somehow felt that if we really needed to be gone, Rick would have left. This, of course, was a mistake. Rick Swenson was the only four-time winner of the race and normally had a dog team fast enough to reel in other teams almost at will. I wasn't the musher he was. Several of us decided to leave at midnight, including Rick Swenson and Sonny Lindner. I hoped I could fall in behind them and perhaps draft along with their teams since I expected them to be a little bit faster.

My sled was packed and my dogs hitched when I heard Rick command his team back out onto the trail. Sonny was right behind him. I was almost ready but didn't yet have my face mask on. I decided to start after them and finish putting myself together as we traveled up the river. The temperature had again dropped below minus fifty degrees Fahrenheit and it was then that I realized just how cold that could be. My nose and cheeks instantly experienced a sharp burning sensation, an obvious warning that frostbite was imminent.

I threw back my parka hood, pulled off my mitts and started trying to put on my face mask. The speed of the sled was probably eight or nine miles an hour, creating a breeze as the dogs whisked along the trail. My fingers and hands experienced the same burning sensation as my face, and before I could get the face mask Velcro attached, my hands were in obvious danger of frostbite. Within seconds they were numb to the point of making it impossible to attach the Velcro. I quickly replaced my parka hood, got back into my mitts and bent my head to my chest to provide as much protection from the slight breeze as pos-

Iditarod was great fun, even in the cold. The ruff on Burt's light parka was not made of wolverine so it frosted up at warmer temperatures. During extreme cold, he needed both parkas at the same time.

sible. My hands soon warmed because of the residual heat in my mitts and I made another try at the face mask. This attempt was even more painful than the first. Although I'd been determined to keep up with Sonny and Rick, it was obvious that if I didn't stop my sled and turn downwind, I would likely frostbite my hands and face before I got the face mask in place. This kind of stupidity can haunt you farther down the trail, so I stopped the team, got myself together and then continued.

By then, Rick and Sonny were out of sight, which didn't really matter all that much. I'd traveled mostly alone until now and really enjoyed it more than I did traveling with someone else. The northern sky was again brightened by the Northern Lights and waves of Jack London stories came flooding back to keep me company. I was again in the world of the *Malamute Kid* and *Sitka Charlie*. Tales of the Alaskan gold rush flooded my memory and I could hardly wait to get to Kaltag. It was there that I would pick up the trail to Unalakleet, where other dog mushers had made the heroic run carrying life-saving serum to Nome during 1925.

Burt checks the notebook he always carried to keep track of dog care issues. There were charts in it that helped him keep track of the dogs' feet and medication requirements. He was meticulous in dealing with every issue of dog care. Even with the exertion of cooking and tending the dogs, you knew it was cold when one needed to wear everything you had to stay warm. *Jeff Schultz photo.*

I rested a few hours in Kaltag while I fed the dogs a huge meal. The cold took as much out of the dogs as their work. In spite of the energy drain, I'd managed to keep the dogs fat and happy. Maybe I still had a chance.

We left under clear skies with a tail wind. The miles flew by and we stopped at the site of Old Woman Roadhouse only long enough to snack the dogs. The dogs and I seemed caught up on our rest and were full of vinegar. This high, subarctic tundra was beautiful under clear skies. Only a few puffy clouds drifted along. I could occasionally feel the wind pounding on the back of my parka while snow spindrift skated along the surface indicating a strong east wind.

Chapter Seventeen
Blizzard Out of Shaktoolik, Pinned Down on the Icepack, 1985

We had been in second place at Grayling on the Yukon River but had slipped several places between there and Kaltag. We were now trying to catch up with a steady sustained push across the portage to Unalakleet. We were definitely walking a thin line; we needed to push hard enough to catch up but not so hard as to overextend the dogs. A good, strong team would still be needed when we approached Nome and the finish line.

The moon had dimly lit up the landscape as I continued across the portage from Kaltag to Unalakleet. The dogs moved briskly along and I still had hopes of a good finish. I'd become conscious of a faint sound behind us but couldn't make anything out. The moon wasn't quite bright enough to see anything and my musher's hat and parka hood muffled any sound from behind. But I knew something was there. The dogs picked up the pace, which was more proof that something was following. It must be a team in sneak mode, headlight turned off.

Then I turned around to find a team with a riderless sled, the leaders almost touching me. Some poor soul was back there afoot. Aha! Another team bites the dust! I could just coast along and let this team gain a few miles on its pedestrian musher and then maybe find a place where I could securely anchor my team, maybe a big rock or something. Without that, I didn't dare stop my team and walk back. While it was funny to think about, it wasn't in me to let this team get any further away from its musher.

With a good place to anchor, I could go behind the sled to deal with the other musher's team. The thin snow cover on the portage would never hold my snow hook. If I went back and my team broke loose, two mushers would be afoot. I tried to coax his leaders past me so when the empty sled came even with me I could possibly set its hook. No dice. The leaders wouldn't go past without a driver on the sled to urge them past.

The team approaches Shaktoolik to check in and take a short break before proceeding across the ice pack to Koyuk. The 1985 blizzard struck before Burt and the other teams could leave. Only Libby Riddles got out ahead of other mushers.

Bottom line, the only way to help this unknown competitor was to stop my team, hold his team there and wait for him. If I did this, his mistake would cost me whatever time it took him to walk up here and I had no idea how far back he was. If he was ten miles back and shuffling along at a mile or two an hour, it could be hours.

Actually, there was no debating the issue. I'm just not into taking advantage of people in trouble, even in a race. I set my hook firmly in the thin snow and waited, and waited, and waited. If another team was doing okay, I'd probably try to ditch them to get away, but I couldn't derail someone, and I sure couldn't leave a musher in trouble, which this guy clearly was.

Then off in the distance I could hear the shuffling of feet and somebody coming toward us. In a moment, Tim Osmar came huffing along, gasping for air.

"Hi, Burt."

"Hi, Tim."

"Thanks, Burt."

"You're welcome, Tim."

Dawn broke. It was seven o'clock in the morning as I hurried my dog team toward Unalakleet on the western coast of Alaska. Clear skies and a bright morning sun made the first sight of the village's homes and shops a cheerful setting after ninety miles of wilderness travel across the portage from Kaltag, back on the Yukon River. Mushing down wind, coupled with the beautiful setting, lessened the effect of the sharp wind and blowing snow swirling at our feet. Still, I was concerned over what could signal violent winds and a ground blizzard later on the flats heading toward Shaktoolik. I anticipated an hour or two of visiting with my friends Larry and Tia Wilson but wouldn't take the time if it meant dealing with a ground blizzard after dark.

With Unalakleet in sight, we dropped down onto the Unalakleet River, blown bare by the strong easterly wind. The sled caught up with the dogs as the wind blew me like a sailboat, faster than the dogs could trot on the slick surface. I worried about conditions farther along out of Shaktoolik with this high wind, not to mention the still extreme cold.

The checker was there to greet us into Unalakleet. The required gear was quickly inspected by the checker and before long I was cooking for my dogs at the Wilson's. While the mixture of commercial dog food and mutton soaked, I inspected the dogs for sore feet, unusual stiffness, and other signs of wear and tear. Aside from a couple of minor foot abrasions, which were quickly tended to, the dogs were in excellent condition.

When the dogs were fed, I went inside to find a wonderful breakfast of freshly baked bread, bacon and eggs, juice and coffee, and warm hospitality. After a quick conversation with a reporter who stopped by, I asked for a weather report. If the weather was bad and the wind was blowing as I suspected, I would leave in a couple of hours to assure that I would arrive at Shaktoolik in daylight. If the weather was good, I'd rest a couple of extra hours here. The weather report indicated lots of sunshine and blue sky overhead at Shaktoolik. Nothing was said about the thirty to forty knot winds and blowing snow out of the northeast.

Although my arrival in Unalakleet placed me eleventh, I was only an hour behind musher number five. My hope was to make a quick trip across the forty miles to Shaktoolik and then hustle the next fifty-eight miles across the ice of Norton Bay to Koyuk. In that way, I might possibly regain my position among the top five teams. If all went well, I would find myself in Koyuk ahead of most of the other teams and in a position to rest until the most opportune time for a final push to Nome and the finish line.

It would probably be a six-hour run to Shaktoolik, four hours over rolling hills to the base of the spit south of Shaktoolik with a two-hour mush across open tundra into the village. Since the weather was good, I would awaken at three and be on the trail by four. That would put me in Shaktoolik by ten in the evening and back out on the trail by midnight. The dogs would do better traveling across the ice of Norton Sound in the cool of the night, and with luck we would be in Koyuk by mid-morning the following day.

I learned later that the people giving me the weather report thought they were doing me a favor when they failed to tell me about the wind and blowing snow. They thought if they told me about the wind, I would be hesitant to leave and might waste time in Unalakleet. The opposite would have happened—I'd have left sooner if I'd known about the bad weather to avoid mushing out on the flats in the dark. It was well intended but it cost me dearly.

As it happened, I rested in Unalakleet during the heat of the day and then pushed on during cooling temperatures in the late afternoon. Tia awakened me at three as planned and I began loading pots, pans, sleeping bag, and other gear into the sled. The dogs were hitched and Larry showed me the way out of town on his snowmachine. Across the slough, through a narrow gap in the alders and we were once again on the trail to Nome. My eyes swept the first hill ahead as well as the trail behind for signs of another team but none was in sight. There were seasoned, gritty mushers with strong dog teams somewhere ahead and behind, giving an added sense of urgency to our journey.

One might expect deep snow along the Arctic coast, but that is not necessarily the case. A relative lack of snow makes much of the Arctic arid, almost a frozen desert. Tireless winds out of the north had left little snow on the hills along our path. Snowmachine and dog team traffic between villages had packed what little snow there was on the trail itself, so a thin ribbon of white marked our trail. An occasional tripod placed by villagers gave added reassurance that we were on the right track.

Two hours out of Unalakleet, we faced continuing warnings of things to come. A sharp, bitter wind nipped at my face each time we crossed a ridge. As we came abeam Besboro Island, a large, rocky island approximately ten miles off shore, I could see a huge plume of snow blowing south from its upper reaches. While the trail was somewhat protected from the wind by the low, rolling hills and sparse vegetation, Besboro Island was exposed to the full force of what was obviously an intense Arctic gale. The last two hours into Shaktoolik would be no picnic in daylight and impossible after dark.

The frozen ocean can be a lonely place. Burt veered off the trail onto the ice pack the previous night when blowing snow blinded his headlight beam. Pressure ridges and open water make this a dangerous place when your dogs are confused by the gale and the driver can't see.

Dusk settled as we descended the hill onto the flats through scattered groves of stunted arctic spruce and willow. As we emerged onto the flat open tundra, we were instantly enveloped in a ground blizzard of swirling wind and snow. Particles of snow were driven with such force as to feel like sand against exposed flesh. Eskimos from Shaktoolik had placed a series of markers approximately 300 feet apart along this section of the trail so they could find their way home during these fierce subarctic storms. The storm's intensity made it impossible to see from one marker to the next. I maintained a general heading into the wind, keeping the marker just past in view until the next one came into view through the cloud of white fury. This was more than a whiteout. I had no visibility whatsoever and, of course, I couldn't see the horizon so I couldn't tell up from down.

Neither the dogs nor I had ever experienced such violent arctic conditions. Our training was quite a contrast with the situation we now found ourselves in. Severe winds, blowing snow, and poorly defined trail were having a significant impact on the team's mood and on our progress. Ivor, the lead dog, kept veering off from the wind, at first gently and then with a rush, taking the rest of the team with him. My sled brake was almost useless on the frozen ground, making it difficult to stop and to control the dogs. I would set my snow hook in the ground and repeatedly swing the team back onto the trail. Dealing with Ivor became too much of a headache in the rapidly developing gloom.

One dog that hadn't been up front much, though, was Puddin. She was the two-year-old I had purchased from Joee Redington the previous summer. Not wishing to push her too hard during her first big race and possibly spoil her attitude, I had mostly left her back in the team with her girlfriends until now. She'd proven herself to be an outstanding command leader during training, however, as she was obedient and anxious to please. This, coupled with the fact that she was well rested, made her about the only choice left in spite of her relative youth and inexperience. The prospects weren't good for making Shaktoolik that night under those conditions, but it was worth a try.

I moved her up in lead and moved two swing dogs into positions that would follow her every move. Our progress improved one hundred percent. Puddin, bless her heart, kept forging ahead into that wind as though it were just another training run.

As darkness fell, it became more and more difficult to see the markers and the sparse evidence of the trail that would lead us into Shaktoolik. I rummaged in my kit bag for the headlight and adjusted its beam with fingers that quickly became cold when removed from my warm beaver mitts. The moment I turned it on, I was blinded by its glare as the light reflected off the blowing snow. My vision was instantly reduced from approximately two hundred feet to about fifty feet. I turned off the light but, with darkness almost complete, travel became even more difficult.

A good lead dog can normally be counted on to stay on the trail and not let you down. This, however, was different. A leader uses all of its senses when following a trail. It can normally see the trail, feel it with its feet, and most important in a race where other teams are ahead, the leader will follow the scent of the other dogs. In addition, the lead dogs will listen for directions from the musher.

These severe conditions were essentially neutralizing Puddin's senses. Close to the ground, she was in the worst place for taking the brunt of that bitter wind and gritty, blowing snow. The accompanying roar must have made it difficult for her to hear my commands as I tried to guide her from marker to marker. It would have been impossible to see another team unless we fell over it, yet the mushers racing through this storm were never far from my thoughts.

Burt stops to tend a dog on the ice. Note the lack of horizon to the left of the photo which is a sign of approaching whiteout conditions. Mushing across the frozen icepack in whiteout conditions gave one the eerie feeling of mushing inside a ping pong ball because of the total lack of a horizon.

When you're racing, you must develop a sense of urgency and commitment if you are to be competitive. This was particularly important in endurance events where fatigue, dehydration, and a certain amount of malnutrition could lead to depression with a resulting decrease in resolve. You've got to pre-program some intensity to go with your natural competitiveness. Mine was by now turned up to high in my chase to the finish, and the last thing I wanted to do was stop or turn back.

The decision was taken out of my hands. I felt the direction of the wind change; it seemed to be quartering from my right rear rather than into my face. Suddenly the white snow ahead turned black. Puddin hesitated, looked back at me for directions and then turned to the right, back into the wind. I anchored the team and walked ahead to see what had happened. We had reached an open lead on the ocean west of the spit. We were on the open ice and had nearly run into the cold dark water. The water was oily black, and yet clear. My headlight beam couldn't reach the bottom. This water was *deep*. We couldn't risk this kind of disaster out here alone in the dark, so we needed to stop.

291

With Puddin unable to do it by herself and me unable to help her, we simply couldn't continue. The question then became whether to camp out here in the open or retrace our steps back to the shelter of the trees on that last hill. We didn't take a vote; it wasn't necessary. It would have been nonsense to endure the exposure of the storm on the open tundra when at least some shelter could be found just a short distance back. I swung the team and they followed their own tracks unerringly back to the base of the hill.

We proceeded up to a small grove of spruce trees that gave us the shelter we needed. We maneuvered ourselves into a nice spot to camp and I was soon engrossed in my duties as chief medical officer, camp cook, and father confessor. Snow was melted for the dogs' dinner, feet were tended to, and the dogs all got a little TLC to let them know their efforts were appreciated. Puddin, especially, had shown herself to be special.

As I bent to my tasks, the rustle of traces and the whisper of sled runners on snow announced the arrival of John Barron. John was a good friend of mine, but I wasn't that anxious to see him—not until Nome anyway. I wanted to see the guys ahead, not the ones catching me from behind. We talked for a while and I told him what it was like mushing in the dark out on the flats. He decided to camp rather than continue. After a few moments, the dogs and I were all curled up for a good night's sleep.

Dawn found us again making our way toward Shaktoolik with the team sorted out into the more cooperative configuration that we'd settled upon the night before. I couldn't have been happier with Puddin. She led the team unerringly through the still-raging blizzard. Her judgment and courage in the teeth of that storm reduced my job to monitoring the trail markers.

After an hour, we stopped for a few moments to take a breather. Puddin had begun to weave a little, so I wanted to see if she had a problem and give her a little encouragement. As I knelt down beside her, I noticed that her eyes were opaque. It looked like they had frozen heading into that bitter wind. Actually, they weren't frozen, they had completely iced over, a phenomenon I'd never seen before. Common in these arctic blizzards, the extreme blowing snow and the moisture from her eyes had formed a sheath of ice over her eyes, making it difficult to see.

I took off my beaver mitts and began gently picking the icy sheath away from her eyes with my fingertips. Once this was done, she blinked and looked up at me as if to say, "Holy cow, this is tough going."

The accumulation of snow actually forms a shell over the eyes as the dog blinks and squints, doing no damage and actually forming somewhat of a protective shell over the eye. It was necessary to stop periodically and brush this off so it didn't reach the point of impairing visibility as it was doing to Puddin. This situation was different from my experience on the Yukon when blinking caused the eyelashes to freeze together. You didn't dare try to pull that ice off for fear of pulling your eyelashes out. You had to pinch them with your fingers to thaw the ice.

Sled dogs can read their masters like children can read their parents. Puddin had picked up on my concern and interpreted it as softened resolve. For the first time, she lay down and was slow to get up. One firm command, though, and she was up and going.

As we mushed along, we came upon a dog team almost completely covered with drifted snow. When we approached, one of the dogs raised its head from the snow and woofed. The sled canvas moved and Tim Osmar emerged from the snow-covered shelter his sled bag provided. When travel had become impossible for him the night before, he had elected to stay out on the open tundra rather than retrace his steps. Seeing that he was okay, we continued and were soon in sight of the small frame buildings and schoolhouse that were Old Shaktoolik. A mile or so later we arrived at the checkpoint in the new village.

Approaching Koyuk after being pinned down on the ice during the blizzard of 1985.
Note the dog in the basket.

When Lyn Takak, the checker, came out, my first questions for him were, "Who was here?" and "Who is gone?"

Wind swirled around the corners of the small frame houses in Shaktoolik with an intensity that threatened to rip them physically from their pile foundations. The storm's violence made it difficult to stand against the onslaught. Conversation was possible only with heads bent together and loud shouts as the wind roared with a sound resembling that of a freight train hurtling past. Although clear patches of blue sky were visible overhead, one could hardly see the house next door through the ground blizzard's cloud of blowing snow.

Although Libby Riddles had mushed out of Shaktoolik into the fierce coastal blizzard the day before, no other Iditarod mushers had left. All were studying the storm, gauging the ability of their dogs and themselves to cross the ice of Norton Sound with reasonable safety. Every hour we waited, allowed Libby and the $50,000 first-place prize money to get further away.

It took a lot to stop Iditarod mushers racing across Alaska, but this qualified. I leaned into the wind, now gusting to seventy miles per hour. Leaving the safety and warmth of Shaktoolik to drive alone into the jaws of the raging ground blizzard required an act of great personal courage. Libby lived and trained her dogs in the Eskimo village of Teller where this kind of weather wasn't all that uncommon, so she knew what to do and her dogs were in their element. That made her move possible.

It still didn't change the fact that she would be alone on the ice pack of Norton Bay driving her dogs literally head-on into the worst weather that Alaska can muster. She had left Shaktoolik at mid-afternoon, ensuring at least one night out there by herself. The measure of her grit was reflected in the fact that the most competent mushers in Alaska, and the world, were still in Shaktoolik by mid-morning the following day. It was also a measure of the ferocity of this vicious coastal storm.

Lyn and I shouted back and forth in the roaring wind for a couple of minutes, and then I gathered up my food drops and began preparing food for the dogs. Lyn was kind enough to give us all hot water out of his tap and saved us having to try to keep a cooking fire going in this wind. While the dog food soaked, I busied myself removing booties from the dogs' feet and slipping their harnesses off to make them comfortable. Once done with the dogs, I sorted out the things I'd need to make it across Norton Bay in this blizzard. I wanted enough food along to last for three days. I would take some pre-cooked food in the cooler so I could keep the dogs well hydrated. The rest would be in the form of bags of frozen mutton, hamburger, liver, and other treats. And I'd need food for myself.

Things were well arranged when I took a break to go inside. What a relief to be in out of the wind as it roared around the tiny home that was the checkpoint. Several mushers were sitting around relaxing while Jim Strong, a race judge, and Lyn sat on the couch visiting. I asked them about the trail ahead to Koyuk and Lyn said, "Burt, if you can't follow that trail, you've got to be blind."

Jim nodded his head in agreement. Lyn pointed me toward a pot of chili on the stove and I went over and helped myself. No one seemed in any hurry to get going. My dogs and I had little experience driving into this kind of weather, so I was content to wait and see how the other mushers handled it. I had driven the team north and across the saddle in the Peters Hills to give us some experience with wind, but it didn't compare to this.

Time passed quickly and I decided to wait until the next day to see if things eased up a little. I glanced out the window and saw Dewey Halverson and John Cooper hitching up their teams. I went out to watch as they stepped on the runners and hiked the teams up. Dewey led with John close behind. I'd always admired Dewey's ability as a musher. He talked quietly to his dogs, directing them between the houses and out of the village. They trotted quickly down onto the tundra and were soon out of sight.

A couple of other mushers also left, but most were willing to wait until tomorrow. I went out and fed the dogs one more time to get them well loaded with energy and went back in to find a quiet place to sleep. I hung my wet face mask on a line in the living room to dry and went to sleep. Driving into the fierce wind without a face mask would have resulted in severe frostbite making travel impossible.

The next morning when I arose, I headed straight for my face mask to be sure I had it tucked safely in my parka pocket, but it was gone. I still believed in the code of the trail in spite of some bad experiences, but this was lousy. Without a face mask, I couldn't leave the checkpoint.

Fortunately, I carried a spare and was soon packing to leave. I went out, watered the dogs, went back in, and arranged all the little items on Lyn's coffee table that I knew I'd need. I needed to see them all at once so I'd know I had what I needed. The pile included compass, knife, matches, and other items. As I arranged and re-arranged my little pile, a radio announcer from McGrath sat down across from me and casually started rummaging through my little pile, picking up one item after another to study it.

"Uh, please put the stuff down and leave it alone."

"Why, Burt? Just curious."

"I need to focus here and you're a serious distraction."

Approaching the finish line under the burled arch on Front Street in Nome. Family and friends line the chute and a big banner welcoming Burt hangs on the burled arch.
Jeff Schultz photo.

"I'm not taking anything."

"I'm sorting things out so I don't forget anything. You keep moving things around so I can't keep track."

"I didn't think it was that big a deal."

"KEEP YOUR HANDS OFF! . . . DANG!"

I apologized for being abrupt, gathered up my things and went out to water the dogs.

As I did my chores, John Barron, Raymie Redington, and Glenn Findley were just leaving the checkpoint.

A half hour later, I followed.

The weather seemed to have calmed down a little. A mile or so past the shelter cabin about fifteen miles out, I caught sight of the three teams ahead of me. Before long, I caught them and was soon past them and on my way. At this point, none of the teams behind me was in sight and all seemed rosy. My team was fast and strong and I hoped to reel in another team or two before Nome.

The first indication of a developing ground blizzard was the blurring outline of the northeast side of the bay approximately twenty-five miles away. Slowly but surely the eastern coast of Norton Bay became less visible. After a couple of hours, it appeared that the ground blizzard was within a half a mile of me. It seemed to be getting closer except that the northwest corner of the bay was still visible. It was amazing what a straight line the edge of the storm seemed to hold. To the left of me were pressure ridges, which indicated the possibility of open water, something I did not intend to get forced into no matter what that ground blizzard did.

About then my watch told me it was time to snack the dogs, however, it seemed prudent to push on as far as possible before the ground blizzard struck again, which it surely would. I decided to go ahead and snack the dogs on schedule. There was a lot of snowmachine traffic between villages along the coast and the local guys kept the trails well marked for themselves. They didn't want to get lost under blizzard conditions either. We stopped for approximately ten minutes while the dogs ate their snacks and I had a quick cup of coffee and some cookies. As I was getting underway, the storm struck with blinding intensity. The wind increased to approximately fifty miles an hour and blowing snow stung my face like grains of sand in a full-scale desert sandstorm. I felt bad for the dogs, whose faces were a little more than a foot above the ice and hoped they wouldn't be too uncomfortable for the remaining twenty miles or so into Koyuk.

I became conscious of a burning sensation in my urinary tract that seemed to be getting worse by the minute. Was I developing some kind of infection from drinking tainted water back along the trail? Possibly. Then I realized the pain wasn't inside of me but outside; it was my extremity. It was getting cold to the point of frostbite. I couldn't believe it, but that merciless, cold wind was ripping through the zippers of my clothing layers and was about to cause serious damage.

I remembered sitting around a campfire a few years earlier when one of the guys had talked about this happening. He had said that early mushers out along the coast had fashioned penis protectors out of rabbit hide to protect from freezing. It took a few minutes for this to sink in and then I hurriedly rummaged in my kit bag for something that would substitute for a rabbit hide. I found a fleece neck warmer tube and quickly stuffed it down inside my insulated pants.

We continued for a mile or two and then the markers ran out. The State of Alaska, Department of Transportation Maintenance, financed maintenance of these coastal trails under contract with people in the villages. Spruce trees approximately ten feet high were cut and stripped of limbs except for the top two or three feet. These trees had been planted in the ice approximately 400 feet apart. With the bushy tops, they stood out, even in poor visibility and provided a good safe route.

Unbeknownst to me, approximately a mile and half of sea ice containing the trail and those markers had broken away from the shore ice and the large pan had drifted out to sea leaving a gap of open water where the trail should have been. More than one winter traveler had drifted out to sea on an ice floe never to be seen again.

The open sea where the ice had blown out had refrozen into a rubbery thin surface. The difference between hard-frozen pack ice and this treacherous new "green ice" was difficult to see in the chaos of extreme wind and blowing snow.

Burt's son, Jeff, welcomes him with a Champaign toast while partner and good friend Ed McMillan watches. These great moments made the long winter and grueling trip to Nome worthwhile.

I drove the team as far from the last visible marker as possible on a compass heading, then anchored the dogs and proceeded on foot searching for the next marker. I continued trudging northward until I could just barely see my team in the blowing snow behind me. It would be suicidal to be separated from my dogs. I stood for a moment in the howling blizzard and decided to put no more distance between my team and myself. I circled to the right and then the left hoping to see some evidence of a marker, perhaps an outline or shadow, but I found nothing. As I was going back to my dogs after approximately a half hour, two other teams caught up and we held a conference. Glenn Findley from Australia and Raymie Redington were the first to arrive. Ten minutes later, John Barron approached. Visibility by now was so restricted that we didn't see him until he was within fifty feet of us.

All four of us were well seasoned in Alaska winter travel and were extremely competent outdoorsmen. All were capable of dealing with these conditions. Our main concern at that moment was the possibility of getting lost before we could reconnect with the marked trail. Losing position was our biggest concern. We wondered why in hell Lyn and Jim hadn't told us about these missing markers. We could have planned a solution before we ever left Shaktoolik.

Glenn was a cement contractor in his native Australia and was running his second Iditarod with a team he'd leased from Joe Redington. Raymie Redington had virtually grown up with dogs and had spent all of his life as a commercial fisherman and trapper. John Barron lived in a remote cabin on the Yentna River, making his living commercial fishing and trapping. Good company under these circumstances.

We began searching for trail with one team building upon another so each man had a team or the last stake in sight at all times. This allowed us to extend ourselves something more than a quarter mile from the last marker. We were still searching when we heard a shout. It was Raymie hollering that he had found the trail. He waved to us to bring our teams over and fall in behind him. This we did and proceeded northward for a mile or so until we realized that what Raymie had found wasn't the trail at all but an errant snowmachine track that led nowhere.

Now we had completely lost the trail. As we stopped to palaver and develop a plan, we discovered that we were on green ice, just freshly frozen. There was no way to tell exactly how thick the ice was, but it was obvious that it hadn't been frozen too long. I glanced down at my feet to discover that I was standing in about an inch of water. The rubbery ice was sagging under our weight and could collapse at any moment. We immediately headed due east until we again reached firm ice. With the possibility of breaking through the ice and plunging into the icy waters of Norton Bay fresh in our minds, there was no way we would again veer toward the west, even though we knew the trail was in that direction. We proceeded due north by compass, hoping to pick up the shore and follow it into Koyuk.

We learned later that the checker and race official in Shaktoolik had known about this section of blown-out trail and knew its extent. They didn't tell us about it because they thought we might be afraid to leave the village. They didn't want a bunch of teams bottled up in the checkpoint to deal with. Had we known the extent of the missing section of trail, we would have simply mushed north for a couple of miles and then headed back west to rejoin the trail. Without this important information, we didn't dare risk heading back onto green ice with the possibility of plunging through thin ice or driving into open water under these horrific, blinding conditions. Our lack of information would ultimately cost us dearly.

Mile after mile we advanced into the blizzard, first with one team in the lead, then another, hoping to give each musher's lead dogs a chance to rest. After approximately three hours, we noticed occasional tufts of grass sticking up through the icy floor beneath us. At that time we should have headed west, which would have taken us across safe ground to intersect the trail into Koyuk. The transition from the ice pack of Norton Bay to land was so indiscernible that we weren't really confident we were on shore.

We were afraid we were traversing delta-like islands off shore from the mouth of the Koyuk River and were concerned about the safety of turning west too soon. We were in a delicate situation. If we turned west too soon, we might encounter dangerously thin ice, in poor visibility, yet if we continued north, we could end up in the trackless country northeast of Koyuk, where we could become hopelessly lost. If we got too far off the beaten track, we would be difficult to find, much less be able to find our own way. As we went on, our dogs solved the problem for us. They were simply too tired to proceed.

At this point, the wind was blowing with such intensity that it roared even though there were no buildings near for it to roar around. I had to shout at the top of my lungs to make my lead dogs hear the commands. The battering effect on men and dogs was tiring in itself.

After we decided to hole up, we swung our teams downwind to give them some protection with the sleds. We lined up our sleds approximately four feet apart, realizing that we were now in a survival situation. We had been cut off from our back trail by our mistake with the errant snowmachine trail and had no idea what direction Shaktoolik was from our position. Backtracking across the bay in that blizzard wasn't much of an option anyway.

We knew then that unless the wind abated or we were found, we were in serious trouble and it was only a matter of time until exposure began to take effect.

The memory of Herbie Nayokpuk's experience during the 1982 race, dealing with a violent coastal blizzard in this same area, was vivid. Herby hadn't been able to continue north into the storm, which was less severe than this one. Herby was able to return to Shaktoolik. He spoke later of how cold he had become and how cold his dogs were, and he spoke of running short of food.

I had three days of dog food and personal food on my sled for just such an emergency. I believed that I had an adequate cushion but couldn't help thinking of Herbie getting cold to the point of retreating to Shaktoolik. Herbie was an Eskimo from Shishmaref whom I'd met in the early 1970s while hunting polar bears. He and his dogs were used to traveling in this violent coastal weather; so if he had trouble dealing with it, it wouldn't be easy for us.

Burt's friends from Anchorage came to greet him at the finish and enjoy the hoopla and the party that was Nome, Alaska, during Iditarod. The finish was half the fun. The gang included Fred Rosenburg and his wife, Floyd Tetpon, Bette and Ed McMillan, sons Brad and Jeff, wife Jan, and Vi Redington, Joe's wife.

In any case, with no back-trail, we were irrevocably cut off from our trail.

I quickly fed the dogs a hearty meal, ate a good meal myself, and had a cup of coffee from my thermos. As I headed back to my sled, I paused to speak to Raymie. There he was on his sled, sitting up in his sleeping bag and parka. No face peered back. When I spoke, he replied from somewhere down in his parka. I chuckled at the vision of a ghost rider among us and headed for my sled.

I took my mitts off to undo the stuff sack with my sleeping bag, and the effect on my skin was immediate and dramatic. My hands burned like fire as the chill factor, now off the charts, took effect. The skin on my hands was instantly frostbitten and stung as if I'd been sunburned. Thank God for beaver mitts. Putting my hands back into my mitts brought immediate warmth, although the frostbitten skin on my hands burned for several hours. I settled gratefully into my sleeping bag.

Burt was presented with the Halfway Trophy at the finish of the 1985 race. Burt led the field and broke trail through heavy, blowing snow from Ophir to Iditarod through a blizzard so brutal that press and race officials couldn't get through the raging storm to be in Iditarod when Burt arrived. This was the only time this had happened in the history of the race, likely making this the toughest run to halfway in any race.

That year for the first time, I'd had a sled bag made which incorporated a zipper rather than simply flaps that snapped shut. A sled bag was a canvas affair that fit the sled and held all of the gear and food. I had this bag especially constructed so it was big enough for me to stretch my sleeping bag out in and get inside. I could then zip up the sled bag as well as my sleeping bag for a good night's sleep in almost any weather. The top of the sled bag was Gortex so it would breathe, a necessity for this kind of camping. People's bodies lose approximately a quart and a half of fluid during a night of sleep, which would condense inside any nonporous shelter. The insulation value of clothes and sleeping bag would be destroyed by this accumulating moisture.

I was soon comfortably settled into my sleeping bag with that terrible cold, howling wind momentarily cut off. I was sound asleep in moments and didn't waken until midnight. I unzipped the bags and stuck my head out to see what was going on. I estimated wind velocity at approximately fifty or sixty miles an hour. The temperature was zero. The blowing snow lifted momentarily and a dim flashing beacon became visible off to the northwest. I took a compass bearing on it and hunkered back into my bag to wait for morning.

When morning came, the wind had reached a new level. It was obvious that the thing to do was stay under shelter as much as possible, since even a few moments in the raging wind drained energy at an alarming rate. Exposure was our primary threat in the open, but we all had good shelter in our sleds. I remembered being on the Yukon River the year before, mushing into a wind of approximately thirty miles an hour. The temperature then had been zero and the graph showed a wind chill factor of minus fifty degrees. The temperature now was just zero degrees Fahrenheit with winds gusting to at least seventy miles per hour. There was no way of knowing what the wind chill factor might be, but we knew it was cold enough to be deadly.

My head felt cold. Even with my musher's hat on and wearing my parka with the hood covering my head, my head was getting cold as I lay nestled in my sleeping bag inside my sled bag. The wind was blowing so hard that it penetrated all those layers. Your head is an effective radiator with all that blood supply. I had to do something or my core body temperature would drop even faster. I needed to find something to block the wind. The solution was to take the lid from my cooler and jam it behind the bungees that held my sled brake up. The lid was impervious and would completely block the icy wind. I decided to wait until later to install it when I could combine some chores.

I remained nestled in the bag until the need to get out and relieve myself could no longer be ignored. I thought for fifteen minutes on a plan that would get me out of my sleeping bag, out of my sled bag and out of my parka, and then down with my pile pants and my union suit in the quickest possible way to do my business. I would then reverse the order to get back into my sleeping bag when I was done. The humor of this kind of exercise totally escaped me under the circumstances, but with a plan in mind, I leaped forth. Off came my parka, down with my suspenders and pile pants. I fumbled for the handle of the zipper on the trap door of my red polypropylene union suit. The blowing snow of the ground blizzard instantly wetted my hands. By the time I pulled the zipper six inches, the skin of my hand was frostbitten, as stiff as parchment. I quickly tucked it under my arm for a second and then tried again.

After five tries, the trap door was unzipped. Within a few seconds, the skin of my butt was wet from blowing snow and in a few more seconds it was also frostbitten and stiff as rawhide. As I write this, it seems hilarious, but at the time, it was a deadly serious game. I had to get everything put back. The problem was that my rapidly freezing hands made it increasingly difficult to get the trap door zipped and my clothes back on. I rushed back to my sled and, with my rear end facing downwind, I plunged my frostbitten hands into my sleeping bag. The residual warmth from the bag soon warmed my hands and I was able to grab the cooler lid and jam it behind the bungees at the rear of my sled.

Then I began inching the zipper on my long johns shut, giving it a tug, plunging my hands into the sleeping bag, giving it another tug and so on. Back up with my suspenders and on with my inner parka then back into the sleeping bag, which I clutched around me until my hands and torso again felt warm. Then I inched the zipper on the sled bag shut, followed by the zipper on my sleeping bag. I was finally settled into a comfortable nap.

The damage from exposure during this brief interlude drove home a serious issue regarding our survival. We could not leave the shelter of our sleds except for urgent calls of nature or serious emergencies. Nothing else warranted risking our health and possibly our lives. Frostbitten hands can become useless. If we became unable to zip parkas and sleeping bags, we would become even more exposed. In addition, our core body temperatures dropped significantly each time we exited our sleeping bags and were exposed to that vicious driving wind. Fortunately, my frostbite was only superficial and caused no lasting damage, although it felt as though I'd been badly scalded for a few hours.

Meanwhile in Nome people were becoming concerned. My wife had stopped by the community center and spotted a group of friends. As she approached, they suddenly became quiet, obviously talking about something they didn't want her to hear. She asked, "What's going on?"

"Well, we're just worried about Burt and the guys stuck on the ice in that blizzard."

"What are you worried about?"

"Burt could lose his life out there!"

"Well, I'm not worried. You can't kill Burt."

The group thought that was rather callous.

Then Bob Snider, my hunting buddy, wandered in and spotted my wife with the group.

"Heard anything about when Burt's getting in here?"

"No, Bob, they're still stuck out there."

"Well, you tell that lazy son-of-a-bitch when he does get here that I went home. I'm danged if I'm going to hang around this sorry place if he's just going to sit on his butt out there."

The ladies were shocked but Bob and Jan had a good laugh.

When they told me about it later, I said, "Well, the wife probably had the insurance paid up, and Snider expects you to be tough. Actually, I think it's funny." That left the ladies shaking their heads.

My life's been full of strong women and tough buddies. I'm not sure anyone in Nome appreciated the Bomhoff sense of humor.

We were still pinned down when about noon natural functions again entered my consciousness. I had heard tales of Arctic travelers carrying small containers to urinate in when pinned down in fierce blizzards, illustrating just how important it is to avoid exposure. It is already evident that it would have been foolhardy to get out of that sleeping bag for anything but a dire emergency or to feed my dogs. I began to wonder about something handy to use without getting out of my sleeping bag. Unfortunately, most of my utensils were in a rucksack tied to my sled so they wouldn't blow away in the storm. To retrieve them would require exiting my sleeping bag. I planned to feed my dogs again at 2:30 and I was determined not to get out of my sled until then.

I had been rationing my personal food and coffee supply all morning in an effort to make it last as long as possible. Even though I was becoming somewhat uncomfortable, it seemed prudent to continue taking swigs of coffee and a bite of lunch every two or three hours to keep my strength up and avoid dehydrating too badly. I reached for my thermos, unscrewed the cup, which formed its cap, and pulled the cork out. I took a swig and replaced the cork. As I reached for the cup, I had one of my better ideas that day. The thermos cup worked perfectly and I was soon resting comfortably again in my cocoon.

The press wanted to hear the details of the teams pinned down on the ice pack. Four teams had been pinned down in a narrow blow hole, for 36 hours while the blizzard raged. Fans were worried about their safety, but Burt's family and friends figured he'd show up when he got tired of sitting on his butt.

As I lay there resting, listening to the wind howl, I became conscious of how long it was taking me to perform even the simplest tasks inside my sleeping bag. If I unzipped the sleeping bag and the sled bag to peer outside, it seemed to take nearly an hour to zip them back up. I would tug at the zipper, then rest, tug at the zipper, then rest and then tug again each time moving the zipper just three or four inches. The same effort was required to close my sleeping bag. My insides didn't feel the least bit cold, so the thought of hypothermia had not yet entered my mind.

The storm also reminded us of its intensity each time we tried to communicate. It required shouting at the top of our lungs to be heard by the person just four feet away in the neighboring sled. Even with that, it seemed we could survive indefinitely. Then I realized that moisture was beginning to collect inside the mouth of my sleeping bag. A layer of frost approximately a quarter of an inch thick had formed on the inside of my sled bag. The countdown had begun. Hour by hour, moisture from our bodies would continue to accumulate inside our sleeping bags and inside the sled bags until sufficient moisture had formed to destroy the insulating quality of our meager shelters. It was obvious, too, that I was a little weaker than I had been the day before. Although I felt comfortable, a degree of hypothermia must have already established itself.

I resolved even more firmly not to move from that bag except to feed my dogs and to handle an emergency. We could wait a little while longer and then we needed to make a break for it. I did have a compass bearing on that beacon at the Koyuk airport. Exposure is a deadly hazard, so it was worth waiting awhile for the storm to abate.

But there was no way I was going to lie there in my sled until I became incapacitated.

I don't know if those thoughts entered the other mushers' minds because we never talked about it. My shelter was fairly warm and comfortable, as were Glenn Findlay's and John Barron's. Glenn occasionally got up and stomped around to warm his feet and check on things. In fact, that's probably why he survived the best of the four—that, and the fact that he was younger. Glenn, Raymie and I all kept our bunny boots on even when we were in our sleeping bags. John Barron removed his boots and laid them by his sled before crawling into his bag. He seemed fairly comfortable.

Raymie was probably the least comfortable. He had switched to a four-and-a-half-foot racing sled at Shaktoolik for the dash to Nome. His sled was just too short to permit sleeping inside. He was perched on top of the sled in his sleeping bag and remained quietly comfortable, using chemical hand warmers to keep warm. He must have had a lifetime supply in his pockets because he never ran out. Nobody complained.

Raymie is a dear friend and one of the best trailmates ever. He was one of the funniest guys around and always kept us laughing. Even when he was furious and cussing like you never heard before, he was somehow amusing.

We remained thus in our own little worlds until mid-afternoon. We were all holed up in our sleeping bags when someone hollered that they'd heard an airplane. A few minutes later, we all heard it. Within five minutes, a tiny Super Cub appeared overhead being flown by Les Reynolds, a good friend and seasoned Alaskan Bush pilot. His passenger was the race marshal. Within seconds the wind had snatched it away; however, it reappeared within a few minutes. The flight apparently terrorized the race marshal and she tried to punish us later by attempting to disqualify us for "getting ourselves into this mess." The board knew the story and laughed it off.

Someone asked if we should get out and signal that we were okay. I didn't care what anyone else did, but I wasn't getting out of my shelter to satisfy someone's curiosity. I'm a commercial pilot with thousands of hours flying in Alaska, including winter flying out of Point Barrow and other Arctic villages. It was obvious to me that no one could land safely under these conditions. If they tried it, they might crash or not be able to get airborne again. Since there was nothing to anchor an airplane to out here, it might just blow away.

Having someone here with us who was not properly equipped, and possibly injured, would only add to our problems. I hoped they would simply establish our location and leave. Besides that, what if they misinterpreted the signal and somehow thought we needed immediate emergency help? If they tried to land for the wrong reasons and hurt themselves, it wouldn't help anybody and would give us that much more to deal with. It was in our best interest that they head back to where they came from.

Within a few minutes, the Cub was gone and then it was replaced by a Cessna 180. It circled several times. Raymie's impatience got the better of him and he crawled out of his bag and waved to make sure they saw us, after which we all stayed in our sleeping bags to preserve what little energy our bodies still contained. I knew they couldn't safely land. An airplane on this slick surface with these winds, with no way to tie down, might blow away. I didn't want an airplane landing anywhere near us in these conditions anyway. We were far better off without them, no matter how well intended. Again, I've flown many hours in the Arctic and know when it's not safe. We were safer in our sleds than the people in those airplanes.

My pal Tony Oney had landed a film crew next to Herbie Nayokpuk on the ice pack out of Shaktoolik during the 1982 Iditarod blizzard, which wasn't quite as severe as this one. Tony had guided polar bear hunters out of Shishmaref for many years and had lots of experience flying out on the ice pack in winter. Tony was one of the few pilots around with the skill to get an airplane down and then off the ice safely when the weather was like this. He'd done it hundreds of times hunting polar bears during the early years. I knew that whoever was buzzing around overhead now couldn't begin to match Tony's experience and skill.

We knew it was futile for us to be up and around at that point since it might be hours and even days before we could move. The surface wind again appeared to be gusting between fifty and seventy miles an hour with snow blowing at such a rate as to make our lead dogs difficult to see just forty feet away. It was still prudent to remain as sheltered as possible to ensure our survival. We remained holed up as the airplane circled overhead and then left, much to our relief.

The Bomhoff fan club, an informal group of family and friends. Left to right back row: Burt's sons Brad and Jeff, Ed Rosenburg, Rich Prawley, wife Jan, Terri McWilliams, handler Jeff Prawley, his sister Kiersten, Burt's daughter Jill, partner Ed McMillan, Sandy and Suzanne Williams. Ed's wife, Bette, is front row far right. *Jeff Schultz photo.*

Later, someone wrote a book about the heroes of the Iditarod Air Force. He included a chapter on our experience and made it sound like those airplanes had heroically saved us. I have no idea where that baloney came from. Aside from being a distraction and a possible hazard to us, they did little more than satisfy their curiosity. Maybe someone thought it was heroic just to fly around in that weather.

An hour or two later, we were all dozing when someone shouted, "There's a snowmachine." We tore at our zippers to look out. Sure enough, two snowmachines had arrived from downwind and the drivers were approaching us. Kenneth Dewey Jr., a young Eskimo from Koyuk, and John Arnold, one of the official Iditarod snowmachine trailbreakers, who hailed from Wasilla, had found us.

They had been heading out to replace the markers that were missing when the trail blew out and Kenneth spotted one of our brake marks on the frozen surface of Norton Bay. Only a superb tracker could ever have seen the tiny brake mark scratch on the ice that indicated four dog teams had passed that way. He knew that four teams were missing and that these tracks might mark the path of those teams. He followed the trail, one tiny mark after another into ever-worsening wind, often having to look directly beside the snowmachine to avoid losing the sign. He said later that he almost ran over our snow-covered lead dogs in the poor visibility because he was watching so intently to avoid losing our trail.

Kenneth and John rattled our sleds and yanked at our tug lines in an effort to get us moving. My mind was in a dim haze from napping in the cold. I was probably experiencing some of the effects of hypothermia having lowered my core body temperature. I can remember looking at John and telling him to wake me up later.

He just looked at me and rattled my sled a couple of times and told me to get up and get moving. "Koyuk's only eight miles away," he said, "and if you move now, we can make it before dark." Kenneth told us that we had somehow mushed into a blowhole of intense wind that was only a few miles across. We had no way of knowing how narrow the severe weather was, or we would have moved. The main trail just a few miles away had not experienced the severe weather that we had mushed into.

I got out of my sleeping bag, pulled on my outer wind parka and beaver mitts, and started loading my sled.

The six-gallon cooler that I used to prepare my dog food had drifted full of snow and was as hard as a block of ice. The snow around it had hardened like concrete, so I had to chop it out of the hard-packed snow with my axe. Then I chopped the snow out of the cooler to avoid carrying the extra weight. I soon had my gear packed and was ready to go. John Barron was hobbling around with his feet stuck in the tops of his boots unable to pull them on the rest of the way. They had lain flat on the snow by his sled and had frozen shut. John Arnold took a knife and cut the laces so his boots could be wrenched open enough to get his feet into. I often wondered what we would have done had John not been handy with his knife. A man's feet could freeze within moments without the protection of bunny boots or good Native mukluks.

The snowmachines started for Koyuk and, one after another, we headed our dog teams after them. An hour later we broke out of the ground blizzard and could see the low hills behind Koyuk a few miles away. Looking south, we could see Shaktoolik dimly in the far distance.

The intensity of the storm decreased rapidly as we left our camping spot and mushed closer to Koyuk, making it feel like a balmy spring breeze. We fed our dogs and accepted the hospitality of the kind residents of Koyuk. We were each invited to someone's home, where we enjoyed warm food and a place to nap before proceeding to Nome.

Even though many teams passed us while we were trapped out on the ice, all four of us still managed to finish in the money. It was a nice ending to a story that could have ended in tragedy.

Kenneth Dewey Jr. and I became good friends over the years and I value his memory. I asked him how it was that we were pinned down in terrible weather east of Koyuk, while the weather was so much better near the village. He responded that there was a wind hole east of Koyuk where the north wind blew far harder than it did closer to the hills near Koyuk. When we had driven east to get off the treacherous green ice, we drove right into the path of that howling wind tunnel. Kenneth acknowledged that we had to do what we did and were danged lucky the ice didn't give way under the weight of our sleds. We could easily have been drowned and lost forever.

A funny thing happened on my way along the coast from Topkok Hill into Nome. I was mushing along, thinking I was going to finish in twenty-first place, just out of the money. Near Solomon, I saw a dog team coming toward me and thought it must be a local recreational musher heading in this direction, opposite of an Iditarod team. Dogs in the teams of recreational mushers are sometimes undisciplined and like to fight. I couldn't afford something like that happening now, so I watched the dogs intently as they approached. I didn't even look at the musher.

Suddenly the musher shouted, "Burt, you're going the wrong way. Nome is THAT way."

I looked up. It was Raymie. In a flash it occurred to me that there had been twenty teams ahead of me when I left White Mountain, less than a hundred miles from Nome. I needed to eliminate one of those mushers to finish twentieth in the money. I must confess that it occurred to me to just tell Raymie that I was going back to look for a loose dog. An Iditarod musher couldn't officially finish with a dog not accounted for so he'd probably buy it. *And after all, Raymie was the only team standing between me and a finish in the money.*

"Raymie, you're the one going the wrong way. You're ahead of me, remember?"

"No, I'm not, Burt. Turn around. There are other teams behind you. You're losing ground."

Raymie was the only team standing between me and a finish in the money.

"Raymie, think about this. The ocean is on your right. Shouldn't it be on your left?"

Nome, Alaska. It may all be relative, but there is simply no pleasure for a dog or a musher that matches a soft straw bed and a full tummy at the end of the long, tough trail from Anchorage . . . unless it be a toddy at the Board of Trade Saloon on Front Street with old friends.

"Holy shit! How did I do this?" It took him just seconds to swing his team around and head for Nome.

We learned later that Raymie had taken the detour that angled off the trail to Solomon and then in the poor visibility had taken the fork that headed him back the wrong way. John Barron had seen the whole thing and just about died laughing. When he saw Raymie coming, he hunkered down so Raymie wouldn't see him. When he saw Raymie take the wrong trail, he just figured there was one more musher he didn't have to worry about.

One final thought. Kenneth Dewey, the Eskimo who found us, was a loyal and faithful provider for his parents, brothers, and sisters in Koyuk. He hunted and worked seasonally to keep his entire family in good stead. To me he was a fine example of a young Eskimo man who lived a life that combined the traditional and modern in a good way. Kenneth died in a tragic plane crash several years later. I dedicate this chapter to my dear departed friend, Kenneth Dewey Jr.

Chapter Eighteen
The Toughest Musher

Years later, after all that water under the bridge, we were gathered in my log cabin in the foothills south of Mount McKinley—a few veteran mushing pals, sipping our drinks and discussing dog stuff. My visitors' teams were tied outside, fed and nestled into their beds of straw. We had dined on moose roast with mashed potatoes and gravy, my favorite meal when company came. My pal Sandy Williams and I had shot the moose at my camp on the Stony River the previous fall.

The dim light of a gas lantern drove the darkness into the corners. The snow lay deep outside and the thermometer barely registered. The stove gave off the faint smell of wood smoke and warmed us the way woodstoves do, toasty on one side and a little cool on the other. As the wind whistled in the trees, we talked of trails, dogs, and races.

Mushers love to gossip and compare; maybe it comes from the lack of TV and other entertainment. Like farm folks back home, anything is fair game. We talked dog deals, the neighbors, and who liked whom. Eventually, we got around to comparing mushers and teams. As we warmed to the conversation, we began to argue about who was the toughest musher of modern time.

Make no mistake, we *weren't* talking about who was tough and who was not. Any man or woman who can drive a team across Alaska to Nome in the dead of winter is deep down grit-and-gristle tough. What we talked about was the toughest of the tough.

We talked Iditarod mushers because that's what we knew best, but we agreed there was really no "toughest race." That depended on the worst conditions caused by severe weather, an extremely challenging trail, and competition good enough to force one to proceed through these conditions at the fastest possible pace. A race could consist of extremes of weather and trail, but if the competition was lax and permitted teams to proceed at a deliberate pace, then there was no measure. We could work through most anything given enough time.

Burt chats with Rick Swenson at the start of the 2011 race. Rick has the most wins of any Iditarod musher and could arguably be the toughest musher, considering his courageous win during the horrific blizzard of 1991.

As the discussion continued, an informal scoring system developed. Points were lost in this discussion for mushers who made excuses such as poor trail marking, the committee, volunteers, fans, fellow mushers, or your dogs—especially leaders—for any problems. And, finally, it was no fair diminishing the teams ahead by inferring they had some kind of advantage because they trained harder or smarter.

Interestingly, whining often seems to fool the press. If you are one of their favorites, they can spin any story so the markers really did lead you astray or your dogs really did let you down when you needed them most. But mushers know.

The mushing fraternity least respects some of the mushers most revered by the press and the fans.

Now this thing was difficult to decide. So many variables: weather, dogs, competitors, companions, terrain, snow cover, wind, temperature. The list was endless. So who got our title, THE TOUGHEST MUSHER?

We decided that we had to think of a situation where a group of legitimate contenders for the "tough" title was all in it together and one musher rose higher than any other in decisive fashion. He had to beat the pants off anyone else who was there. Part of the measure would be how the winner handled the situation; of secondary interest would be how those behind handled things later when it was all over.

The conversation rolled on with each of us having a strong opinion, with each citing his own special story and each his own personal choice. We talked with great respect because almost all who were mentioned were able, and *all* whose names appear in this chapter qualified. There were some legendary tough guys: Jerry Riley, Roger Nordlum, Bud Smyth, Dean Osmar, Cowboy Smith and Joe Redington, himself. But we needed an incident that could be defined, an incident where the guys were all in it together and one stood out. It couldn't be the dangers of the trail that we all confronted every year, like the Happy River Steps or the dreaded Dalzell Gorge. These areas could be scary and dangerous but most mushers accepted them as part of the trip. If you couldn't handle the trail, you simply wouldn't make it to Nome.

The guys believed that the whole thing could be settled by looking at one of two situations, either out of Shaktoolik during the 1985 Iditarod race or at the finish of the 1991 Iditarod race. Both situations involved a lone musher advancing under terrible blizzard conditions, probably life-threatening, while others remained. During 1985, Libby Riddles left Shaktoolik in a blizzard that was intimidating for everyone. She mushed across the open ice of Norton Bay into a raging storm to claim victory. Two seasoned mushers, Dewey Halverson and John Cooper, chased her but couldn't catch her. No one turned back.

We settled on the 1991 finish because some mushers not only couldn't continue but couldn't even stay out on the trail. They turned back to seek shelter. The story goes something like this. A handful of tough, seasoned mushers arrived in White Mountain just seventy-seven miles from Nome in a vicious Arctic storm. Some questioned if anyone could even survive, much less actually make it to Nome through the violent, bitter cold blizzard.

Our small group in the safety of my cozy, warm cabin in the Peters Hills country had taken a vote and decided that this event truly qualified as defining.

The winner, Rick Swenson, and the second place finisher made it through this brutal storm to the finish line, while all the other contenders turned around and mushed back to the shelter of the White Mountain checkpoint.

Libby Riddles became the 1985 Iditarod champion by streaking out of Shaktoolik ahead of the other teams into a fierce blizzard. With that performance, it could be claimed that she is possibly the toughest woman to drive an Iditarod dog team.

Some wag in Nome printed up a bunch of T-shirts with the inscription, "NEVER TURN BACK." It seemed like half the people in Nome were wearing those T-shirts to honor Rick Swenson and his gutsy performance, and maybe to take a little jab at the ones who turned back.

Was anyone biased as we sat there and argued? Probably. So I decided that to be fair, I would describe the situation here, using the published words of the press and the mushers involved. The reader can then judge as though he was there listening to the people at the scene while it was unfolding.

I viewed the VHS tapes of the 1991 race finish as broadcast by Anchorage NBC affiliate, Channel 2. This seemed to be the most complete and accurate description of events and included interviews with the mushers who were involved. This was how their coverage of the news and interviews described the challenging scenario. It was a study in human behavior under scary conditions and was fascinating to review, even years later.

Wednesday evening Susan Butcher was first into White Mountain with an hour lead. The conversations on camera went something like this. Speaking of her faster team and Rick Swenson who was behind her, Susan said, "I should even feel good if we're leaving together. The wind is coming up; there should be some stormy conditions between here and Nome."

Jerry Riley tends one of his dogs during a rest stop. Joe Sr. told Burt that if you ever found a group of mushers in a terrible life-threatening situation that was so bad only one would survive, that one would probably be Jerry Riley. Jerry had a reputation for being a tough dog man, and Burt always found him to be attentive and kind to his dogs.

After Rick arrived, he responded to a reporter's question about his chances. "We know Susan is faster. You've got to be realistic. You've got a team stronger than mine. Only a lightning bolt would allow me to catch her."

A reporter then said, "At one-thirty in the morning, Susan left the checkpoint to what everyone expected would be her fifth Iditarod victory."

One hour later Rick gave chase, looking for that lightning bolt.

Less than thirty minutes later Joe Runyan left White Mountain, followed by Tim Osmar and Martin Buser.

The next morning a blizzard once again obliterated the trail.

By eight that morning, the three teams of Runyan, Butcher, and Osmar had returned to White Mountain, unable to slice through the storm.

The camera was on Joe Runyan, "It was stupid for us to go. It pisses me off that they even sent us out there. You know that? Stupid. Anyway, we just wasted our day!"

A reporter tells us, "Six miles out of the checkpoint, at temperatures reaching eighty below, mushers hit what Susan Butcher calls a wall." (Eighty below, probably referred to wind chill.)

Susan said, "I'd go five feet and the dogs would go off the trail. It was the first you'd know because you couldn't see the markers."

Susan continued, "I couldn't see the leaders. So I said, okay, I'll wait for Rick. So rather than stay in that really windy place, I decided I'd come back a quarter mile to wait an hour or so for Rick. We were in a place where it was still doable. I wasn't thinking of turning back, I just wanted a partner to go through it with. When I came on him (Rick Swenson), he was having trouble with his light, his hands were freezing, and I had to do his headlight for him. It was a tough situation out there. I found the trail; I found the marker. He was going to be in front and I was going to follow him when we pulled out of there."

Then Susan concluded, "We weren't ten feet away when he pulled the hook and I never saw him again, couldn't find the next stake, and couldn't follow the trail."

Meanwhile, there was a small group of people inside the Safety Roadhouse, just twenty-two miles from Nome, with nothing to do but commiserate and wait.

Official Iditarod trailbreakers were talking about the severity of the blizzard and their difficulties breaking trail. One said, "You couldn't see the stakes; you couldn't find the trail."

Rick Swenson's dad calmly responded to a reporter's question about Rick's chances out in the storm, saying, "Well, I'm not really too worried about him. I'm sure he pulled in someplace. I'm just going to wait for him, that's all."

A reporter continued the narration with the information that, "Meanwhile, back at White Mountain, all the teams but Rick Swenson and Martin Buser had returned to the checkpoint. Then, at seven forty-five a team appeared at Safety Roadhouse. It was as if out of nowhere. The storm had released its grip on Swenson."

Burt visits with Iditarod veteran Bud Smyth who had a reputation for innovative ideas and being one of the toughest guys around. Everybody in the holding area for the 2011 re-start at Willow is bundled up in their winter coats except Bud. It takes a tough musher to hold his coat on his arm during winter in Alaska.

The gamble had paid off. When Rick lost Susan Butcher, he kept on leading his team from trail marker to trail marker. Not even sure if he was going in the right direction and not knowing where Susan Butcher was, he kept going. Now, all he had to do was make it the last twenty-two miles to Nome.

When word reached White Mountain, the mushers who had turned back were interviewed. Tim Osmar said, "I think he deserves it. More power to him. I wish it would have been me, but it wasn't in the cards."

Joe Runyan said, "Got a lot of admiration for him. He went through a bad storm in training, probably figured he could do it and he did it. I've a lot of admiration for him."

The reporter then tells us that at 1:34 AM on Thursday, Rick made it to Nome in twelve and a half days. The only five-time champion, he had won in each of the last three decades. After a nine-year dry spell, Rick was no longer a former champion. He'd not been in the winner's chute since 1982. Rick had just won $50,000 dollars and a new truck.

Rick spoke with feeling as he was interviewed at the finish line. "It was a little scary; it was real stressful. I worked very hard. I walked a long, long way, leading the dogs. It was cold; it was not a pleasant night."

Rick continued, "It surprised me that she (Susan) turned back, knowing that I didn't turn back. But I'm guessing maybe she's softened a little with four victories under her belt. She's going to have to win six now if she wants to be *top* dog!"

What the heck, our little group voted Rick the *toughest*, not necessarily the *most gracious*. But it seemed okay for him to crow a little.

Dewey Halverson visits in Burt's kitchen. Burt would invite his wife Rhea to join them when they got together but she would decline saying she'd heard it all before. She joked about the mutual admiration society and said the conversation was always the same: Dewey, you're great! Yah, but you're greater! Yes, Dewey, but you're the best! Blah, blah, blah . . .

Martin came in second two hours later, having survived the storm. It was his highest finish in six races. He said it was do or die. He decided, why not go for it? If he were pinned down out there, it wouldn't be much different than being back at White Mountain. This way he was moving forward, not back.

Shortly before seven, Susan was interviewed in White Mountain and stated, "Rick is a longtime friend, as opposed to what the press says. We've had a close relationship for years. I know things are not going great in his life, so this is a fantastic boost. It has been nine years since he won a major race. It is a neat thing. As a friend I couldn't be happier for him."

Then the announcer intoned, "The race doesn't always go to the swift, but to those bold enough to take it. This year the race belongs to the musher from Two Rivers who dared to walk where no one else dared."

Nothing in this story diminishes any of the mushers who turned back—I knew them all and knew them to be seasoned, gritty mushers all. They were all genuine tough guys or they would never have been there in the first place, would never have ventured out into the raging blizzard to begin with.

Tim Osmar proved himself many times during Iditarod races, to be an excellent dog man, one of the toughest mushers and a princely gentleman, beginning with his performance at eighteen years of age during the 1985 Iditarod race.

Several years later, Joe Runyan wrote a book in which he opined about the incident.[7] He described it from the standpoint of a participant, so it was an interesting perspective. We pick up his story at the White Mountain checkpoint:

> Up the coast, out of White Mountain, the five of us were right together in the same ferocious storm. Buser and Swenson made the decision to keep going, while Butcher, Osmar and I decided to wait for a better day in White Mountain.
>
> Swenson went on to steal the race and win his fifth Iditarod. He worked his way through the storm and made it to Nome. Buser was second. Both Swenson and Buser had trained on the coast several weeks prior to the race. Their preparation and familiarity with the trail paid off when they beat the wind.
>
> Based on the condition of my team, I have never regretted turning back to White Mountain. It was a good decision for my team. Sometimes you have to hold 'em, and sometimes you have to fold 'em. Better to try again on a better day.
>
> While the storm continued to rage and pound the mushers on the trail, just a few front-runners had made it to Nome. Many mushers were pinned down by the storm and there was considerable concern for the safety of many.
>
> Meanwhile, in Nome a T-shirt had spontaneously appeared which sported the over worn cliché "Never turn back." It apparently was sort of a victory statement for Swenson and Buser. Despite the intrinsic merits of the cliché by itself or the well-intentioned motive for making the T-shirts, it always struck me as one of the nadir low points of sportsmanship of the Iditarod. To glorify a victory by denigrating the efforts of others didn't even escape the sensibilities of children.

After considering everything, our vote went to Rick Swenson, as the toughest musher, with Libby Riddles right behind. Both Rick and Libby left their checkpoints and mushed into raging blizzards with no partner and no one ahead

---

[7] <u>Winning Strategies for Distance Mushers</u>, Joe Runyan, 1997, Published by Joe Runyan

to leave any hint of a dog team's passing. In Rick's case, his would-be partner couldn't even stay with *him*, much less make it on her own until later when the storm eased. A dog team leaves little evidence of its travel during an Arctic blizzard. The snowdrifts are hard so there's not much feel, much less visual sign for other teams to follow. But a dog team would leave a scent trail for the following teams, a huge advantage for those following when visibility was down to zero.

Burt with Raymie Redington, and Raymie's sons Ryan and Ray Jr., in the holding area before Iditarod. Dog men to the core, Burt raced with Raymie and his dad Joe Sr. many times. Note the game face worn by Ray, Jr. and Raymie. Ryan was also a fierce competitor, but always seemed to have an easy going mood about him.

Martin Buser joins legendary mushers like Roger, Bud, Jerry, and Cowboy, since he didn't turn tail when three seasoned veteran mushers did. Dewey Halverson and John Cooper also join the group for forging into the 1985 storm behind Libby when others, this author included, were still sitting in Shaktoolik judging their ability to deal with it. Libby easily won world's toughest woman musher. We thought Rick earned the title honestly through his courage, skill, and experience.

The discussion in my cabin had gone on long into the night. I'm not sure if it was because there'd been so many mushers to consider or if we just couldn't easily agree. We all knew that anyone who finished the race was tough. Somebody started to snore, softly, as we took the final vote. It seemed like a good time for the guys to roll out their sleeping bags and call it a night.

I stood up, banked the fire so it would last all night and turned off the gas light. The covers were soon pulled up to my chin as I listened to the gentle snoring of my buddies and the cold breeze sighing in the spruce tree outside my window. We all looked forward to morning. I'd put the coffee on and womp up some of my special pancakes. The storytelling would begin before the first fork sliced into a hotcake and the first sip of coffee was down. We'd likely have something new to argue about, too.

Oh, by the way, this "toughest musher" award was not official. You judge for yourself. We were just some ol' pals shoot'n the breeze.

Chapter Nineteen
Mentors

Morning came early in dog camp. I could hear the wind whipping the big spruce trees outside. A couple of the guys were still snoring as I slid from under the covers and padded over to the wood stove. That cold wind and banked fire had cooled the place down to the point I could almost see my breath. I poked the ashes, tossed a couple of logs in and opened the vents. I headed for the window as the fire roared to life. I could already feel its heat as I checked the weather outside. A raging ground blizzard could be seen out on the meadow away from the trees that sheltered the cabin. It looked like a good day to stay inside and visit. Training season was past, so we had no schedules to keep.

I put the coffee pot on and started breakfast as the boys began to stir. They set their dog food out to soak and we sat down at the big walnut table for breakfast. When done, we all went out and fed our dogs and came back in to visit. The guys would likely stay until mid-afternoon and then hitch up their dogs for the journey home.

Talk turned to a time when we were all just starting to mush dogs. We all agreed that some of the most rewarding memories we had were of great people who took the time to not only teach us what we needed to know—but to mentor. Men and women who took us in as a friends and let us see this great life from the inside. I remember so well how eager I was to be one of the group, not just a spectator, but a *musher*.

I told the guys how inspired I was when I first learned of THE LAST GREAT RACE ON EARTH! How that resonated through my head, through my soul, through the whole of what and who I was. So many years ago now. It was as though my entire life had been on a trajectory that led only to that location in time and place. My sense of adventure, my love of this great state called Alaska were all encapsulated in these few words, *the Last Great Race on Earth*.

Iditarod dogs move at a quick, mile-eating trot across a frozen slough. The flats are great for developing speed but hills are needed to maintain strength on the uphill sections and fast speeds downhill. Burt always whistled when the dogs picked up speed on the downhill sections. Eventually, the dogs picked up speed anytime he whistled, handy when passing other teams.

In fact, these few words held far more meaning than any of us could know in just a year or two, or even a dozen. Maybe not until now. What we did know, and it's obvious to my readers by now, is that Iditarod was far more than just a race. Iditarod was a window into a time long ago when Alaska was the land of our dreams, a land of prospectors, gold miners, fur traders, and trappers, dog teams and card sharks and maybe even ladies of the night. Where winter temperatures plummeted through the bottom of the thermometer just outside a tiny wilderness cabin and spit froze with a crack before it even hit the snow.

All of this is right here in Alaska today, the cold, the life and the characters. That was obvious that day, right there at my cabin. But it is a bit hard for most to find and it is a hard life. That's because it is out in the woods where the malamute howls and snow is deep, where a trapper's set holds a marten beside the trail and overflow on an icy creek bottom can soak your boots and freeze your feet miles from camp. Even when you know where that life is, you can't always get there anymore.

Leaving my routine to race Iditarod was a huge challenge. I loved my routine. I was CEO of a large engineering/surveying company and lived a comfortable life within the establishment. But something was missing. There was a hole that couldn't be filled, an itch that couldn't be scratched.

This journey started with baby steps that would change my life forever. They would create a lifestyle that was rewarding and fulfilling but would burn a bridge behind that was already beginning to smolder. That bridge would burn day by day until it was impossible to cross back over the ashes. The bridge would never be re-built.

BEGINNINGS

We all had our stories to tell and I told mine. I'd been an Iditarod fan for a long time, but my first important contact with dog mushing, *when I saw the bridge beginning to burn*, began in a most unexpected way. My engineering firm was doing preliminary work on a large subdivision tucked back in a valley in the Chugach Mountains near Anchorage. Our client was a well-known Anchorage developer whose land occupied a beautiful valley surrounded on three sides by Chugach State Park. It was through his land that one of the few points of access to the park could be achieved, making it extremely important to the State Division of Parks. They did not want to route people into this beautiful park through a subdivision. Terri McWilliams, a well-known musher, was the director of the Division of Parks. She feared that we might even attempt to block access to the park and that the development might create blight to the pristine valley.

Battles between developers and environmentalists in Alaska over the years had made it extremely difficult to discuss development issues in a constructive manner. Although Miss McWilliams herself was a reasonable woman, some members of her staff, in their zealous desire to protect the park had pretty much trashed me as the developers' representative. It had polarized the issue.

In any case, we knew that whatever our client might eventually develop, it would be first class and would enhance the park, not detract from it. A number of my friends who worked for the Division of Parks kept me informed of my image over there. As developers, we were considered archenemies of a decent society and fully intent on inflicting our evil purposes on everything and everyone in our path. Terry, herself, had ultimately become vitriolic. I could hardly believe some of the things she reportedly said about me personally. We'd never laid eyes on each other, but that needed to change. Everyone's interests would be best served by putting personalities aside and keeping to the issues.

We found ourselves in court with our client's attorneys on one side of the court-room and Parks staff and attorneys on the other. I asked one of my engineers to identify the individuals on the other side. One of them was Terri McWilliams, whom I still hadn't met. As I glanced back, our eyes met. *She knew who I was.* If looks could kill. I decided to be brash in my approach to Ms. McWilliams. The first time the judge called a recess, I sauntered toward her group.

They shuffled uneasily when they discovered I was moving toward them and Terri fixed me with the look of a schoolteacher about to come down on a naughty child. I gave her my warmest smile, said, "Hello, Ms. McWilliams, my name is Burt Bomhoff," and stuck out my hand. There's not one person in a thousand who won't take your hand when offered, no matter how despicable they think you are. Terri was no exception. Out came her hand, the scowl still on her face. I grasped it warmly but firmly and refused to let go.

Terri McWilliams talks dogs with Burt at a post-Iditarod race party. Burt was privileged that Terry wore her fan club hat since she was virtually his first mentor when he began mushing dogs. She gave him his first ride in a dog sled.

Looking her in the eye, I told her how long I'd been a fan of hers and how closely I'd followed her mushing career. At that time, she was the official dog driver for Dick Tozier's Beartoe Kennels, a competitive sprint racing team. Dick, one of the most respected men in sled dog racing, was the race marshal for the Anchorage Fur Rendezvous Sled Dog Race and other events. Dick was always busy officiating, so he needed a top musher to drive his team. Terri was that musher.

I asked her about her mushing and she began to thaw. I've never met a musher who won't drop everything to talk dogs. I was not going to let go of her hand until she thawed out. She finally did just before the judge came back. In the end, the economy collapsed, our client dropped the development project, and once again, the staff at the Division of Parks could sleep well. And I'd made a new friend.

Then the phone rang and it was Terri. She was calling to ask if I would like to go for a tour of Beartoe Kennels. I said I would and stopped by a couple of days later. I shook hands with Dick and met his dogs. Dick was a big, imposing guy wearing a twenty-gallon Stetson. He was busily hitching a "cart" to the back of his dog truck so it could be towed to the training area. The cart consisted of a small, chopped-down foreign car that had been reworked into a vehicle a team of dogs could pull on bare ground. The top had been cut off and the motor and gear train had been removed to make it lighter. The cart enabled Dick and Terri to begin training before the snow fell. With the cart firmly attached, we loaded sixteen dogs into the truck and away we went.

Terri McWilliams finishes with a dog in the basket at Tudor Track. Dogs are given a ride home if they have problems keeping up during a race.

We stopped on a backcountry road in the hills east of Anchorage, unhitched the cart from the back bumper hitch of Dick's truck and tied its rear to the truck with a rope and slip knot. This was the safety line in case the parking brake on the training cart didn't hold. He then strung out his gang line, grabbed a bundle of harnesses, and started hitching dogs. We soon had sixteen furiously barking huskies lunging at their tug lines screaming to go. Dick instructed us to get into the cart while he got behind the wheel with his foot firmly on the brake.

While Dick stood on the brake, Terry yanked the snub line loose and away we went. Dick and Terri sat in the front with Dick steering. Dick's daughter, Christine, and I sat on couch cushions in the back of the little Fiat as we careened up the narrow road. We had to be one of the funniest sights in Anchorage bouncing along with Dick at the wheel and the rest of us hanging on for dear life. Dick was still wearing his Hoss Cartwright hat. The dogs made almost no sound except for an occasional yelp and the soft rustle of their traces.

As we rounded a corner, we saw a pickup ahead of us with a man bent under the hood tinkering with his engine. As we silently veered towards him, Dick turned to Terri and said, "Watch this." Just as the first dog passed the guy, Dick yelled "howdy!" Looking under his arm, the unsuspecting mechanic saw sixteen dogs towing a beat up rusty convertible driven by Hoss Cartwright. He straightened up so fast that he banged his head on the hood with a tremendous clang. And we were gone.

Another mile farther and the team suddenly stopped. "What in the hell is going on now?" Dick wanted to know.

Both he and Terri stood up to see what was happening. One of the lead dogs had stopped to take a dump. Terri leaped from the car, grabbed a switch off the bushes beside the road, and ran forward hollering, "Go ahead. Go ahead!" and switched the pup a couple of times. Then Terri made a flying leap into the cart as it flew by and we were on our way. Racing dogs must learn to do their business on the fly or not do it at all. Most of them learn to get the job done galloping full tilt.

Terri asked me if I could tell which of the dogs were pulling hard, and which weren't. I looked at the dogs carefully trying to figure it out but I couldn't tell. All of the tug lines appeared taut and all the dogs were loping. She pointed out that one dog's tail was in the air, which mushers call "flagging." Some dogs develop the ability to lope in their traces keeping their tug taut while not really exerting any pull. Thus relaxed, their tail goes up in the air and is a dead give-away. Dick barked the dog's name, which resulted in a marked change in the dog. The head went down and the tail went down as it obviously began straining against the harness.

I asked Dick how the dogs all knew their names. "The first thing a dog is taught is his name. If you can't teach a sled dog his name, you probably can't teach him to work anyway. You have to be able to communicate with the dogs in the team individually. That way you can single them out as you go with a word of encouragement or a word of criticism and they all know who you're talking to."

We must have looked like a cross between the Beverly Hillbillies and a clown car flying along in our muddy, beat up stripped-down cart with Hoss Cartwright at the wheel. Dick was a perfect replica of the TV star with his 250-pound frame and huge, domed cowboy hat. Within moments, we had reached the turnaround and were heading back toward the pickup. As we flew by, the guy at the pickup just stood in the middle of the road rubbing the bump on his head, gazing at us with a quizzical expression.

The day ended all too soon. I loaded gear and latched doors while Dick and Terri loaded the dogs. We drove back and put the dogs away. Then we had a cup of coffee in Dick's kitchen and discussed the day. This coffee thing seemed to be a ritual among dog mushers. I was happy to hear everything I could about mushing dogs.

It was awhile before I was invited again. A rainy fall made the back roads too muddy for cart training, so we had to wait for snowfall. Finally, it snowed and on Saturday, November 24, Terri called. They would be hitching the dogs and told me to meet them at Dick Tozier's house. The temperature was ten degrees above zero Fahrenheit. Terri asked me to open all the doors on the dog boxes while they started bringing dogs. When the dogs were tossed into the boxes, I would quickly shut the door and snap the clasp on the door. The snaps were attached from the bottom up so that the solid part of the snap was toward the door. In that way, if the little spring broke on the snap or didn't catch just right, the door still wasn't likely to open.

We drove the truck to a trail that runs near Service High School and began setting up the sleds. Each was rigged with a gang line, a snub line, and a   line attached to a ring on the bridle. The snow hook was placed in the sled and the snub line was tied to a post with a knot that was unique to dog mushing. It was sort of like a bowline but with a tag end, which was jerked to untie the sled so the dogs could run.

Terri showed me how the dogs were harnessed, although I didn't harness any dogs that day. The dogs were then hitched to the gang line with a short neckline snapped to their collar and finally a tug line was snapped to the back of the harness.

Terri told me to hop into the sled and sit on the cushion. She yanked the snub line and hollered, "Go ahead!" The eight-dog team took off at a gallop. It was exhilarating to watch the dogs running for all they were worth. Visions of Alaskan mushers Scotty Allen and Leonard Seppala danced in my head as our team moved quickly through the snowy birch woods.

Terri explained that you could slow the sled down a little bit on steeper hills by dragging a heel. Sprint mushers don't want brake grooves on the trail for fear that a dog might sprain an ankle. We missed our turn on the loop at the end of the trail and careened full tilt into the Service schoolyard. The dogs didn't want to make the "haw" turn to go back, so I went forward, and brought the leaders back around. Back down the trail we went.

Terri and I had taken off first, so we met Dick head-on as we headed back toward the truck. When meeting, both teams pass on the right or "gee" side with mushers hollering, "Go ahead!" Racers keep the sled on the "gee" side of the trail to assure that they don't collide and tangle the teams. When passing a team that is going in the same direction, you holler for trail and then pass the slower team on the "gee" side. That way the passing team was trained to always pass on the same side. It avoids tangles.

Seasoned Iditarod mushers, left to right: Dewey Halverson, Fred Agree, Raymie Redington, and Burt gathered to visit at the race re-start in Willow.

We mushed again on Sunday, November 25. When we got to the trail, Dick decided I was ready to drive a team of my own and that I would be using the larger freight sled. His daughter, Chris, would be my passenger. Although young, Christine was experienced with dogs, she was probably my babysitter. I was to have a six-dog team consisting of Stubby and Jasper in lead, Hooslia and Ruby in swing, and Rachel and Sundance in wheel.

I lined out the gang line, hooked the snub line and the snow hook line to the bridle, and tied the snub line firmly to a post. We had to be just as careful removing the dogs from the truck as we were putting them in. We would open a door a crack, put a hand in, and grab a dog's collar before the dog could push the door open. The dogs would come leaping out of the boxes and onto the ground wild with excitement.

Gripping the dog firmly but not too tightly with our legs, we slipped the web harness over its head, placing its front legs through the appropriate place in the harness. A gentle tug backwards on the harness straightened it and set it properly, and the dog was hitched to the gang line. The neckline snapped on to the dog's collar while the tug line snapped onto the rear of its harness.

Never once from the time the dog box door was open a crack until the dog was firmly hitched to the gang line was it given the opportunity to get loose. The dogs didn't mind pulling the sled, it was just that the racing husky was so crazy to run, that if you ever let it go, it might run off down the trail and never be recovered. The commands they learned were "go ahead," "gee," "haw" and "whoa," but few of them know what it means to "come here."

When we had them all hitched, I yanked the snub line knot and the sled was loose. I hollered, "Go ahead!" and the dogs were running. The trail ran approximately fifty yards on the level, after which it went down a steep hill and then took a jump almost all in one breath. It astounded me. We seemed out of control but this was nothing like it would be years later driving a twenty-dog team in Iditarod. The run was terrific with all the dogs pulling except for Ruby, who had a loose tug line most of the way. Stubby and Rachel were trotters, so they would trot anytime the team had to slow down, especially going uphill. The other dogs tried to lope most of the way, a characteristic of sprint dogs.

Burt ready to train Dick Tozier's dogs at Tudor Track. Trails didn't get much icier than this during Iditarod. Anchorage's occasional warm winter weather often resulted in trails that were icy and treacherous. It was amazing how skilled those sprint mushers were at negotiating icy trails at race speeds.

All too soon, we were back at the truck unhitching the team. During one of our "chalk talks" at his home, Dick had instructed me to occasionally stop during a run, set the snow hook and go pet each dog and give him a word of encouragement. He said the dogs should have fun when they run. They should run out of excitement and the pure enjoyment of it, which is much better than having to push them. There is a time for discipline, but it is not early in the season when you want the dogs to have a good time.

I began to love the routine. I would help train the dogs during the week and then lend a hand on race days. On race day, this meant loading dogs at the lot, hitching them at the track, helping hold them back as they approached the chute, and helping them get back to the truck after they crossed the finish line.

We continued our routine, training three or four evenings each week. As we glided along, lost in thought and enjoying the beauty of an Alaska winter night, it occurred to me that mushing dogs was a lot like flying airplanes, hours upon hours of boredom punctuated by moments of adrenaline rush. You are always aware of the dogs and your surroundings, but your mind can be somewhere else.

Joe Redington Sr. stopped by Tozier's one night to drop off Susan Butcher's Iditarod sled. Susan had run into a telephone guy wire line, breaking the brush bow and several cross members in her sled. Joe and I had never met, so it was nice to meet him and visit. He picked up a couple of snow hooks and ordered a new Iditarod sled for Susan. It was a treat to meet such a famous musher and the man they call the Father of Iditarod.

I realized more and more what a highly respected and well-liked musher Dick Tozier was. The opportunity to help Dick train dogs and learn mushing from him was a rare privilege and greatly appreciated. Now, as I write this many years later with my hair turned white, I miss Dick, and Terri, and Joe, and Norm, and all those other sourdoughs a great deal. One of the wonderful aspects of Alaska in those days was that our heroes were often our friends.

We continued the nightly regimen and the dogs liked me better and better all the time. We were beginning to establish a bond.

Our first official race of the season was January 1, 1980. Even though I'd been able to run dogs for several months, I still found that I had a lot to learn. Terri had so many fans that showed up at the race, all wanting to help and all wanting her attention. Dick was race marshal, so he was occupied with managing the race itself. We finally had to almost drag Terri bodily away from everyone to get her to help us hitch up the dogs and get to the starting line.

I spent the winter watching the clock in my office and then racing home from work. A quick change of clothes and I'd be hotfooting it over to Tozier's, where we would load dogs and make our evening run. There would be time afterward for coffee and a post mortem of the evening's runs. It was a wonderful winter, training dogs during the week and then heading for Tudor Track on Sundays to handle Terri's dog team in the races she entered. I was getting closer to my dream of racing Iditarod. Terri became a dear friend and later came to Nome to cheer me across the finish line. This was a nice change from the look she gave me the first time we met.

Although sprint mushing was not really the same sport as long-distance mushing, there were similarities. I was able to learn a great deal about training dogs and the mechanics of sled dog racing and equipment. We would glide along those Alaskan trails and my dreams were on next year when I hoped to put an Iditarod team of my own together. I dreamed of racing the Iditarod Trail Sled Dog Race from Anchorage to Nome and I dreamed of life in the wild back-country of Alaska.

The Tudor Track race season ended with the approach of the Anchorage Fur Rondy. Dick didn't enter his team in the Rondy races, so our training season ended.

CONVERSATIONS

I couldn't help but chuckle on opening day of the 1980 Fur Rondy race. My wife and I were sitting in the Petroleum Club having lunch with Congressman Don Young and his wife, Lou. We enjoyed the warmth and luxury of the Petroleum Club, as well as discussing dogs and dog mushing. Don had lived for years at Fort Yukon and had years of experience mushing dogs. There I was with a few months of experience. Each of us had tales to tell.

Don told about a lead dog that belonged to Lou that would work just fine unless he decided that the load was too heavy. Whenever that happened, he would stop and turn around. No amount of argument or struggle would get him to move or do anything that he didn't want to do.

A musher can feel frustrated when racing a team that gets lazy and slacks off. Don said that when he used to race dogs, and they didn't want to run, he'd dream up outlandish ideas. He thought about running a copper wire up the gang line with leads going up each individual dog's tug line. From there the copper wire would be soldered to a copper penny, which would be inserted in the dog's butt. This whole contraption would be attached to a battery on the sled with an array of buttons, one for each dog. As he mushed down the trail, if any of the dogs slacked off a bit he could call the dog's name and zap. Instant tuning without stopping. He said the beauty of it would be when he came upon another team and wanted to pass. He would wait until he got up to the other sled, and then push all of the buttons at once, *overdrive*.

Another ploy would be to dig up all the yellow snow from around the dog-house of a bitch in heat, put it in a bag to be taken along on race day. Then as you proceeded around the course grab a few crystals of yellow snow from the bag and sprinkle them along the trail. It would be interesting to watch the reaction of the following teams when all the male dogs hit their brakes and started sniffing around the trail, looking for that foxy female.

Of course, Don would never mistreat his dogs. It was just fun to think wicked thoughts when the dogs think they know more than the musher does. Mushing dogs is a lot of fun and so is talking about it.

Dick Tozier called me a week or so after the Rondy to invite me along on a trip to Fairbanks. Dick's good buddy, Bill Taylor, had some dogs for sale and Dick was interested. I leaped at the opportunity. We would go in Dick's truck and stop for the night at Dale Redlington's home in Nenana. We would then proceed to Taylor's to spend the next night and maybe deal dogs. Dick spoke highly of both men and said that both had good dogs.

We drove Dick's dog truck in case we bought dogs. After spending every other night with Dick for the past several years, we'd become good friends. Usually, we talked dogs but Dick also had a horse and was president of the Alaska Sled Dog Racing Association that put on all of the Tudor Track Races and the Anchorage Fur Rondy World Championships. We talked about all of that as the miles rolled by. Then I mentioned that I wanted to race Iditarod. Dick knew it and just shook his head. "Burt, sprint mushers race in the afternoon and sleep in a warm bed at night. Iditarod mushers drive all day and all night and sleep in a snow bank under a spruce tree. It doesn't take a genius to figure out what's best."

We arrived at Dale's and he showed us to our rooms. As we visited after dinner, Dick mentioned that I was going to be racing Iditarod and was interested in distance mushing. Dale said that Nenana had an Iditarod champion who lived just down the street and that they should introduce Burt to him.

We threw on our parkas and walked over to Jerry Riley's house. Margaret answered the door and invited us in.

"Jerry! Company!"

Jerry stuck out his hand in greeting and invited us in.

"Jerry, Burt's putting a team together to run the Iditarod," Dick said.

"Well, Burt, you'll have about as much fun as a man can have. Have you got it all figured out?"

"Not even close. I've handled for Dick the past few years so have part of it under control, but I've got no clue about driving a dog team to Nome and keeping them healthy."

"Well, Burt, I'll tell you what I know."

Over the next several hours, Jerry explained what he fed his dogs, both in training and during the race. He talked about what shots he gave his dogs, what medications kept them healthy and even told me what clothes he wore. As he went over his personal race diet, Margie chimed in. I used what Margie told me about Jerry's personal food menu for every Iditarod race that I entered and never changed a thing.

During a break in the conversation, I asked Jerry what the secret was to negotiating the dreaded Dalzell Gorge. He responded, "Go at night so you can't see the bad stuff before you're in it. It looks worse than it is."

Burt's parents came all the way from Iowa to visit and watch Burt start the Iditarod. Burt loved to hunt until Iditarod began to occupy his spare time.

I appreciated Jerry taking me under his wing when I knew nothing about long-distance mushing, something I never forgot. When Jerry needed a hand with anything from that day forward until today, I tried to be there for him. Jerry has taken some criticism for the way he treats his dogs over the years, but a lot of old-timers like Dick and Dale had a lot of respect for him.

We went from Dale's home in Nenana the next morning and headed for Bill Taylor's house. Bill took us mushing and sold me a nice leader.

That was one trip I hated to see end. Terri McWilliams and Dick Tozier became two of my closest friends and Iditarod supporters. Terri occasionally helped me train my Iditarod dogs when she could get away from her work, and she came to Nome to cheer me across the finish line.

Summer in front of Gerald Riley's handler's cabin in the dog yard on the outskirts of Nenana. Rustic, but with all the comforts of home, lawn chairs, propane grill, bicycle and an old van to store stuff in.

Dick died a premature death and Terri moved out of Alaska. I'm sad when they come to mind but privileged to have had them as my good friends while they were here. Tudor Track was renamed Tozier Track in honor of this wonderful man who did so much for sled dog racing.

I later bought fifteen dogs from Duke Bertke, the guy I'd met at Dick's that night. Some were good dogs and others probably average.

My goal was to put a team together and attempt racing Iditarod in 1981. I realized that no one could put a winning team together in one year. I would be competing with mushers who had been racing Iditarod since 1973 when the first Anchorage-to-Nome race was run. I did feel, though, that I could put my faith in some good mushers and put together a team that might at least finish in the top half.

I then owned twenty dogs, which probably varied on both sides of average with none of them being outstanding. My job would be to see that they had a proper diet and a proper training program so I could get the most out of them. If I continued to be enthusiastic about mushing, I'd develop a breeding program and try to develop good dogs of my own. Most of the mushers who did well had been at it for at least a few years, so I was not kidding myself.

JOE MAY

On Monday, February 18, 1980, I drove to Trapper Creek, a small community west of Talkeetna, Alaska, to visit Joe May. Joe had lived in Alaska approximately seven years. He was a retired merchant marine from Michigan who had always dreamed of coming to Alaska. He was a trapper, and ran his trapline using a dog team. In 1976, Joe ran the Iditarod race from Anchorage to Nome, coming in eleventh. He lay off a few years and then ran the race again in 1979 coming in fifth. Joe was an interesting guy with his Alaskan lifestyle and mushing success. Because of this, he had attracted a fair amount of attention in the press.

Having heard and read a lot about Joe, I pictured a man who loved dogs, enjoyed running them, and approached the racing thing in a relaxed way. I had a feeling that he was more interested in his dogs and seeing what they could do, and that the competition was secondary. I pictured a man of integrity who liked to talk about mushing sled dogs in Alaska.

I drove to Joe's place on Oil Well Road and parked my car by the road. It was a short hike up to his cabin approximately a hundred yards from the road. Joe and Jan, his handler, had just finished a fifty-mile run from his cabin to the Forks Roadhouse. They invited me to sit down for a cup of coffee and a little conversation, which turned into dinner and a bottle of burgundy. Most of the conversation involved middle and long-distance sled dog racing. I asked many questions and Joe was generous in answering.

Once the training season had advanced, Joe generally trained his dogs over a forty- to fifty-mile course, running the course two days and laying off one. The day off was used to get caught up on everything that went by the board during the two long training days. He started the season training the dogs on shorter runs, building them up as they became more conditioned until he reached the fifty-mile mark. When that became a standard day, he went two days on and one off.

There were a hundred questions on my mind. I asked Joe if he used booties during training or just during a race. He explained that he used them whenever needed, and had gone through thirty pairs of booties that day. He examined the dogs every day for signs of limping or other troubles, and then treated the problems. He kept a chart on a clipboard with each dog's name on the left, with columns for each paw so that he could make notations for each dog's feet. He used that chart to go out and make the rounds of the dogs, treating cuts and worn spots on the pads. It was clear that you needed an adequate supply of booties when running dogs over a rough training trail.

He used salve to rub on any injuries that existed. Common problems were bent toenails, worn pads, and splits or tears between the pads. He put boots on the dogs that had foot problems so they could run while at the same time have a chance to heal. People occasionally criticize the sport of dog racing, believing that humans have a choice while dogs don't. On the contrary, a dog could express himself every bit as well as a person. As long as he liked what he was doing, he would tolerate those minor cuts and abrasions, because overall he was enjoying it more than he would if he stayed home. When it got to the point where that wasn't the case, he'd let you know.

Always ready to help, Iditarod Champion Joe May spent hours talking dogs with Burt when he stopped by Joe's cabin at Trapper Creek in 1980. Afternoon gave way to an incredible dinner of moose steaks that were chain-sawed off a frozen hindquarter that hung from a tree in the yard. Wine and potatoes baked on an open fire topped it off.

We talked of other things, too. Many dog teams go sour sometime early in the season. Some mushers just keep driving the dogs until they are conditioned and then drive on new trails to revive the dogs' interest. Other mushers try to keep the dogs happy all season by mushing variable distances on different trails, always keeping it interesting.

Joe had developed a handy arrangement for his headlamp. All mushers who drive at night use small, electric miner's headlamps. These lamps have a switch on the lamp and are mounted on the forehead. The switch is small and a little bit hard to work, especially with mitts on. Joe said there was nothing worse than coming down a mountain in the dark, when you need to hang on with both hands, but you had to let go with one hand to try to find your light switch. Because of this, he mounted a push-button switch right on the battery case. The battery case was mounted to his belt where he could turn on his headlamp simply by bumping the battery case with his elbow.

Joe liked to pick good rough trails with lots of ups and downs to train on. He said it was like training football players by making them run through the tires because it developed agility. He also liked to run along unpacked trails at times because the dogs were going to have to push through fresh snow on the Iditarod and traverse punchy trails. They might as well get used to it. It was also important to vary the terrain because there were many up-and-down sections on the Iditarod Trail. The dogs needed to get used to it and develop sufficient strength to handle it without surprises.

Talk turned to nutrition. Most experts agree that the calories needed for dogs involved in long-distance dog mushing are the kind of calories stored in animal fats as opposed to the kind of calories that were stored in carbohydrates. Carbohydrate calories tend to be utilized more rapidly and don't provide the staying power that fatty meats provide. Foods that contain more than fifty percent fat include most cuts of beef, pork, chicken, cheese, and sausage. Most dog mushers feel that beaver meat was just about the ideal food for dogs under working stress. And dogs love it.

Many believe it takes about four hours for a bite of food to pass through the digestive track and be converted into energy. During races, a musher should try to give the dogs a continuous supply of energy so the dogs don't feel the drop in energy they might feel with no stops to eat.

Often dogs need to be trained to drink water. Dogs tend to dehydrate during a race. Mushers need to ensure a sufficient supply of fluids. Some products on the market add aroma to the water to encourage the dogs to drink more.

Joe stated, "The National Academy of Science had a great deal of diet information, which was important for working dogs and dogs in stress situations."

I began to realize that Joe's approach to mushing and racing sled dogs was far from casual. He knew a lot and all of it was based on sound scientific principles.

In those days, most racing dog diets consisted of fish and red meat, along with commercial dog foods. Red meat could be warmed and fed to the dogs uncooked. Fish would give the dogs parasites, so it needed to be boiled before feeding. After the fish is boiled, it must be allowed to cool.

Most of what Joe fed was a slurpy, sloppy soup containing chunks of beaver or whatever. In this way, the dogs got used to drinking and taking in lots of water. Dehydration took a tremendous toll on working dogs, zapping their strength and bringing down their physical and mental processes.

To evaluate a sled dog, a musher needs to stand back a ways and watch how a dog moves to judge whether it is a good dog, or is lame, or has sore feet. In this way, you can analyze a dog's gait to evaluate whether anything is wrong. Don't stand too close or it'll be difficult to judge. You can tell a lot watching a dog run around its post in the yard.

Joe pointed out the importance of a racing dog having small, tight feet as opposed to having large feet with long toes. A foot that is big and tends to spread is more subject to injury such as sprains and tears. Toenails need to be trimmed during training and prior to races to avoid breaking and tearing. Don't trim into the quick when cutting toenails for it is extremely painful for the dog and may bleed. Jack Morris, an Iditarod Trail veterinarian, told me later that no more than one-eighth inch of nail be trimmed at a time. The toenail should be almost long enough to touch the ground with the dog standing flat-footed.

The topic of moose attacks always came up and that night was no exception. Most mushers agree that when a moose spots a dog team, it reacts as though the team is a pack of wolves. The moose will high tail it away if it can, but it may also charge into the team and attempt to kill the dogs. Since the dogs are hitched front and rear to a gang line, they have no way of escaping or defending themselves. Therefore, a musher should always carry a firearm capable of killing a moose and be prepared to use it. It was interesting that we encountered so many moose on the Anchorage trails and never had one get belligerent. City life with its traffic, barking dogs, and people smells must have conditioned them to be more relaxed about sharing the trail.

Joe began fixing dinner. He went outside and trimmed several moose steaks off a frozen carcass with his chainsaw. He opened the door to the woodstove and put them on the coals to broil. Homemade Thousand Island dressing was served over salad with lots of wine and coffee to wash it down. What a terrific evening! I invited Joe to come and stay with us in Anchorage and let me return the favor.

Joe grabbed a bucket of warm water to prime the pump and went out to fetch a pail of water. The well was a sand point with a pitcher pump. Joe took the bucket of warm water along to soak the pump's diaphragm. When done pumping, the prime was released so the water was let out of the pump housing and the pump wouldn't freeze solid. When the next person went out to fetch water, he took a bucket of hot water to soak and thaw the diaphragm. In this way, the outdoor pump worked all winter with a minimum of problems.

Training carts were invaluable for training dogs in the off season. Iditarod dogs developed tremendous strength pulling a chopped down car up hill. John Barron, veteran Iditarod musher, chopped this old Volkswagen for Burt by cutting off all extraneous metal and removing everything but the brakes. Teams that pull these carts all summer have no trouble pulling a sled up the steepest mountain trails when the snow flies.

The final advice Joe gave me that evening was to give Ralph Mann a call. He believed that Ralph had a number of good dogs for sale. It was after midnight when Joe asked if I'd like to spend the night, but I pulled on my coat and boots and started for home.

The more I was around dogs, the more intimately involved I got with them until they seemed almost human. It was funny listening to a musher talking to his dogs when he didn't think anyone was listening, or when he forgot you were standing there. I went up to Trapper Creek to buy some dogs from Ralph Mann as Joe had suggested.

When I arrived, Ralph took me to his dog yard and told me about the dogs that were for sale. His dogs were happy to see him and set up a tremendous clamor. The racket was so intense that I couldn't hear Ralph talking. He got an exasperated look on his face, turned around to his twenty dogs and hollered, "Shut up, goddamn it, I don't want to hear about it!" Then he turned to me and said with a sheepish look, "Sometimes they just don't know when to be quiet."

I bought Egor and Mibbs from Ralph and before long wished that I had bought more from him. They were the best dogs I'd seen yet and the price was fair. I added them to the growing string of dogs I was accumulating. The week before, I'd bought Sundance from Dick, since Sundance liked to trot and wasn't needed for Dick's sprint team.

During the last week in March, after the 1980 Iditarod was over, Joe May called me at the office and took me up on my invitation to stay at our house when he was in Anchorage. I suggested that he stop by early so that we could have dinner and visit during the evening. This was again one of the most interesting conversations imaginable. Joe had just won the 1980 Iditarod, setting a new record on one of the most difficult trails in memory. It was a pleasure listening to this soft-spoken man who had accomplished so much.

Joe emphasized the importance of traveling light more than any other Iditarod racer I have ever listened to. A down sleeping bag was spread inside his toboggan sled and the sled bag was pulled tight around Joe's neck to serve as a tent. He cooked on a lightweight two-burner Coleman stove from which he had removed the cover, the folding legs and every second wire in the grill. He had an aluminum cooking pot the same shape as the Coleman stove with a lid to help retain heat. He tried to carry as little food as possible for his personal diet and described my sheep-hunting diet almost to the letter. He ate a light breakfast of warmed cereal and fluids. Sausage, cheese, and dried fruit were lunch, and something light and warm was dinner.

Fluids were important. You usually needed to water the dogs morning and evening, so it was a simple matter to heat your personal fluids, too. You needed to fill your thermos with hot chocolate or coffee, which would keep warm.

LIBBY

On Friday, March 28, 1980, Duke Bertke called me to say he had just heard from Libby Riddles. She had a dog named Buff for sale. Buff was a bitch and the sister of Zinger, my second leader, and a dog named Mayberry, who was a good Iditarod dog. Duke recommended I buy the dog for the $300 Libby was asking. I called Libby that evening and made an appointment with her to see the dog in the morning. She suggested I try the dog over the weekend and either buy it or return it if it didn't fit in.

I stopped by Libby's home on Hillside Drive on Saturday morning and was treated with friendly Alaskan hospitality. Libby brewed up a pot of coffee and asked me if I would like it black or with cream and sugar. I told her black, which she said was going to be *very* black and she wasn't kidding. I have not tasted stronger coffee since drinking chicory in New Orleans. I told her I thought that cup of coffee would probably keep me awake until the next day. It sure was good and hit the spot. She introduced me to her friend, Charlie, and the three of us sat and visited for about an hour in Libby's kitchen.

Libby had done a lot of her training near Eureka, Alaska, which is an excellent place to train dogs. There were plenty of rough trails and enough overflow to give the dogs a chance to see most of the conditions they were going to see during Iditarod. She said that after the training she had experienced, the Iditarod felt like a piece of cake, which was the way she wanted it. All the mushers I talked to who have finished in the money have emphasized the need for training on rough trails.

Libby warned me to be wary of traps anytime I mushed dogs where other people might be. Some trappers, especially wolf trappers, set their traps in the middle of the trail hoping to catch something running the trail. She said her dogs had gotten into traps twice. One of her wheelers got a hind foot caught in a trap, which must have been murderously painful. Before she could put on the brakes, the rest of the team had stretched the poor wheel dog to the point where his leg must have been ten feet long.

She said it was extremely difficult to remove the dog from the trap because of its pain, which caused it to snap, bite, and growl every time she got near it. She finally got it loose. Libby strongly recommended I take a couple of C-clamps along, so I would have some way of getting a trap off if it was too big to release by hand.

Libby also strongly urged taking a moose gun along anytime I mushed. She said she had gotten involved with moose several times and found it to be a totally terrifying experience. In her view, it would be irresponsible to be unable to protect your dogs when they were helpless.

RICK SWENSON

Rick Swenson and his wife joined us at our home for dinner a couple of nights before the start of the 1983 Iditarod. I'd bought several dogs from Rick and had invited him to stay at our home with his dogs at race time. He had loaned me OB, one of his famous leaders, now too old to stay ahead of Rick's own competitive team but deserving of another race. OB could easily stay ahead of my team. Over dinner, the topic turned to training programs. Rick looked at mine and shook his head. He then drew up a schedule for me that I used from that time forward.

A week or so later I was cooking food for my dogs at the Ophir checkpoint when Rick wandered over to visit. I'd put all of my meat and kibble in my cook pot and filled it with water. I had to stir it constantly while the water came to a boil to avoid scorching the meat. Rick shook his head and asked me if I had an extra pair of poly-gloves. "Rick, I'm an engineer. We wear a belt *and* suspenders! Of course, I have an extra pair."

Rick Swenson helped Burt with the loan of a seasoned leader, OB, and designed a dog training schedule that Burt used until he retired from mushing. Note the Velcro on Rick's hat for attaching various items, including facemasks and headlights.

Rick responded that he'd show me how to cook dog food in trade for my extra pair of gloves.

The right way is to bring the water to a boil and pour it into the cooler over the frozen meat and kibble. Let it soak and feed it. It's a lot less work with no danger of scorching anything.

My early conversations with these experienced dog people helped a lot in my transition from office to dog camp.

Chapter Twenty
The Final Chapter?

O nce again, I find myself reminiscing in a small cabin in the Alaska wild country north of Willow. I purchased the cabin for my handler's from Lavon years ago. No handler here now—no need. Snow covers the ground and the tree limbs are loaded with great clumps of snow. Dog posts stand in orderly rows and a few old, rotting, broken-down doghouses seem ready to sag back into the ground whence they sprang. No sled dogs in sight, just my English setter, Hunter, resting quietly at my feet. And no hard-packed trail leading out the back of the yard. The place is quiet and lonely. It's amazing how time marches on without us even noticing.

I decided that there had been enough dogs in my life to last a lifetime, and it was time to go back to the city life in Anchorage.

I was offered a job as project manager on a large fuel storage and pipeline construction project on the North Slope. I took it. Fuel facilities at all eight North Slope Borough villages were obsolete and ready to fall apart. We rebuilt all of the storage facilities, pipelines, and dispensing stations. It took four and one-half years at a cost of millions to complete the work. It felt great to be back engineering and there wasn't a day that I didn't get up and look forward to going to work. I especially liked having an excuse to spend time in the villages.

The problem was that I lived in town and didn't have dogs. I would drive up into the Mat-Su Valley to visit my dog-mushing buddies just to get a little contact.

When we completed construction, the company asked me to manage the engineering and facilities departments for the Alaska Long-Range Radar System.

I took it. The job involved managing the design, engineering, construction, and maintenance of fourteen radar sites across Alaska. These sites constituted the original DEW (Distant Early Warning system) line, which had been constructed years earlier. In aggregate, the facilities on these fourteen sites combined to constitute the largest military base in PACAF—with facilities valued at $4,000,000,000.

I was proud of my work and my crew. The company presented me with a commendation award that holds an American flag that flew over all fourteen radar sites that I managed. The plaque reads:

BURT BOMHOFF
May 18, 1997 — June 17, 2005
In grateful appreciation for eight years of
your dedicated service to the Alaska Radar System
and our nation's defense.

Still no dogs. So I moved twenty miles out of Anchorage to Chugiak where I could keep a few dogs and still get back and forth to work. More than seventy years old then, I still dreamed of driving a dog team across this great wilderness of Alaska. I was going to train in my spare time, because I had to work to support my racing.

Riding a sled behind a strong fast team out of my yard was one thrilling experience. My place is on top of a low ridge so the trail is downhill with twists and turns for the first quarter mile. We would leave the yard wide open with me standing on the brakes with all my weight. An immediate hard, snappy turn to the left and we were parallel to the railroad tracks. Fifty yards farther and it was a hard, tight right turn and across the railroad tracks. Then downhill with a couple sharper turns where we crossed a narrow footbridge and picked up the Birch Lake Mushing Trails.

The trail out of the yard would keep me sharp for those hair-raising trails through the Alaska Range during the Iditarod race. As the dogs gained strength, I needed to train longer miles, so I looked for a place with more trails in the Willow area. Lynwood Fiedler offered to let me use his dog yard. I would train the dogs out of my backyard in Chugiak after work all week and then make the trip to Willow on Saturday and Sunday to get longer training miles. Miles of driving on weekends began to take their toll, so I searched for some land for a training camp, a place I could drive to on Friday after work and stay until Sunday night.

Burt and Joe Redington checking out Joe's new pups in 1998. Joe loved his dogs 'til he died on June 12, 1999, just a year after this picture was taken. Close friends could see that Joe's health had already begun to fail.

Burt eulogizes Joe Redington Sr. before a somber crowd at the memorial service for Joe at Iditarod headquarters in Wasilla. It was Burt's sad honor to serve as a pallbearer at Joe's funeral. A bronze statue of Joe graces the front yard of Iditarod headquarters.

Burt served as executive director for the 1993 race and presented famed explorer Col. Norman Vaughan with a banner at the drawing banquet in Anchorage to take along on his 1993 Antarctic expedition. The banner identified the expedition and was composed of an Alaska flag, an American flag, and an Iditarod Official Finishers patch. Norm's goal was to climb 10,302-foot Mount Vaughan, towering above him in Antarctica, at the age of eighty-eight. He accomplished this remarkable feat.

I found the perfect piece of land at Willow for training an Iditarod team. To begin with, I could drive to it. It was just an hour from home. Although it wasn't nearly as good for the soul as training in true wilderness, like my camp on the Kahiltna or in the Peters Hills country south of Mount McKinley, it was handy. *And I was training a dog team again!* I could cart-train on the local road system before snow fell and had a huge winter trail system to the north to use.

We set up a tent to serve as my abode and I bought the cabin I'm sitting in now. We hauled it in with a wrecker. I figured that since the handler was there permanently and I was just there a few nights a week, I'd sleep in the tent. Years of camping out on the trail with my dogs made this tent seem plush.

Now the routine changed. I drove up to Willow after work three nights each week and spent weekends at Willow when I ran the longer miles. This meant that I got home from my training camp around one in the morning three nights a week and then got up at seven for work.

I felt tired most of the time and chalked it up to the rigorous schedule. Driving a dog team five times a week was just about the nicest life imaginable. The dogs were great and our camp couldn't have been better.

I entered the 2004 Iditarod Trail Sled Dog Race with high hopes. The dogs had many miles on them so were tough and fast. Turns out, they were better than I was. I felt great at the start but tired quickly. I wondered if I had some latent fatigue from all those long days and short nights or maybe it was just age catching up to me. I was nearly seventy at the time but knew I was still tough. Maybe I'd feel better down the trail.

By the time we reached Rainy Pass, I could hardly drag myself around the checkpoint. It must have been obvious because several people offered to give me a hand. I refused. That's grounds for disqualification and I sure wasn't going to risk that. It was likely to be my last race and I desperately wanted to finish.

Burt with Norm, a friend who is sorely missed, at Norm's cabin at Petersville on a warm, sunny afternoon. Even after he was confined to a wheel chair, Norm loved to get out in his beloved Alaska to enjoy his log cabin home and the beautiful Peters Hills. Even in failing health, Norm always had a big smile and "Dreamed Big & Dared to Fail." Norm wanted to live at home with his wife Carolyn for the rest of his life, and did not want to be in a care facility. Carolyn made sure this happened the way Norm wanted. *Carolyn Vaughan photo.*

It wasn't to be. I scratched at Rainy Pass and flew my dogs back home.

Two weeks later, I was diagnosed with a particularly viral form of prostate cancer. My doctors recommended that I schedule surgery immediately and I obliged. Now several years later, there's no sign of the cancer.

I ponder all of this as I sit in my snug cabin. Would I do as my pal Norman Vaughan suggested so many years ago and build an Iditarod team as strong as the one I built before? Probably not. My memory bank is full to the brim with a thousand trips down cold, lonely wilderness trails, dogs that gave great love and loyalty, friends like Joe Redington Sr. and Norman Vaughan, Dick Tozier, Terri McWilliams, and Raymie—too many to list, but all in my memory.

How could you ask for more than a yard full of faithful sled dogs creating a mood that was purely old-time, bush Alaska? Burt's big smile is proof of how happy it gets.

My mind traveled back to a cold night in Galena on the Yukon River during the 1986 race. I was president of the Iditarod Trail Committee at that time, and had flown the race trail and stopped at Galena to spend the night in the community center. As I sat in the large room, I was keenly aware of my surroundings. This was dog country and had been for more than a century. The room was full of Iditarod mushers, eating and sleeping, fixing gear and doing other chores. If ever the ghosts of mushers past swirled about a room, it was here.

Then a courtly gentleman entered the room with a gust of cold winter air. He knocked the snow off his pants with a couple of swats of his beaver mitts and took off his frost-covered marten fur hat revealing a shock of snow-white hair. He was an old man, and his gaze scanned the room with the look of familiarity and pleasure of one at home. He'd been around dog drivers before and obviously had come here tonight to be with his kind. A feeling swept over me similar to what I felt when those ghost mushers came near me while I raced—*except this was no ghost.* Beneath this image of a frail, elderly gentleman stood one who was obviously a giant. Here was a man who had trod this great frozen land as one who belonged, a man who was equal to any challenge.

Home sweet home at Willow. Burt lived in this tent and the handler got the cabin. This was an especially cozy tent with a door that actually opened and closed. It is always fun to have a litter of new pups to remind one of how life renews itself.

As he scanned the room, our eyes met in recognition. It was Edgar Nollner, a hero who was one of two surviving mushers from the famed relay that had carried diphtheria serum to Nome. Along with my earlier reveries, Edgar's appearance just about overwhelmed me. At eighty-two years old, Edgar attracted no attention from the dozen or so Iditarod mushers scattered about the room. We shook hands and I took him around the room and introduced him to the other mushers. They needed to meet this man.

We sat down to visit as people drifted in and out of the community hall. We spoke of trails, dogs and the mushers we knew, some still living and some long gone. We talked of his run from Whisky Creek into Galena during the serum run. He'd been a competitive sprint musher at the time so was more than ready for the task and seemed to count it as just something one would do because he was asked to. What I saw as heroism, Edgar acknowledged with modesty.

The serum run is part of Iditarod history, and what a story it is. A diphtheria epidemic struck Nome, Alaska, during January 1925. This epidemic had horrendous potential consequences since the Native population had almost no immunity to this disease. This was during the period when airplane travel was still in its infancy in Alaska and mail was carried by dog team. It was decided that antitoxin could be shipped to Seward and carried by rail to Nenana. From there, a relay of dog teams would carry the serum down the Tanana River to the Yukon River and on to Nome. Kenneth Ungermann told the exciting story in his book, *The Race to Nome.*[8]

Burt leaves the restart for his last Iditarod race in 2004. The dogs were tough, eager, and ready to run. *Ken Stout photo*

Edgar Nollner was a twenty-one-year-old musher who was to take the serum from Billy McCarty at Whisky Creek upstream from Galena and drive it to Galena. At the creek, Edgar Nollner waited patiently. The mercury in the thermometer outside the cabin registered -40 degrees. It was ten o'clock Thursday night and would probably get colder before morning. Twenty-one-year-old Nollner was counting on his eight-year-old lead dog, Dixie, to set a fast pace to Galena. A few years before, Dixie had led his team to victory in a six-mile race at Ruby, beating his nearest competitor by the wide margin of six minutes.

---

[8] The Race to Nome, Kenneth A. Ungermann, 1963, Harper & Row

Finally, McCarty and his panting dogs came in view around a bend in the trail. A few minutes later Ed Nollner was on his way to Galena, twenty-four miles away.

Nollner pushed his seven big gray malamutes as fast as they would go. His older brother George was waiting at Galena as the next relay driver. Ed was making sure no one could criticize his speed on the serum drive.

The two brothers spoke briefly as they transferred the precious cargo to George's sled.

And the serum continued to Nome, carried by one dog team after another. I asked Edgar if he'd been to Nome lately and he responded that he'd *never* been to Nome. Not once during his entire life.

I asked him if he would like to go to Nome and be my guest at the Finishers' banquet. He said he sure would, so I looked up Danny Davidson, one of the Iditarod Air Force pilots, to see if he'd fly Ed into Nome for the banquet. He said sure.

When we got to Nome, I asked Edgar to sit next to me at the head table as my guest of honor. I did my best to introduce Edgar to the crowd with a hero's welcome. While he stood beside me, I addressed the crowd:

Friends of Iditarod, tonight at this banquet I am thrilled to honor our Iditarod mushers. We have a musher with us who was not in this race but was part of an important race decades ago. This musher magnifies our thrill tonight beyond imagination because of that more important race. That was the race of 1925, rushing precious, life-saving vaccine to the people of Nome where a diphtheria epidemic had struck. Edgar Nollner is one of two surviving members of that historic relay and stands beside me now. This is the first time he has *ever* been to Nome—a man who helped save the people of Nome so many years ago is in Nome now for the first time in his life. Please welcome him and take the opportunity later this evening to become his friend. I can think of no greater privilege for us who are members of today's mushing family.

The crowd gave him a standing ovation that was long and enthusiastic. It was a great moment for Edgar and it brought important Alaska history to life for the people in Nome. Of the things I am proud of during the 1986 race, this is right at the top of the list. It warms my heart to this day.

As more warm memories came and went in my cabin north of Willow, my eyes wandered to the bookshelf where I spotted another of Norm's books. The book is *With Byrd at the Bottom of the World.*[9] I opened the cover and read his inscription dated September 1, 1999.

> *To Burt*
>
> *The only death you die is the death you die every day, by not living. One never fails until he quits. Dream Big and Dare to Fail.*
>
> *Norman D. Vaughan*

The inscription continued:

> *Burt, you were a great friend and thanks again and again for building your log cabin, which is now our home.*
>
> *Norman and Carolyn*

I have lived a great life full of great people, great challenges, and great adventures. I have known many of Alaska's early day heroes, dog mushers, bush pilots, gold miners and trappers. The best parts so far were the years living in a small cabin in the heart of Alaska's great winter wilderness. But like Norm, I believe that the best is yet to come. That was part of the secret of his long life—always a dream of the next big adventure.

What next? Well, I have this buddy out in the Ophir gold country who has a placer mine. He says that with gold prices out of sight this might be a good time to dig out that rusty gold pan and look for some color.

Or . . . wait a minute . . . maybe I'll get to do what I love to do most, run one *last great race on earth.* I'd need a good sponsor. Who knows?

---

[9] With Byrd at the Bottom of the World, Norman D. Vaughn, with Cecil B. Murphey, 1990, Stackpole Books, 1st Ed.

A MUSHER'S PRAYER

Help us, Lord, to live our lives
in such a manner that when we harness up
for that last inevitable dog sled ride,
to the hills high up, where the snow is hard,
and the wolves still howl
that you, our last Judge, will tell us
that our entry fees are paid.

Author unknown

IDITAROD ALASKA

Iditarod Committee Service

BOOK TWO

Author's note: This section of my book takes a hard turn away from stories along the race trail and of living in the Alaska bush training and mushing dogs. It is about the work that goes on behind the scenes by volunteers and staff to put the race on.

IDITAROD COMMITTEE SERVICE

The Iditarod Official Finishers Club

After the 1981 finish in Nome, I sat in the back row at the post-race meeting of the Iditarod Official Finishers Club. It was a privilege and a thrill to be there for the first time. All of my heroes were in view as the meeting progressed from old business to new and then to the election of officers. I saw Rick Swenson and his buddy, Sonny Lindner, along with Roger Nordlum and Cowboy Smith, Herbie Nayokpuk and Clarence Towarak, Dewey Halverson, Jerry Austin, and many others. Some of them I had already met and some I was anxious to meet.

Joe Redington Sr. sat next to me. I had to chuckle as the meeting rolled on because of comments Joe had made to me before we even entered the room. "Burt," he had said, "the worst threat to Iditarod is these mushers. If anyone ever manages to pull this race down, it will be mushers. They know dogs and they know the Alaska wilderness, and they know all about running the race. And most of the fans will support them, no matter what they do. Mushers are romantic folk heroes, so the fans will believe them when they say anything whatsoever about Iditarod. But Iditarod is a big, complicated, international business, and most mushers don't know crap about that. They just think they do. But sponsors and activists take a harder view. Fans will overlook behavior that sponsors and activists won't."

I was to hear that several times during the coming years at board meetings and musher meetings. As various mushers pushed certain Iditarod issues and did things in their private lives that reflected badly on the race and were contrary to Joe's vision for the race, he would grumble those words. And I have to admit, I agreed with Joe a lot of the time. He had but a sixth-grade education so it was a measure of his genius that he had such panoramic vision and the ability to motivate people to make his vision a reality.

That evening, I was nominated and elected to be president of the Finishers Club. I had held political office and served on a host of committees over the years but really didn't want to get involved with Iditarod committee work. I'd seen too much controversy, hard feelings, and strife on volunteer committees. I wanted to keep my dog mushing free of those traps. But by the time the vote came, I didn't have the heart to decline. The opportunity to give something back to the Iditarod honored and pleased me.

As it turned out, I served six terms as president of the Iditarod Official Finishers Club during the races from 1982 through 1987. I am proud of what we accomplished with much help during those years. I took my marching orders from the mushers themselves at the annual meetings in Nome, returning to the Trail Committee Board of Directors with the issues. They approved most of our suggestions. Race management, on the other hand, ignored most of them.

Burt, as president of the Iditarod Official Finishers Club called a mushers' meeting at Rainy Pass during the 1985 race to talk about the race freeze and the lack of food drops ahead at the next checkpoint at Rohn River. Some mushers had threatened to leave anyway and hope that the food drops would be delivered by the time they arrived in Rohn. After a good discussion, the consensus was that it was foolish to put the dogs at risk and proceed against the marshal's direction. The mushers blamed the race marshal for not delivering the food on time but all agreed not to risk the possibility of getting pinned down away from any source of dog food. *Jeff Schultz photo.*

As the years went by, I continued to work hard to present race problems that only mushers could understand, and I always offered suggestions for improvement. There was much concern over management of the 1983 race, so the meeting in Nome that year was especially intense. The mushers discussed all the issues they felt needed attention and I presented them to the Board of Directors in a lengthy and detailed letter.[10] (See Appendix B.)

As the years went by, we spent a lot of time talking about rules at those Nome Finishers Club meetings. We thought the rules that had been written for the first Iditarod race in 1973 were good, so most of our discussions revolved around specific problems that arose during each race. For example, we wrote a Good Samaritan rule to protect a musher who might inadvertently break a rule while helping another musher in an emergency.

While serving as president, I tried to find ways to earn money for the Finishers Club without requiring more effort or money from the mushers. One idea was to use games of chance. Alaska law permits non-profit corporations to engage in games of chance for fund-raising purposes if they have been in existence for more than four years. I called a mushing pal, Myron Angstman, who practiced law in Bethel, Alaska, and ran the idea by him. He agreed that it would work and offered to prepare the corporate documents at no charge. Under the signatures of Myron, Joe Redington Sr., Sue Firmin, and me, the Finishers Club received its official *Certificate of Non-profit Corporation* on January 21, 1985. Then, all we had to do was wait the mandatory four years and fund-raising could begin with no hassle for our mushers. The corporation was kept active until my last term as president of the Official Finishers Club ended in 1987.

When it came time to elect new officers during the Iditarod Official Finishers Club meeting in Nome at the end of the 1987 race, I reminded the group that I'd been president for six years. "I'll continue to serve if no one else wants to, but I'd be happy if someone else would do it." A couple of mushers said they wanted to take charge, so we elected their slate of officers. By that time, I had served as president of both the Official Finishers Club and the Iditarod Board of Directors, so I was happy to take a break.

---

[10] APPENDIX B, The Anchorage Times, May 21, 1985

I briefed the new officers and, of course, provided them with copies of the Finishers Club documents and files. By that time, there was only one year to go before we could begin our games of chance.

There had been a constant call among a handful of mushers to establish a dues system, with all mushers paying $25 per year to belong. I objected for a number of reasons. First, if you were an official finisher, you were automatically a member of the Iditarod Official Finishers Club in my opinion. Also, many Iditarod families had to make hard choices regarding where their money was spent. The decision for them often came down to whether to buy needed family items or dog food and harnesses. Iditarod was their dream of living a lifestyle like *the early Alaska, the traditional Alaska.* Sometimes a new harness took priority over a treat for the kids or even a new coat.

Also, it seemed to me that our non-profit gaming potential would easily fund the Finishers Club. I had images of the good we could do, even a Mushers Relief Fund to assist finishers in dire straits. Also, we could hold other fund-raising events if it was determined more money was needed. After all, I had run the club for six years with no need for dues money. However, there was no dissuading the new officers who seized on the idea and immediately put the $25 dues requirement into effect.

That was years ago and I have never changed my mind nor paid dues to this day. Several hundred finishers have never received a meeting notice since then because they didn't pay dues. In fact, less than seventy mushers out of the hundreds who have finished the race ever paid the $25, and only those few mushers receive meeting notices and information from the Club.

To top it off, club officers have since let the Iditarod Official Finishers Club non-profit corporate status lapse.

The Iditarod Trail Committee Board of Directors

I had served a couple of years on the Iditarod Trail Committee Board of Directors and as chairman of the Race Rules Committee when Joe Sr. asked me to serve as president of the Board after the 1985 race. It wasn't my plan to get further involved in committee work, which would take me even further away from the reason I got involved with mushing dogs in the first place. However, Joe and the other mushers felt that the 1985 race had been such a poorly run fiasco that something needed to be done.

Race management that year had totally ignored the Finishers' recommendations. Food drops hadn't been shipped out on schedule so weren't in place by race time. In fact, they still weren't in place as the mushers approached the halfway point at Iditarod. Of course, Alaska weather did what it usually does—snow and blow. Mushers were ordered to stay in place by the Race Marshal twice during that race, once at Rainy Pass and again at Ophir, while the Race Manager was still trying to get his food drops delivered. When the race was finally restarted, all teams were made to restart in confusing fashion so that leaders lost any advantage they had gained by pushing hard up to that point.

One of the worst problems was dwindling food supplies for teams stuck at the checkpoint. We were running out of dog food at Rainy Pass when I called my wife and asked her to have one of my buddies fly some dog food out. The weather was too bad to fly so we started rationing food. Then one of my pals made it through and brought an airplane load of meat, which I shared with my pals, Joe Sr. and Jan Masek and with the seven Native teams in the race who were all camped out on the knoll behind the checkpoint. I figured Native teams were least able to get help since they lived in the bush and had few contacts in Anchorage.

I told Joe Sr. I would think about the presidency and sat down to make a list of all the things that needed to be done if the race was to remain an exciting, world-class event. The list was a long one, with many difficult challenges. The race needed to be managed much better than it had been recently and the entire operating structure of Iditarod needed some management systems. To accomplish this would take a year of full-time effort if I were to get it done. After much soul-searching, I decided to volunteer the time.

The Board elected me to serve as president for the 1986 race. There was so much to do that I did, in fact, take the year off from work to serve as Iditarod President.

I believed that we needed to write manuals for all the important volunteer functions such as Race Marshal and trailbreakers. We needed to better prepare rookies for the arduous trail to Nome. My first sled dog race had been the 1981 Iditarod. While I had no difficulties I couldn't cope with, making it to Nome, it was because I'd spent a lifetime outdoors camping, hunting, fishing, snow machining, and flying. It was obvious to me that many rookies didn't have that experience.

Outgoing Iditarod president, Dr. Bob Sept, passed the gavel to incoming president Burt Bomhoff to begin his term as president for the 1986 race.

And most important of all, the Iditarod Race needed a headquarters that would serve as a permanent home, something truly Alaskan that would give us a permanent identity.

The Iditarod Headquarters

People had been talking about a permanent headquarters for Iditarod since the race began, but Iditarod was primarily a volunteer organization and no one had the time or experience to make it happen. I decided to make the building of a permanent headquarters for Iditarod my top priority. (Teelands store in Wasilla had graciously allowed us to occupy the second floor of their building for some years.)

I contacted Wasilla Mayor Charles Bumpus, a good friend, to see if the city might donate land for our new headquarters. He located a ten-acre parcel of park land and scheduled me to appear before the city council to make my pitch. Dorothy Page, known as the Mother of the Iditarod, was a council member, so I knew that I had at least two friends, counting the mayor. The pitch was simple: We needed a new headquarters and Wasilla wanted to be "The Home of the Iditarod." Together we could achieve both goals.

Burt showing Wasilla Mayor Charlie Bumpus and State Representative Ron Larson the site of the new Iditarod headquarters building in Wasilla. The City of Wasilla donated a ten-acre site for the Iditarod Headquarters Project which it still occupies today.

I didn't trust future Iditarod boards of directors to protect this new headquarters. I felt that a future board might find itself short of funds and attempt to mortgage our headquarters to borrow operating capital. In a worst-case scenario, the headquarters could be mortgaged and then lost if a default occurred. We found an easy solution. The city provided the land to be available only so long as it was used for Iditarod headquarters. Title to the land remained with the city.

The next step was to arrange funding. I went to Juneau to plead with the legislature. Several good friends held high-level positions in the legislature at that time, so I was confident of success. I took Iditarod's executive director along to witness the process.

Senator Jan Faiks met us at the airport and gave us a ride to our hotel. She co-chaired the powerful Senate Finance Committee that I would appear before the following morning. The Committee graciously heard my plea and reminded me that Alaska was in the depths of a severe recession and that money was tight. I convinced them that Iditarod was one of the highest-profile attractions for Alaska's tourism business and helping us build an attractive headquarters would pay dividends right then as well as for years to come. The leadership was enthusiastic and allocated $50,000 toward construction of a new Iditarod headquarters. We needed more, however.

We stopped by Representative Al Adams's office to talk to him. He was chairman of the House Finance Committee. We had previously served together on the Board of Directors of a bank in Anchorage and were good friends. When I told him we needed to see him over funding for a new Iditarod headquarters, he ordered coffee and invited us in. We discussed the project and our need for funds. The tight money situation came up again. When we discussed what a great attraction Iditarod was for tourism as well as for our own people, the result was the same enthusiastic support. Representative Adams supported us and decided that the place to get the money from was the tourism budget. He called Don Dickey, head of the Division of Tourism, and told him to allocate $50,000 from his budget for a new Iditarod headquarters. I could hear Don, who'd been a friend of mine for twenty-five years, explode over the phone. He told Al that his budget was already tight and that every penny was committed. Don was so upset that we could easily hear both sides of the telephone conversation from our seats. I admired Don's passion but still thought he could help us out a little.

Of course, Al won out in the end and we got the $50,000. After all, Al was chairman of the House Finance Committee; Don was not going to win that argument.

While in Juneau, we also talked with other people I hoped would give us the political support we needed. They included Governor Bill Sheffield, Representative Ron Larson, Senator Jay Kurtulla, and Representative Frank Ferguson. All were supportive. Before it was over, the State of Alaska had donated $140,000 to Iditarod during a year of seriously declining revenues. I am proud of the accomplishment, proud of our political leaders, and proud that Iditarod had a shiny image, able to attract that kind of money during hard times.

Iditarod president, Burt Bomhoff, addressed the crowd at the headquarters' ribbon cutting ceremony while incoming president, Les Reynolds, waited in the wings. Les is a seasoned bush pilot and had been chief pilot for the Iditarod Air Force

We now had a site for our headquarters and substantial funds, but that still wasn't enough. So we returned to Anchorage to continue raising money. I stopped by the executive offices of National Bank of Alaska and talked to Edward Rasmussen, the bank's president. Ed had been branch manager at the Spenard Branch when I was just starting in business. That was during the 1970s.

Ed reminded me that Alaska was suffering a depression and that money was tight. He said he would do some due diligence and get back to me. Although we'd known each other for a long time, he was a savvy banker who didn't take chances. He made a couple of calls and then invited me back in and donated $50,000 for our construction budget. Then he committed to loaning us the remainder of the funds needed for construction. Since the land for the building couldn't be mortgaged, Ed loaned us that money over my signature. We paid back every penny he loaned us.

We were all proud of Iditarod and the wonderful way it enabled everyone to relive Alaska's pioneer heritage vicariously from our living room chairs.

Next, we needed a design for the building, so we did a search and hired an outfit out of Fairbanks who seemed qualified. Their instructions from us were to design a facility that would be Alaskan and reflect the spirit of Iditarod and the importance of dog teams in our early history. They came back with a design for a two-story frame building that looked like a row house in Boston. If it resembled anything Alaskan, it was a hard rock mine facility similar to the buildings at Kennecott mine. Kennecott isn't dog country; it's railroad country.

Burt had the honor of presenting Joe Redington Sr. with his lifetime membership in the Iditarod Trail Committee to honor his founding of the race and many years of dedicated service. This highlight was observed by Sen. Jay Kurtulla, Sen. Jan Faiks, and the mother of the Iditarod, Dorothy Page. *Jeff Schultz photo.*

We were meeting in a café in Eagle River, so I pulled out a pencil and drew a log building on a napkin. I told the architects that we would construct our headquarters out of huge natural logs, reminiscent of bush Alaska—in other words, dog country. Then I drew a floor plan with an entrance into a large main area suitable for merchandise. The building provided offices for staff in a wing to the right and a museum/meeting room to the left. I drew elevations on the napkin to assure that the view of the building would reflect Alaska. We needed a huge area to store merchandise and the cheapest way to get that was with a basement. Log buildings are most beautiful when they are long and low. They need to nestle into the surrounding wilderness. Iditarod headquarters would be big, but it needed to be cozy. Every good Alaskan artist knows this. Check it out. The designers came back with a set of plans that we actually built at Wasilla based on the sketch I drew on that napkin.

The best constructor of log buildings at that time was Log Weavers of Alaska out of Nenana. They used huge logs that were cut and hewed near Nenana. They then hauled the logs to the site and erected them. Iditarod Headquarters was built exactly as we envisioned it within the available budget. Some things could have been bigger or a little better, but I believe we got maximum facility for the money we were able to obtain. And I didn't know where to get one more penny. No one else with Iditarod had any suggestions for doing anything other than what we did.

Iditarod headquarters is one of my proudest Iditarod achievements. To conceive of the idea, fund it, and build it with donated and public funds all in one year was, I believe, an impressive achievement for a non-profit organization.

HSUS WARS OF THE 1990s

Before we get off the subject of Ed Rasmussen's benevolence, let's jump ahead to the HSUS wars of the 1990s. An interesting story developed years after Ed helped us build Iditarod Headquarters, and I was no longer on the board. In the early '90s, Iditarod found itself under attack by the Humane Society of the United States (HSUS). Society officials accused Iditarod of being cruel to animals. Nothing could have been further from the truth, but HSUS had the potential to damage our image, something our sponsors and many fans wouldn't tolerate.

A nasty public battle ensued. Quotes by Iditarod board members like, "Tell them to go to hell," and "You're fussing with our heritage here" and "This is our event. If you don't like it, I don't care," started to appear in the press.

The fans remained loyal, but sponsors, the press and former Iditarod leaders were alarmed. Referring to the board of directors, writer Lew Freedman complained of mushers on the board and editorialized that *"The Board of Directors has musher Matt Desalernos on it. And musher Martin Buser. And musher Joe Runyan. And musher Joe Redington. And Dave Monson, once-and-future musher and husband of Susan Butcher. Musher Lavon Barve is president of the board."* He continued, *"It's time to kick them all out and start over.*[11] Craig Medred referred to the *"The dumb as stone Iditarod Trail Committee,"* in their handling of the HSUS issue.[12]

Meanwhile a petition was being circulated nationwide, urging the Iditarod Board of Directors to resign. It accused the board of a variety of blunders, conflicts of interest and unprofessional conduct. The petition said, "the board has bungled efforts to communicate with the Humane Society and failed to work effectively with three executive directors in two years." The petition was circulated by four people, including Rosemary Phillips, a former board member and executive director, Dr. Bob Sept, former chief veterinarian and board president along with Phil Meyer and Leo Rasmussen.

Matt Desalernos was elected president to replace Lavon Barve. He sent race sponsor Timberland a hostile nine-page letter for siding with HSUS. He accused Timberland of lacking courage and of conduct that was indefensible. He referred to HSUS as nothing more than a well-organized cult who seduced members by preying on the weaknesses of innocent and lonely people who are vulnerable and starving for affection. Matt went on to set requirements on Timberland if Iditarod was to accept money from them in the future. These included Iditarod's right to approve all of their publicity releases regarding animal care, public validation by Timberland of Iditarod's existing commitment to animal care, and a multi-year agreement.[13]

The letter was apparently the last straw. Alaska fans remained loyal, but the sponsors were fed up. Timberland withdrew its $400,000 sponsorship, then IAMs Dog Food refused to renew its $175,000 sponsorship and ABC Sports dropped its $40,000 sponsorship, leaving a $615,000 shortfall. Iditarod

---

[11] Anchorage Daily News, Marcdh 28, 1993

[12] Anchorage Daily News. March 19, 1993

[13] Matt Desalernos letter of June 4, 1994 to Jay Steere, The Timberland Company

would have to sell more than $6,000,000 in hats and T-shirts at 10% profit, to make this up . . . for just the current year. Multiply that by years into the future when these sponsors might have remained loyal and the loss is in the millions. The president stated, "I don't think we'll be one dollar poorer. I'll lay that down as a challenge to Alaskans."[14]

Fortunately, Ed Rasmussen had the generosity and the means to meet the challenge. He donated sufficient funds to Iditarod to make up these lost sponsor fees until Iditarod could recover. He did this by donating more than a half million dollars for each of several years, assuring that the purse remained intact and Iditarod and its officers didn't suffer a disastrous embarrassment.

The Iditarod Organization

Returning to 1986, I discovered that the Iditarod financial books had not been audited since the race began in 1973. We needed an annual audit if we were to retain the trust of our sponsors and volunteers. First, we needed to change the fiscal year-end from April 30 to June 30, so we would have time to accumulate income and expenses for a given race before the annual financial report was prepared. Up to this point, the books were a mess, with bills still coming in after the books for a given race were closed. We needed to have an accurate financial picture of each race so finances wouldn't overlap from race to race.

Also, the accounting system had been carried out on a cash basis rather than an accrual basis. Under the existing system, payables were entered into the system when the mail was opened, not when the obligation for them was made, sometimes months earlier. This resulted in a lag in entrees for liabilities, which didn't give a true picture of how much we actually owed. When the bookkeeper wanted us to look good while she prepared the monthly financial statement, she could simply hold bills in a drawer until after that month's statement was prepared. This had created a "rolling wave" of debt that never really showed up on the books.

I actually found a drawer full of invoices, some that were several months old, waiting for sufficient funds for payment. None had been entered in the

---

[14] Anchorage Daily News, April 24, 1994

books. Although I was concerned about slow pay, I was even more concerned about liabilities existing with only the bookkeeper knowing how much they were. There was no way the Board of Directors could function without this knowledge. So we hired the firm of Milton D. Johnson to set up an accrual system of bookkeeping and to audit our books. Now, when the Board, creditors, the bank, or our members want information regarding what is owed and what we have, the correct data is available.

Iditarod had pretty much operated on a "seat of your pants" basis. We developed an organization chart and a timeline chart to ensure that nothing fell through the cracks. With a timeline chart, we could list everything we needed to do ahead of the race in chronological order so we weren't getting ahead of ourselves and so we knew when things needed to be done to assure they were in place at race time. We hoped to avoid waiting until the last minute to ship food drops and then have them stalled due to weather as what happened in 1985. With this, our organizing efforts followed a logical sequence. The Race Coordinator had done an excellent job of organizing the race, but we felt we needed more structure.

Along with that, we prepared job descriptions for all the staff and the most important volunteer positions. We were trying to avoid overlap and duplication of effort.

Our retail business needed a little work. Iditarod had not obtained trademarks to protect its name, nor the logos that Bill Devine had designed. I retained a lawyer to obtain the necessary trademarks and copyrights. We also worked to expand our merchandising through advertising and marketing efforts. The merchandise program had always done well so this was mostly tying up loose ends, although our new programs did increase sales and profits.

It seemed to me that the *Iditarod Runner*, our official publication, could stand a little spiffing up. I asked race founder Joe Redington Sr. and famed explorer and musher Norman Vaughan to each write a column every month about the early days. We asked teenager Will Barron, a cartoonist and a dog musher, to give us a mushing cartoon for each issue. Pamela Tarver, a talented young writer, interviewed some of our most interesting mushers and wrote a profile for each issue. I invited Iditarod champions such as Rick Swenson and Martin Buser to write about their adventures. We even included a regular column by chief veterinarian James Leach, who had a great deal of experience with doctoring racing dog teams. In my own president's column, I tried to use mushing experiences to make a point rather than just to report the news. The *Runner* had become sort of a news magazine, but we wanted it also to be a window into the world of mushing and bush Alaska at a more personal level. It seemed to me that fans would be more likely to turn the pages if more mushing lore were included.

We needed a more effective means of soliciting sponsors. Our sponsors were a dedicated group of businesses who enthusiastically supported us; however, with a world-class event we needed to branch out to national and international organizations. Proposals to represent us were solicited from groups that represented athletes and teams. We settled on High Bar Productions, Inc. of New York to represent us in soliciting large national and international sponsors.

While in New York meeting with them, I also met with executives at NBC, who were then producing our television race coverage. We discussed ways to improve coverage and broaden viewership. We also discussed problems they had in their dealings with us.

The Board had become factionalized early in its existence, with members from the Anchorage/Wasilla area and outlying areas often at odds with each other. Members from Nome and Fairbanks referred to the local group as the Wasilla Mafia. Because the "Mafia" was close to headquarters and, therefore, more readily involved in the decision-making process, they simply had more stroke in running the show. This created jealousies when members from Nome and elsewhere perceived themselves as being left out of the loop. Issues were often decided along personal and geographical lines rather than by reasoned discussion.

In an effort to alleviate some of this, I organized a retreat to be held at Chena Hot Springs Resort outside Fairbanks. The resort was operated by Iditarod musher Jan Masek, who gave us a special deal to meet there. Jim Leach, Les Reynolds and I flew our Super Cubs up and landed on the resort's strip. I wanted the meeting to be held away from Wasilla on neutral ground. We hired a professional facilitator to lead the discussions. We hoped she would lead us to a new spirit of cooperation. The retreat helped in some respects; however, the basic issue that created the problem in the first place was hard to overcome. Participation just wasn't as easy for a person in Nome or Fairbanks as it was for those who could be in headquarters in thirty minutes by auto.

We arrived back from our retreat with a host of issues left to address. I appointed several committees to work on those issues, from by-laws to rookies.

The First Rookie Seminar

As race time approached, it became imperative that we address the issue of preparing rookies for the race. We encouraged all interested mushers to enter the race, but we knew that some were simply not prepared for this race across Alaska in winter. A competent dog musher wasn't necessarily competent to handle the rigors that the Alaska wilderness could serve up over a two-week period.

I formed a committee to determine what information was necessary and began rounding up experts in various fields. Dr. Mills of Anchorage was the most prominent expert in cold weather medicine at that time. He agreed to discuss the dangers of extreme cold weather exposure and how to cope with them. Of particular importance were dealing with frostbite and hypothermia while functioning outside for an extended period in Alaska's icy winter. He talked not only about how to avoid injuries but what to do if you suffered these potentially debilitating conditions. Although there were always people on the trail during a race, a musher could be seriously alone when weather made travel difficult or impossible. We were in the early stages of cold weather medicine, so much of what Dr. Mills brought to us was cutting edge and totally at odds with conventional wisdom. His research on thawing frozen extremities was priceless.

I invited Dewey Halverson and Jerry Austen to talk generally about racing a dog team across Alaska. Jerry talked about winter camping, gear, musher food, food for the dogs, harnesses, sleds, sleeping bags, clothing from boots to parkas, tools, spare parts, and a host of other topics that would help a musher drive his team safely and quickly to Nome.

I had always considered Dewey to be a pro when it came to driving dogs. Most mushers started training dogs in early fall, using carts before snow fell. Dewey usually worked construction at remote locations, so he didn't even get home until late November. He'd start training dogs about Thanksgiving and miraculously have a competitive team trained in time for Iditarod. And his dogs were always happy, all the way to Nome. So I picked him to talk about the complex issues of driving a dog team across Alaska while keeping the dogs healthy and happy to run.

Rookies were encouraged to stop and enjoy the checkpoints. After all, they weren't likely to be competitive so why not maximize the experience. It was a unique opportunity that few have to interact with some of our most interesting Alaskans, and those living along the trail were always anxious to interact with an Iditarod musher. Dewey and Jerry also talked about race etiquette and dealing with fellow mushers.

The Race Marshal conducted a thorough seminar on race rules. Much of this would be duplicated at the musher meeting to be held later, but we wanted special emphasis on interpretations that rookies might have trouble with.

We invited race veterinarian James Leach to discuss medical issues common to dogs racing the Iditarod. I had won the Leonard Seppala Award for best treatment of a competitive team in the 1984 race. Humane dog care was one of my special interests. Dr. Leach talked about food and nutrition for the dogs and the need for massive doses of calorie-rich food. Each dog needed huge amounts of calories each day to keep him healthy and eager to run. Jim talked about proper-fitting harnesses and how to avoid harness burns and the best treatment if they occurred. He spent a lot of time on foot care; after all, "an army marches on its feet." And he talked about first aid for racing dogs, including what supplies to bring and *when to ask the vet.*

Since this was the first Iditarod Rookie Seminar held, it was necessary to conduct it just before the race when all the rookies were in town. This would be too late for some of the information to be of value to rookies. Because of that, I retained a professional videographer to film the seminar. He was to provide copies on VHS to be distributed to rookies in future races as soon as they signed up. It was my hope that this would give them a head start on knowledge and skills that would help them get safely to Nome. We would then conduct the live Rookie Seminar at race time to fill in the gaps. In this way, we would avoid requiring rookies to make a special trip to attend the seminar, making the race even more expensive. Knowing how much time and money was involved in entering a team in Iditarod, I did everything in my power to avoid unnecessary expenses for teams or the race itself.

The Rules Committee

I'd served on the Rules Committee for several years, so I knew what the rules meant. We were constantly seeing examples of Race Marshals interpreting them to fit their own point of view. Rules Committee members, all experienced racers, were often confronted with rulings by the marshals or judges that had nothing to do with the actual intent of the Rules Committee or the Board of Directors. Rulings were often overly punitive, as though the official was on some kind of power trip. I sat down and wrote an explanation for each rule and how it was to be administered, and called it the Official Handbook. Each rule had an interpretation. After the Rules Committee had a chance to review it and grant their approval, the Official Handbook was presented to the Board for final approval, which they granted.

Even with the Official Handbook, however, things sometimes went awry. Before the race a couple of years later, Joe Sr. and I invited the Race Marshal, Bobby Lee, to lunch at the Cattle Company in Anchorage to discuss rules and our intent. I was chairman of the Rules Committee and Joe was a committee member. We had written a rule that required mushers to make an effort to maintain a reasonable rate of progress.

We were only concerned with mushers who deliberately wasted time. A Nome musher had bragged about the "forty below and we don't go" club during the final Iditarod banquet at the finish of the 1981 race in Nome. He and some buddies had made a leisurely trip, stopping to relax at every opportunity. If it was dark, they wouldn't go. If it was cold, they wouldn't go. In the process, they drove race officials nuts and seriously strained the patience and sense of humor of villagers along the way. These guys would show up days after the food drops were put away and villagers had all headed to Nome for the finish so those left behind were stuck retrieving food supplies and cleaning up the mess afterward. Officials constantly had to retrace their steps and fly back miles and miles to see if these mushers were okay.

We decided that making a vacation out of the race was beyond reasonable, so we wrote a rule to control it. We explained to the marshal that we were concerned the Race Marshal could abuse this rule and boot some musher out of the race who was making an honest effort to get to Nome. We explained that many mushers spent a year and all of their cash to get their team to the starting line. We felt it was our job to *help* them finish so long as the rules were obeyed and they were making a sincere effort to make progress. We only wanted to discourage a musher from deliberately delaying his own progress.

The things that could not be tolerated were cruelty or neglect of the dogs, and cheating. We *absolutely* did not want a musher disqualified if he was making a sincere effort to get to Nome, no matter how long it took. If a team had so much invested in giving us this great Alaskan adventure, we could give them our support for a couple of weeks. We believed that we owed it to each musher to protect his efforts the best we could. Our *only* concern was preventing *deliberate* abuse of the system.

We saw this as probably the most dangerous rule in the book. I explained in detail to the race marshal that this rule was only for one purpose, to control blatant abuse. No one making an honest effort to make it to the finish should be disqualified, even if they were behind. Rate of progress wasn't the issue, an honest attempt was.

Joe and I both made a special point of telling Bobby that this rule did not apply to Colonel Norman Vaughn, who was in his eighties and always proceeded at a deliberate pace. It was no secret that he was the oldest and the slowest. Norm had been the dog handler for Admiral Byrd during his 1926 expedition to Antarctica. Norm was an inspiration to millions of seniors. One of the truly meaningful things that Iditarod could give the world was the inspiration of Norm. If he was taking good care of his dogs, and plugging along, leave him alone. If he got in trouble, it was his own dang fault and he knew it going in. And if we had to rescue him, it wouldn't be the first time we rescued someone. It would be worth it.

Our point was that if Norm, then in his eighties, could drive a dog team across this great frozen state of Alaska, maybe some senior citizen out there might just be inspired to roll off the couch and get a little exercise. Norm deserved all the help we could give him. Under no circumstances was he to be disqualified unless he wasn't able to care for his dogs. If he couldn't make it to Nome, he'd drop out voluntarily. He deserved that dignity. Norm had so much experience in arctic conditions that we weren't worried about him, anyway.

So Norm and his adventuresome wife, Carolyn, were entered in the race and were moving along just fine at the back of the pack, slow but sure. Everyone adored Norm, so he and Carolyn got a hero's welcome at every village. He was exceedingly popular and was as much anticipated as the front-runners. Although he was at the back of the pack, no one considered him an inconvenience.

Now, after all this discussion, the marshal removed Norm and Carolyn from the race on the Yukon River. His reason? Norm wasn't going to make it to Nome anyway so it wasn't worth Iditarod's effort to continue its support. The fact was that Norm's dogs were fine, as were Norm and Carolyn. Bless their hearts, Norm and Carolyn simply rose above this sanctimonious insulting nonsense and pointed their teams toward Nome. They crossed the finish line just like the other teams, *without Iditarod's help*. And the villagers loved them for it!

The marshal refused to reinstate them, even though they finished, and the Iditarod Board refused the Vaughans' appeal for reinstatement. To this day, I believe that decision should be reconsidered so Carolyn could receive her Official Finisher's patch and buckle. She worked hard to get it and she deserves it. Maybe the existing Board of Directors will reconsider the issue.

In a later race, Bobby disqualified race champion Rick Swenson for an accidental dog death; Rick appealed the ruling and was reinstated. Bobby hasn't been seen around Iditarod since.

Race Management

Work on the Official Rules Handbook and the Race Manual was important; however, a host of other issues also needed work to correct problems that surfaced during the 1985 race. During the first part of the twentieth century, dog teams traveled the trails all winter keeping them open all the way from Seward to Iditarod and on to Nome. And the Alaska Road Commission had kept the trails cleared of brush and flagged the trail with red ribbons so teams wouldn't get lost during severe weather. At present, parts of the Iditarod Trail are used only during the race, so they are trackless up until race time. Even sections that are in use aren't always well marked. Iditarod trailbreakers go out ahead of the teams with snowmachines to pack a trail for the teams and hang flagging so drivers won't be confused over exactly where the trail is.

Trail maintenance during the 1985 race was not good. There were many incidents, but one in particular has always stuck in my mind. We had been held up at Rainy Pass for a couple of days because food drops hadn't been sent out to the checkpoints far enough ahead. After the delay, we were allowed to continue toward Rohn River by an alternate, little-used trail through a narrow pass called Ptarmigan Pass or Hell's Gate. Travel through there and you'll know where the name came from.

Joe Redington and I had dropped down from Hell's Gate and were mushing along the South Fork of the Kuskokwim River when the trail became confusing. In a dog race, teams follow the markers. I'd learned that the hard way during the 1981 Iditarod. We came to an area that was loaded with ribbons off to our left; we headed for them. A sharp turn and we immediately found ourselves in waist-deep water with a current. The lead dogs were swimming in the current before we even saw the water. Fortunately, our lead dogs swam through the current to the other side, then they and each succeeding pair that regained footing pulled the team and sled across, and we made it through. Once in the water, there was no way to call the dogs back without risking them being swept downstream with drastic consequences.

We were soaked to the waist but we made it into Rohn checkpoint okay and told officials they needed to get back there and rearrange the flagging or someone could drown some dogs. Then we thawed out. We couldn't figure out what the trailbreakers were thinking when they led us into open water, so we asked the chief trailbreaker. He responded that this was how they marked dangerous trail in a snowmachine race, with lots of ribbons. We explained that in a sled dog race, the trail is flagged for the teams to follow. Heavy flagging indicates a place of extra importance for the teams to head for.

No one had told the trailbreakers about these procedures prior to the 1985 race. All they were told was that there would be flagging sent ahead, so they simply took off and started breaking trail. I was determined that 1986 would be a whole lot better.

So I wrote a manual for trailbreakers. It included a lot of information, but the most important requirement was a *clearly marked, well-broken trail ahead of the lead mushers*. We did not want a musher getting lost and we surely didn't want a lead team's chances impaired because he couldn't find the trail while following teams approached. I personally wrote this section and still have my notes in the diary I kept as president. This policy made a major improvement in our race trail. I specified exactly what a marker should mean in every type of terrain along the way, whether in timber, on the tundra, or on the sea ice. I even set spacing for the various types of terrain to assure a team could find its way in any weather. Markers need to be closer together on open ice or treeless tundra but can be farther apart in timbered areas where the trail is obvious.

Bill Sherwonit interviewed me a few days before the start of the 1986 race to ask about the current state of the race. He had covered the race for several years for the Anchorage Times and knew the race intimately. The interview appears in Appendix E.[15]

Along the Race Trail to Nome

I flew my ski-equipped Piper Super Cub during the 1986 race to observe the race first-hand and see how much improvement our year of effort had produced. I landed the Cub at every checkpoint as well as at any place along the trail where I could land near a team. I spent the night wherever I found the lead teams.

I flew into McGrath just ahead of the leader, Joe Garney. Joe was an Eskimo musher from Teller, Alaska. His partner, Libby Riddles, had won the 1985 race with the same dog team he now drove. She had mushed through an incredible blizzard to win. Joe was determined to equal or better Libby's performance. With Joe almost in the checkpoint, I walked over to where the trail left McGrath and found no sign that the trailbreakers had left town. This was the problem we had hoped to eliminate with the new manual. I searched for the trailbreakers and found them relaxing. I told the chief trailblazer that Joe Garney was approaching McGrath and might blaze on through. I told him that he needed to leave immediately and make sure the trail was marked. If Joe mushed right on through McGrath and headed for Takotna, it could be a disaster for him with no markings to follow.

He told me that they'd worked hard to get to McGrath and deserved a little relaxation. A heated argument ensued, with him making the point that there was a lot of traffic between McGrath and the next checkpoint at Takotna, so anyone could

---

[15] The Anchorage Times, February 23, 1986

follow the trail. I told him there were confusing trails criss-crossing everywhere between McGrath and Takotna. They finally said they would leave right away. Floyd Tetpon was flying along the trail, also, and was there in McGrath. Feeling uneasy, I located Jack Niggemyer, the race manager and had the same discussion with him. He assured me that he'd get the trailbreakers out on the trail right away.

Burt relaxed on a ridge above the race trail and watched the teams belonging to Susan Butcher and Joe Garney as they made their way out of White Mountain during the 1986 race. Floyd Tetpon's Cub is parked nearby. Burt and Floyd would land on a low ridge near the trail and watch the teams go by after which they flew on to the next ridge and repeated the process. They thought they had the best seats in the house.

Meanwhile, the worst happened. Joe Garney went straight through McGrath, pausing only to feed his dogs, and got lost among the maze of trails between McGrath and Takotna. After spending hours flogging around in the dark, he eventually followed the glow of McGrath's lights in the sky and found his way back to McGrath. Joe wasted more than four hours on those confusing trails trying to find Takotna in the dark. Those hours took their toll on his team, disproportionately greater than the actual time spent. A racing team normally spends as much time resting as running, so Joe actually lost about eight hours.

Burt and Joe at Joe Garney's dog yard in Teller. The dog posts are fashioned from water pipes that were surplussed from the gold dredge at Nome. They are tall to stay above huge winter snow drifts. Dogs keep moving up the poles as the drifts get higher.

Even worse, dogs know when things aren't right. Reversing direction to return to a checkpoint bums a dog team out and causes them to lose confidence in their driver. Joe likely lost far more than those eight hours because of this incident. He finished second, less than an hour behind the winner, using the same team that Libby Riddles had won with the year before. Many believed that Joe would have won the 1986 Iditarod race had we not let him down. Joe never complained, not wanting to diminish the win for the person who eventually did finish first. I'd rank him more than a good sport for not complaining or placing blame.

Twenty-five years later, Floyd Tetpon and I were visiting at his home in Eagle River when this incident came up in conversation. A warm fire crackled in the fireplace and the coffee pot was on. Floyd commented on how important this incident really was to people out in the bush. Joe's win would have been especially inspiring to thousands of good people in villages across Alaska, who could have used a little inspiration.

Joe Redington had told me that he was first inspired to found the Iditarod race when he worked in villages in the early days. He had observed that snow-machines had replaced dog teams and were parked where dog teams had once been. He was proud of bringing sled dogs back to the bush into native culture, so Joe Sr.'s own words confirmed Floyd's opinion.

From McGrath, I flew my airplane on to Iditarod and then to Cripple, and then landed at Sulatna Crossing. Sulatna Crossing was a true wilderness checkpoint with not even a cabin to mark the spot. It was simply located at a nice spot for a camp near the trail. There was a slough nearby where a ski plane could land and take off. But the checkpoint material was hauled in by snowmachine since the slough was marginal for airplanes. The checkers had set up a great camp with a snug wall tent, a good supply of firewood, and trails that were broken out with snowshoes so teams would have a handy place to park if they elected to spend some time there. I had a nice visit and a cup of tea with the checkers, after which I went on to Ruby and then Galena.

I spent the night in Galena, sleeping on a pad in the community center, which served as Galena's command post during the race. I loved sitting in the community center visiting with mushers, race staff, and fans from the village. I couldn't help but feel a sense of history knowing that mushers and sled dogs had been a part of this community forever.

As I mentioned earlier in the book, my reverie was interrupted as a courtly gen-tleman entered the community center. As he scanned the room, our eyes met with mutual recognition. It was Edgar Nollner, one of only two surviving mem-bers of the historic serum relay that saved Nome in 1925. We visited long and I learned that he'd never been to Nome, the town he helped save. Several days later, I had him flown to Nome so the Iditarod family could meet him personally.

I left Galena the next morning and flew down the Yukon. We continued west to Nulato, Kaltag, and then on to Unalakleet. Then we flew north to Shaktoolik and Koyuk. I stopped at every village to see how the race was going, to visit with good friends, and to see how the teams were doing. Every musher I visited with gave us rave reviews on the condition of the trail, which had been perfect except for the incident out of McGrath. They assured me that all food drops had been delivered on time. I believe that the 1986 race was well managed.

Burt and his pal, Floyd Tetpon, an Eskimo who grew up in Unalakleet, watch the teams from an upturned boat in White Mountain. Floyd, a professional land surveyor, flew his Super Cub as a member of the Iditarod Air Force. *Jeff Schultz photo.*

I hooked up with my buddy Floyd Tetpon at Koyuk and we agreed to fly to White Mountain and then the rest of the way into Nome together. Floyd also flew a ski-equipped Super Cub. We flew about the same speed so it was easy to stay reasonably close together as we continued toward Nome. A Super Cub on skis is a wonderful airplane for flying across the Alaska Bush. With reasonable care, you could find a place to land just about anywhere. Floyd was an Eskimo who had grown up in Unalakleet. He and I had worked together since the early '70s and had been partners in a surveying business and a hunting cabin in the Stony River country out west of the Alaska Range.

We left White Mountain at about the same time the leaders, Susan Butcher and Joe Garney, were leaving. They were now in a duel to see who would win and who would be runner-up. Floyd and I flew a few miles out of White Mountain and then landed our Cubs on a low ridge near the trail and waited for the teams. We watched them wend their way toward us and then past us until they were out of sight. Then we took off, flew a few miles past the teams, and landed again on the snow-covered tundra. It was fascinating to watch the teams traveling at virtually the same speed, always the same distant apart. The dogs trotted briskly along, but Joe wasn't able to pull ahead of Susan. Nor could she pull away from him.

We repeated the scenario over and over, landing on a spot where we could watch the teams coming and going, then taking off to find another vantage point. As we noted how closely matched the teams were, we talked about Joe getting lost in the maze of confusing, unmarked trails out of McGrath and couldn't help speculating over the possibility that Joe Garney might have passed through this area earlier and we'd now be watching Susan in a solo effort to finish second.

Floyd and I arrived in Nome, tied up our airplanes and kicked back to enjoy the end of the race. We wandered around town visiting with friends and enjoying watching the teams cross the finish line. We were at the airport checking on our airplanes when we spotted a group of people across the runway preparing for a flight. It was one of our pilots who was flying the assistant director of marketing at corporate headquarters for Chrysler Corporation in Dearborn, Michigan. I had met with him in Dearborn a few months earlier and had invited him and his wife to visit us in Nome for the finish of the Iditarod. I had asked the pilot to give them a ride down the trail to see the country and see what the teams looked like out on the trail. We were hosting them to an up-close and personal look at the race with the prospect of a major sponsorship in mind.

As we stood watching at a distance, the pilot moved about the Cessna aircraft. He was at the front of the airplane turning the propeller when the engine started with a roar. He jumped aside and then rushed to the passenger-side door. He attempted to open it but those Cessna doors could be hard to open, especially if the aircraft was moving. The airplane surged forward and the tail hit the pilot with a thud. He was knocked flying as the airplane leaped forward and began to accelerate, straight toward us. Neither Floyd nor I had seen anyone enter the pilotless airplane and hoped nobody had. Dave was still lying there where the whole thing began and we thought we could see the executive and his wife still standing there. We hoped one of them wasn't in the out-of-control airplane.

It all happened in a flash with the airplane still coming right at us, engine roaring at what sounded like full throttle. I'd lived on Campbell Lake for many years and had listened many times to Cessna 185 aircraft taking off right past my windows with those powerful Continental engines. In fact, I'd owned a Cessna 185 for several years, so I knew what they sounded like at take-off power. We frantically looked for some place to hide, but we were pinned against the airport boundary fence and weren't sure whether to run left or right.

Then the airplane left the ground and made a slow turn to its left. As we watched in horror, it flew pilotless down the taxiway and right toward a cluster of planes tied up on the ramp. Then it made another left turn and flew headlong into a huge pile of icy snow that had been plowed off the Nome Airport surface. It hit with a resounding bang and settled back on its wheels, with wings seriously munched forward. No one was in the airplane when we got there except for an Iditarod Air Force pilot who got there first. He had the door open and was bent inside doing something.

Although the local Dodge dealer had always sponsored Iditarod, corporate at Dearborn elected not to get involved.

Burt greeted all the teams at the finish line. Here he welcomes Joe Runyan who finished a very respectable fourth place. *Jeff Schultz photo.*

There was a lot to talk about at the Official Finishers banquet in Nome. Race heroes were introduced, dignitaries recognized, volunteers acknowledged and mushers honored. Many volunteers received special recognition at the Finishers banquet.

Burt enjoyed the honor of presenting outgoing champion Libby Riddles to the crowd at the 1986 awards banquet in Nome. A very popular champion, she received a long, standing ovation. Libby spends her summers giving lectures and entertaining visitors to Alaska with her fascinating Iditarod tales. *Jeff Schultz photo.*

Summary

When Joe Sr. asked me to serve as president, he caught me at a time when my enthusiasm for Iditarod knew no bounds. So much needed to be done for Iditarod to achieve its true potential as an exciting, world-class Alaskan adventure. There were so many issues of such huge magnitude that I didn't think being just a part-time president would get the job done. I could imagine my term ending with no long-term progress having been made. To get the big important things done, I believed I needed to take a year off from my business interests and do nothing but manage Iditarod. I wanted to look back and know that my time had been well spent. So I did; and now I believe that I can.

During my tenure as president, much was accomplished. The most important was building a permanent headquarters for Iditarod with donated land and funds.

Incidentally, I established the Gold Coast Trophy to be awarded the first team to arrive in Unalakleet on the shore of the Bering Sea. At first, I sponsored it through Golden Horn Lodge, which I then owned. Later, Ed Rasmussen continued to sponsor the trophy through NBA after I sold the lodge.

The second important accomplishment was conceiving the idea of a rookie seminar and then organizing and conducting the first one. Most agree that this seminar is the most important thing we do for new Iditarod mushers.

Other improvements include obtaining trademark protection for our names and logos; writing operating manuals for the volunteer functions, which resulted in some notable improvements, including a much better trail most of the way to Nome; and writing job descriptions for staff positions. We put a bookkeeping system in place and arranged for the first audit of the Iditarod books. I developed an organization chart and critical path charts for all the race functions, and expanded the merchandising. We also interviewed multinational sports agents and hired one to assist in obtaining and expanding the list of large corporate sponsors for the Iditarod race.

Aside from committee service, it was good to have been selected by the State of Alaska to survey the alignment of the first eighty-six miles of the Iditarod Trail from Knik through Rabbit Lake to Skwentna.

My happiest accomplishment of all was in bringing Edgar Nollner to Nome for his first visit.

Some of these accomplishments have been lost, but I hope the big ones will endure.

###

APPENDIX A

The conversation over *Susan Butcher's encounter with the moose* re-surfaced several years later when she passed judgment on the Northwest Passage sled-dog expedition and urged its sponsors to bail out. Craig Medred, outdoors editor for the Anchorage Daily News, reacted to her remarks in an editorial dated December 23, 1991, which follows.

Editorial, by Craig Medred, <u>Anchorage Daily News</u>, December 23, 1991

The words of Susan Butcher have haunted me since the day she passed judgment on the Northwest Passage sled-dog expedition and urged sponsors to bail out.

Without question, this trek across the top of North America from Alaska to Churchill, Manitoba, had deteriorated into a fiasco.

Fifteen dogs were dead from starvation or hypothermia. Several mushers might be dead, too, if not for a chance encounter with a caribou hunter who guided the expedition into the village of Paulatuk, Northwest Territories.

The World Society for the Protection of Animals and the Humane Society has demanded an investigation. Expedition sponsors worried about bad publicity have disavowed the adventure.

Into the morass stepped Butcher, the world's best-known dog driver, an authority on racing dogs, and a woman to be admired for her skill and determination. Her verdict: "The mushers have gone on an expedition unprepared for the terrain and climate they would obviously encounter."

OK. Certainly, most wilderness tragedies could be traced back to poor planning somewhere along the line. Nobody should know that better than Butcher.

During the 1985 Iditarod Trail Sled Dog Race, she watched powerless and in horror as a moose stomped around on her team for 20 minutes. One dog was killed outright, another suffered a slower death. Several were injured.

There was no telling how bad the carnage might have been if Dewey Halverson of Trapper Creek hadn't arrived on the scene and shot the moose dead.

Butcher couldn't do that. Despite the fact mushers had been warned about moose that year, she did not pack a gun.

"Going out there without a gun was like going out there without a parka," Halverson would say later.

Butcher made a bad decision when she decided to leave the gun behind to shave weight. And we've all been guilty of making bad decisions at one time or another.

The Northwest Passage expedition seems guilty of several bad decisions, and it was hard to feel sympathy for expeditions that spend as much time groveling for publicity as preparing for the wilderness.

In fact, I could almost convince myself the Northwest Expedition deserves the public whipping it had taken.

Only the haunting words of Butcher stop me short: "I know the trust dogs have in their owners, and to be put in a situation where that trust was totally broken. The mental pain of what happened to those dogs was to me as horrible as the physical pain. I couldn't stand to think of what those dogs went through."

Such profound and absolute garbage. Worse, some people would believe this bunkum.

That the dogs in question endured physical pain before their deaths was certain. That the pain was especially horrible was possible, but doubtful. That there was, beyond all that, some terrible mental anguish was pop psychology at its worst.

I know. I have been there close to the edge. Not even people suffer such trauma.

I have interviewed dozens of adventurers who barely escaped death and read the journals of some who didn't make it.

Nowhere was there great mental pain. There was simply no time for that. Survival is an overpowering thought for any and all animals.

People in survival situations keep going until they can't go anymore, and then they die. It can't be much different for dogs.

That dogs could somehow put aside the overwhelming desire to survive in order to conceptualize the future, recognize the inevitability of their deaths and then anguish over that is pure poppycock.

If you want to talk about mental anguish for dogs, put them in harness and trap them on a narrow trail facing a moose trying to stomp them to death while the person they trust for their survival stands there watching, unable to help.

That's mental anguish. That's something about which you could truly say, "The mental pain of what happened to those dogs was to me as horrible as the physical pain. I couldn't stand to think of what those dogs went through."

And all I could say was that Susan Butcher ought to be thankful there was no Susan Butcher around to send a telegram to her sponsors.

Craig Medred was the *Daily News* outdoors editor.

APPENDIX B

THE ANCHORAGE TIMES
Tuesday, May 21, 1985

Iditarod Race Rules Adopted

Changes reflect concern for dogs

"The safety and well-being of dogs is our main concern. It transcends any other part of the race, including the competitive aspect."

Burt Bomhoff, president Iditarod Trail Committee

By Bill Sherwonit, Times Outdoors Writer

Iditarod Trail Sled Dog Race officials leave absolutely no room for doubt: the Iditarod's No. 1 priority is care of the dogs. Everything else including the race for first is secondary. That's the way it is, always has been and always will be.

To that end, the Iditarod's rulebook is constantly scrutinized. And each year the race regulations are revised, amended and improved to insure the best possible care of the dogs, says Burt Bomhoff, the Iditarod Trail Committee's newly elected president and spokesman.

"The Iditarod is still a developing sport," Bomhoff said. "We attempt to solve problems as they come along. I want to emphasize that these rules (dealing with the safety and care of the dogs) is not something that just suddenly happened. It's always been a concern. Each year, improvements are made."

During the ITC's May meeting at the Sheraton Anchorage Hotel last weekend, several rules were added or changed for the 1986 race to "further secure the safety of the dogs." Among the more significant changes, additions or amendments:

Dog Minimums: *A musher may not drop more than 30 percent of his dogs.*

The 'thirty-percent rule' was added to put the burden back on the mushers to take care of their dogs," ITC member Susan Butcher said at Saturday's Board of Directors' meeting. "Unless you're pushing your dogs too hard, or not caring for the dog's feet, or doing something else that's wrong, no musher should have to drop 50 percent of his dogs."

Dog Care: *The chief veterinarian may penalize a musher if proper dog care is not maintained.*

"This rule takes dog care one step beyond 'cruel and inhumane,'" Bomhoff explained.

"At times it's obvious that a musher is not being cruel, but may still be acting carelessly or negligently (with regard to the health of the dogs). This gives the chief veterinarian a tool by which he can impose a penalty himself, in a manner that fits the crime."

Driverless Team: A driver seeking to recover a lost team either on foot, with assistance from another musher or mechanized vehicle and continue the race. *If a dog team is picked up during an emergency, it must be returned to that point if it is to continue. Motorized assistance must be reported to an official at the next checkpoint.*

"This is another effort to protect the safety of the dogs," Bomhoff said. "If a team does get separated from a driver, he can take whatever steps are necessary to get back to the dogs as quickly as possible.

"We're trying to achieve a balance. What we're saying here is that the safety of the team is most important. In the past, this has been a kind of gray area. Drivers might be afraid to get help for fear of being disqualified. What we're saying is that in such an emergency, a driver should take the most immediate and direct steps to recover a team without having to worry about being disqualified. Later there may be some sort of action taken to assure fairness of competition (which is why any motorized assistance must be reported). But if a team is loose, we want to recover it as quickly as possible."

Injured, Fatigued or Sick Dogs: *A veterinarian may prevent a dog from leaving a checkpoint for medical reasons.*

"By holding a dog at a checkpoint, a veterinarian ensures humane treatment of the dog. But at the same time, it provides the musher with an option. He can either wait until the veterinarian says the dog can continue, or he can drop the dog," Bomhoff said.

"The dog isn't automatically pulled from the race in such a case. There's a choice involved."

Good Samaritan Rule: *A musher will not be penalized for aiding another musher in an emergency. Incidents must be reported to race officials at the next checkpoint.*

"We don't want a situation where a musher is afraid to help out in an emergency because of a fear of being disqualified," Bomhoff said. "Again, it's mostly dog-related. We don't want a team in trouble sitting between checkpoints because people are afraid to help out."

Checkpoints: *In case of medical emergency or life threatening situation, a dog may be dropped at any checkpoint with the approval of a veterinarian.*

Not all checkpoints along the trail are designated dog drops. This rule allows mushers the chance to drop a dog at a non-drop checkpoint, if warranted by a severe injury or other health problem, rather than risk further injuries or medical complications.

Other notable rule changes for 1986 not specifically dealing with dog care include:

Race Freeze: *The race marshal may freeze the race. When a freeze is called, the teams will all proceed forward at their own pace to a single designated checkpoint. The teams will depart the checkpoint based on their order and time of arrival into that checkpoint.*

"This year (1985) was the first time we've ever had to freeze (halt) the race," Bomhoff said. "Donna Gentry, the race marshal, had to improvise as she went along. This rule defines the freeze process. Also, it says that freezes will be at one site only, to prevent any possible confusion (as took place this year when mushers were frozen at two different checkpoints and then restarted in different ways at the two sites)."

Censure: *A written warning, monetary penalty or disqualification must have occurred before a censure.*

"This is to ensure fairness to the mushers," Bomhoff said. "There have been times when mushers have been censured after a race, when no previous action had been taken. This can no longer happen."

Disqualifications: *Mushers may be disqualified for rule infractions involving cruel and inhumane treatment of animals or for deliberate rule infractions which give a musher an unfair advantage over another musher.*

"The word 'deliberate' was added so that mushers aren't subject to disqualification for inadvertent mistakes. The whole idea there was to prevent cheating," Bomhoff said.

Disqualifications: *It is intended that the nearest involved official be included on the (three-member) panel. The musher will be given the opportunity to present his case to each member of the panel prior to the decision.*

"The nearest involved official in an incident has not always been on the panel," Bomhoff said. "Since that person is the most involved, that's the one with the most knowledge and the one you most want on the panel.

"As far as a musher talking to each member of the panel, that's to ensure fairness. We want to make sure that the musher has a chance to tell his side of the story."

APPENDIX C

The Anchorage Times
Sunday, August 4, 1985

Swenson forgives Iditarod woes, plans '86 run

"Whatever happens, I'm not running this race again. I'm just not going to put up with the crap they (race organizers) put you through. They can find some other sucker."

Rick Swenson, near the end of the 1985 Iditarod Race

The wounds have healed. Sort of.

The disorganized mess that was the 1985 Iditarod Trail Sled Dog Race is nothing much more than a bad memory for Rick Swenson, although he may not completely forget the problems. He'll instead forgive.
And he'll be back in '86.

If there were any real doubts, Swenson ended them earlier this summer by mailing his $1,249 entry fee into Iditarod Race Headquarters in Wasilla. The check arrived on July 1—the first day of sign-ups.

Swenson's angry outburst at Koyuk in the 1985 Iditarod wasn't a fake or a ploy. He meant what he said in referring to the Iditarod's fouled restarts, poorly broken trails, and botched dog food shipments into several checkpoints. Swenson's remark was more the bitter backlash of a scorned lover than a blanket condemnation of the Last Great Race.

Truth is, Swenson does love the Iditarod. And it hurts when he sees it being fouled up. Especially when he's one of the people to pay the price for what he sees as organizational incompetence.

Recently, at his home in Eureka, the four-time Iditarod champion talked about his decision to return for another try at the fifth title.

"I have several reasons for competing in 1986," he said. "First of all, what I said (at Koyuk) was a spur-of-the-moment remark—although my complaints were valid. I'm sure that things will never be that bad again. I have faith in the new administration, particularly the new president (former Iditarod musher Burt Bomhoff).

"I think there'll be a lot of changes. They'll work hard to eliminate the black eye that the Iditarod got last year."

There's more reasons, though, why Swenson will be back.

"The Iditarod is where my heart is," Swenson admitted. "And the race suits where I live—on top of a big hill at the end of the road. The workouts that my dogs get here are right for the Iditarod."

The Iditarod suits the Swenson lifestyle.

First and foremost, Swenson is an outdoorsman. He's the quintessential Alaskan sourdough: trapper, gold miner, musher. All three of his hobbies/ occupations have ties that bind. They get him into the outdoors. They allow him independence. They keep him happy.

Swenson traps and mines gold by his own schedule. And he trains and races sled dogs the same way.

"I like to be in the outdoors a lot. I've always liked to camp, ever since I was a kid," Swenson said. "That's all part of the Iditarod. Seeing the country, camping out.

"And I'm in a hurry enough in my life. I don't need to be in a hurry when I'm racing. In long-distance races, you have to get from Point A to Point B, but you do it at your own pace, by your own schedule. I like that."

Swenson is justifiably proud of his mushing accomplishments: the race records he's accumulated; the four Iditarod victories—no one else has more than one; and the fact that "in all the races I've run, I hold the record (for the fastest time)."

If Rick Swenson has a fault, it's that he's bluntly honest; he speaks his mind. That honesty sometimes gets him in trouble—with the press, with the Iditarod organization and, perhaps, with potential sponsors.

He seems somewhat embittered by the fact that his "unsurpassed" long-distance mushing record hasn't been rewarded with more lucrative sponsorships or endorsements, but at the same time insists, "I ain't complaining. I came up here with nothing and got everything I could want to have.

"I don't need the publicity, the notoriety anymore," he said. "The only real reasons (to keep going for no. 1) are to prove the quality of my dogs and my own personal motivations."

Swenson's ultimate mushing motivation is the Iditarod—for all the reasons listed above and one other.

"You do what you're best at, right? I've acquired a tremendous amount of experience in my 10 years of running the Iditarod," he said. "It's to my own advantage, businesswise, to use the knowledge that I've acquired. It makes sense for me to run the Iditarod."

This year, the Iditarod will again be the No. 1 goal. But Swenson, now in his mid-thirties, is making at least one major change. This year, he'll be running dogs for more than just himself. He'll be racing to raise money for muscular dystrophy.

"I guess, it's time to try something a little different," he says. "Now what I'm doing can help somebody else, too."

Bill Sherwonit is the outdoors writer at *The Anchorage Times*.

APPENDIX D

The Anchorage Daily News
Thursday, March 14, 1985

Restart snafu penalizes some Iditarod mushers, helps others

The second freeze of the 1985 Iditarod Trail Sled Dog Race lasted just a bit over 24 hours from 7:45 p.m. Sunday to 8 p.m. Monday.

But it may take forever and a day before anyone understands the effects that the freeze and the two-way restart have on the race and the mushers competing for a $200,000 purse.

Clearly, some mushers were penalized and some were helped by the double standard for getting the race started again for the third time. (The first freeze last week was applied equally to all competitors.)

Race officials said the two methods resulted from poor communications. Iditarod Trail Committee President Bob Sept, in McGrath, had one system for restarting the race. Race marshal Donna Gentry, in Ophir, had another.

Neither has spoken at length of the reasons for the foul-up. Only Sept has admitted an error took place.

Here's what happened.

Officials were forced to halt the contest because no dog food could be flown to Iditarod, half-way point of the race. The heaviest snowfall and foulest weather in the Iditarod's 13-year history have kept airplanes grounded off and on since the race began March 2.

Without food in Iditarod, many dogs would be racing at least 155 miles from Ophir, where they last were fed, to Shageluk, the checkpoint after Iditarod—on empty stomachs.

So a freeze was called to allow food to be brought in to Iditarod.

The problem was in how to calculate the most equitable method of restarting the race once the weather cleared.

More than 40 of the 58 mushers remaining in the race Sunday night were located in a 61-mile stretch between Ophir and McGrath. By the time of the freeze, 7:45 p.m., leaders Burt Bomhoff and Tim Osmar had been in Ophir for 50 minutes. More were on the way.

A group of 17 mushers were already in McGrath, and Joe Redington Sr., the first of that bunch into McGrath, was just about to leave for the next checkpoint, Takotna.

A handful of mushers were in or coming into Takotna.

Race officials decided that Ophir and McGrath would be the two restart points.

Gentry in Ophir decided that the mushers would leave in the same order they arrived, and in the same time differences in which they arrived.

Osmar and Bomhoff, for instance, would leave a the restart time of 8 p.m., while Guy Blankenship would leave at 9:06 p.m. because he had arrived in Ophir an hour and six minutes after the two leaders. Emmitt Peters, who followed Blankenship into Ophir by 12 minutes, departed at 9:18.

And so it went for the 25 mushers who were already in Ophir or managed to get there after the freeze was called. Because Osmar and Bomhoff had been in Ophir for 50 minutes when the race was halted, they lost that time. It was never figured into the restart schedule.

Meanwhile, in McGrath, Sept decided to peg the restart not on where mushers were located relative to each other at the time of the freeze, but on when they got into McGrath compared with when Joe Redington Sr. got there. He had led the rest of the mushers into McGrath.

Fred Jackson, for example, left McGrath at 9:40 p.m. Monday evening, an hour and 40 minutes after Redington, even though he and 15 other drivers were already in the Innoko River checkpoint when the race was frozen.

The waiting time became a new factor in the race solely because of the freeze. Had there been no halt, any of the McGrath mushers could have left any time he or she wanted. He or she could have bolted out of McGrath on Redington's heels, for instance, if driver and dogs were up to the hustle.

Instead, some mushers were delayed out of McGrath for upwards of 10 hours.

APPENDIX E

The Anchorage Times, February 23, 1986

Iditarod chief wants race 'integrity'

Editor's note: Anchorage musher Burt Bomhoff, a veteran of four Iditarods, is highly respected by his fellow sled dog racers and president of the Official Iditarod Finishers Club (which includes all mushers who have completed the 1,100 mile Iditarod Trail Sled Dog Race from Anchorage to Nome). Last spring, Bomhoff was unanimously elected as president of the Iditarod Trail Committee, the organization which runs the Last Great Race. Recently, Bomhoff talked at length about the Iditarod with Times Outdoors Writer Bill Sherwonit

Times: What is the current "state" of the Iditarod?

Bomhoff: It's an event with great, great potential, far more than any other in Alaska.

Alaska has such a mystique that's recognized around the world. It's a mystical place that takes you back in time. The Iditarod is a way of resenting that to people. The media covering the race show the best parts of Alaska: its biggest cities, its villages and towns, the tundra, mountain ranges, the arctic coast. The Iditarod captures the spirit of adventure, it shows people of all economic, social and cultural backgrounds working together. In addition, it gives us all a history lesson on Alaska every year. We learn again about the serum run, the Iditarod Trail, the gold rush.

Through all that runs a spirit of competition that is second to none.

We have the ingredients and the raw materials; that just leaves the people and their vision. The race is at a turning point. It can be a great event. I want the people involved in the race to believe in it as that kind of event.

That's one reason I pushed for the $200,000 purse. And why I'd like to see it increased to $250,000 next year and ultimately $500,000. Our competitors spend $1½ to 2 million every year. People like Susan Butcher and Rick Swenson spend $55,000 to $60,000. Even the less competitive mushers can spend $15,000 to $20,000. The competitors are willing to put everything into it, their lives, their money. (The organization) should do the same.

Times: The Iditarod is sometimes criticized for receiving financial aid from the state. How much are you getting? And what's your answer to critics who say the money can be better used elsewhere?

Bomhoff: Last year we got something like $72,000. This year we're asking for $90,000.

There are very, very good reasons for state assistance. The publicity, the notoriety that the Iditarod brings to Alaska is unmatched by any other event. State tourism is often mentioned as an alternative to the oil industry. There is nothing that brings the excitement of Alaska across the country and around the world like the Iditarod. There's nothing that depicts the scenery, the people and the pioneering spirit like this race. I'm sure that for every dollar the state spends on the Iditarod, it gets at least $10 in return.

Second, from an educational standpoint, we have the computer system. We have kids involved in the project all along the trail. The data is collected, put into the computer and then made available to the public. Anyone can just pick up the phone, dial a number, and the information is right there. We even have it now where the computer talks to you.

Another thing is that the Iditarod is a cabin-fever remedy. It's the biggest festival, all across Alaska. So often we have arguments between different groups. We tend to get people factionalized. But the Iditarod gets us together. It's the only event that brings us all together with a common event, working toward a common goal.

Times: What does your experience as a musher contribute in you position as president of the ITC?

Bomhoff: I understand the importance of the competition from the point of view of a musher. Mushers are the key ingredient. Having been president of the mushers (the finishers club), I have a strong loyalty to them and an appreciation of what they go through. A lot of people don't seem to realize the magnitude of their effort. Without the mushers, we don't have a race. Getting them to Nome should be the No. 1 priority.

Times: You're still the president of the Official Iditarod Finishers Club. Are there any concerns about a possible conflict of interest between that position and your job as president of the ITC?

Bomhoff: It has never come up that someone has said "you have a conflict of interest." I've recognized the potential for a conflict of interest. But I can't think of a specific example where the best interest of the race isn't also the best interest of the mushers and vice versa.

I know that the mushers would just a soon have me as both. I asked at the mushers' meeting (after the 1985 Iditarod) and they wanted me again. The mushers know I will go to bat for them. I always put the ushers first. If we have that good competition, everyone will benefit. Actually, the board gets tired sometimes of me always talking about the importance of the mushers.

Times: What are some of the major changes that have taken place within the Iditarod organization during the past year?

Bomhoff: First, we have new headquarters (along Knik Road). That gives us our own home, makes it more of a family. It also gives us a place for people to see what the Iditarod is all about. It's an anchor and symbol. It's almost done. All that's left is the finishing touches.

Second, we've taken a lot more trouble with the trail. This year we've had local people all along the trail working on it and marking it. Plus we've had four snowmachiners, led by Eric Halverson (one of last year's snowmobiling trailbreakers), straightening it out. We will have very close marking in open areas where the wind blows, so mushers can follow the trail.

The idea is to keep the teams rolling. I want a race track. It ain't the great camping trip. People don't want to watch teams out on a camping trip, they want to see a race.

We're also improving dog food drops. We're farming out that job to local air carriers all along the route. Not only does that help us, it helps the local economies and gets us working together to an even greater degree with the local people. It increases our reliability to virtually 100 percent.

Another new thing is a four hour rookie seminar, to improve musher safety and competition. We're inviting all other mushers too. We'll have experts talking on all sorts of topics. Rick Swenson our premier musher (and winner of four Iditarod championships) will talk about techniques of driving and handling a team. Jim Leach, our head veterinarian for the '86 race, will talk about animal care. Dr. William Mills will discuss frostbite, hypothermia and the physiology of coping with cold and fatigue. And Dr. Bob Martin will talk about cold weather gear.

Finally, we've expanded our full time personnel, making it broader and more professional.

Times: The Iditarod Trail Committee has always been known as a volunteer organization. Do these changes mean that the trend is away from volunteer effort?

Bomhoff: We're still a volunteer group and will continue to remain one. But now we'll be managing the volunteers better. We'll continue to depend on volunteers; they're still our major source of energy. It's just that we'll be able to work with them more effectively.

Times: Every year it seems as if someone proposes that the Iditarod be reversed and run from Anchorage to Nome. What's your reaction to that?

Bomhoff: It won't happen. There are so many reasons why it shouldn't go from Nome to Anchorage and no good reasons why it should.

Spring breakup follows the direction of the race. Starting in Anchorage and finishing in Nome is the natural way to go. If we reversed directions, we'd have even bigger trail and snow problems.

And how would the finish be handled? It would probably have to end in Wasilla and not Anchorage. You couldn't tie up the streets waiting for mushers to arrive. Anchorage is the natural starting place, but not a good place to finish the race

There are other reasons. There are lots of reasons not to change directions.

Times: Is there a chance that limits will ever be place on the size of the Iditarod field?

Bomhoff: There's always that chance. There's a practical limit to what we can handle. I don't know how many people entered the first Boston Marathon, but it reached a point where they had to place limits on the field. We only have so much capacity at checkpoints.

Another problem is making sure the pack stays tight. Officials and racers have to move together. And there's also a strain on checkpoints. We can't conduct the race over the entire 1,000 miles. If we find the mushers getting too spread out, we may need to make some changes. There's no reason for teams to drop back so far if the mushers are willing to work. We just can't handle a pack that's so spread out if that becomes a problem, we may have to make some changes, either limiting the size of the pack or regulating how far the tail-enders can fall behind the leaders at each checkpoint.

Times: Although a, as you say, the entire state seems to get involved in the Iditarod, have you considered the possibility of village burnout along the race course?

Bomhoff: There has always been that potential. The Iditarod is a high-profile, high-visibility occurrence. Basically a lot of good comes from it, but obviously some people who are not fans of the race might get tired of all the people and dogs underfoot. You can't ignore it. This year we've tried to get more of our people up and down the trail, communicating with the checkpoints and emphasizing the fun aspects of the race. Plus we're trying to make it help benefit them (the towns and villages used as checkpoints).

It also helps that we have two routes (northern and southern, used on alternating years_. That helps some checkpoints from having to deal with it every year.

Times: There's always a great deal of concern about dog deaths. The number of deaths has been small during the 1980s. but last year was an exception, as 12 dogs died.

Bomhoff: Last year was abnormal. Somehow the law of averages went nuts. Each of the deaths were investigated individually and, except for one case, they were all found to be unpreventable.

One thing I'd like to mention. I don't think we realize the hazards that dogs face in an urban environment. I really feel that an Iditarod dog's life is immensely preferable to that of a pet. Our dogs, when they don't run they go nuts. When they do, you can see the glee. They love to run. It's true that they get fatigued during the race, but there's nothing cruel about fatigue. Competitive person's most pleasurable experiences involve fatigue. And these dogs whether it's the breeding or not, will perform when tired.

We do have to careful to maintain humane treatment of the dogs. I certainly wouldn't perceive a repeat of last year. We just have to continually increase our efforts to educate the mushers.

Times: What is your no. 1 priority during your year as president of the ITC?

Bomhoff: My goal, when I leave the Iditarod, is to leave it well organized. And most of all, I want to leave it so that the competitive integrity of the race is ensured. That is, the best team comes in first, the second best team comes in second, and so on.

Now the best team does not necessarily mean the fastest or the toughest team. It's the team that is best trained and the best prepared to cope with the problems that are faced out on the trail. It's the team that best handles those problems.

You don't want outside factors to play a role. The trail should be properly marked, the dog food should be delivered on time. That's our job. Then the mushers need be only concerned with racing.

If we don't ensure the integrity of the race, the mushers become discouraged.

I also want to ensure an event that's exciting for everyone in the world to watch and have the race achieve its potential. The Iditarod is the one thing that can bring all Alaskans together. I want to see that happen.

Times: One final question. Who's going to win the 1986 Iditarod?

Bomhoff: Of course I can't pick a winner. But I can name the people I consider the top contenders for No. 1. Rick Swenson of course; he's the best there is. Dewey Halverson; he finished second last year, plus he bought my team. And I showed I had a pretty good team last year by being the first musher to the half-way point. Joe Garnie; he's got the same team Libby used last year and Joe finished third two years ago. Susan Butcher. Joe Redington Sr. Jerry Austin. And Rick Mackey, who does just an excellent job with his dogs.

Index